SCIENCE
FICTION
QUOTATIONS

SCIENCE FICTION QUOTATIONS

From the Inner Mind to the Outer Limits

edited by Gary Westfahl

With a foreword by Arthur C. Clarke

Yale University Press / New Haven and London

Designed by Mary Valencia

Set in Minion type by Tseng Information Systems, Inc.

Printed in the United States of America by Vail-Ballou Press

Library of Congress Cataloging-in-Publication Data

Science fiction quotations : from the inner mind to the outer limits / edited by Gary Westfahl ; with a foreword by Arthur C. Clarke.

    p.   cm.

Includes index.

ISBN 0-300-10800-1 (paperback : alk. paper)

1. Science fiction — Quotations, maxims, etc. I. Westfahl, Gary.

PN6084.S34S35 2005

808.83′876 — dc22

2005003195

#57669983

A catalogue record for this book is available from the British Library.

The paper in this book meets the guidelines for permanence and durability of the Committee on Production Guidelines for Book Longevity of the Council on Library Resources.

10 9 8 7 6 5 4 3 2 1

CONTENTS

Contents

FOREWORD

Arthur C. Clarke

Let me open with a quotation from that most prolific source, Anonymous: "If you have to ask what science fiction is, you'll never know."

In spite of this, attempts to define science fiction will continue as long as people write Ph.D. theses. Meanwhile, I am content to accept Damon Knight's magisterial: "Science Fiction is what I point to and say '*That's* science fiction.'"

Much blood has also been spilled on the carpet in attempts to distinguish between science fiction and fantasy. Somewhere in the literary landscape, science fiction merges into fantasy, but the frontier between the two is as fuzzy as the boundary of fractal images like the famous Mandelbrot Set. I have therefore suggested an operational definition: science fiction is something that could happen — but usually you wouldn't want it to. Fantasy is something that couldn't happen — though often you wish it would.

The writer of science fiction is faced with a problem which the writers of so-called mainstream fiction — devoted to a tiny subsection of the real universe — don't have to worry about. They seldom need to spend pages setting the scene: sometimes one sentence will do the trick. When you read "It was a foggy evening in Baker Street," you're there in a millisecond. The science fiction writer, constructing a totally alien environment, may need several volumes to do the job: the classic example is Frank Herbert's masterwork *Dune* and its sequels.

Notwithstanding this slight handicap, many of the finest works of science fiction are short stories. I can still recall the impact of Stanley Weinbaum's "A Martian Odyssey" when the July 1934 *Wonder Stories* arrived. When I close my eyes, I can still see that characteristic Frank R. Paul cover: never before or since did I read a story — and then go straight back to the beginning and read it right through again . . .

So perhaps the short story is to science fiction what the sonnet is to the epic poem. The challenge is to create perfection in as small a space as possible — something I have often dabbled in, with varying degrees of success. This enrichment process is carried to a new level when works of science fiction are littered with witty remarks, "gems" that offer profound (or hilarious) insights into a wide range of topics and subjects covering God, the Universe and everything else.

Science Fiction Quotations offers a fascinating collection of such quotations, culled from a large number of literary, media and entertainment sources and neatly categorised. It is a massive undertaking that would have daunted but the most indefatigable of researchers—and one for which generations of science fiction writers and enthusiasts would be extremely grateful.

Browsing through the manuscript brought back a kaleidoscope of memories from my own lifelong association with the *genre* in its various manifestations—pulp magazines, books, television series, films and, most recently, interactive games and Web sites. It has once again confirmed something I have always felt: mine will be the last generation that was able to read all the noteworthy works of science fiction.

I am naturally delighted to see that editor Gary Westfahl has included several of my own quotations—including some that I had long forgotten! And here is my less known Clarke's Sixty-fourth Law that he might have added to the relevant section: "Reading software manuals without the hardware is as frustrating as reading sex manuals without the software."

Of course, a single volume like this can only skim the surface of the vast reservoir of quotable quotes found in different realms of science fiction. It is only a matter of time—probably just a few years—before smart computer programs can be tasked to scan everything that has ever been printed in search of quotes. The next edition of this dictionary might well be a collaboration between carbon and silicon based compilers . . .

For every quote in this impressive dictionary, there must be a few more that science fiction enthusiasts wish had also been included. On a cursory glance through the manuscript, I didn't spot that piece of sage advice from Sam Goldwyn that no writer should ever forget: "If you gotta message, use Western Union."

Indeed, the primary function of any story is to entertain—not to instruct or to preach. Promoting a particular scientific concept or technology or a utopian worldview should be the secondary aim of a science fiction story. In fact, we can apply this to discern good science fiction. Some years ago, I suggested that the acid test of any story comes when you reread it, preferably after a lapse of some years. If it's good, the second reading is as enjoyable as the first. If it's great, the second reading is more enjoyable. And if it's a masterpiece, *it will improve with every reading.* Needless to say, there are very few masterpieces in or out of science fiction.

Fortunately, there is no further need to defend science fiction against the illiterates who, until recently, were prone to attack it. However, many long-time enthusiasts such as myself still have automatic defence mechanisms; it is hard to ignore the instincts of a lifetime. I can still remember the days when I used to hide the covers of my 1930 *Wonder* and *Amazing Stories.*

By mapping out possible futures, as well as a good many improbable ones, the science fiction writer does a great service to the community. He encourages in his readers flexibility of mind, readiness to accept and even welcome change—in one word, adaptability. Perhaps no attribute is more important in this age. The dinosaurs disappeared because they could not adapt to their changing environment. We shall disappear if we cannot adapt to an environment that now contains spaceships, computers—and thermonuclear weapons.

Nothing could be more ridiculous, therefore, than the accusation some-times made against science fiction that it is escapist. That charge can indeed be made against much fantasy—*so what?* There are times (the last century has provided a more than ample supply) when some form of escape is essential, and any art form that supplies it is not to be despised. And as C. S. Lewis (creator of both superb science fiction and fantasy) once remarked to me: "Who are the people most opposed to escapism? *Jailors!*"

C. P. Snow ended his famous essay "Science and Government" by stressing the vital importance of "the gift of foresight." He pointed out that men often have wisdom without possessing foresight. Science fiction has done much to redress the balance. Even if its writers do not always possess wisdom, the best ones have certainly possessed foresight.

And that is an even greater gift from the gods.

ACKNOWLEDGMENTS

I must first thank Fred Shapiro, who recruited me to edit this volume and who regularly provided advice and feedback throughout the long process of researching and preparing the manuscript. He is the reason why this book exists, and I could not have completed the project without his assistance.

To find and verify science fiction quotations, I primarily relied upon the J. Lloyd Eaton Collection of Science Fiction and Fantasy Literature housed in the Tomàs Rivera Library of the University of California, Riverside. Everyone working there deserves thanks for help and support, including Melissa Conway, Darien Davies, and Sheryl Davis, but Sara Stilley merits special mention for her many diligent efforts to provide the books and magazines that I requested. For texts not in the Eaton Collection, I turned to the library's indefatigable Interlibrary Loan Department, and I thank its staff members — Maria Mendoza, Janet Moores, Kimberly Noon, and Deborah Snow — for their fine efforts.

Although I endeavored to resolve all questions raised by this project through my own research, I sometimes sought information and guidance from colleagues. An incomplete list of those who helped in some way includes Mike Ashley, Jerry Bails, Gregory Benford, Richard Bleiler, Cuyler Brooks, John Clute, William C. Contento, Arthur B. Evans, Martin Feldman, Fiona Kelleghan, David Langford, Arthur Lortie, Sharlyn Orbaugh, John S. Partington, David Pringle, Steve Rowe, David N. Samuelson, Andy Sawyer, and Darrell Schweitzer. While preparing the manuscript, I benefited from the support and assistance of several people at Yale University Press, including database analyst John C. Colucci, acquisitions editor Mary Jane Peluso, and assistant editor Lauren Shapiro.

I also appreciated the supportive work environment provided by Roger Hayes and other staff members of the UCR Learning Center, as well as David Werner and other faculty members of the University of LaVerne's Educational Programs in Corrections. My final words of heartfelt thanks go to my children, Allison and Jeremy, and my wife, Lynne, who suffered through many hours of neglect while I devoted myself to this project. No quotation in this volume can fully convey how much I have appreciated their love and support during this time and throughout my career.

INTRODUCTION

I have devoted much of my life to science fiction, first as an enthusiastic reader and more recently as a scholar and commentator. When Fred Shapiro contacted me to say that he was editing a book of quotations for Yale University Press and would like me to edit an accompanying volume of science fiction quotations, I felt well prepared for the task. Still, I could not have anticipated just how humbling, enlightening, and exhilarating the experience of preparing this book would be.

My first priority was to establish a working definition of a "science fiction quotation." The immediate answer—a quotation from a work of science fiction—raised potentially contentious questions: When did science fiction originate? How does one define a work of science fiction? A book representing an entire field of literature should also represent the shared attitudes of its readers and writers, so I followed the consensus opinion that science fiction originated in the nineteenth century and blossomed as a genre in the twentieth century, excluding by fiat works published before 1800, such as Thomas More's *Utopia* and Jonathan Swift's *Gulliver's Travels* (which are, in any event, represented in other books of quotations). I also resolved to accept as science fiction any work that at least some readers and scholars had previously accepted as such. I would seek quotations primarily from novels, short stories, films, and television programs, with limited attention to plays, radio dramas, and comic books.

I originally intended to include numerous quotations from science fiction's sister genre, fantasy, which has so often shared its writers, readers, and publishing venues; this seemed especially appropriate since there were no plans for a companion volume of fantasy quotations. As it happens, many of these quotations were removed during final editing because they pertained to topics of little relevance to science fiction, such as magic and witches, but a sizable number were retained; in light of their contributions to the volume, I trust that their presence will not unduly upset dedicated science fiction readers.

Clearly, this volume could not consist entirely of quotations *from* science fiction works, since there was definitely a place for quotations *about* science fiction, to be drawn primarily from editorials, articles, and critical studies.

It further seemed fitting to include quotations from science fiction *writers,* even if these quotations appeared in works other than their science fiction stories. One way to epitomize the contents of this volume, then, would be as a compilation of quotations from the science fiction community, taken from works which members of that community have written or embraced, with an emphasis (of course) on science fiction itself.

Having characterized the project in that fashion, I was driven to a critical decision regarding its organization. The original design was to organize quotations by author, placing all quotations from one author in one section; such an organization would implicitly present science fiction as a collection of isolated individual voices, each offering its own brand of wisdom. But science fiction, as many have noted, is better described as an ongoing conversation: writers and commentators constantly toss out ideas that other writers and commentators respond to, in turn inspiring additional responses. It did not seem right, for example, to place Arthur C. Clarke's First Law in one section and Isaac Asimov's Corollary to that law in another section. By bringing together statements from different authors under topical headings, the book could better embody and convey the atmosphere of dialogue and discussion that is one of the genre's distinctive strengths.

An additional goal of this volume was to provide accurate, verified versions of its quotations. Over the years, many quotations have been passed from source to source, sometimes accumulating errors along the way; for instance, an inaccurate version of Harlan Ellison's 1968 statement about Robert A. Heinlein's dilating door has appeared in several critical studies, and no one has troubled to seek out Ellison's article to see what words he actually chose. Here, I resolved to locate and reproduce definitive texts for all quotations. Since some texts have appeared in variant forms, occasionally igniting scholarly debates about which version should be regarded as definitive—debates I could not delve into—I developed and followed these guidelines. For novels, I privileged first book publication, ignoring earlier serializations (except in cases when several years elapsed between serialization and book publication); for some older novels, I trusted scholarly editions from university presses; for foreign works, I relied on either first American translations or, when these were suspect, other recommended translations; and for recent novels from British, Canadian, or Australian writers (since university scholars cannot indefinitely overburden their interlibrary loan departments), I accepted first American editions as definitive. For short stories, I privileged the first published versions, usually in magazines; in a few cases when magazines were not available, I accepted the story's second publication as definitive. For films and television programs, except in rare instances when shooting scripts were available, I watched videocassettes to obtain accurate transcriptions. As with all human endeavors, the final volume will still include errors, but I have worked strenuously to ensure that these are as few as humanly possible.

In theory, the process of assembling a book of science fiction quotations is straightforward enough: the editor would read through or watch every single work of science fiction, every single work about science fiction, and every single work by science fiction authors, recording every single worthwhile quotation and eventually selecting only the best ones. As a practical matter, however, one editor, or a dozen editors, could not possibly fulfill this agenda in a finite period of time because of the vast dimensions of the field, so my survey of relevant materials was necessarily more selective. I relied on memories of earlier reading to seek out and record certain quotations, and I looked for quotations in compilations published as books or available online. These references proved a mixed blessing: books yielded some valuable quotations but generally seemed to endlessly recycle the same small number of noteworthy quotations from a handful of science fiction writers. Online sources were more variegated in their quotations, but quotations were sometimes misattributed or riddled with errors. Most frustrating was their common policy of failing to provide sources for quotations, which meant that I had to pore through the author's complete works to locate definitive texts for desired quotations. Several quotations are not in this volume because, despite considerable labors, I could not determine their original published source.

Having exhausted secondary resources, I shifted to detailed examinations of primary texts. I scanned every page of major novels, as well as numerous anthologies of stories, jotting down quotations as I noticed them. I regularly visited the J. Lloyd Eaton Collection of Science Fiction and Fantasy Literature at the University of California, Riverside, asking to examine books and magazines to locate or verify quotations. While striving to be methodical in covering significant works, I also incorporated elements of serendipity: while visiting a local library, I might examine a book on the shelf next to the book I was looking for, or while reading a story in a magazine, I might look at other stories in the same issue. One quotation came to me when a student worker at the Eaton Collection accidentally handed me a magazine that I had not requested; before returning it, I took a few minutes to scan through its contents and happened upon a gem.

I might have continued this process for years and years, reading texts and finding interesting quotations; but when my deadline was approaching and I already had far more quotations than I could possibly use, I necessarily stopped researching and started preparing the manuscript, haunted by the knowledge that there remained innumerable authors and works that I should have examined. Now I faced a new set of challenges. Having initially established hundreds of possible topical headings, I needed to eliminate or combine categories to achieve a reasonable number of cohesive chapters; then, I had to remove some seventy thousand words of quotations from the manuscript to achieve the desired length. Some quotations were not particularly strong and I felt no remorse in deleting them; other deletions were more painful and problematic. Quotations were eliminated for several reasons: some made points that other quotations on the subject seemed to make more eloquently or concisely; some were powerful in their original contexts but had less impact as stand-alone statements; some were very long and not amenable to editing; and some came from authors who were already well represented in a given category. Certainly, if I am ever asked to compile a second volume of science fiction quotations or a revised and expanded edition of this volume, there will be no shortage of worthwhile materials to draw upon.

Before anyone examines the quotations in this volume, I should issue two warnings. First, readers should bear in mind that, to paraphrase Clarke, the opinions expressed in these quotations are not necessarily those of their authors. There is no reason to believe that William Shakespeare disliked lawyers—in fact, he was probably quite fond of them—but he wrote words of a different nature to be spoken by a clearly unsympathetic character, leading many people to say, infelicitously, "It's like Shakespeare said—let's kill all the lawyers." Similarly, some quotations in this volume represent the views of characters or narrative voices that manifestly are not the views of the author who created them. A particular problem is that, in an effort to allow room for as many quotations as possible, some quotations are given without introductory language along the lines of "She had come to believe that" or "He often suspected that," so the statement as presented here may project an air of conclusiveness that its author did not intend.

Second, though such judgments may be inevitable, the presence or absence of a given author in this volume, or the number of quotations from an author, should not be taken as a measure of the author's talents—for two reasons. As already noted, my survey of science fiction was incomplete, and I know I have neglected any number of meritorious authors and texts. In addition, certain authors may be more likely to generate stimulating quotations for reasons unrelated to their talents. One author may prefer to pause periodically and ponder the broader significance of the story or may allow characters to drift into extended conversations that have little to do with the story—resulting in a rambling, sloppily written story that happens to yield several memorable quotations. Another author may be intent solely upon telling the story as effectively as possible, with every word dedicated to that goal—resulting in a tightly focused, eloquent story that happens to include no statements capable of standing on their own as quotations. While working on this project, I was sometimes surprised to find myself jotting down numerous quotations from writers I do not particularly admire and relatively few quotations from other writers who are among my favorites; I learned through experience that there is not necessarily a correlation between quotability and literary value.

A few words about the format of this volume: within a given category, quotations are usually arranged in chronological order, though I violate this a few times to juxtapose closely related quotations. If there are several quotations from one year, they are arranged alphabetically by authors' last names; on rare occasions when there are quotations from two or three works by the same author published in the same year, they are arranged alphabetically by title. Titles in quotation marks are short stories and italicized titles are books, unless otherwise noted parenthetically; the phrase "episode of" signals a television series unless noted otherwise. For the most part, quotations are reproduced exactly as they originally appeared, including original spellings, though I silently correct typographical errors and, when editing out portions of sentences, sometimes adjust the punctuation or capitalization. Unbracketed ellipses are the author's; bracketed ellipses are mine. All quotations are attributed to officially credited authors, even in cases when evidence suggests an uncredited coauthor; for authors who have published under different names, the best-known name is regularly employed. When novels have appeared under different titles in different countries, I use the titles of the American editions.

If someone wishes to track down and read quotations in their original contexts, the novels, films, and television programs should not be difficult to locate, but short stories may prove more elusive. Two online resources—the Locus Index to Science Fiction (http://www.locusmag.com/index/) and the Internet Speculative Fiction DataBase (http://www.isfdb.org/)—should provide information on most, if not all, of the stories.

Most topic headings are self-explanatory, with two exceptions. In "The

Introduction

Laws of Science Fiction," I gather together some rules and general principles articulated by science fiction authors, such as Asimov's Three Laws of Robotics, Clarke's Three Laws, *Star Trek*'s Prime Directive, and Theodore Sturgeon's Law. And under the imperfect heading "Surrealism," I celebrate science fiction's noted ability to generate, due to its innovative subject matter, statements that are delightfully absurd or incongruous; a few such statements are in other sections, but most ended up in this category.

I said at the beginning that I found working on this project to be humbling, enlightening, and exhilarating. Humbling—because I have become more aware than ever of just how vast the field of science fiction is, of just how many books, stories, films, and television programs people should be familiar with before daring to call themselves experts in the field. I will approach all future research with a new and sobering awareness of how little I or any other person really knows about this genre.

Enlightening—first, because this project forced me to reread many of the field's classic works and to read for the first time other texts that I should have read long ago. More broadly, compiling these quotations brought a new understanding of science fiction's characteristic attitudes and concerns. As I anticipated, I found many intriguing quotations about subjects like "Aliens," "Space," and "Time Travel"; I did not anticipate that "History" would become one of the book's largest and most stimulating sections—at times, science fiction writers seem as fascinated by the past as they are by the future. There were many quotations about "Science" but an equal number about "Religion," reinforcing the view of some scholars that this is, surprisingly, one of the genre's central preoccupations. One might imagine that science fiction writers and readers would be unanimous in strongly supporting the space program; yet I discovered many statements that pondered humanity's conquest of space in a more jaundiced, even critical, fashion. In these and innumerable other ways, the quotations here indicate that the more our knowledge of science fiction expands, the less confidence we can have in stereotypical preconceptions about the genre.

Exhilarating—because this project has convinced me, more than ever before, that my youthful impulse to focus my attention and energies on science fiction was a wise decision. Science fiction works are well worth reading and watching. Because of the field's uniquely broad range of interests and perspectives, even the awkward words of untalented writers in pulp magazines can command attention, and the more skillful authors of recent decades may achieve rhetorical heights that they could not have attained in other genres. Perhaps there is something in the very nature of science fiction that inspires a special sort of eloquence no other form of literature can achieve. However, rather than developing such an argument at length, I will stop talking now, and allow science fiction to speak for itself.

SCIENCE FICTION QUOTATIONS

A

There are times in life when the most comfortable thing is to do nothing at all. Things happen to you and you just let them happen.
    —James Hilton, *Lost Horizon* (1933)

Always act on instinct, Burke. It puts the sparkle in existence.
    —Gordon R. Dickson, "The Monkey Wrench" (1951)

Such is oft the course of deeds that move the wheels of the world: small hands do them because they must, while the eyes of the great are elsewhere.
    —J. R. R. Tolkien, *The Fellowship of the Ring* (1954)

"He knows his leaders are not corrupted by intellectual paralysis."
    "What's that mean?" Syd asked dryly.
    "It means they act first and think second."
    —Philip K. Dick, *The World Jones Made* (1956)

Once human beings realize something can be done, they're not satisfied until they've done it.
    —Frank Herbert, "Cease Fire" (1958)

What I do I do because I like to do.
    —Anthony Burgess, *A Clockwork Orange* (1962)

Confucius once said that a bear could not fart at the North Pole without causing a big wind in Chicago.
    By this he meant that all events, therefore, all men, are interconnected in an unbreakable web. What one man does, no matter how seemingly insignificant, vibrates through the strands and affects every man.
    —Philip José Farmer, "Riders of the Purple Wage" (1967)

Actions

Every intelligent creature was curious—and curiosity prompted it to act when something incomprehensible took place.
    —Stanislaw Lem, "The Hunt" (1968), translated by Michael Kandel (1977)

Orr had a tendency to assume that people knew what they were doing, perhaps because he generally assumed that he did not.
    —Ursula K. Le Guin, *The Lathe of Heaven* (1971)

If the human race ever stops acting on the basis of what it thinks it knows, paralyzed by the fear that its knowledge may be wrong, then Homo sapiens will be making its application for membership in the dinosaur club.
    —Hank Davis, "To Plant a Seed" (1972)

Each deed you do, each act, binds you to itself and to its consequences, and makes you act again and yet again.
    —Ursula K. Le Guin, *The Farthest Shore* (1972)

Do nothing because it is righteous or praiseworthy or noble to do so; do nothing because it seems good to do so; do only that which you must do and which you cannot do in any other way.
    —Ursula K. Le Guin, *The Farthest Shore* (1972)

He had felt not that he was doing all the things he did, but that they were doing him. He had been in other people's hands. His own will had not acted.
    —Ursula K. Le Guin, *The Dispossessed: An Ambiguous Utopia* (1974)

Do, or do not. There is no try.
    —Leigh Brackett and Lawrence Kasdan, *The Empire Strikes Back* (film, 1980)

All of us are either doers or voyeurs, isn't that right?
    —Jack Dann, "Going Under" (1981)

There are no mistakes. The events we bring upon ourselves, no matter how unpleasant, are necessary in order to learn what we need to learn; whatever steps we take, they're necessary to reach the places we've chosen to go.
    —Richard Bach, *The Bridge across Forever* (1984)

Second thoughts can generally be amended with judicious action; injudicious actions can seldom be recovered with second thoughts.
    —C. J. Cherryh, *Cyteen* (1988)

Honor is only a label they use for what they want you to do, Chernon. They want you to stay, so they call staying honorable.
    —Sheri S. Tepper, *The Gate to Women's Country* (1988)

Tenar sighed. There was nothing she could do, but there was always the next thing to be done.
    —Ursula K. Le Guin, *Tehanu: The Last Book of Earthsea* (1990)

She saw Culhane's conviction, shared by Lord Director Brill and even by such as Lady Mary, that what they did was right because they did it. She knew that look well.
    —Nancy Kress, "And Wild for to Hold" (1991)

It was a world of acts, and words had no more influence on acts than the sound of a waterfall has on the flow of the stream.
    —Kim Stanley Robinson, *Red Mars* (1992)

"Jesus," said Chevette Washington, like somebody talking in their sleep, "what are you *doing*?"
    He didn't know, but hadn't he just gone and done it?
    —William Gibson, *Virtual Light* (1993)

Of all the forces in the universe, the hardest to overcome is the force of habit. Gravity is easy-peasy by comparison.
    —Terry Pratchett, *Johnny and the Dead* (1993)

ALIENS

No one would have believed, in the last years of the nineteenth century, that human affairs were being watched keenly and closely by intelligences greater than man's and yet as mortal as his own; that as men busied themselves about their affairs they were scrutinized and studied, perhaps almost as narrowly as a man with a microscope might scrutinize the transient creatures that swarm and multiply in a drop of water. With infinite complacency men went to and fro over this globe about their little affairs, serene in their assurance of their empire over matter. It is possible that the infusoria under the microscope do the same. No one gave a thought to the older worlds of space as sources of human danger, or thought of them only to dismiss the idea of life upon them as impossible or improbable. It is curious to recall some of the mental habits of those departed days. At most, terrestrial men fancied there might be other men upon Mars, perhaps inferior to themselves and ready to welcome a missionary enterprise. Yet, across the gulf of space, minds that are to our minds as ours are to those of the beasts that perish, intellects vast and cool and unsympathetic, regarded this earth with envious eyes, and slowly and surely drew their plans against us.

— H. G. Wells, *The War of the Worlds* (1898)

Those who have never seen a living Martian can scarcely imagine the strange horror of their appearance. The peculiar V-shaped mouth with its pointed upper lip, the absence of brow ridges, the absence of a chin beneath the wedge-like lower lip, the incessant quivering of this mouth, the Gorgon groups of tentacles, the tumultuous breathing of the lungs in a strange atmosphere, the evident heaviness and painfulness of movement, due to the greater gravitational energy of the earth — above all, the extraordinary intensity of the immense eyes — culminated in an effect akin to nausea. There was something fungoid in the oily brown skin, something in the clumsy deliberation of their tedious movements unspeakably terrible. Even at this first encounter, this first glimpse, I was overcome with disgust and dread.

— H. G. Wells, *The War of the Worlds* (1898)

[On Martians:] "It's a pity they make themselves so unapproachable," he said. "It would be curious to learn how they live on another planet; we might learn a thing or two."

— H. G. Wells, *The War of the Worlds* (1898)

I think we're property.

I should say we belong to something.

That once upon a time, this earth was No-man's Land, that other worlds explored and colonized here, and fought among themselves for possession, but that now it's owned by something.

That something owns this earth — all others warned off.

— Charles Fort, *The Book of the Damned* (1919)

"I've always wanted to see a Martian," said Michael, stiltedly. "Where are they, Dad? You promised."

"There they are," said Dad, and he shifted Michael on his shoulder and pointed straight down.

The Martians were there, all right. It sent a thrill chasing through Timothy.

The Martians were there—in the canal—reflected in the water. Timothy and Michael and Robert and Mom and Dad.

The Martians stared back up at them for a long, long silent time from the rippling water . . .

—Ray Bradbury, "The Million-Year Picnic" (1946)

The great pods were leaving a fierce and inhospitable planet. [. . .] Did this incredible alien life form "think" this or "know" it? Probably not, I thought, or anything our minds could conceive. But it had sensed it; it could tell with certainty that this planet, this little race, would never receive them, and would never yield. And Becky and I, in refusing to surrender, but instead fighting their invasion to the end, giving up any hope of escape in order to destroy even a few of them, had provided the final and conclusive demonstration of that unchangeable fact. And so now, to *survive*—their one purpose and function—the great pods lifted and rose, climbing up through the faint mist, and out toward the space they had come from.

—Jack Finney, *The Body Snatchers* (1955)

The human race had long ago overcome its childhood terror of the merely alien in appearance. That was a fear which could no longer survive after the first contact with friendly extraterrestrial races.

—Arthur C. Clarke, *The City and the Stars* (1956)

Perhaps they have been living there inside the Sun since the Universe was born, and have climbed to peaks of wisdom which we shall never scale. [. . .] One day they may discover us, by whatever strange senses they possess, as we circle round their mighty, ancient home, proud of our knowledge and thinking ourselves lords of creation. They may not like what they find, for to them we should be no more than maggots, crawling upon worlds too cold to cleanse themselves from the corruption of organic life.

—Arthur C. Clarke, "Out of the Sun" (1958)

Aliens

Once upon a time there was a Martian named Valentine Michael Smith.
 — Robert A. Heinlein, *Stranger in a Strange Land* (1961)

Where there are no men, there cannot be motives accessible to men.
 — Stanislaw Lem, *Solaris* (1961), translated by Joanna Kilmartin and
 Steve Cox (1970)

He recalled an earlier hope he had had of [the aliens]: that they might be superior beings, beings of wisdom and enlightened power, coming from a better society where higher moral codes directed the activities of its citizens. He had thought that only to such a civilization would the divine gift of traveling through interplanetary space be granted. But perhaps the opposite held true: perhaps such a great objective could be gained only by species ruthless enough to disregard more humane ends.
 — Brian W. Aldiss, "The Saliva Tree" (1965)

[Dr. McCoy on tribbles:] The nearest thing I can figure out is that they're born pregnant. It seems to be a great timesaver . . .
 — David Gerrold, "The Trouble with Tribbles," episode of *Star Trek* (1967)

I was ambassador to a planetful of things that would tell me with a straight face that two and two are orange.
 — Terry Carr, "The Dance of the Changer and the Three" (1968)

Eerie, Joe thought. A chitinous multilegged quasiarachnid and a large bivalve with pseudopoedia arguing about Goethe's *Faust*.
 — Philip K. Dick, *Galactic Pot-Healer* (1969)

Life got awfully boring with only humans to talk to.
 — Larry Niven, *Ringworld* (1970)

Entering the dock Redleaf has a vision: the aliens will look exactly like his wife and their mouth bent into the accusatory *o* they will say to him, "what the hell are you doing in here looking like that? you barely have any right to the universe let alone our quarters, you clean yourself up right this moment or we'll throw you out and take away your oxygen mask!"
 — Barry N. Malzberg, "Conquest" (1971)

"For Christ's sake, Ruth, they're *aliens*!"

"I'm used to it," she says absently.

—James Tiptree, Jr., "The Women Men Don't See" (1973)

I found the head Rock and I stood there in that valley, all surrounded by Rocks going *slurp!* and *squish!* and sucking up bug food. This was not the best part of my life I'm telling you about.

—Harlan Ellison, "I'm Looking for Kadak" (1974)

He strolled out of the alley, trying not to look like an alien who had just buried his spaceship under the forsythia bushes.

—Ted Reynolds, "Boarder Incident" (1977)

Somewhere in the cosmos, he said, along with all the planets inhabited by humanoids, reptiloids, fishoids, walking treeoids and superintelligent shades of the color blue, there was also a planet entirely given over to ballpoint life forms. And it was to this planet that unattended ballpoints would make their way, slipping away quietly through wormholes in space to a world where they knew they could enjoy a uniquely ballpointoid life-style, responding to highly ballpoint-oriented stimuli, and generally leading the ballpoint equivalent of the good life.

—Douglas Adams, *The Hitchhiker's Guide to the Galaxy* (1979)

Why is any object we don't understand always called a "thing"?

—Harold Livingston, *Star Trek: The Motion Picture* (film, 1979)

"The *aliens*," Dominguez said, frowning at Paul, "are still a mystery to us. We exchange facts, descriptions, recipes for tools, but the important questions do not lend themselves to our clumsy mathematical codes. Do they know of love? Do they appreciate beauty? Do they believe in God, hey?"

"Do they want to eat us?" Paul threw in.

—Michael Swanwick, "Ginungagap" (1980)

There was a fear of the non-human intelligence of the Birleles, even a fear of their strange shadowed beauty. Not everyone was attracted by the alien. Many were frightened and repelled by it.

—Sydney J. Van Scyoc, "Bluewater Dreams" (1981)

Why does he have to come here, with his birdcalls and his politeness? Why can't they all go someplace else besides here? There must be lots of other places they can go, out of all them bright stars up there behind the clouds.

    —Nancy Kress, "Out of All Them Bright Stars" (1985)

For a moment, she saw Nikanj as she had once seen Jdahya—as a totally alien being, grotesque, repellant beyond mere ugliness with its night crawler body tentacles, its snake head tentacles, and its tendency to keep both moving, signaling attention and emotion. [. . .] She stared at it for a moment longer, wondering how she had lost her horror of such a being.

    Then she lay down, perversely eager for what it could give her.

    —Octavia E. Butler, *Dawn* (1987)

All aliens are just personifications of our neuroses, physical manifestations of what we fear or desire.

    —Alexander Jablokov, "The Place of No Shadows" (1990)

THE BORG: Strength is irrelevant. Resistance is futile. We wish to improve ourselves. We will add your biological and technological distinctiveness to our own. Your culture will adapt to service ours.

    —Michael Piller, "The Best of Both Worlds" Part 1, episode of
    Star Trek: The Next Generation (1990)

Suddenly, without warning, the Other reaches out and seizes Carvalho's right hand in his own.

    And shakes it.

    Which in reaction sets Earthman and Other, still enthusiastically shaking one another's hand, to turning lazy, laughing cartwheels among the stars.

    —James Stevens-Arce, "Oscar Carvalho, *Spacial*" (1990)

The figures the telescope was producing were all that was left of an exploding star twenty million years ago. A billion small rubbery things on two planets who had been getting on with life in a quiet sort of way had been totally destroyed, but they were certainly helping Adrian get his Ph.D. and, who knows, they might have thought it all worthwhile if anyone had asked them.

    —Terry Pratchett, *Johnny and the Dead* (1993)

Do not attempt to judge an extraterrestrial race or its artifacts on the basis of human experience.
  —Christopher Anvil, "A Question of Identity" (1995)

There are beings in the universe billions of years older than either of our races. Once, long ago, they walked among the stars like giants, vast, timeless. Taught the younger races, explored beyond the rim, created great empires, but to all things, there is an end. Solely, over a million years, First Ones went away. Some passed beyond the stars never to return. Some simply disappeared.
  —J. Michael Straczynski, "In the Shadow of Z'ha'dum," episode of
  Babylon 5 (1995)

The thing about aliens is, they're alien.
  —Gregory Benford, "A Hunger for the Infinite" (1999)

ALIEN WORLDS

I was transplanted to a dark planet where the first germs of creation were struggling together. From a clay that was still soft rose gigantic palm trees, poisonous euphorbias and acanthus twined about cactus—the arid forms of rocks stuck out like skeletons from this sketch of creation, and hideous reptiles squirmed, enlarged, or grew round in the midst of an inextricable web of wild vegetation. The pale light of the stars alone illuminated the bluish distances of this strange horizon; and yet, as the creations were formed, a more luminous star gathered from them the germs of light.
  —Gérard de Nerval, *Aurelia* (1854), translated by Richard Aldington (1932)

[On the Moon:] He sighed and looked about him. "This is no world for men," he said. "And yet in a way—it appeals."
  —H. G. Wells, *The First Men in the Moon* (1901)

I perceived the moon no longer as a planet from which I most earnestly desired the means of escape, but as a possible refuge for human destitution. [. . .] "We must annex this moon," I said. "There must be no shilly-shally. This is part of the White Man's Burthen."
  —H. G. Wells, *The First Men in the Moon* (1901)

Alien Worlds

I opened my eyes upon a strange and weird landscape. I knew that I was on Mars; not once did I question either my sanity or my wakefulness.
— Edgar Rice Burroughs, *A Princess of Mars* (1917)

You and I have drifted to the worlds that reel about the red Arcturus, and dwelt in the bodies of the insect-philosophers that crawl proudly over the fourth moon of Jupiter.
— H. P. Lovecraft, "Beyond the Wall of Sleep" (1919)

Other memories encroached, cold, fear-etched memories that reached for him like taloned, withered claws.
Memories of alien lands acrawl with loathesomeness and venom. Strange planets that were strange not because they were alien, but because of the abysmal terror in the very souls of them. Memories of shambling things that triumphed over pitiful peoples whose only crime was they could not fight back.
— Clifford D. Simak, "Shadow of Life" (1943)

There they go, off to Mars, just for the ride, thinking that they will find a planet like a seer's crystal, in which to read a miraculous future. What they'll find, instead, is the somewhat shopworn image of themselves. Mars is a mirror, not a crystal.
— Ray Bradbury, "A Few Notes on *The Martian Chronicles*" (1950)

[First words said on the Moon:] By the grace of God, and the name of the United States of America, I take possession of this planet on behalf of, and for the benefit of, all mankind.
— Robert A. Heinlein, Rip von Ronkel, and James O'Hanlon,
Destination Moon (film, 1950)

I knew what it was like to walk on alien soil.
— Leigh Brackett, "The Woman from Altair" (1951)

Alien worlds have alien rules, you either learn quickly or not at all.
— Michael Shaara, "The Holes" (1954)

It was a fresh young world, Hubert thought sadly; a virgin world, waiting innocently for the first immigrants to despoil it; waiting, like a young and

tender girl, to be picked up on the stellar street and sold into galactic prostitution.
— Robert F. Young, "Report on the Sexual Behavior on Arcturus X" (1954)

The Lord sure makes some beautiful worlds.
— Cyril Hume, *Forbidden Planet* (film, 1956)

Every world was a miracle, if your eyes were good enough.
— Chad Oliver, "North Wind" (1956)

They were a vast historical panorama [of Mars], clockwise around the room. A group of skin-clad savages squatting around a fire. Hunters with bows and spears, carrying the carcass of an animal slightly like a pig. Nomads riding long-legged, graceful mounts like hornless deer. Peasants sowing and reaping; mud-walled hut villages, and cities; processions of priests and warriors; battles with swords and bows, and with cannon and muskets; galleys, and ships with sails, and ships without visible means of propulsion, and aircraft. Changing costumes and weapons and machines and styles of architecture. A richly fertile landscape, gradually merging into barren deserts and bush-lands — the time of the great planet-wide drought. The Canal Builders — men with machines recognizable as steam-shovels and derricks, digging and quarrying and driving across the empty plains with aquaducts [*sic*]. More cities — seaports on the shrinking oceans; dwindling, half-deserted cities; an abandoned city, with four tiny humanoid figures and a thing like a combat-car in the middle of a brush-grown plaza, they and their vehicle dwarfed by the huge lifeless buildings around them. [. . .]
  "Wonderful!" von Ohlmhorst was saying. "The entire history of this race."
— H. Beam Piper, "Omnilingual" (1957)

Poor old Dim kept looking up at the stars and planets and the Luna with his rot wide open like a kid who'd never viddied any such thing before, and he said:
  "What's on them, I wonder. What would be up there on things like that?"
  I nudged him hard, saying: "Come, gloopy bastard as thou art. Think thou not on them. There'll be life like down here most likely, with some getting knifed and others doing the knifing."
— Anthony Burgess, *A Clockwork Orange* (1962)

Alien Worlds

He was at home on those alien worlds, without time, those worlds where flowers copulate and the stars do battle in the heavens, falling at last to the ground, bleeding, like so many split and shattered chalices, and the seas part to reveal stairways leading down, and arms emerge from caverns, waving torches that flame like liquid faces.

— Roger Zelazny, "He Who Shapes" (1965)

He awoke—and wanted Mars. The valleys, he thought, what would it be like to trudge among them? Great and greater yet; the dream grew as he became fully conscious, the dream and the yearning.

— Philip K. Dick, "We Can Remember It for You Wholesale" (1966)

The grass is always greener under an alien star.

— John DeCles, "Cruelty" (1970)

Blossoms opened, flamboyance on firethorn trees, steel-flowers rising blue from the brok and rainplant that cloaked all hills, shy whiteness of kiss-me-never down in the dales. Flitteries darted among them on iridescent wings; a crownbuck shook his horns and bugled.

— Poul Anderson, "The Queen of Air and Darkness" (1971)

Carry me back to Titan.
That's where I want to be.
I want to repose
On the methane snows
At the edge of a frozen sea.

— Eleanor Arnason, "The Warlord of Saturn's Moons" (1974)

Don't you understand, this is the first time I've actually stood on the surface of another planet . . . a whole alien world . . . ! Pity it's such a dump though.

— Douglas Adams, *The Hitchhiker's Guide to the Galaxy* (1979)

We have labored to produce a planet which, taken as a whole, would obey the Three Laws of Robotics. It does nothing to harm human beings, either by commission or omission. It does what we want it to do, as long as we do not ask it to harm human beings. And it protects itself, except at times and in places where it must serve us or save us even at the price of harm to itself.

— Isaac Asimov, *The Robots of Dawn* (1983)

We all want different things from Mars.
  —Kim Stanley Robinson, *Red Mars* (1992)

AMBITION AND HOPE

Mark his perfect self-contentment, and hence learn this lesson, that to be self-contented is to be vile and ignorant, and that to aspire is better than to be blindly and impotently happy.
  —Edwin A. Abbott, *Flatland: A Romance of Many Dimensions* (1884)

Have you never wanted to do anything that was dangerous? Where should we be if nobody tried to find out what lies beyond? Have you never wanted to look beyond the clouds and the stars, or to know what causes the trees to bud? And what changes the darkness into light? But if you talk like that, people call you crazy. Well, if I could discover just one of these things, what eternity is, for example, I wouldn't care if they did think I was crazy.
  —Garrett Fort and Francis Edward Faragoh, *Frankenstein* (film, 1931)

The humans have a curious force they call ambition. It drives them, and, through them, it drives us. This force which keeps them active, we lack. Perhaps, in time, we machines will acquire it.
  —John Wyndham, "The Lost Machine" (1932)

It was better to live with disappointment and frustration than to live without hope.
  —Robert A. Heinlein, "Waldo" (1942)

There is a special sadness in achievement, in the knowledge that a long-desired goal has been attained at last, and that life must now be shaped toward new ends.
  —Arthur C. Clarke, *The City and the Stars* (1956)

He never gave up his search for the Door into Summer.
  —Robert A. Heinlein, *The Door into Summer* (1956)

Hope clouds observation.
  —Frank Herbert, *Dune* (1965)

Ambition and Hope

After a time, you may find that having is not so pleasing a thing, after all, as wanting. It is not logical, but it is often true.
  —Theodore Sturgeon, "Amok Time," episode of *Star Trek* (1967)

Why can I never set my heart on a possible thing?
  —Ursula K. Le Guin, *The Left Hand of Darkness* (1969)

How strange human nature is: confronted with a ladder, man feels compelled to climb to the very top. It's cold and drafty up there—bad for the health— and a fall can be fatal. The rungs are slippery. It's a funny thing: you're aware of the dangers, and you're practically ready to drop from exhaustion, yet you keep fighting your way up. Regardless of the situation, you keep climbing; contrary to advice, you keep climbing; despite the resistance of your enemies, you keep climbing; against your better instincts, your common sense, your premonitions, you climb, climb, climb. If you don't keep climbing, you fall to the bottom. That's for sure. But if you do keep climbing, you fall anyway.
  —Arkady Strugatsky and Boris Strugatsky, *Prisoners of Power* (1969),
    translated by Helen Saltz Jacobson (1977)

All her life she had made her own mistakes and her own successes, both usually by trying what others said she could not do.
  —Vonda N. McIntyre, "Aztecs" (1977)

Hope is a punishable offense. The verdict is always death; one more death of the heart.
  —Tanith Lee, "Medra" (1984)

Your dream is a good one. [. . .] The desire that is the very root of life itself: To grow until all the space you can see is part of you, under your control. It's the desire for greatness.
  —Orson Scott Card, *Speaker for the Dead* (1986)

There is that within a man that drives him ever onwards, just as the power of the seasons drives the roots of flowers into the hard earth; and so he decided, against his better judgment, to open his eyes and find out what was going to happen to him next.
  —Tom Holt, *Ye Gods!* (1992)

"He has been positively growing tusks trying to create a breed of human insect which will continue to live on this accursed planet."

"Everyone needs a goal."

—Steve Aylett, *Atom* (2000)

ANIMALS

Listen to them [wolves] — the children of the night. What music they make!

—Bram Stoker, *Dracula* (1897)

I sometimes think, Mary, that it is a mistake to have a dog for a nurse.

—J. M. Barrie, *Peter Pan* (play, 1904)

Lions, and tigers, and bears! Oh, my!

—Noel Langley, Florence Ryerson, and Edgar Allan Woolf, *The Wizard of Oz* (film, 1939)

The creatures outside looked from pig to man, and from man to pig, and from pig to man again; but already it was impossible to say which was which.

—George Orwell, *Animal Farm: A Fairy Story* (1945)

[Referring to the birds:] Nat listened to the tearing sound of splintering wood, and wondered how many million years of memory were stored in those little brains, behind the stabbing beaks, the piercing eyes, now giving them this instinct to destroy mankind with all the deft precision of machines.

—Daphne du Maurier, "The Birds" (1952)

I have spent too much of my life opening doors for cats — I once calculated that, since the dawn of civilization, nine hundred and seventy-eight man-centuries have been used up that way.

—Robert A. Heinlein, *The Door into Summer* (1956)

The wild black scavengers of the skies laid their eggs in season and lovingly fed their young. They soared high over prairies and mountains and plains, searching for the fulfillment of that share of life's destiny which was theirs according to the plan of Nature. Their philosophers demonstrated by unaided reason alone that the Supreme *Cathartes aura regnans* had created the world especially for buzzards. They worshipped him with hearty appetites for many centuries.

—Walter M. Miller, Jr., *A Canticle for Leibowitz* (1959)

A man who has *been* an animal has infinitely more knowledge of that animal than a man who has merely dissected one.

—Jack Sharkey, "Arcturus Times Three" (1961)

The reptiles had taken over the city. Once again they were the dominant form of life.

Looking up at the ancient impassive faces, Kerans could understand the curious fear they roused, rekindling archaic memories of the terrifying jungles of the Paleocene, when the reptiles had gone down before the emergent mammals, and sense the implacable hatred one zoological class feels towards another that usurps it.

—J. G. Ballard, *The Drowned World* (1962)

Stupefaction overrode all other emotion when I saw this creature on the lookout, lying in wait for the game. For it was an ape, a large-sized gorilla. It was in vain that I told myself I was losing my reason: I could entertain not the slightest doubt as to his species. But an encounter with a gorilla on the planet Soror was not the essential outlandishness of the situation. This for me lay in the fact that the ape was correctly dressed, like a man of our world, and above all that he wore his clothes in such an easy manner.

—Pierre Boulle, *Planet of the Apes* (1963), translated by Xan Fielding (1963)

Rabbits (says Mr. Lockley) are like human beings in many ways. One of these is certainly their staunch ability to withstand disaster and to let the stream of their life carry them along, past reaches of terror and loss. They have a certain quality which it would not be accurate to describe as callousness or indifference. It is, rather, a blessedly circumscribed imagination and an intuitive feeling that Life is Now.

—Richard Adams, *Watership Down* (1972)

When you've seen one pterodactyl you've seen them all.

—Edward Wellen, "Down By the Old Maelstrom" (1972)

You become what you live.
   She lived shark.
    —Edward Bryant, "Shark" (1973)

Never try to outstubborn a cat.
    —Robert A. Heinlein, *Time Enough for Love* (1973)

The literature of the emperor penguin is as forbidding, as inaccessible, as the frozen heart of Antarctica itself. Its beauties may be unearthly, but they are not for us.
    —Ursula K. Le Guin, "The Author of the Acacia Seeds and Other Extracts from the *Journal of the Association of Therolinguistics*" (1974)

She had always known that all lives are in common, rejoicing in her kinship to the fish in the tanks of her laboratories, seeking the experience of existences outside the human boundary.
    —Ursula K. Le Guin, *The Dispossessed: An Ambiguous Utopia* (1974)

Who would have thought the bees would have been the first alien force to invade America?
    —Stirling Silliphant, *The Swarm* (film, 1978)

It was none the less a perfectly ordinary horse, such as convergent evolution has produced in many of the places that life is to be found. They have always understood a great deal more than they let on. It is difficult to be sat on all day, every day, by some other creature, without forming an opinion about them.
    —Douglas Adams, *Dirk Gently's Holistic Detective Agency* (1987)

Animals never spend time dividing experience into little bits and speculating about all the bits they've missed. The whole panoply of the universe has been neatly expressed to them as things to (a) mate with, (b) eat, (c) run away from, and (d) rocks.
    —Terry Pratchett, *Equal Rites* (1987)

[On dolphins:] Never trust a species that grins all the time. It's up to something.
    —Terry Pratchett, *Pyramids* (1989)

Animals

The gorillas are not yet sufficiently advanced in evolutionary terms to have discovered the benefits of passports, currency-declaration forms, and official bribery, and therefore tend to wander backward and forward across the border as and when their beastly, primitive whim takes them.
  —Douglas Adams, *Last Chance to See* (1990)

Eric: You liked dinosaurs back then.
Dr Grant: Well, back then they hadn't tried to eat me yet.
  —Peter Buchman, Alexander Payne, and Jim Taylor, *Jurassic Park III* (film, 2001)

Animals do neither good nor evil. They do as they must do. We may call what they do harmful or useful, but good and evil belong to us, who chose to choose what we do. [. . .] The animals need only be and do. We're yoked, and they're free. So to be with an animal is to know a little freedom.
  —Ursula K. Le Guin, *The Other Wind* (2001)

Humans, eh? Think they're lords of creation. Not like us cats. We *know* we are. Ever see a cat feed a human? Case proven.
  —Terry Pratchett, *The Amazing Maurice and His Educated Rodents* (2001)

It's hard to be an ornithologist and walk through a wood when all around you the world is shouting: "Bugger off, this is my bush! Aargh, the nest thief! Have sex with me, I can make my chest big and red!"
  —Terry Pratchett, *Monstrous Regiment* (2003)

APOCALYPSE

The more I think of a people calmly developing, in regions excluded from our sight and deemed uninhabitable by our sages, powers surpassing our most disciplined modes of force, and virtues to which our life, social and political, becomes antagonistic in proportion as our civilisation advances— the more devoutly I pray that ages may yet elapse before there emerge into sunlight our inevitable destroyers.
  —Edward Bulwer-Lytton, *The Coming Race* (1871)

The darkness grew apace; a cold wind began to blow in freshening gusts from the east, and the showering white flakes in the air increased in number. From the edge of the sea came a ripple and whisper. Beyond these lifeless sounds the world was silent. Silent? It would be hard to convey the stillness of it. All the sounds of man, the bleating of sheep, the cries of birds, the hum of insects, the stir that makes the background of our lives—all that was over.

    —H. G. Wells, *The Time Machine: An Invention* (1895)

How small the vastest of human catastrophes may seem, at a distance of a few million miles.

    —H. G. Wells, "The Star" (1897)

I felt the first inkling of a thing that presently grew quite clear in my mind, that oppressed me for many days, a sense of dethronement, a persuasion that I was no longer a master, but an animal among the animals, under the Martian heel. With us it would be as with them, to lurk and watch, to run and hide; the fear and empire of man had passed away.

    —H. G. Wells, *The War of the Worlds* (1898)

By millions of years, time winged onward through eternity, to the end—the end, of which, in the old-earth days, I had thought remotely, and in hazily speculative fashion. And now, it was approaching in a manner of which none had ever dreamed.

    —William Hope Hodgson, *The House on the Borderland* (1908)

The world was held in a savage gloom—cold and intolerable. Outside, all was quiet—quiet! From the dark room behind me, came the occasional, soft thud of falling matter—fragments of rotting stone. So time passed, and night grasped the world, wrapping it in wrappings of impenetrable blackness.

    —William Hope Hodgson, *The House on the Borderland* (1908)

Every time we mention the world, we must remember it is going to end.

    —Edwin Balmer and Philip Wylie, *When Worlds Collide* (1932)

It is a new intoxication—annihilation. It multiplies every emotion.

    —Edwin Balmer and Philip Wylie, *When Worlds Collide* (1932)

"This storm you talk of . . ."

"It will be such a one, my son, as the world has not seen before. There will be no safety by arms, no help from authority, no answer in science. It will rage till every flower of culture is trampled, and all human things are leveled in a vast chaos."

—James Hilton, *Lost Horizon* (1933)

This is written in the elder days as the Earth rides close to the rim of eternity, edging nearer to the dying Sun, into which her two inner companions of the solar system have already plunged to a fiery death. The Twilight of the Gods is history; and our planet drifts on and on into that oblivion from which nothing escapes, to which time itself may be dedicated in the final cosmic reckoning.

—Clifford D. Simak, "The Creator" (1935)

Even if this is the end of humankind, we dare not take away the chances some other life-form might have to succeed where we failed. If we retaliate, there will not be a dog, a deer, an ape, a bird or fish or lizard to carry the evolutionary torch. In the name of justice, if we must condemn and destroy ourselves, let us not condemn all life along with us! We are heavy enough with sins. If we must destroy, let us stop with destroying ourselves!

—Theodore Sturgeon, "Thunder and Roses" (1947)

"Look," whispered Chuck, and George lifted his eyes to heaven. (There is always a last time for everything.)

Overhead, without any fuss, the stars were going out.

—Arthur C. Clarke, "The Nine Billion Names of God" (1952)

They are so confident that they will run on forever. But they won't run on. They don't know that this is all one huge big blazing meteor that makes a pretty fire in space, but that some day it'll have to *hit*.

—Ray Bradbury, *Fahrenheit 451* (1954)

The intense heat is turning Metaluna into a radio-active sun. The temperature must be thousands of degrees by now. A lifeless planet. And still, its existence is useful to someone. As a sun, its heat is, I hope, warming the surface of some other world, giving light and warmth to those who may need it.

—Franklin Coen and Edward G. O'Callaghan, *This Island Earth* (film, 1955)

The world had gone darker and grimmer and heavier in this moment while history turned around me in the silence and the night. A new world lay ahead. All I could be sure of was that it would be a harsh world, full of sweat and bloodshed and uncertainty. But a real world, breathing and alive.

—C. L. Moore, *Doomsday Morning* (1957)

The Planet drifts to random insect doom.

—William S. Burroughs, *Naked Lunch* (1959)

So he left the lagoon and entered the jungle again, within a few days was completely lost, following the lagoons southward through the increasing rain and heat, attacked by alligators and giant bats, a second Adam searching for the forgotten paradises of the reborn Sun.

—J. G. Ballard, *The Drowned World* (1962)

I, uh, don't think it's quite fair to condemn a whole program because of a single slip-up, sir.

—Stanley Kubrick, Terry Southern, and Peter George, *Dr. Strangelove, or, How I Learned to Stop Worrying and Love the Bomb* (film, 1963)

A terrible cold world of ice and death had replaced the living world we had always known. Outside there was only the deadly cold, the frozen vacuum of an ice age, life reduced to mineral crystals. [. . .] I drove at great speed, as if escaping, pretending we could escape. Although I knew there was no escape from the ice, from the ever-diminishing remnant of time that encapsuled us.

—Anna Kavan, *Ice* (1967)

She thinks of the Heat Death of the Universe. A logarithmic of those late summer days, endless as the Irish serpent twisting through jewelled manuscripts forever, tail in mouth, the heat pressing, bloating, doing violence. The Los Angeles sky becomes so filled and bleached with detritus that it loses all colour and silvers like a mirror, reflecting back the fricasseeing earth. Everything becomes warmer and warmer, each particle of matter becoming more agitated, more excited until the bonds shatter, the glues fail, the deodorants lose their seals. She imagines the whole of New York City melting like a Dali into a great chocolate mass, a great soup, the Great Soup of New York.

—Pamela Zoline, "The Heat Death of the Universe" (1967)

Silence. It flashed from the woodwork and the walls; it smote him with an awful, total power, as if generated by a vast mill. It rose from the floor, up out of the tattered gray wall-to-wall carpeting. It unleashed itself from the broken and semi-broken appliances in the kitchen, the dead machines which hadn't worked in all the time Isidore had lived here. From the useless pole lamp in the living room it oozed out, meshing with the empty and wordless descent of itself from the fly-specked ceiling. It managed in fact to emerge from every object within his range of vision, as if it — the silence — meant to supplant all things tangible. Hence it assailed not only his ears but his eyes; as he stood by the inert TV set he experienced the silence as visible and, in its own way, alive. Alive! He had often felt its austere approach before; when it came it burst in without subtlety, evidently unable to wait. The silence of the world could not rein back its greed. Not any longer. Not when it had virtually won.
— Philip K. Dick, *Do Androids Dream of Electric Sheep?* (1968)

Various Horsemen are abroad, doing their various Apocalyptic things.
— George Alec Effinger, "Wednesday, November 15, 1967" (1971)

The line between inner and outer landscapes is breaking down. Earthquakes can result from seismic upheavals within the human mind. The whole random universe of the industrial age is breaking down into cryptic fragments.
— William S. Burroughs, preface to *Love and Napalm: Export U.S.A.*
by J. G. Ballard (1972)

In his mind Vaughan saw the whole world dying in a simultaneous automobile disaster, millions of vehicles hurled together in a terminal congress of spurting loins and engine coolant.
— J. G. Ballard, *Crash* (1973)

The past seems like a long horror story of grinding toil, men and women teeming like rodents — and, of course, the final self-inflicted end as the world went up in flames, roasting the men and women in it like the corpses of animals over one of their own spits.
— Hilary Bailey, "The Ramparts" (1974)

Let me tell you about the end of the world. It happened fifty years ago. Maybe a hundred. And since then it's been lovely. I mean it. Nobody tries to bother you. You can relax. You know what? I *like* the end of the world.
 —Thomas M. Disch, *334* (1974)

The day came. The wrath descended. Sin, guilt, and retribution? The manic psychoses of those entities we referred to as states, institutions, systems — the powers, the thrones, the dominations — the things which perpetually merge with men and emerge from them? Our darkness, externalized and visible? However you look upon these matters, the critical point was reached. The wrath descended.
 —Philip K. Dick and Roger Zelazny, *Deus Irae* (1976)

The catastrophe story, whoever may tell it, represents a constructive and positive act by the imagination rather than a negative one, an attempt to confront the terrifying void of a patently meaningless universe by challenging it at its own game. [. . .] Each one of these fantasies represents an arraignment of the finite, an attempt to dismantle the formal structure of time and space which the universe wraps around us at the moment we first achieve consciousness.
 —J. G. Ballard, "Cataclysms and Dooms" (1977)

Nothing like a little cosmic cataclysm to take my mind off jammed sinuses.
 —Edward Bryant, "Particle Theory" (1977)

I can see we're in for a fabulous evening's apocalypse.
 —Douglas Adams, "Fit the Fifth," episode of *The Hitch-Hiker's Guide to the Galaxy* (radio series, 1978)

Apocalypse is the eye of a needle, through which we pass into a different world.
 —George Zebrowski, *Macrolife* (1979)

Kids! Bringing about Armageddon can be dangerous. Do not attempt it in your own home.
 —Neil Gaiman and Terry Pratchett, *Good Omens: The Nice and Accurate Prophecies of Agnes Nutter, Witch* (1990)

Apocalypse

Some people dote on contemplating disasters.
—William Gibson and Bruce Sterling, *The Difference Engine* (1991)

Chaos is found in greatest abundance wherever order is being sought. It always defeats order, because it is better organized.
—Terry Pratchett, *Interesting Times* (1995)

Night is falling. The gods have left us for those who please them better. Our time in the world is passed, and we are as wasted as the wind against the mountains. Shadows are falling, the gods have left us.
—Jim Grimsley, "Free in Asveroth" (1998)

If you look at the whole life of the planet, we—you know, Man—has only been around for a few blinks of an eye. So if the infection wipes us all out, that is a return to normality.
—Alex Garland, *28 Days Later* (film, 2002)

THE ARTS

This has ever been the fate of energy in security; it takes to art and to eroticism, and then come languor and decay.
—H. G. Wells, *The Time Machine: An Invention* (1895)

Once there was a race, quite unlike the human race—quite. I have no way of describing to you what they looked like or how they lived, but they had one characteristic you can understand: they were creative. The creating and enjoying of works of art was their occupation and their reason for being.
—Robert A. Heinlein, "The Unpleasant Profession of Jonathan Hoag" (1942)

I chose the world's great literature, and painting, and sculpture, and music— those mediums which best portray man lifting to the stars.
—Mark Clifton, "What Have I Done?" (1952)

The moment when one first meets a great work of art has an impact that can never again be recaptured.
—Arthur C. Clarke, "Jupiter Five" (1953)

I think great art should play a part in the ordinary man's life, don't you?
It can make his existence so much richer and more meaningful.
—Philip K. Dick, *Eye in the Sky* (1957)

Around the time of the Terran Caesar Augustus, a Martian artist had been
composing a work of art. It could have been called a poem, a musical opus,
or a philosophical treatise; it was a series of emotions arranged in tragic,
logical necessity. Since it could be experienced by a human only in the sense
in which a man blind from birth might have a sunset explained to him, it
does not matter which category it be assigned.
—Robert A. Heinlein, *Stranger in a Strange Land* (1961)

One does have to learn to look at art. But it's up to the artist to use language
that can be understood. Most of these jokers don't *want* to use language you
and I can learn; they would rather sneer because we "fail" to see what they
are driving at. If anything. Obscurity is the refuge of incompetence.
—Robert A. Heinlein, *Stranger in a Strange Land* (1961)

Life is short, he thought. Art, or something not life, is long, stretching out
endless, like [a] concrete worm. Flat, white, unsmoothed by any passage over
or across it.
—Philip K. Dick, *The Man in the High Castle* (1962)

There is in all things a pattern that is part of our universe. It has symmetry,
elegance, and grace—those qualities you find always in that which the true
artist captures. You can find it in the turning of the seasons, in the way sand
trails along a ridge, in the branch clusters of the creosote bush or the pattern
of its leaves. We try to copy these patterns in our lives and our society,
seeking the rhythms, the dances, the forms that comfort. Yet, it is possible
to see peril in the finding of ultimate perfection. It is clear that the ultimate
pattern contains its own fixity. In such perfection, all things move toward
death.
—Frank Herbert, *Dune* (1965)

Science explains the world, but only Art can reconcile us to it.
—Stanislaw Lem, "King Globares and the Sages" (1965), translated by
   Michael Kandel (1977)

All art is a form of controlled schizophrenia.
 —William F. Temple, "The Legend of Ernie Deacon" (1965)

An artist's life is supposed to lead toward his masterpiece, not away from it.
 —John Sladek, "The Happy Breed" (1967)

Good evening, and welcome to a private showing of three paintings, displayed here for the first time. Each is a collectors' item in its own way—not because of any special artistic quality, but because each captures on a canvas, and suspends in time and space, a frozen moment of a nightmare.
 —Rod Serling, *Night Gallery* (TV movie, 1969)

The laborers—the Producers—of the world had gotten fed up with doing all the work while a large portion of the population—the goddamn queer Artists—did nothing but eat up all the fruits of honest nine to five work. Artists contributed nothing, and wasted large amounts of our precious resources.
 —George Alec Effinger, "All the Last Wars at Once" (1971)

How could she have believed such an artificial life as the theatre was suitable?
 —Anne McCaffrey, "Prelude to a Crystal Song" (1974)

She danced because she needed to. She needed to say things which could be said in no other way, and she needed to take her meaning and her living from the saying of them.
 —Spider Robinson and Jeanne Robinson, "Stardance" (1977)

All the history of the stage is a struggle, the gasping of a beautiful child born at the point of death. The moralists, censorship and oppression, technology, and now poverty have all tried to destroy her. Only we, the actors and audiences, have kept her alive.
 —Gene Wolfe, "Seven American Nights" (1978)

"Actors," said Granny, witheringly. "As if the world weren't full of enough history without inventing more."
 —Terry Pratchett, *Wyrd Sisters* (1988)

We are dreamers, shapers, singers, and makers. We study the mysteries of laser and circuit, crystal and scanner, holographic demons and invocations of equations. These are the tools we employ and we know many things.

   —J. Michael Straczynski, "The Geometry of Shadows," episode of
     Babylon 5 (1994)

The artist had captured a moment that went on suggesting other moments in the mind of the beholder. This, Timmon told me, was what every painter, every singer, every craftsman sought to create.

   —Jim Grimsley, "Free in Asveroth" (1998)

ASTRONAUTS AND SPACE TRAVELERS

Thanks to the courage and devotion of three men, this project of sending a bullet to the moon, once seen as a futile enterprise, had already produced concrete results, with incalculable consequences. The voyagers, imprisoned in their new satellite, had not reached their destination, but at least they had become part of the lunar world; they were in orbit around the celebrity of the night, and, for the first time, the human eye could penetrate all her mysteries. The names of Nicholl, Barbicane, and Michel Ardan would be forever celebrated in the annals of astronomy, for these bold explorers, eager to widen the circle of human knowledge, had audaciously launched themselves into space, gambling their lives in the strangest undertaking of modern times.

   —Jules Verne, *From the Earth to the Moon* (1865), translated by
     Walter James Miller (1978)

Thousands of men have spun a trail of daring adventure and pioneering in the spaceways. There are statues in virtually every park on the planet dedicated to their truly magnificent achievements. Statues of rugged men, with set chins and purposeful eyes. Pioneers who blasted open the greatest frontier of them all, so you cannot blame us if doggedly we persist in revering their magic names; to honor their memories.

   —Sam Moskowitz, "Man of the Stars" (1941)

Spacemen die if they stay in one place.

   —Robert A. Heinlein, "The Green Hills of Earth" (1947)

Astronauts were not the impulsive daredevils so dear to the stereopticon-loving public. They couldn't afford to be. The hazards of the profession required an infinite capacity for cautious, contemplative thought.
　—Eric Frank Russell, "Hobbyist" (1947)

Spacemen—men who work in space, pilots and jetmen and astrogators and such—are men who like a few million miles of elbow room.
　—Robert A. Heinlein, "Gentlemen, Be Seated!" (1948)

David will never go to space again.
　I'm glad. What did it gain the McQuarries? What has it ever gained men? Have men ever brought back more happiness from the stars? Will they ever?
　—Leigh Brackett, "The Woman from Altair" (1951)

You know what they say about *bold* spacemen never becoming *old* spacemen. They don't live that long.
　—Poul Anderson, "Garden in the Void" (1952)

We'd sat cooped up in a prison-cell that flew, that was all—but now we were "spacemen."
　—Edmond Hamilton, "What's It Like Out There?" (1952)

The *Stone* trembled and threw herself outward bound, toward Saturn. In her train followed hundreds and thousands and hundreds of thousands of thousands of restless, rolling Stones . . . to Saturn . . . to Uranus, to Pluto . . . rolling on out to the stars . . . outward bound to the ends of the Universe.
　—Robert A. Heinlein, *The Rolling Stones* (1952)

Constantly working outward, putting system after system inside the known universe, they were the bright hungry wave of mankind reaching out to gather in the stars.
　—Algis Budrys, "Lower Than Angels" (1956)

We're *free* out here, really free for the first time. We're floating, literally. Gravity can't bow our backs or break our arches or tame our ideas. You know, it's only out here that stupid people like us can really think. The weightlessness gets our thoughts and we can sort them. Ideas grow out here like nowhere else—it's the right environment for them.

Anyone can get into space, if he wants to hard enough. The ticket is a dream.
  —Fritz Leiber, "The Beat Cluster" (1961)

"You spin in the sky, the world spins under you, and you step from land to land, while we . . ." She turned her head right, left, and her black hair curled and uncurled on the shoulder of her coat. "We have our dull, circled lives, bound in gravity, *worshiping* you!"
  —Samuel R. Delany, "Aye, and Gomorrah" (1967)

If space people didn't have curiosity, they probably wouldn't be space people.
  —Stephen Tall, "The Bear with the Knot on His Tail" (1971)

Up here [in space], you're free. Really free, for the first time in your life. All the laws and rules and prejudices they've been dumping on you all your life . . . they're all *down there*. Up here it's a new start. You can be yourself and do your own thing . . . and nobody can tell you different.
  —Ben Bova, "Zero Gee" (1972)

Once you've grown up in space, moving on means moving out, not going back to Earth. Nobody wants to be a groundpounder.
  —Gregory Benford, "Dark Sanctuary" (1979)

"What was being on the moon literally like?" [. . .]
  "Being on the moon?" His tired gaze inspected the narrow street of cheap jewellery stores, with its office messengers and lottery touts, the off-duty taxi-drivers leaning against their cars. "It was just like being here."
  —J. G. Ballard, "The Man Who Walked on the Moon" (1985)

Nonetheless, Scranton had travelled in space. He had known the loneliness of separation from all other human beings, he had gazed at the empty perspectives that I myself had seen.
  —J. G. Ballard, "The Man Who Walked on the Moon" (1985)

You're all astronauts on some kind of star trek.
  —Brannon Braga and Ronald D. Moore, *Star Trek: First Contact* (film, 1996)

BEAUTY

Only the rational and useful is beautiful.
— Yevgeny Zamiatin, *We* (1924), translated by Mirra Ginsburg (1972)

[On King Kong's death:] It wasn't the airplanes. It was beauty killed the beast.
— James Ashmore Creelman and Ruth Rose, *King Kong* (film, 1933)

Beauty is a luster which love bestows to guile the eye. Therefore it may be said that only when the brain is without love will the eye look and see no beauty.
— Jack Vance, *The Dying Earth* (1950)

The novels were all right for a while until she found out that most of them were like the movies — all about the pretty ones who really own the world.
— Theodore Sturgeon, "Saucer of Loneliness" (1953)

When beauty is universal, it loses its power to move the heart, and only its absence can produce any emotional effect.
— Arthur C. Clarke, *The City and the Stars* (1956)

The deer knew that the boy thought her beautiful. For it was the purpose of the deer in this world on that morning to be beautiful for a young boy to look at.
— Craig Strete, "Time Deer" (1974)

We know truth for the cruel instrument it is. Beauty is infinitely preferable to truth.
— George R. R. Martin, "The Way of Cross and Dragon" (1979)

We each have a moral obligation to conserve and preserve beauty in this world; there is none to waste.
— Robert A. Heinlein, *Friday* (1982)

You are horror and beauty in rare combination.
  —Octavia E. Butler, *Dawn* (1987)

They gave me eyes. All of you are beautiful; you shine like stars. But I must
go away with them.
  —Joan Slonczewski, *The Wall around Eden* (1989)

Beauty was the promise of happiness, not happiness itself; and the anticipated
world was often more rich than anything real.
  —Kim Stanley Robinson, *Red Mars* (1992)

How was it that destruction could be so beautiful? Was there something in
the scale of it? Was there some shadow in people, lusting for it? Or was it just
a coincidental combination of the elements, the final proof that beauty has no
moral dimension?
  —Kim Stanley Robinson, *Red Mars* (1992)

People give up the earth for beauty.
  —Esther M. Friesner, "Big Hair" (2000)

It was her scars that made her beautiful.
  —Mary Gentle, *Ash: A Secret History* (2000)

BELIEF

There was the class of superstitious people; they are not content simply to
ignore what is true, they also believe what is not true.
  —Jules Verne, *From the Earth to the Moon* (1865), translated by
    Walter James Miller (1978)

Feeling is believing.
  —Edwin A. Abbott, *Flatland: A Romance of Many Dimensions* (1884)

Of course she believed the blessed lie, for in times of extreme peril it is
human to be optimistic.
  —R. F. Starzl, "The Planet of Despair" (1931)

People believe in God because they've been conditioned to believe in God.
— Aldous Huxley, *Brave New World* (1932)

People make mistakes in life through believing too much, but they have a damned dull time if they believe too little.
— James Hilton, *Lost Horizon* (1933)

The capacity of humans to believe in what seems to me highly improbable — from table tapping to the superiority of their children — has never been plumbed. Faith strikes me as intellectual laziness.
— Robert A. Heinlein, *Stranger in a Strange Land* (1961)

I knew nothing, and I persisted in the faith that the time of cruel miracles was not past.
— Stanislaw Lem, *Solaris* (1961), translated by Joanna Kilmartin and Steve Cox (1970)

Disbelief is catching. It rubs off on people.
— Ray Bradbury, "A Miracle of Rare Device" (1962)

He hungered to believe in the marvelous. (Who doesn't?)
— Edgar Pangborn, "The Children's Crusade" (1974)

There must be few indeed who don't cherish a faith in some things, because all knowledge remains incomplete; even though faith is only the fantasy of things hoped for, the invention of things not seen. I have faith in the good will of myself and certain others, faith in the rightness of love and virtue and mercy. That faith will sustain me as it has in the past, while I live.
— Edgar Pangborn, "The Children's Crusade" (1974)

A personal god, a father-model, man needs that. Dave draws strength from it and we lean on him. Maybe leaders have to believe.
— James Tiptree, Jr., "Houston, Houston, Do You Read?" (1976)

An exaggerated and solemn respect always indicates a loss of faith.
— Gene Wolfe, "Seven American Nights" (1978)

The truths, the great truths — and most of the lesser ones as well — they are unbearable for most men. We find our shield in faith. Your faith, my faith, any faith. It doesn't matter, so long as we *believe,* really and truly believe, in whatever lie we cling to. [. . .] They may believe in Christ or Buddha or Erika Stormjones, in reincarnation or immortality or nature, in the power of love or the platform of a political faction, but it all comes to the same thing. They believe. They are happy. It is the ones who have seen truth who despair, and kill themselves.
　　— George R. R. Martin, "The Way of Cross and Dragon" (1979)

Some things were too hard to believe, however entertaining they might be to hear or read.
　　— Hal Clement, *The Nitrogen Fix* (1980)

In reduced circumstances you have to believe all kinds of things. I believe in thought transference now, vibrations in the ether, that sort of junk.
　　— Margaret Atwood, *The Handmaid's Tale* (1986)

This is how humans are: We question all our beliefs, except for the ones we *really* believe, and those we never think to question.
　　— Orson Scott Card, *Speaker for the Dead* (1986)

The Electric Monk was a labor-saving device. [. . .] Electric Monks believed things for you, thus saving you what was becoming an increasingly onerous task, that of believing all the things the world expected you to believe.
　　— Douglas Adams, *Dirk Gently's Holistic Detective Agency* (1987)

Belief is a force. It's a weak force, by comparison with gravity; when it comes to moving mountains, gravity wins every time. But it still exists.
　　— Terry Pratchett, *Pyramids* (1989)

It is always hard when reality intrudes on belief.
　　— Alan Dean Foster, *Cyber Way* (1990)

Religious revivals have been endemic on the Number One World ever since the gods retired and went to live in the sun. Nobody is exactly sure why. One view is that mankind has a desperate need to believe in something, preferably something so blatantly absurd that only blind, unquestioning faith will suffice — for example, the belief which sprang up in the late nineteenth century and was still widely current in Jason Derry's time and which held that human beings were not in fact created at all but were somehow the descendants of bald, mutant monkeys. The other view is that there is never anything much on television during the summer.

—Tom Holt, *Ye Gods!* (1992)

To learn a belief without belief is to sing a song without the tune.

A yielding, an obedience, a willingness to accept these notes as the right notes, this pattern as the true pattern, is the essential gesture of performance, translation, and understanding. The gesture need not be permanent, a lasting posture of the mind or heart; yet it is not false. It is more than the suspension of disbelief needed to watch a play, yet less than a conversion. It is a position, a posture in the dance.

—Ursula K. Le Guin, *The Telling* (2000)

Belief is the wound that knowledge heals, and death begins the Telling of our life.

—Ursula K. Le Guin, *The Telling* (2000)

STORM: Sometimes anger can help you survive.
NIGHTCRAWLER: So can faith.

—Michael Dougherty, Dan Harris, and David Hayter, *X2: X-Men United* (film, 2003)

THE BODY

The Martians may be descended from beings not unlike ourselves, by a gradual development of brain and hands (the latter giving rise to the two bunches of delicate tentacles at last) at the expense of the rest of the body. Without the body the brain would of course become a more selfish intelligence, without any of the emotional substratum of the human being.

—H. G. Wells, *The War of the Worlds* (1898)

There are so many disadvantages in human construction which do not occur in us machines. [. . .] Some little thing here or there breaks — they stop work-

ing and then, in a short time, they are decomposing. Had he been a machine, like myself, I could have mended him, replaced the broken parts and made him as good as new, but with these animal structures one is almost helpless.
　—John Wyndham, "The Lost Machine" (1932)

The human heart is more complex than any other part of the body.
　—William Hurlbut, *Bride of Frankenstein* (film, 1935)

You must admit that it might be confusing to have one brain and two bodies.
　—Edgar Rice Burroughs, *Synthetic Men of Mars* (1940)

I am still young and ill-formed, running to slenderness instead of to the corpulence that is the universal mark of beauty.
　—James V. McConnell, "All of You" (1953)

Madge borrows a body once a month and dusts the place, though the only thing a house is good for now is keeping termites and mice from getting pneumonia.
　—Kurt Vonnegut, Jr., "Unready to Wear" (1953)

The body, he reflected, possesses ways of its own, sometimes in contra-distinction to the purposes of the mind.
　—Philip K. Dick, *Clans of the Alphane Moon* (1964)

Within his body there throbbed the contributions of many a young Vorster volunteer: a film of lung tissue from one, a retina from another, kidneys from a pair of twins. He was a patchwork man, and he carried the flesh of his movement about with him.
　—Robert Silverberg, "Open the Sky" (1966)

Harrison Wintergreen was inside his own body.
　It was a world of wonder and loathsomeness, of the majestic and the ludicrous. Wintergreen's point of view, which his mind analogized as a body within his true body, was inside a vast network of pulsing arteries, like some monstrous freeway system. The analogy crystallized. It *was* a freeway, and Wintergreen was driving down it. Bloated sacs dumped things into the teeming traffic: hormones, wastes, nutrients. White blood cells

35

careened by him like mad taxicabs. Red corpuscles drove steadily along like stolid burghers. The traffic ebbed and congested like a crosstown rush hour. Wintergreen drove on, searching, searching.
—Norman Spinrad, "Carcinoma Angels" (1967)

Seagrave's slim and exhausted face was covered with shattered safety glass, as if his body were already crystallizing, at last escaping out of this uneasy set of dimensions into a more beautiful universe.
—J. G. Ballard, *Crash* (1973)

You're gaining weight finally. Thinness is dangerous.
—Octavia E. Butler, "Bloodchild" (1984)

The body was meat. Case fell into the prison of his own flesh.
—William Gibson, *Neuromancer* (1984)

Almost everything which corrupts the soul, must also decay the body.
—William Gibson and Bruce Sterling, *The Difference Engine* (1991)

The molecules of your body are the same molecules that make up this station and the nebula outside, that burn inside the stars themselves. We are starstuff, we are the universe made manifest, trying to figure itself out.
—D. C. Fontana, "A Distant Star," episode of *Babylon 5* (1994)

I was nodding off on the streetcar home from work when I saw the woman getting on. She was wearing the body I used to have!
—Nalo Hopkinson, "A Habit of Waste" (1996)

BOOKS

"What is the use of a book," thought Alice, "without pictures or conversations?"
—Lewis Carroll, *Alice's Adventures in Wonderland* (1865)

Squatting upon his haunches on the table top in the cabin his father had built—his smooth, brown, naked little body bent over the book which rested in his strong slender hands, and his great shock of long, black hair falling

about his well shaped head and bright, intelligent eyes — Tarzan of the apes, little primitive man, presented a picture filled, at once, with pathos and with promise — an allegorical figure of the primordial groping through the black night of ignorance toward the light of learning.
    —Edgar Rice Burroughs, *Tarzan of the Apes* (1914)

Books are opium.
    —Aldous Huxley, *Eyeless in Gaza* (1936)

The best books, he perceived, are those that tell you what you know already.
    —George Orwell, *Nineteen Eighty-Four* (1949)

The opinions expressed in this book are not those of the author.
    —Arthur C. Clarke, *Childhood's End* (1953)

A book is a loaded gun in the house next door.
    —Ray Bradbury, *Fahrenheit 451* (1954)

The books say *nothing*! Nothing you can teach or believe. They're about non-existent people, figments of imagination, if they're fiction. And if they're nonfiction, it's worse, one professor calling another an idiot, one philosopher screaming down another's gullet.
    —Ray Bradbury, *Fahrenheit 451* (1954)

Books were only one type of receptacle where we stored a lot of things we were afraid we might forget. There is nothing magical in them, at all. The magic is only in what books say, how they stitched the patches of the universe together into one garment for us.
    —Ray Bradbury, *Fahrenheit 451* (1954)

What traitors book can be! you think they're backing you up, and they turn on you.
    —Ray Bradbury, *Fahrenheit 451* (1954)

She came over and sniffed at one of the books, baring her teeth as though it were a dangerous adversary.
    —Pierre Boulle, *Planet of the Apes* (1963), translated by Xan Fielding (1963)

Books

Somehow, the burning of millions of books felt more brutally obscene than the killing of people. All men must die, it was their single common heritage. But a book need never die and should not be killed; books were the immortal part of man.

—Robert A. Heinlein, *Farnham's Freehold* (1964)

A classic is a book that has never finished saying what it has to say.

—Italo Calvino, "Why Read the Classics?" (1981), translated by
   Patrick Creagh (1987)

They had a sad smell, old books.

—William Gibson, *Mona Lisa Overdrive* (1988)

Grandad was superstitious about books. He thought that if you had enough of them around, education leaked out, like radioactivity.

—Terry Pratchett, *Johnny and the Dead* (1993)

BUILDINGS AND ARCHITECTURE

Oh, great, divinely bounding wisdom of walls and barriers! They are, perhaps, the greatest of man's inventions. Man ceased to be a wild animal only when he built the first wall.

—Yevgeny Zamiatin, *We* (1924), translated by Mirra Ginsburg (1972)

A dweller in a house may impress his personality upon the walls, but subtly the walls too, may impress their own shape upon the ego of the man.

—C. L. Moore, "No Woman Born" (1944)

He looked down into a night that was alive with radiance. The streets and walls glowed, strings of colored lamps flashed and flashed against a velvet dark, fountains leaped white and gold and scarlet, a flame display danced like molten rainbows at the feet of a triumphal statue. Star architecture was a thing of frozen motion, soaring columns and tiers and pinnacles to challenge the burning sky.

—Poul Anderson, "Ghetto" (1954)

Hill House, not sane, stood by itself against its hills, holding darkness within; it had stood so for eighty years and might stand for eighty more. Within, walls continued upright, bricks met neatly, floors were firm, and doors were sensibly shut; silence lay steadily against the wood and stone of Hill House, and whatever walked there, walked alone.
  —Shirley Jackson, *The Haunting of Hill House* (1959)

He had moved up a floor, and the sequence of identical rooms he had occupied were like displaced images of himself seen through a prism. Their common focus, that elusive final definition of himself which he had sought for so long, still remained to be found.
  —J. G. Ballard, "The Cage of Sand" (1962)

Cheops' Law: Nothing *ever* gets built on schedule or within budget.
  —Robert A. Heinlein, *Time Enough for Love* (1973)

"Think of it [1930s architecture]," Dialta Downes had said, "as a kind of alternate America: a 1980 that never happened. An architecture of broken dreams."
  —William Gibson, "The Gernsback Continuum" (1981)

Buildings were just the world's furniture, and he didn't care how it was arranged.
  —John Varley, "The Pusher" (1981)

Case watched the sun rise on the landscape of childhood, on broken slag and the rusting shells of refineries.
  —William Gibson, *Neuromancer* (1984)

The sitting room is subdued, symmetrical; it's one of the shapes money takes when it freezes. Money has trickled through this room for years and years, as if through an underground cavern, crusting and hardening like stalactites into these forms.
  —Margaret Atwood, *The Handmaid's Tale* (1986)

Do not look for revelations in the ancient ruins. You will find here only what you bring: bits of memory, wisps of the past as thin as clouds in the summer,

fragments of stone that are carved with symbols that sometimes almost make sense.
    —Pat Murphy, *The Falling Woman* (1986)

The walls and floor of the great room were hers to reshape as she pleased. They would do anything she was able to ask of them except let her out.
    —Octavia E. Butler, *Dawn* (1987)

A ruin is a ruin, a toppled remnant, and its final statement is failure.
    —George Turner, *Drowning Towers* (1987)

There was something vampiric about the room, she decided, something it would have in common with millions of similar rooms, as though its bewilderingly seamless anonymity were sucking away her personality.
    —William Gibson, *Mona Lisa Overdrive* (1988)

Lammiela's house was the abode of infinity. The endless rooms were packed with the junk of a hundred worlds.
    —Alexander Jablokov, "The Death Artist" (1990)

Buildings express values, they have a sort of grammar, and rooms are the sentences.
    —Kim Stanley Robinson, *Red Mars* (1992)

BUSINESS AND ECONOMICS

Strangely late in the world's history, the obvious fact was perceived that no business is so essentially the public business as the industry and commerce on which the people's livelihood depends, and that to entrust it to private persons to be managed for private profit is a folly similar in kind, though vastly greater in magnitude, to that of surrendering the functions of political government to kings and nobles to be conducted for their personal glorification.
    —Edward Bellamy, *Looking Backward, 2000–1887* (1888)

Buying and selling is essentially anti-social in all its tendencies. It is an education in self-seeking at the expense of others, and no society whose citizens

are trained in such a school can possibly rise above a very low grade of civilization.
— Edward Bellamy, *Looking Backward, 2000–1887* (1888)

Nothing about your age is, at first sight, more astounding to a man of modern times than the fact that men engaged in the same industry, instead of fraternizing as comrades and co-laborers to a common end, should have regarded each other as rivals and enemies to be throttled and overthrown. This certainly seems like sheer madness, a scene from bedlam.
— Edward Bellamy, *Looking Backward, 2000–1887* (1888)

I explained that the laws of nature require a struggle for existence, and that in the struggle the fittest survive, and the unfit perish. In our economic struggle, I continued, there was always plenty of opportunity for the fittest to reach the top, which they did, in great numbers, particularly in our country; that where there was severe economic pressure the lowest classes of course felt it the worst.
— Charlotte Perkins Gilman, *Herland* (1915)

We earth men have a talent for ruining big, beautiful things. The only reason we didn't set up hot-dog stands in the midst of the temple of Karnak on Egypt is because it was out of the way and served no large commercial purpose.
— Ray Bradbury, "And the Moon Be Still As Bright" (1948)

The hawkers were ignored by the hurrying throngs of people; anybody with a genuine system of prediction would be using it, not selling it.
— Philip K. Dick, *Solar Lottery* (1955)

Junk is the ideal product . . . the ultimate merchandise. No sales talk necessary. The client will crawl through a sewer and beg to buy . . .
— William S. Burroughs, *Naked Lunch* (1959)

Politics is the enemy of a sound economic entity.
— Philip K. Dick, *The Crack in Space* (1965)

"Tanstaafl." Means "there ain't no such thing as a free lunch."
— Robert A. Heinlein, *The Moon Is a Harsh Mistress* (1966)

A profit is not without honor.
— Philip José Farmer, "Riders of the Purple Wage" (1967)

He tried to read an elementary economics text; it bored him past endurance, it was like listening to somebody interminably recounting a long and stupid dream.
— Ursula K. Le Guin, *The Dispossessed: An Ambiguous Utopia* (1974)

It's a well-known economic phenomenon but tragic to see it in operation, for the more shoe shops there were, the more shoes they had to make and the worse and more unwearable they became. And the worse they were to wear, the more people had to buy to keep themselves shod, and the more the shops proliferated, until the whole economy of the place passed what I believe is termed the Shoe Event Horizon, and it became no longer economically possible to build anything other than shoe shops. Result — collapse, ruin and famine.
— Douglas Adams, *The Restaurant at the End of the Universe* (1980)

Power, in Case's world, meant corporate power. The zaibatsus, the multinationals that shaped the course of human history, had transcended old barriers. Viewed as organisms, they had attained a kind of immortality. You couldn't kill a zaibatsu by assassinating a dozen key executives; there were others waiting to step up the ladder, assume the vacated position, access the vast banks of corporate memory.
— William Gibson, *Neuromancer* (1984)

Every transaction is for gain on one side or both, and the transaction that pretends to fair play is corrupt by definition. Corruption is the normal state of a society that restrains its excesses by law or morality.
— George Turner, *Drowning Towers* (1987)

Their society is based on *ownership*. Everything that you see and touch, everything you come into contact with, will *belong* to somebody or to an institution; it will be theirs, they will own it. [. . .] The ownership of humans is possible too; not in terms of actual slavery, which they are proud to have abolished, but in the sense that, according to which sex and class one belongs to, one may be partially owned by another or others by having to sell one's labour or talents to somebody with the means to buy them.
— Iain M. Banks, *The Player of Games* (1988)

That's a large part of what economics is—people arbitrarily, or as a matter of taste, assigning numerical values to non-numerical things. And then pretending that they haven't just made the numbers up, which they have. Economics is like astrology in that sense, except that economics serves to justify the current power structure, and so it has a lot of fervent believers among the powerful.
   —Kim Stanley Robinson, *Red Mars* (1992)

The weakness of businessmen was their belief that money was the point of the game.
   —Kim Stanley Robinson, *Red Mars* (1992)

It's often easiest for us to identify at the retail level, Laney. We're a shopping species.
   —William Gibson, *Idoru* (1996)

History, as every mature Aten knew, was simply the evolution of economics.
   —Ralph A. Sperry, "On Vacation" (1998)

CHANGE

The horror of the Same Old Thing is [. . .] an endless source of heresies in religion, folly in counsel, infidelity in marriage, and inconstancy in friendship. The humans live in time, and experience reality successively. To experience much of it, therefore, they must experience many different things; in other words, they must experience change. And since they need change, the Enemy (being a hedonist at heart) has made change pleasurable to them.

   —C. S. Lewis, *The Screwtape Letters* (1942)

"At least half of mankind," he observed, "still makes an unconscious equation in its thinking, and assumes that change—any sort of change—is identical with progress. It is not so; and any student of the course of evolutionary history on Terra could tell you of change which has been regressive, change which has led to an ultimately fatal specialization, change which has been overadaptation to an ecological niche which no longer existed, or did not yet exist."

   —Margaret St. Clair, *Agent of the Unknown* (1952)

"Things don't stay the way they are," said Flanerty. "It's too entertaining to try to change them." [. . .]

   "Most fascinating game there is, keeping things from staying the way they are."

   —Kurt Vonnegut, Jr., *Player Piano* (1952)

It was a pleasure to burn.

   It was a special pleasure to see things eaten, to see things blackened and *changed*. With the brass nozzle in his fists, with this great python spitting its venomous kerosene upon the world, the blood pounded in his head, and his hands were the hands of some amazing conductor playing all the symphonies of blazing and burning to bring down the tatters and charcoal ruins of history.

   —Ray Bradbury, *Fahrenheit 451* (1954)

Those who don't build must burn. It's as old as history and juvenile delinquents.
—Ray Bradbury, *Fahrenheit 451* (1954)

When you tire of living, change itself seems evil, does it not? for then any change at all disturbs the deathlike peace of the life-weary.
—Walter M. Miller, Jr., *A Canticle for Leibowitz* (1959)

The mind of man was uncommonly stubborn and slow to change. Reformers, including himself, were always prone to forget that. Victory always seemed just around the corner. But generally it was not, after all.
—Philip K. Dick, *The Crack in Space* (1965)

She was not accustomed to thinking about things changing, old ways dying and new ones arising. She did not find it comfortable to look at things in that light.
—Ursula K. Le Guin, *The Tombs of Atuan* (1971)

Change is what's boring, monotonous. Sameness is a continual challenge, almost impossible to maintain. Repetition, knowing that you've done it right before and can do it right again, is satisfying.
—Robert Thurston, "Good-Bye, Shelley, Shirley, Charlotte, Charlene" (1972)

A new thing is always interesting, in its trivial fashion.
—Ursula K. Le Guin, "The Direction of the Road" (1973)

Death was in him, under him; the earth itself was uncertain, unreliable. The enduring, the reliable, is a promise made by the human mind.
—Ursula K. Le Guin, *The Dispossessed: An Ambiguous Utopia* (1974)

It is change, continuing change, inevitable change, that is the dominant factor in society today. No sensible decision can be made any longer without taking into account not only the world as it is, but the world as it will be—and naturally this means that there must be an accurate perception of the world as it will be. This, in turn, means that our statesmen, our businessmen, our everyman must take on a science fictional way of thinking, whether he likes it or not, or even whether he knows it or not. Only so can the deadly problems of today be solved.

> —Isaac Asimov, foreword to *Encyclopedia of Science Fiction*, edited by Robert Holdstock (1978)

Nothing in the universe ever stops except the human politic, the human solution to this problem or that. And when we stop, we fail. Stopping is the only unnatural thing there is; every force in nature, every object in the universe is in motion, changing, changing . . .

> —Theodore Sturgeon, "Why Dolphins Don't Bite" (1980)

Of all the species, yours cannot abide stagnation. Change is at the heart of what you are.

> —Maurice Hurley and Gene Roddenberry, "Hide and Q," episode of *Star Trek: The Next Generation* (1987)

Her strength is in staying put. God, what strength! But it's all in that. So the shit piles up around her, and she never clears it away. Hell, she builds walls of it! Fecal fortifications. Defending her from, God forbid, change. From, God forbid, freedom . . .

> —Ursula K. Le Guin, "Half Past Four" (1987)

The essence of human good lay in its fleeting poignancy. Only things mech-like built and shaped. [. . .] Humanity today knew the true division between the sweet passing beauties of things human, and the cruel hard mech ways.

The knowledge of certain death, that nothing could be caught, that each fleeting instant had to be savored in its passing—that was the essence of wisdom. Not holding on, but instead, living fully.

> —Gregory Benford, "At the Double Solstice" (1988)

Changing was necessary. Change was right. He was all in favor of change.

What he was dead against was things not staying the same.

> —Terry Pratchett, *Diggers* (1990)

All that you touch
You Change.

All that you Change
Changes you.

The only lasting truth
Is Change.

God
Is Change.
    —Octavia E. Butler, *Parable of the Talents* (1998)

Our lives are about development, mutation and the possibility of change; that is almost a definition of what life is: change. [. . .] If you disable change, if you effectively stop time, if you prevent the possibility of the alteration of an individual's circumstances—and that must include at least the possibility that they alter for the worse—then you don't have life after death; you just have death.
    —Iain M. Banks, *Look to Windward* (2000)

CHILDREN AND YOUNG PEOPLE

"It would have made a dreadfully ugly child; but it makes rather a handsome pig, I think." And she began thinking of other children she knew, who might do very well as pigs.
    —Lewis Carroll, *Alice's Adventures in Wonderland* (1865)

I want always to be a little boy and to have fun; so I ran away to Kensington Gardens and lived a long time among the fairies.
    —J. M. Barrie, *Peter Pan* (play, 1904)

Children are the boldest philosophers. They enter life naked, not covered by the smallest fig leaf of dogma, absolutes, creeds. This is why every question they ask is so absurdly naive and so frighteningly complex.
    —Yevgeny Zamiatin, "On Literature, Revolution, Entropy, and Other
        Matters" (1923), translated by Mirra Ginsburg (1970)

We are two different breeds of animals, children and adults. [. . .] There is no meeting of the minds. Jeez. There is nothing but war. It is why all children grow up hating their childhoods and searching for revenges.
    —Alfred Bester, "The Starcomber" (1954)

Like paternal parent, like male offspring.
—Roger Dee, "The Poundstone Paradox" (1954)

People did not remember their childhoods clearly enough to take seriously the rages and frustrations that shook children.
—James Blish, *A Case of Conscience* (1958)

Homo sapiens is a unique animal. Physically he matures at approximately the age of thirteen. However, mental maturity and adjustment is often not fully realized until thirty or even more. Indeed, it is sometimes never achieved. Before such maturity is reached, our youth are susceptible to romantic appeal. Nationalism, chauvinism, racism, the supposed glory of the military, all seem romantic to the immature. They rebel at the ordinariness of present society. They seek entertainment in excitement.
—Mack Reynolds, "Gun for Hire" (1960)

Youth must go, ah yes. But youth is only being in a way like it might be an animal. No, it is not just like being an animal so much as being like one of these malenky toys you viddy being sold in the streets, like little chellovecks made out of tin and with a spring inside and then a winding handle on the outside and you wind it up grrr grrr grrr and off it itties, like walking, O my brothers. But it itties in a straight line and bangs straight into things bang bang and it cannot help what it is doing. Being young is like being like one of these malenky machines.
—Anthony Burgess, *A Clockwork Orange* (1962)

Babies are man's birthright, and it is his bounden duty to create as many of them as he possibly can.
—Robert F. Young, "There Was an Old Woman Who Lived in a Shoe" (1962)

People who say they want children later always mean they want children never.
—Bob Shaw, "Light of Other Days" (1966)

How fortunate for the species, Sarah muses or is mused, that children are as ingratiating as we know them. Otherwise they would soon be salted off for the leeches they are, and the race would extinguish itself in a fair sweet flowering, the last generations' massive achievement in the arts and pursuits of high civilization.

 —Pamela Zoline, "The Heat Death of the Universe" (1967)

When a species becomes terrified of its own young, it appears to be scheduled for the grand disposall down which went the dinosaurs.

 —John Brunner, *Stand on Zanzibar* (1968)

The young are an alien species. They won't replace us by revolution. They will forget and ignore us out of existence.

 —William S. Burroughs, *The Wild Boys: A Book of the Dead* (1971)

These kids, that I have known, lived with, still know, in California, are my science fiction stories of tomorrow, my summation, at this point of my life as a person and a writer; they are what I look ahead to—and so keenly desire to see prevail. What, more than anything else I have ever encountered, I believe in. And would give my life for. My full measure of devotion, in this war we are fighting, to maintain, and augment, what is human about us, what is the core of ourselves, and the source of our destiny.

 —Philip K. Dick, "The Android and the Human" (1972)

"Do they expect students not to be anarchists?" he said. "What else can the young be?"

 —Ursula K. Le Guin, *The Dispossessed: An Ambiguous Utopia* (1974)

Kids don't get invited to the events that make history. Until very recently all they ever did was work. Worked until they grew old or worked until they starved or worked until they were killed by a passing war.

 —P. J. Plauger, "Child of All Ages" (1975)

"Of course growing up," I said. "Rae is one more year away from being a child. What is so hard to understand about that?" Hawk landed at last upon a lonely beach. "One more year away from being a child? That does not sound like growing!"

 —Richard Bach, *There's No Such Place as Far Away* (1979)

Kids are bent. They think around corners. But starting at roughly age eight, when childhood's second great era begins, the kinks begin to straighten out,

one by one. The boundaries of thought and vision begin to close down to a tunnel as we gear up to get along. [. . .] The job of the fantasy-horror writer is to make you, for a little while, a child again.
  —Stephen King, *Danse Macabre* (1981)

There is something enormously powerful in the child's ability to withstand the fraudulent. A child has the clearest eye, the steadiest hand. The hucksters, the promoters, are appealing for the allegiance of these small people in vain.
  —Philip K. Dick, "How to Build a Universe That Doesn't Fall Apart Two
    Days Later" (1985)

Children aren't pets—they're little animals that have to be watched as well as loved.
  —George Turner, *Drowning Towers* (1987)

Youth is stupidly resilient.
  —George Turner, *Drowning Towers* (1987)

"A child is a kind of immortality," Selna muttered. "A link forged. A bond."
  —Jane Yolen, "The White Babe" (1987)

It is always, somehow, a surprise to find that an adult child still loves you.
  —Nancy Kress, "In Memoriam" (1988)

A boy's heart is a natural altar and many strange deities ask for sacrifice there.
  —Jane Yolen, "The Quiet Monk" (1988)

I was old the day I was born and I'll be young the day I die.
  —Kim Stanley Robinson, *Green Mars* (1994)

CHOICE

All we have to decide is what to do with the time that is given to us.
  —J. R. R. Tolkien, *The Fellowship of the Ring* (1954)

Just because you have a choice, it doesn't mean that any of them *has* to be right.
  —Norton Juster, *The Phantom Tollbooth* (1961)

When a man cannot choose he ceases to be a man.
—Anthony Burgess, *A Clockwork Orange* (1962)

The only thing she was conscious of lacking was a direction, and what was that but a matter of pointing a finger?
—Thomas M. Disch, *334* (1974)

What is an anarchist? One who, choosing, accepts the responsibility of choice.
—Ursula K. Le Guin, "The Day Before the Revolution" (1974)

A promise is a direction taken, a self-limitation of choice. As Odo pointed out, if no direction is taken, if one goes nowhere, no change will occur. One's freedom to choose and to change will be unused, exactly as if one were in jail, a jail of one's own building, a maze in which no one way is better than any other. So Odo came to see the promise, the pledge, the idea of fidelity, as essential in the complexity of freedom.
—Ursula K. Le Guin, *The Dispossessed: An Ambiguous Utopia* (1974)

Drug misuse is not a disease, it is a decision, like the decision to step out in front of a moving car. You would call that not a disease but an error in judgment.
—Philip K. Dick, author's note to *A Scanner Darkly* (1977)

Welcome to the human race. Nobody controls his own life, Ender. The best you can do is choose to be controlled by good people, by people who love you.
—Orson Scott Card, *Ender's Game* (1985)

I've always tried to walk the path of honor. But what do you do when all choices are evil? Shameful action, shameful inaction, every path leading to a thicket of death.
—Lois McMaster Bujold, *Shards of Honor* (1986)

The only way to avoid all frightening choices is to leave society and become a hermit, and that is a frightening choice.
—Richard Bach, *One* (1988)

Choice

We can have excuses, or we can have health, love, longevity, understanding, adventure, money, happiness. We design our lives through the power of our choices. We feel most helpless when we've made choices by default, when we haven't designed our lives on our own.
  —Richard Bach, *One* (1988)

Don't bother with the sardines when Leviathan looms.
  —Ray Bradbury, *Green Shadows, White Whale* (1992)

The past tempts us, the present confuses us, and the future frightens us. And our lives slip away, moment by moment, lost in that vast terrible in-between. But there is still time to seize that one last fragile moment. To choose something better, to make a difference, as you say. And I intend to do just that.
  —J. Michael Straczynski, "The Coming of Shadows," episode of
  Babylon 5 (1995)

The trouble is, humans do have a knack of choosing precisely those things which are worst for them.
  —J. K. Rowling, *Harry Potter and the Sorcerer's Stone* (1997)

It is our choices, Harry, that show what we truly are, far more than our abilities.
  —J. K. Rowling, *Harry Potter and the Chamber of Secrets* (1999)

CITIES

A town, like an individual, has a right to live.
  —J. T. McIntosh, "Katahut Said No" (1952)

The city hovered, then settled silently through the early morning darkness toward the broad expanse of heath which the planet's Proctors had designated as its landing place.
  —James Blish, "Earthman, Come Home" (1953)

She was aware of the life-noise of the city, the hard-breathing giant who never inhales.
  —Theodore Sturgeon, "Saucer of Loneliness" (1953)

The bigger the town, the more evil it seemed to hold, three centimeters under the frontal bone.
—Poul Anderson, "Journeys End" (1957)

Sinharat was a city without people, but it was not dead. It had a memory and a voice. [. . .] Sometimes the voice of Sinharat was soft and gentle, murmuring about everlasting youth and the pleasures thereof. Again it was strong and fierce with pride, crying *You did, but I do not!* Sometimes it was mad, laughing and hateful. But always the song was evil.
—Leigh Brackett, "The Road to Sinharat" (1963)

New York is a seething hell of hate and despair. It is a knife that flays each of us daily, reducing us to raw, quivering nerve ends. Such a witch's caldron of agony, terror and rage can't help but to boil over sooner or later.
—Jerrold J. Mundis, "Do It for Mama!" (1971)

The city was extraordinary, Breckenridge admitted: an ultimate urban glory, a supernal Babylon, a consummate Persepolis, the soul's own hymn in brick and stone.
—Robert Silverberg, "Breckenridge and the Continuum" (1973)

"Urban life is the ultimate human tragedy," said Alice. "People can't escape except through catastrophe."
—Jack Vance, "Assault on a City" (1974)

To wound the autumnal city.
—Samuel R. Delany, *Dhalgren* (1975)

The City was unable to provide for all of man's needs. There was something missing, something primal and liberating, something that was now only a dessicated memory out of man's dark history.
—Thomas F. Monteleone, "Breath's a Ware That Will Not Keep" (1976)

I went out into the night and the neon and let the crowd pull me along, walking blind, willing myself to be just a segment of that mass organism, just one more drifting chip of consciousness under the geodesics.
—William Gibson, "Burning Chrome" (1982)

Cities

Night City was like a deranged experiment in social Darwinism, designed by a bored researcher who kept one thumb permanently on the fast-forward button. Stop hustling and you sank without a trace, but move a little too swiftly and you'd break the fragile surface tension of the black market; either way, you were gone, with nothing left of you but some vague memory in the mind of a fixture like Ratz, though heart or lungs or kidneys might survive in the service of some stranger with New Yen for the clinic tanks.

— William Gibson, *Neuromancer* (1984)

It was one of those nights, I quickly decided, when you slip into an alternate continuum, a city that looks exactly like the one where you live, except for the peculiar difference that it contains not one person you love or know or have even spoken to before.

— William Gibson, "The Winter Market" (1985)

Bobby climbed down behind him, into the unmistakable signature smell of the Sprawl, a rich amalgam of stale subway exhalations, ancient soot, and the carcinogenic tang of fresh plastics, all of it shot through with the carbon edge of illicit fossil fuels.

— William Gibson, *Count Zero* (1986)

The city seemed to stretch about them like some pitiless abyss of geologic time.

— William Gibson and Bruce Sterling, *The Difference Engine* (1991)

Neighborhoods that mainly operated at night had a way of looking a lot worse in the morning.

— William Gibson, *Virtual Light* (1993)

The city sprawled like roadkill, spreading more with each new pressure.

— Steve Aylett, *Atom* (2000)

CIVILIZATION AND BARBARISM

"Are you surprised, professor, at setting foot on land, any land, and finding savages there? Where aren't there savages? Are they any worse than men elsewhere, the local natives you call savages?"

"But captain—"

"All I can say, professor, is that I have encountered savages everywhere."

—Jules Verne, *Twenty Thousand Leagues under the Sea* (1870), translated by Walter James Miller and Frederick Paul Walter (1993)

"Transportation is Civilization," our motto runs.

—Rudyard Kipling, "With the Night Mail" (1905)

This was life! ah, how he loved it! Civilization held nothing like this in its narrow and circumscribed sphere, hemmed in by restrictions and convenionalities. Even clothes were a hinderance and a nuisance. At last he was free. He had not realized what a prisoner he had been.

—Edgar Rice Burroughs, *Tarzan of the Apes* (1914)

Ten minutes later they were crossing the frontier that separated civilization from savagery. Uphill and down, across the deserts of salt or sand, through forests, into the violet depth of canyons, over crag and peak and table-topped mesa, the fence marched on and on, irresistibly the straight line, the geometrical symbol of triumphant human purpose.

—Aldous Huxley, *Brave New World* (1932)

"Cleanliness is next to fordliness," she insisted.

"Yes, and civilization is sterilization."

—Aldous Huxley, *Brave New World* (1932)

You can't have a lasting civilization without plenty of pleasant vices.

—Aldous Huxley, *Brave New World* (1932)

Tumithak had to learn that in no matter what nation or age one finds oneself, he will find gentleness if he looks, as well as savagery.

—Charles R. Tanner, "Tumithak of the Corridors" (1932)

He moved with the dangerous ease of a panther; he was too fiercely supple to be a product of civilization, even of that fringe of civilization which composed the outer frontiers.

—Robert E. Howard, "Beyond the Black River" (1935)

Civilization and Barbarism

"Barbarism is the natural state of mankind," the borderer said, still staring somberly at the Cimmerian. "Civilization is unnatural. It is a whim of circumstance. And barbarism must always ultimately triumph."
   — Robert E. Howard, "Beyond the Black River" (1935)

The very basis of human civilization was leisure . . . spare time in which to indulge curiosity and experiment.
   — Edmond Hamilton, "The Ephemerae" (1938)

The tides of civilization rolled in century-long waves across the continents, and each particular wave, though conscious of its participation in the tide, nevertheless was more preoccupied with dinner.
   — Henry Kuttner and C. L. Moore, "The Piper's Son" (1945)

One of the shortcomings of modern civilization—ancient civilization too, for that matter—is that the average man never gets all he wants of the most desirable products, never makes his life fit his dreams.
   — Jack Vance, "I'll Build Your Dream Castle" (1947)

It is impossible to found a civilization on fear and hatred and cruelty. It would never endure.
   — George Orwell, *Nineteen Eighty-Four* (1949)

Our civilization is flinging itself to pieces. Stand back from the centrifuge.
   — Ray Bradbury, *Fahrenheit 451* (1954)

All languages carry in them a portrait of their users and the idioms of every language say over and over again, "He is a stranger and therefore a barbarian."
   — Robert A. Heinlein, *The Star Beast* (1954)

I wonder how harmless such people are? To what extent civilization is retarded by the laughing jackasses, the empty-minded belittlers?
   — Robert A. Heinlein, *Have Space Suit—Will Travel* (1958)

Is civilization always a woman's choice first, and only later a man's?
   — Cordwainer Smith, "On the Gem Planet" (1963)

What was that epigram that he had trotted forth too often, about civilization being the distance man placed between himself and his excreta? But it was nearer the truth to say that civilization was the distance man had placed between himself and everything else.

—Brian W. Aldiss, *The Dark Light Years* (1964)

The same old hypocrisy. Life is a fight, and the strongest wins. All civilization does is hide the blood and cover up the hate with pretty words!

—Ursula K. Le Guin, *The Dispossessed: An Ambiguous Utopia* (1974)

An army, and sometimes a civilization, must proceed at the pace of its weakest marcher.

—Edgar Pangborn, "The Children's Crusade" (1974)

"From spaceman to caveman in three days," she meditated aloud. "How we imagine our civilization is in ourselves, when it's really in our things."

—Lois McMaster Bujold, *Shards of Honor* (1986)

She felt as she had felt in Havnor as a girl: a barbarian, uncouth among their smoothnesses. But because she was not a girl now, she was not awed, but only wondered at how men ordered their world into this dance of masks, and how easily a woman might learn to dance it.

—Ursula K. Le Guin, *Tehanu: The Last Book of Earthsea* (1990)

Some of these island farms were very ancient places of civilisation, drawing for their comfort and provision on inexhaustible sun, wind, and tide, settled in a way of life as immemorial as that of their plowlands and pastures, as full and secure. Not the show-wealth of the city, but the deep richness of the land, was in the steaming pitcher she brought him, and in the woman who brought it.

—Ursula K. Le Guin, "Olders" (1995)

He soon concluded New Orleans' idea of civilized hours had nothing to do with those kept by the rest of the world, or possibly that New Orleans defined civilization as unending revelry.

—Harry Turtledove, "Must and Shall" (1995)

CLASS SYSTEM

As for seeing the town, he did not even think of it, being of that breed of Britons who have their servants do their sightseeing for them.

— Jules Verne, *Around the World in Eighty Days* (1873), translated by
     William Butcher (1995)

To give the reader some general impression of the way people lived together in those days, and especially of the relations of the rich and poor to one another, perhaps I cannot do better than to compare society as it then was to a prodigious coach which the masses of humanity were harnessed to and dragged toilsomely along a very hilly and sandy road. The driver was hunger, and permitted no lagging, though the pace was necessarily very slow. Despite the difficulty of drawing the coach at all along so hard a road, the top was covered with passengers who never got down, even at the steeper ascents. These seats on top were very breezy and comfortable. Well up out of the dust, their occupants could enjoy the scenery at their leisure, or critically discuss the merits of the straining team. Naturally such places were in great demand and the competition for them was keen, every one seeking as the first end in life to secure a seat on the coach for himself and to leave it to his child after him.

— Edward Bellamy, *Looking Backward, 2000–1887* (1888)

"In the moon," says Cavor, "every citizen knows his place. He is born to that place, and the elaborate discipline of training and education and surgery he undergoes fits him at last so completely to it that he has neither ideas nor organs for any purpose beyond it."

— H. G. Wells, *The First Men in the Moon* (1901)

There can be no understanding between the hands and the brain [workers and management] unless the heart acts as mediator.

— Fritz Lang and Thea von Harbou, *Metropolis* (film, 1926), translator
     unknown (1926)

It was in this world that we found in its most striking form a social disease which is perhaps the commonest of all world-diseases — namely, the splitting of the population into two mutually unintelligible castes through the influence of economic forces.

— Olaf Stapledon, *Star Maker* (1937)

In earlier ages, class distinctions had been not only inevitable but desirable. Inequality was the price of civilization.

—George Orwell, *Nineteen Eighty-Four* (1949)

Ponse was not a villain. He was exactly like the members of every ruling class in history: honestly convinced of his benevolence and hurt if it was challenged.

—Robert A. Heinlein, *Farnham's Freehold* (1964)

She looked beyond me, as if at our village, at the Norsemen loading their boats with weeping slaves, at all the villages of Germany and England and France where the poor folk sweat from dawn to dark so that the great lords may do battle with one another, at castles under siege with the starving folk within eating mice and rats and sometimes each other, at the women carried off or raped or beaten, at the mothers wailing for their little ones, and beyond this at the great wide world itself with all its battles which I had used to think so grand, and the misery and greediness and fear and jealousy and hatred of folk one for the other.

—Joanna Russ, "Souls" (1982)

He disliked him because he found the idea of someone who was not only privileged, but was also sorry for himself because he thought the world didn't really understand the problems of privileged people, deeply obnoxious.

—Douglas Adams, *Dirk Gently's Holistic Detective Agency* (1987)

When the gap between the rich and poor is vast and the middle ground the haunt of an endangered species, snobbery was a defence against terror.

—George Turner, *Drowning Towers* (1987)

It has been a psychological refuge of the poor to denigrate their so-called betters, to satirize their excesses and manners and behaviour and pretend *they* were above such an artificial existence. [. . .] The contempt was a pretence, a shelter to make poverty bearable, even honourable, and so make pride possible.

—George Turner, *Drowning Towers* (1987)

CLOTHING AND NUDITY

Though he was now quite naked, you must not think that he was cold or unhappy. He was usually very happy and gay.
　—J. M. Barrie, *The Little White Bird, or, Adventures in Kensington Gardens* (1902)

Clothes, therefore, must be truly a badge of greatness; the insignia of the superiority of *man* over all other animals, for surely there could be no other reason for wearing the hideous things.
　—Edgar Rice Burroughs, *Tarzan of the Apes* (1914)

Soon he did not miss his clothing in the least, and from that he came to revel in the freedom of his unhampered state.
　—Edgar Rice Burroughs, *The Son of Tarzan* (1917)

Following Derringer's advice he had traveled [through time] naked—"the one costume common to all ages," the scientist had boomed.
　—Anthony Boucher, "The Barrier" (1942)

He wore nothing but a loincloth, but dignity clothed him amply.
　—Ursula K. Le Guin, *The Farthest Shore* (1972)

She was quite naked, the way I'd seen her at the first, but she had the sort of nakedness that seems like clothes, clean-cut, firm and flawless.
　—Tanith Lee, "The Thaw" (1979)

Clothing was a language and Coretti a kind of sartorial stutterer, unable to make the kind of basic coherent fashion statement that would put strangers at their ease. His ex-wife told him he dressed like a Martian; that he didn't look as though he belonged anywhere in the city.
　—John Shirley and William Gibson, "The Belonging Kind" (1981)

She was dressed in her own beauty, like Mother Eve before the Fall. She made it seem so utterly appropriate that I wondered how I had ever acquired the delusion that freedom from clothing equals obscenity.
　—Robert A. Heinlein, *Job: A Comedy of Justice* (1984)

I marvel again at the nakedness of men's lives: the showers right out in the open, the body exposed for inspection and comparison, the public display of privates. What is it for? What purposes of reassurance does it serve? The flashing of a badge, look, everyone, all is in order; I belong here. Why don't women have to prove to one another that they are women?
— Margaret Atwood, *The Handmaid's Tale* (1986)

You can think clearly only with your clothes on.
— Margaret Atwood, *The Handmaid's Tale* (1986)

"You see, jewelry isn't just something she wears," said the ghost of Teppicymon XXVII. *"It's part of who she is."*
— Terry Pratchett, *Pyramids* (1989)

All across the multiverse there are backward tribes. [. . .] Considered backward, that is, by people who wear more clothes than they do.
— Terry Pratchett, *Witches Abroad* (1991)

Clothing seems to be an encumbrance for alien beings.
— Nancy Johnston, "The Rendez-Vous: The True Story of Jeannetta (Netty) Wilcox" (1998)

COMMUNICATION AND SPEECH

If you would talk less nonsense, you would remember more sense.
— Edwin A. Abbott, *Flatland: A Romance of Many Dimensions* (1884)

In civilised life domestic hatred usually expresses itself by saying things which would appear quite harmless on paper (the *words* are not offensive) but in such a voice, or at such a moment, that they are not far short of a blow in the face.
— C. S. Lewis, *The Screwtape Letters* (1942)

They walked along, two continents of experience and feeling, unable to communicate.
— William Golding, *Lord of the Flies* (1954)

You can find out more about someone by talking than by listening.
— William S. Burroughs, *Naked Lunch* (1959)

How do you expect to communicate with the ocean, when you can't even understand one another?
— Stanislaw Lem, *Solaris* (1961), translated by Joanna Kilmartin and Steve Cox (1970)

People have to talk about something just to keep their voice boxes in working order, so they'll have good voice boxes in case there's ever anything really meaningful to say.
— Kurt Vonnegut, Jr., *Cat's Cradle* (1963)

The universe must be full of voices, calling from star to star in a myriad tongues. One day we shall join that cosmic conversation.
— Arthur C. Clarke, "To the Stars" (1965)

It is not easy — talking to dragons.
— Ursula K. Le Guin, *The Farthest Shore* (1972)

Touch was a main channel of communication among the forest people. Among Terrans touch is always likely to imply threat, aggression, and so for them there is often nothing between the formal handshake and the sexual caress. All that blank was filled by the Athsheans with varied customs of touch.
— Ursula K. Le Guin, "The Word for World Is Forest" (1972)

The Store's front steps and porch in summer, its stove in the softening winters, drew the lonely in their hunger for talk, that limping substitute for love.
— Edgar Pangborn, "The Children's Crusade" (1974)

Like other people they communicated as much with their bodies and hands as with speech.
— Vonda N. McIntyre, "Aztecs" (1977)

The poor Babel Fish, by effectively removing all barriers to communication between different races and cultures, has caused more and bloodier wars than anything else in the history of creation.
    —Douglas Adams, "Fit the First," episode of *The Hitch-Hiker's Guide to the Galaxy* (radio series, 1978)

She was so graceful and supple in her movements, so deft at getting her meaning across. It was beautiful to watch her. It was speech and ballet at the same time.
    —John Varley, "The Persistence of Vision" (1978)

Smell is the essence of communication. Look at that word *essence* itself. When you smell another human being, you take chemicals from his body into your own, analyze them, and from the analysis you accurately deduce his emotional state. You do it so constantly and so automatically that you are largely unconscious of it, and say simply, "He seemed frightened," or "He was angry."
    —Gene Wolfe, "Seven American Nights" (1978)

On his way back to the lobby, his cigarettes forgotten, he had to walk the length of the ranked phones. Each rang in turn, but only once, as he passed.
    —William Gibson, *Neuromancer* (1984)

Some problems are best let be, not chewed over with words. This modern compulsion to "talk it out" is a mistake at least as often as it is a solution.
    —Robert A. Heinlein, *Job: A Comedy of Justice* (1984)

"It is true, then, what the villagers say, *When a dead tree falls, it carries with it a live one.*"
    "You speak too often with another's mouth."
    —Jane Yolen, "The White Babe" (1987)

Most people don't listen. They use the time when someone else is speaking to think of what they're going to say next. True Listeners have always been revered among oral cultures, and prized for their rarity value.
    —Terry Pratchett, *Pyramids* (1989)

The gods of the Disc have always been fascinated by humanity's incredible ability to say exactly the wrong thing at the wrong time.
— Terry Pratchett, *Pyramids* (1989)

People didn't understand that true intimacy did not consist of sexual intercourse, which could be done with strangers and in a state of total alienation; intimacy consisted of talking for hours about what was most important in one's life.
— Kim Stanley Robinson, *Red Mars* (1992)

After so many years together it is not necessary for us to speak aloud to say much.
— Carrie Richerson, "The City in Morning" (1998)

COMMUNITIES

As men grow more civilized, and the subdivision of occupations and services is carried out, a complex mutual dependence becomes the universal rule. Every man, however solitary may seem his occupation, is a member of a vast industrial partnership, as large as the nation, as large as humanity. The necessity of mutual dependence should imply the duty and guarantee of mutual support; and that it did not in your day constituted the essential cruelty and unreason of your system.
— Edward Bellamy, *Looking Backward, 2000–1887* (1888)

"We" is from God, and "I" from the devil.
— Yevgeny Zamiatin, *We* (1924), translated by Mirra Ginsburg (1972)

We are not alone.
  No one ever is alone.
  Not since the first faint stirring of the first flicker of life, on the first planet in the galaxy that knew the quickening of sentiency, has there ever been a single entity that walked or crawled or slithered down the path of life alone.
— Clifford D. Simak, *Time and Again* (1950)

Man needs freedom, but few men are so strong as to be happy with complete freedom. A man needs to be part of a group, with accepted and respected relationships. Some men join foreign legions for adventure; still more swear on a bit of paper in order to acquire a framework of duties and obligations, customs and taboos, a time to work and a time to loaf, a comrade to dispute with and a sergeant to hate—in short, to *belong*.

    —Robert A. Heinlein, *Between Planets* (1951)

A man is morally responsible to his community. That's a good idea. But his community is also morally responsible to him.

    —Philip K. Dick, *The Man Who Japed* (1956)

Assembled in a crowd, people lose their powers of reasoning and their capacity for moral choice.

    —Aldous Huxley, *Brave New World Revisited* (1958)

No man is an island, but I have met many isthmuses and a few peninsulas.

    —Susanna Jacobson, "Notes from Magdalen More" (1973)

We spread among the community and we became a part of them, sharing in their consciousness and directing them in their total integration. [. . .] They had integrated their group personality on a level that we could perceive and understand. This is the natural evolution of men and truly their one salvation in the total hostile universe.

    —Thomas N. Scortia, "The Armageddon Tapes—Tape 1" (1974)

The bond that links your true family is not one of blood, but of respect and joy in each other's life.

    Rarely do members of one family grow up under the same roof.

    —Richard Bach, *Illusions: The Adventures of a Reluctant Messiah* (1977)

Lev felt the strength of his friends and the whole community, supporting and upholding. It was as if he were not Lev alone, but Lev times a thousand—himself, but himself immensely increased, enlarged, a boundless self mingled with all the other selves, set free, as no man alone could ever be free.

    —Ursula K. Le Guin, "The Eye of the Heron" (1978)

"If human beings are all monsters, why should I sacrifice anything for them?"

    "Because they are beautiful monsters," he whispered. "And when they live in a network of peace and hope, when they trust the world and their deepest

hungers are fulfilled, then within that system, that delicate web, there is joy. That is what we live for, to bind the monsters together, to murder their fear and give birth to their beauty."
—Orson Scott Card, *Wyrms* (1987)

I'm not good in groups . . . It's difficult to work in a group when you're omnipotent.
—Richard Danus, "Deja Q," episode of *Star Trek: The Next Generation* (1990)

These are the people who hold a community together, who lead. Unlike the sheep and the wolves, they perform a better role than the script given them by their inner fears and desires. They act out the script of decency, of self-sacrifice, of public honor—of civilization. And in the pretense, it becomes reality.
—Orson Scott Card, *Xenocide* (1991)

Even after two separate years of enforced togetherness they were, like any other human group, no more than a collection of strangers.
—Kim Stanley Robinson, *Red Mars* (1992)

Here is the truth. What human life *is*, what it's *for*, what we *do*, is create communities.
—Orson Scott Card, *Pastwatch: The Redemption of Christopher Columbus* (1996)

COMPUTERS

No computer can duplicate the performance of a human brain.
—James Blish, "Solar Plexus," revised (1952)

He turned to face the machine. "Is there a God?"
The mighty voice answered without hesitation, without the clicking of a single relay.
"Yes, *now* there is a God."
—Fredric Brown, "Answer" (1954)

The study of thinking machines teaches us more about the brain than we can learn by introspective methods. Western man is externalizing himself in the form of gadgets.

—William S. Burroughs, *Naked Lunch* (1959)

"Once men turned their thinking over to machines in the hope that this would set them free. But that only permitted other men with machines to enslave them."

"'Thou shalt not make a machine in the likeness of a man's mind,'" Paul quoted.

—Frank Herbert, *Dune* (1965)

If was one thing all people took for granted, was conviction that if you feed honest figures into a computer, honest figures come out. Never doubted it myself till I met a computer with sense of humor.

—Robert A. Heinlein, *The Moon Is a Harsh Mistress* (1966)

That's the trouble with computers, Deirut thought. *Too logical.*

—Frank Herbert, "Escape Felicity" (1966)

HAL 9000: I am putting myself to the fullest possible use, which is all I think that any conscious entity can ever hope to do.

—Stanley Kubrick and Arthur C. Clarke, *2001: A Space Odyssey* (film, 1968)

HAL 9000: Dave. Stop. Stop, will you? Stop, Dave. Will you stop, Dave? Stop, Dave. I'm afraid. I'm afraid, Dave. Dave, my mind is going. I can feel it. I can feel it. My mind is going. There is no question about it. I can feel it. I can feel it. I can feel it. I'm a . . . fraid.

—Stanley Kubrick and Arthur C. Clarke, *2001: A Space Odyssey* (film, 1968)

Bastards, he thought. All robot servo-mechanisms and all computers are bastards.

—Philip K. Dick, *Galactic Pot-Healer* (1969)

Don't dismiss the computer as a new type of fetters. Think of it rationally, as the most liberating device ever invented, the only tool capable of serving the multifarious needs of modern man.
　—John Brunner, *The Shockwave Rider* (1975)

Cyberspace. A consensual hallucination experienced daily by billions of legitimate operators, in every nation, by children being taught mathematical concepts . . . A graphic representation of data abstracted from the banks of every computer in the human system. Unthinkable complexity. Lines of light ranged in the nonspace of the mind, clusters and constellations of data. Like city lights, receding . . .
　—William Gibson, *Neuromancer* (1984)

He'd used decks in school, toys that shuttled you through the infinite reaches of that space that wasn't space, mankind's unthinkably complex consensual hallucination, the matrix, cyberspace, where the great corporate hotcores burned like neon novas, data so dense you suffered sensory overload if you tried to apprehend more than the merest outline.
　—William Gibson, *Count Zero* (1986)

In the hard wind of images, Angie watches the evolution of machine intelligence: stone circles, clocks, steam-driven looms, a clicking brass forest of pawls and escapements, vacuum caught in blown glass, electronic hearthglow through hairline filaments, vast arrays of tubes and switches, decoding messages encrypted by other machines . . . The fragile, short-lived tubes compact themselves, become transistors; circuits integrate, compact themselves into silicon . . .
　—William Gibson, *Mona Lisa Overdrive* (1988)

In cyberspace, she noted, there are no shadows.
　—William Gibson, *Mona Lisa Overdrive* (1988)

Rule 1: Only overrule the tactical computer if you know something it doesn't. Rule 2: The tac comp always knows more than you do.
　—Lois McMaster Bujold, *The Vor Game* (1990)

Donna can feel computers dreaming, or so she says. She collects the dreams of machines, or so she thinks. The dreams of people are in the machines, a planet network of active imaginations hooked into their made-up, make-believe worlds. Artificial reality is taking over; it has its own children. Donna feels the dreams of people. There are others like her. She is not unique.

—Storm Constantine, "Immaculate" (1991)

COSMOLOGY AND ESCHATOLOGY

"Now," said Arcot, looking at it [the cube he had mentally created], "Man can do what never before was possible. From the nothingness of Space he can make anything.

"Man alone in this space is Creator and Destroyer.

"It is a high place.

"May he henceforth live up to it."

And he looked out toward the mighty star-lit hull that had destroyed a solar system—and could create another.

—John W. Campbell, Jr., *Invaders from the Infinite* (1932)

He knew where the seesaw would stop. It would end in the very remote past, with the release of the stupendous temporal energy he had been accumulating with each of those monstrous swings.

He would not witness, but he would cause the formation of the planets.

—A. E. van Vogt, "The Seesaw" (1941)

It came to pass that AC learned how to reverse the direction of entropy.

But there was now no man to whom AC might give the answer of the last question. No matter. The answer—by demonstration—would take care of that, too.

For another timeless interval, AC thought how best to do this. Carefully, AC organized the program.

The consciousness of AC encompassed all of what had once been a Universe and brooded over what was now Chaos. Step by step, it must be done.

And AC said, "LET THERE BE LIGHT!"

And there was light—

—Isaac Asimov, "The Last Question" (1956)

I was continuing to shrink, to become . . . what? The infinitesimal? What was I? Still a human being? Or was I the man of the future?

If there were other bursts of radiation, other clouds drifting across seas and continents, would other beings follow me into this vast new world? So close—the infinitesimal and the infinite. But suddenly, I knew they were really the two ends of the same concept. The unbelievably small and the unbelievably vast eventually meet—like the closing of a gigantic circle. I looked up, as if somehow I would grasp the heavens. The universe, worlds beyond number, God's silver tapestry spread across the night. And in that moment, I knew the answer to the riddle of the infinite. I had thought in terms of man's own limited dimension. I had presumed upon nature. That existence begins and ends is man's conception, not nature's. And I felt my body dwindling, melting, becoming nothing. My fears melted away. And in their place came acceptance. All this vast majesty of creation, it had to mean something. And then I meant something, too. Yes, smaller than the smallest, I meant something, too. To God, there is no zero. I still exist!

—Richard Matheson, *The Incredible Shrinking Man* (film, 1957)

What if the world isn't scattered around us like a jigsaw puzzle—what if it's like a soup with all kinds of things floating around in it, and from time to time some of them get stuck together by chance to make some kind of whole? What if everything that exists is fragmentary, incomplete, aborted, events with ends but no beginnings, events that only have middles, things that have fronts or rears but not both, with us constantly making categories, seeking out, and reconstructing, until we think we can see total love, total betrayal and defeat, although in reality we are all no more than haphazard fractions. [. . .] Using religion and philosophy as the cement, we perpetually collect and assemble all the garbage comprised by statistics in order to make sense out of things, to make everything respond in one unified voice like a bell chiming to our glory. But it's only soup . . .

—Stanislaw Lem, *The Investigation* (1959), translated by Adele Milch (1974)

The Cosmic Command, obviously no longer able to supervise every assignment on an individual basis when there were literally trillions of matters in its charge, had switched over to a random system. The assumption would be that every document, circulating endlessly from desk to desk, must eventually

hit upon the right one. A time-consuming procedure, perhaps, but one that would never fail. The Universe itself operated on the same principle.
— Stanislaw Lem, *Memoirs Found in a Bathtub* (1961), translated by
Michael Kandel and Christine Rose (1973)

Once there lived a certain engineer-cosmogonist who lit stars to dispel the dark.
— Stanislaw Lem, "Uranium Earpieces" (1965), translated by
Michael Kandel (1977)

Little eggs within bigger eggs within great eggs within a megamonolith on a planetary pear within an ovoid universe, the latest cosmogony indicating that infinity has the form of a hen's fruit. God broods over the abyss and cackles every trillion years or so.
— Philip José Farmer, "Riders of the Purple Wage" (1967)

"Kipple is useless objects, like junk mail or match folders after you use the last match or gum wrappers or yesterday's homeopape. When nobody's around, kipple reproduces itself. For instance, if you go to bed leaving any kipple around your apartment, when you wake up the next morning there's twice as much of it. It always gets more and more. [. . .]

"No one can win against kipple," he said, "except temporarily and maybe in one spot, like in my apartment I've sort of created a stasis between the pressure of kipple and nonkipple, for the time being. But eventually I'll die or go away, and then the kipple will again take over. It's a universal principle operating throughout the universe; the entire universe is moving toward a final state of total, absolute kippleization."
— Philip K. Dick, *Do Androids Dream of Electric Sheep?* (1968)

No structure, even an artificial one, enjoys the process of entropy. It is the ultimate fate of everything, and everything resists it.
— Philip K. Dick, *Galactic Pot-Healer* (1969)

In the beginning there was the sun and the ice, and there was no shadow. In the end when we are done, the sun will devour itself and shadow will eat light, and there will be nothing left but the ice and the darkness.
— Ursula K. Le Guin, *The Left Hand of Darkness* (1969)

Deep Thought: All right. The Answer to Everything . . .
Two: Yes . . . !
Deep Thought: Life, the Universe, and Everything . . .
One: Yes . . . !
Deep Thought: Is . . .
Three: Yes . . . !
Deep Thought: *Is* . . .
One/Two: Yes . . . !!!
Deep Thought: Forty-two.
 — Douglas Adams, "Fit the Fourth," episode of *The Hitch-Hiker's Guide to
 the Galaxy* (radio series, 1978)

In the beginning the Universe was created. This has made a lot of people very
angry and been widely regarded as a bad move.
 — Douglas Adams, "Fit the Fifth," episode of *The Hitch-Hiker's Guide to
 the Galaxy* (radio series, 1978)

There is a theory which states that if ever anyone discovers exactly what the
Universe is for and why it is here, it will instantly disappear and be replaced
by something even more bizarrely inexplicable. There is another theory
which states that this has already happened.
 — Douglas Adams, "Fit the Seventh," episode of *The Hitch-Hiker's Guide to
 the Galaxy* (radio series, 1978)

As a matter of cosmic history, it has always been easier to destroy, than to
create.
 — Jack B. Sowards, *Star Trek II: The Wrath of Khan* (film, 1982)

In a distant and second-hand set of dimensions, in an astral plane that was
never meant to fly, the curling star-mists waver and part . . .
 See . . .
 Great A'Tuin the turtle comes, swimming slowly through the interstellar
gulf, hydrogen frost on his ponderous limbs, his huge and ancient shell
pocked with meteor craters. Through sea-sized eyes that are crusted with
rheum and asteroid dust He stares fixedly at the Destination.
 In a brain bigger than a city, with geological slowness, He thinks only of
the Weight.

Most of the weight is of course accounted for by Berilia, Tubul, Great T'Phon and Jerakeen, the four giant elephants upon whose broad and star-tanned shoulders the disc of the World rests, garlanded by the long waterfall at its vast circumference and domed by the baby-blue vault of Heaven.

Astropsychology has been, as yet, unable to establish what they think about.

— Terry Pratchett, *The Colour of Magic* (1983)

In the beginning, there was nothing, which exploded.

— Terry Pratchett, *Lords and Ladies* (1992)

"The Constructors could have owned a universe; but it was not enough. So they challenged Finitude, and touched the Boundary of Time, and reached through that, and enabled Mind to colonize and inhabit all the many universes of the Multiplicity. But, for the Watchers of the Optimal History, even *this* is not sufficient; and they are seeking ways of reaching beyond, to further Orders of Infinity . . ."

"And if they succeed? Will they rest?"

"There is no rest. No limit. No end to the *Beyond*—no Boundaries which Life, and Mind, cannot challenge, and breach."

— Stephen Baxter, *The Time Ships* (1995)

COURAGE AND COWARDICE

Physical courage and the love of battle, for instance, are no great help—may even be hindrances—to a civilized man. And in a state of physical balance and security, power, intellectual as well as physical, would be out of place.

— H. G. Wells, *The Time Machine: An Invention* (1895)

He was not, as he knew well from experience, one of those persons who love danger for its own sake. There was an aspect of it which he sometimes enjoyed, an excitement, a purgative effect upon sluggish emotions, but he was far from fond of risking his life.

— James Hilton, *Lost Horizon* (1933)

COWARDLY LION: Courage! What makes a king out of a slave? Courage! What makes the flag on the mast to wave? Courage! What makes the elephant charge his tusk in the misty mist, or the dusky dusk? What makes the muskrat guard his musk? Courage! What makes the sphinx the seventh wonder? Courage! What makes the dawn come up like thunder? Courage! What makes the Hottentot so hot? What puts the "ape" in apricot? What have they got that I ain't got?

ALL: Courage!

COWARDLY LION: You can say that again! Huh?

—Noel Langley, Florence Ryerson, and Edgar Allan Woolf,
   The Wizard of Oz (film, 1939)

Courage is not simply *one* of the virtues, but the form of every virtue at the testing point, which means, at the point of highest reality. A chastity or honesty, or mercy, which yields to danger will be chaste or honest or merciful only on conditions.

—C. S. Lewis, *The Screwtape Letters* (1942)

We have a tradition of freedom, personal freedom, scientific freedom. That freedom isn't kept alive by caution and unwillingness to take risks.

—Robert A. Heinlein, *Rocket Ship Galileo* (1947)

There is a seed of courage hidden (often deeply, it is true) in the heart of the fattest and most timid hobbit, waiting for some final and desperate danger to make it grow.

—J. R. R. Tolkien, *The Fellowship of the Ring* (1954)

The brave things in the old tales and songs, Mr. Frodo: adventures, as I used to call them. I used to think that they were things the wonderful folk of the stories went out and looked for, because they wanted them, because they were exciting and life was a bit dull, a kind of a sport, as you might say. But that's not the way of it with the tales that really mattered, or the ones that stay in the mind. Folk seem to have been just landed in them, usually—their paths were laid that way, as you put it. But I expect they had lots of chances, like us, of turning back, only they didn't. And if they had, we shouldn't know, because they'd have been forgotten. We hear about those as just went on— and not all to a good end.

—J. R. R. Tolkien, *The Two Towers* (1955)

If a grasshopper tries to fight a lawnmower, one may admire his courage but not his judgment.
  —Robert A. Heinlein, *Farnham's Freehold* (1964)

There is no safety, and there is no end. The word must be heard in silence; there must be darkness to see the stars. The dance is always danced above the hollow place, above the terrible abyss.
  —Ursula K. Le Guin, *The Farthest Shore* (1972)

Timidity can be as dangerous as rashness.
  —Poul Anderson, "The Saturn Game" (1981)

Almost everything about a human creature is ridiculous, except its ability to suffer bravely and die gallantly for whatever it loves and believes in.
  —Robert A. Heinlein, *Job: A Comedy of Justice* (1984)

Leadership is mostly a power over imagination, and never more so than in combat. The bravest man alone can only be an armed lunatic. The real strength lies in the ability to get others to do your work.
  —Lois McMaster Bujold, *Shards of Honor* (1986)

Cowardice, properly judged, may be a survival trait.
  —George Turner, *Drowning Towers* (1987)

CULTURES AND ANTHROPOLOGY

There is some wisdom, and some foolishness in every people's way.
  —Walter M. Miller, Jr., "The Soul-Empty Ones" (1951)

No one person can change a whole culture.
  —Poul Anderson, "Ghetto" (1954)

When two alien cultures meet, the stronger must transform the weaker with love or hate.
  —Damon Knight, "Stranger Station" (1956)

Customs tell a man who he is, where he belongs, what he must do. Better illogical customs than none; men cannot live together without them.

—Robert A. Heinlein, *Citizen of the Galaxy* (1957)

Through a Moses, or through a Hitler, or an ignorant but tyrannical grandfather, a cultural inheritance may be acquired between dusk and dawn, and many have been so acquired.

—Walter M. Miller, Jr., *A Canticle for Leibowitz* (1959)

Can we any more postulate a separate culture? Viewing the metastasis of Western Culture it seems progressively less likely. Sarah Boyle imagines a whole world which has become like California, all topographical imperfections sanded away with the sweet smelling burr of the plastic surgeon's cosmetic polisher; a world populace dieting, leisured, similar in pink and mauve hair and rhinestone shades. A land Cunt Pink and Avocado Green, brassiered and girdled by monstrous complexities of Super Highways, a California endless and unceasing, embracing and transforming the entire globe.

—Pamela Zoline, "The Heat Death of the Universe" (1967)

Maybe there is a recurrent mental fatigue in human cultures, induced by the short periods of enterprise. You push on with your grand vigor for a while, and then—slump; abdication of intelligence as the governing force, and of course if that's complete enough it drags down virtually everything in a long ruin.

—Edgar Pangborn, "Mount Charity" (1971)

The anthropologist cannot always leave his own shadow out of the picture he draws.

—Ursula K. Le Guin, "The Word for World Is Forest" (1972)

When one culture has the big guns and the other has none, there is a certain predictability about the outcome.

—Joanna Russ, "When It Changed" (1972)

My profession is supposed to be understanding cultures—every culture, when most people don't even comprehend their own.

—Gene Wolfe, "Alien Stones" (1972)

They never went so far as to maintain anything like the old society and culture. Music, sculpture, art, and the oral literary tradition were dead and gratefully lost. These things just got in the way of making one's living.
— George Alec Effinger, "Contentment, Satisfaction, Cheer, Well-Being, Gladness, Joy, Comfort, and Not Having to Get Up Early Any More" (1976)

She'd killed him with culture shock.
— William Gibson, "Johnny Mnemonic" (1981)

A dying culture invariably exhibits personal rudeness. Bad manners. Lack of consideration for others in minor matters. A loss of politeness, of gentle manners, is more significant than is a riot.
— Robert A. Heinlein, *Friday* (1982)

"Anthropology," Tate said disparagingly. "Why did you want to snoop through other people's cultures? Couldn't you find what you wanted in your own?"
— Octavia E. Butler, *Dawn* (1987)

Some cultures send their young people to the desert to seek visions and guidance, searching for true thinking spawned by the openness of the place, the loneliness, the beauty of emptiness.
— Pat Murphy, "Rachel in Love" (1987)

A wise man should always respect the folkways of others, to use Carrot's happy phrase, but Vimes often had difficulty with this idea. For one thing, there were people in the world whose folkways consisted of gutting other people like clams and this was not a procedure that commanded, in Vimes, any kind of respect at all.
— Terry Pratchett, *The Fifth Elephant* (1999)

There are only two things I can't stand in this world: people who are intolerant of other people's cultures — and the Dutch.
— Mike Myers and Michael McCullers, *Austin Powers in Goldmember* (film, 2002)

DARKNESS AND LIGHT

No man knows till he has suffered from the night how sweet and how dear to his heart and eye the morning can be.
　—Bram Stoker, *Dracula* (1897)

Night, the Mother of Fear and Mystery, was coming upon me.
　—H. G. Wells, *The War of the Worlds* (1898)

Two lights for guidance. The first, our little glowing atom of community, with all that it signifies. The second, the cold light of the stars, symbol of the hypercosmical reality, with its crystal ecstasy. Strange that in this light, in which even the dearest love is frostily assessed, and even the possible defeat of our half-waking world is contemplated without remission of praise, the human crisis does not lose but gains significance. Strange, that it seems more, not less, urgent to play some part in this struggle, this brief effort of animalcules striving to win for their race some increase of lucidity before the ultimate darkness.
　—Olaf Stapledon, *Star Maker* (1937)

History had, without question, been changed.
　Darkness would not fall.
　—L. Sprague de Camp, *Lest Darkness Fall* (1939)

With the slow fascination of fear, he lifted himself on one arm and turned his eyes toward the blood-curdling blackness of the window.
　Through it shone the Stars!
　Not Earth's feeble thirty-six hundred Stars visible to the eye—Lagash was in the center of a giant cluster. Thirty thousand mighty suns shone down in a soul-searing splendor that was more frighteningly cold in its awful indifference than the bitter wind that shivered across the cold, horribly bleak world. [. . .]
　On the horizon outside the window, in the direction of Saro City, a

crimson glow began growing, strengthening in brightness, that was not the glow of a sun.

The long night had come again.

—Isaac Asimov, "Nightfall" (1941)

My night is your day.

—Jean Cocteau, *Beauty and the Beast* (film, 1946), translated by
Francis Howard (1946)

We shall meet in the place where there is no darkness.

—George Orwell, *Nineteen Eighty-Four* (1949)

Even here, Martin Ashley thought, so far from home, the night still came.

—Chad Oliver, "Rite of Passage" (1954)

"Faithless is he that says farewell when the road darkens," said Gimli.

"Maybe," said Elrond, "but let him not vow to walk in the dark, who has not seen the nightfall."

—J. R. R. Tolkien, *The Fellowship of the Ring* (1954)

The night belonged to me and my droogs and all the rest of the nadsats, and the starry bourgeois lurked indoors drinking in the gloopy worldcasts.

—Anthony Burgess, *A Clockwork Orange* (1962)

The sunlights differ, but there is only one darkness.

—Ursula K. Le Guin, *The Dispossessed: An Ambiguous Utopia* (1974)

There is no place bereft of the light, the comfort and radiance of the creator spirit. There is no place that is outcast, outlawed, forsaken. There is no place left dark.

—Ursula K. Le Guin, "The Stars Below" (1974)

To know the abyss of the darkness and not to fear it, to entrust oneself to it and whatever may arise from it—what greater gift?

—Ursula K. Le Guin, "The New Atlantis" (1975)

Now the world has gone to bed,
Darkness won't engulf my head,

Darkness and Light

I can see by infrared,
How I hate the night.
  —Douglas Adams, *Life, the Universe, and Everything* (1982)

Where, she wondered, would the darkness go? She knew. It would retreat to the edge of the world, and into the people she knew, and into her; she could feel it lurking there even now, hiding in her mind's shadows with her fears.
  —Pamela Sargent, "The Old Darkness" (1983)

"You dead awhile there, mon."
  "It happens," he said. "I'm getting used to it."
  "You dealin' wi' th' darkness, mon."
  "Only game in town, it looks like."
  —William Gibson, *Neuromancer* (1984)

There is no greater dark than the dark between the stars.
  —Frederik Pohl, *Heechee Rendezvous* (1984)

You who sought our land for so long, welcome to the realm of the cold and the dark.
  —Joan Slonczewski, *The Wall around Eden* (1989)

It's important to have a way of seeing through a dark time. To keep waiting, for the light to come.
  —Joan Slonczewski, *The Wall around Eden* (1989)

"The darkness is where danger comes from," Peter said, "and from the fire comes only illusion."
  —Neal Stephenson, *The Diamond Age, or, A Young Lady's Illustrated Primer* (1995)

DEATH

I thought I saw Elizabeth, in the bloom of health, walking in the streets of Ingolstadt. Delighted and surprised, I embraced her; but as I imprinted the first kiss on her lips, they became livid with the hue of death; her features appeared to change, and I thought that I held the corpse of my dead mother in

my arms; a shroud enveloped her form, and I saw the grave-worms crawling in the folds of the flannel.
— Mary Shelley, *Frankenstein, or, The Modern Prometheus* (1818)

Earth is to me a tomb, the firmament a vault, shrouding mere corruption. Time is no more, for I have stepped within the threshold of eternity; each man I meet appears a corse, which will soon be deserted of its animating spark, on the eve of decay and corruption.
— Mary Shelley, *The Last Man* (1826)

All England slept; and from my window, commanding a wide prospect of the star-illumined country, I saw the land stretched out in placid rest. I was awake, alive, while the brother of death possessed my race.
— Mary Shelley, *The Last Man* (1826)

Death must be so beautiful. To lie in the soft brown earth, with the grasses waving above one's head, and listen to silence. To have no yesterday, and no to-morrow. To forget time, to forgive life, to be at peace.
— Oscar Wilde, "The Canterville Ghost" (1887)

What is death? In death life lives, and among the dead you shall find the life you lost.
— H. Rider Haggard, "Black Heart and White Heart" (1896)

To die will be an awfully big adventure.
— J. M. Barrie, *Peter Pan* (play, 1904)

Only the man who has died many times begins to live.
— Edwin L. Arnold, *Lieut. Gullivar Jones: His Vacation* (1905)

That is not dead which can eternal lie
And with strange aeons even death may die.
— H. P. Lovecraft, "The Nameless City" (1921)

To die — to be really dead — that must be glorious.
— Garrett Fort, *Dracula* (film, 1931)

Death

There was death afoot in the darkness. It crept furtively along a steel girder. [. . .] Girders lifted a gigantic steel skeleton. The naked beams were a sinister forest.

It was in this forest that Death prowled.

Death was a man.

—Lester Dent, *The Man of Bronze* (1933)

When you rave of your insane desire to create living men from the dust of the dead, a strange apparition has seemed to appear in the room. It comes, a figure like Death, and each time it comes more clearly—nearer. It seems to be reaching out for you, as if it would take you away from me.

—William Hurlbut, *Bride of Frankenstein* (film, 1935)

Go. You live. Go. You stay. We belong dead!

—William Hurlbut, *Bride of Frankenstein* (film, 1935)

"Death," said Mark Staithes. "It's the only thing we haven't succeeded in completely vulgarizing."

—Aldous Huxley, *Eyeless in Gaza* (1936)

Earth and sky and water, he thought. I am one with them. Death has made me one with them. For death brings one back to the elementals, to the soil and trees, to the clouds and sky and the sun dying in the welter of its blood in the crimson west.

—Clifford D. Simak, "Eternity Lost" (1949)

To mourn is to pity oneself. The dead feel nothing. The mourner does not pity the dead. He pities himself for having lost the living.

—Walter M. Miller, Jr., "The Soul-Empty Ones" (1951)

All Egyptian culture was colored by the feeling for the dead. Their finest buildings were tombs and mortuary structures. Instead of repressing their emotions about death, they dramatized them. They brought them out in the open where they could look at them.

The dramatization was definitely conducive to mental health. The psychologists tell us that it is no accident that no other human culture has yet lasted as long as the Egyptian did.

—Margaret St. Clair, *Agent of the Unknown* (1952)

Perhaps that was death — the discovery that nothing existed save oneself in the midst of torture.
— Charles Dye, "The Seventh Wind" (1953)

One grows used to anything, he thought, even to one's death. You could probably chop off a man's head three times a day for twenty years and he'd grow used to it, and cry like a baby if you stopped.
— Robert Sheckley, *Immortality, Inc.* (1958)

Sorensen had done well in choosing a profession in which he associated mainly with the dead.
— Stanislaw Lem, *The Investigation* (1959), translated by Adele Milch (1974)

"Now, then," said the psychiatrist, looking up from his note pad, "when did you first discover that you were dead?"
— Charles Beaumont, "Blood Brother" (1961)

Death is merely a matter of definition. Once the definition was very simple: you were dead when you stopped moving for a long time. But now the scientists have examined this antiquated notion more carefully, and have done considerable research on the entire subject. They have found out that you can be dead in all important respects, but still go on walking and talking.
— Robert Sheckley, *Journey beyond Tomorrow* (1962)

Nobody really believes in death until he sees a dead man.
— Murray Leinster, "Third Planet" (1963)

The meeting between ignorance and knowledge, between brutality and culture — it begins in the dignity with which we treat our dead.
— Frank Herbert, *Dune* (1965)

Consider how erroneous and unwise it is to fear death, a state that deserves, rather, vindication! For what can equal the perfection of nonexistence?
— Stanislaw Lem, "Automatthew's Friend" (1965), translated by Michael Kandel (1977)

Death

Why does man so zealously guard his dead? Is it because this is the monumentally democratic way of immortalization, the ultimate affirmation of the power to hurt—that is to say, life—and the desire that it continue on forever?
—Roger Zelazny, "He Who Shapes" (1965)

[First use of phrase:] He's dead, Jim.
—Richard Matheson, "The Enemy Within," episode of *Star Trek* (1966)

The death of a great mage, who has many times in his life walked on the dry steep hillsides of death's kingdom, is a strange matter: for the dying man goes not blindly, but surely, knowing the way.
—Ursula K. Le Guin, *A Wizard of Earthsea* (1968)

Death is very close, he thought. [. . .] Nothing is killing me; I have no enemy, no antagonist; I am merely expiring, like a magazine subscription: month by month. Because, he thought, I am too hollowed out to participate any longer.
—Philip K. Dick, *Galactic Pot-Healer* (1969)

"The child is father to the man"; remember? And the man is father to the corpse.
—Philip K. Dick, *Galactic Pot-Healer* (1969)

An earthquake does not frighten a man who died in an earthquake.
—Ursula K. Le Guin, "Nine Lives" (1969)

He cursed this world where he was so alone and helpless, where the dead were dead forever, where there was no way of restoring them to life.
—Arkady Strugatsky and Boris Strugatsky, *Prisoners of Power* (1969), translated by Helen Saltz Jacobson (1977)

Life and death. What's the difference, I always say . . .
—Norman Kagan, "The Dreadful Has Already Happened" (1971)

You have no idea what an inconvenience it is, to be dead.
—Joanna Russ, "Poor Man, Beggar Man" (1971)

The static qualities of death oppressed him; he felt that mutability was mankind's only hope, even though it took the flowers and pleasures of one's time.

Most terrible about the dead was the way in which they did not, could not, could never, could never even hope to change.
— Joanna Russ, "Poor Man, Beggar Man" (1971)

What we're here for
is death
Somebody accidentally
wound us up
("I told you
to leave that alone")
and we must
wait
to run down.
— George Alec Effinger, "Things Go Better" (1972)

Life rises out of death, death rises out of life; in being opposite they yearn to each other, they give birth to each other and are forever reborn.
— Ursula K. Le Guin, *The Farthest Shore* (1972)

Cetians died eagerly, curious as to what came next.
— Ursula K. Le Guin, "The Word for World Is Forest" (1972)

The Deathbird closed its wings over the Earth until at last, at the end, there was only the great bird crouched over the dead cinder. Then the Deathbird raised its head to the star-filled sky and repeated the sigh of loss the Earth had felt at the end. Then its eyes closed, it twitched its head carefully under its wing, and all was night.
— Harlan Ellison, "The Deathbird" (1973)

To die was merely to go on in another direction.
— Ursula K. Le Guin, "The Day Before the Revolution" (1974)

To a dead the whole universe is plastic, nothing's real, nothing matters a hell of a lot, it's all only a joke.
— Robert Silverberg, "Born with the Dead" (1974)

Drowning is my occupation now.
— Robert Silverberg, "A Sea of Faces" (1974)

Death

Death seemed more like an old friend than an interruption. It was sleep.
— Craig Strete, "Time Deer" (1974)

"*Every*one's entitled to go on living," Novins said, vehemently. "That's why we live. To say no to death."
— Harlan Ellison, "Shatterday" (1975)

It is enough to make you understand why most languages have a word like "soul." There are various degrees of death, and time spares us none of them. Yet something endures, for which a word is needed.
— Ursula K. Le Guin, "The New Atlantis" (1975)

He had never been at the side of someone dying before, but he knew it was the human way of ceasing to function. It was an involuntary and irreversible dismantling.
— Isaac Asimov, "The Bicentennial Man" (1976)

He thought, correcting the old saying to make it come out the more wisely: Of the dead only speak evil.
— Philip K. Dick and Roger Zelazny, *Deus Irae* (1976)

I don't want to die now, I've still got a headache! I don't want to go to heaven with a headache, I'd be all cross and wouldn't enjoy it.
— Douglas Adams, "Fit the Second," episode of *The Hitch-Hiker's Guide to the Galaxy* (radio series, 1978)

What is most mortal is most alive.
— Ursula K. Le Guin, "The First Report of the Shipwrecked Foreigner to the Kadanh of Derb" (1978)

I went back to the stretcher with the fear of death like a cold compress on the back of my neck.
— Cherry Wilder, "Mab Gallen Recalled" (1978)

Death, he has learned, is only a slow walk through icefields.
— Jack Dann, "Camps" (1979)

Death is the ultimate insecurity to a conscious being, the break that takes away all productivity and vitality, the meaning of all further growth.
　—George Zebrowski, *Macrolife* (1979)

When all the elements of a system are ordered, it's dead—administrative—totally organized, totally communicative, and wholly uninformative. But it doesn't know it's dead until that information comes from a higher state of disorder.
　—Carter Scholz, "The Johann Sebastian Bach Memorial Barbecue" (1980)

Death was a black wall. It lay before her, extending to infinity in all directions, smooth and featureless and mysterious. She could almost reach out an arm and touch it.
　—Michael Swanwick, "Ginungagap" (1980)

Death is the ultimate sensory experience.
　—Joan D. Vinge, *The Snow Queen* (1980)

I've seen things you people wouldn't believe. Attack ships on fire off the shoulder of Orion. I watched C-beams glitter in the dark near the Tannhauser Gate. All those moments will be lost in time, like tears in rain. Time to die.
　—Hampton Fancher and David Webb Peoples, *Blade Runner* (film, 1982)

There is no death. It is only a transition to a different sphere of consciousness.
　—Steven Spielberg, Michael Grais, and Mark Victor, *Poltergeist* (film, 1982)

Some people die, but they don't know that they're gone.
　—Steven Spielberg, Michael Grais, and Mark Victor, *Poltergeist* (film, 1982)

When it's time to die, it's time to die.
　—Ian Watson, "Slow Birds" (1983)

Why, he thought, is anything here? Why is there a world and sky and stars? Why shouldn't there simply be nothing for ever and ever?
　Perhaps that was the nature of death: nothing for ever and ever.
　—Ian Watson, "Slow Birds" (1983)

Death

What he taught was a kind of passivity, a blissful waiting for a death that was more than merely personal, a death which was also the death of the sun and stars and of all existence, a cosmic death which transfigured individual mortality.

— Ian Watson, "Slow Birds" (1983)

"I'm dead, Case. Got enough time in on this Hosaka to figure that one."
  "How's it feel?"
  "It doesn't."
  "Bother you?"
  "What bothers me is, nothin' does."

— William Gibson, *Neuromancer* (1984)

No individual death among human beings is important. Someone who dies leaves his work behind and that does *not* entirely die. It never entirely dies as long as humanity exists.

— Isaac Asimov, *Robots and Empire* (1985)

It was such an easy thing, death. He saw that now: It just happened.

— William Gibson, *Count Zero* (1986)

Gordon Way was dead, but he simply hadn't the slightest idea what he was meant to do about it. It wasn't a situation he had encountered before.

— Douglas Adams, *Dirk Gently's Holistic Detective Agency* (1987)

He had nothing against ghosts personally, didn't think a person should be judged adversely simply for being dead, but — he didn't like it.

— Douglas Adams, *Dirk Gently's Holistic Detective Agency* (1987)

The worst thing about knowing that Gary Fairchild had been dead for a month was seeing him every day at work.

— Barbara Hambly, *The Silicon Mage* (1988)

If you're not ready to die, then how can you live?

— Charles De Lint, *Svaha* (1989)

KIRK: I've always known I'll die alone.

— David Loughery, *Star Trek V: The Final Frontier* (film, 1989)

People always come back from the dead in such a bad temper.
  — Terry Pratchett, *Pyramids* (1989)

The rings were a matching pair of gold bands, left to Daniel by his parents, who had known he could never afford to buy his own. It gave her pause for thought, how after all these years, somehow, the dead still looked after the living.
  — Joan Slonczewski, *The Wall around Eden* (1989)

Death had subtler vectors than direct touch.
  — Lois McMaster Bujold, *The Vor Game* (1990)

Death is a fine performance, but there's no reason to perform it at a dinner party.
  — Alexander Jablokov, "The Death Artist" (1990)

The ways of dead people are not our ways. They have a very oblique way of expressing themselves, and often they'll tell you something that can be interpreted many ways; it gives them a way out while preserving their reputation for infallibility.
  — S. P. Somtow, "Lottery Night" (1990)

They skid. Broadside. Toward the onrushing trucktrain, the fiery red letters on its sides screaming: FLAMMABLE.
  Just like that, in the midst of life, we are in death.
  — James Stevens-Arce, "Scenes from a Future Marriage" (1995)

He thought of coral, of the reefs that grew around sunken aircraft carriers; perhaps she'd become something like that, the buried mystery beneath some exfoliating superstructure of supposition, or even of myth.
  It seemed to him, in Visitors, that that might be a slightly less dead way of being dead. And he wished her that.
  — William Gibson, *Idoru* (1996)

I am Death, not taxes. *I* turn up only once.
  — Terry Pratchett, *Feet of Clay* (1996)

Death came in on sixteen legs.
  —Gregory Benford, "A Hunger for the Infinite" (1999)

Cole Sear: I see dead people.
Malcolm Crowe: In your dreams? *(Cole shakes his head no.)*
Malcolm: While you're awake? *(Cole nods.)*
Malcolm: Dead people like, in graves? In coffins?
Cole: Walking around like regular people. They don't see each other. They
    only see what they want to see. They don't know they're dead.
Malcolm: How often do you see them?
Cole: All the time. They're everywhere.
  —M. Night Shyamalan, *The Sixth Sense* (film, 1999)

DESTINY

A blind fate, a vast pitiless mechanism, seemed to cut and shape the fabric
of existence, and I, Moreau (by his passion for research), Montgomery (by
his passion for drink), the Beast People, with their instincts and mental
restrictions, were torn and crushed, ruthlessly, inevitably, amid the infinite
complexity of its incessant wheels.
  —H. G. Wells, *The Island of Doctor Moreau* (1896)

A star a billion miles away explodes . . . and human civilization falls like a
house of cards. The fantastic, inexorable mathematics of fate.
  —Edmond Hamilton, "The Ephemerae" (1938)

We are all doomed to commit acts of cruelty or violence or evil; that is our
destiny, due to ancient factors. Our karma.
  —Philip K. Dick, *The Man in the High Castle* (1962)

"Statistics aren't the same thing as destiny, Bennie. Everybody makes his
own."
  "Statistics or destiny?"
  "Both, I guess."
  —Roger Zelazny, "He Who Shapes" (1965)

Rarely is it given man to know the day or the hour when fate intervenes in his destiny, but, because he had checked his watch just before he saw the girl with the hips, Haldane IV knew the day, the hour, and the minute. At Point Sur, California, on September 5, at two minutes past two, he took the wrong turn and drove down a lane to hell.

—John Boyd, *The Last Starship from Earth* (1968)

I am not a person and I am not an animal. There is something I am here for something I have to do before I can go.

—William S. Burroughs, *The Wild Boys: A Book of the Dead* (1971)

The city is necessity. The future is built. The gears move us toward it. I am Fate.

—Katherine MacLean, "The Missing Man" (1971)

To deny the past is to deny the future. A man does not make his destiny: he accepts it or denies it.

—Ursula K. Le Guin, *The Farthest Shore* (1972)

"If they're dead there's nothing I can do about it," she said. "And if they're alive, there's nothing I can do about it. So I shan't."

—Terry Pratchett, *Pyramids* (1989)

Tiff believed that you are what happens to you. The rich and strong must have virtue; one to whom evil has been done must be bad, and may rightly be punished.

—Ursula K. Le Guin, *Tehanu: The Last Book of Earthsea* (1990)

DIMENSIONS

Hasheesh helped a great deal, and once sent him to a part of space where form does not exist, but where glowing gases study the secrets of existence. And a violet-coloured gas told him that this part of space was outside what he had called infinity. The gas had not heard of planets and organisms before, but identified Kuranes merely as one from the infinity where matter, energy, and gravitation exist.

—H. P. Lovecraft, "Celephais" (1922)

Dimensions

There were boundless, unforeseeable realms, planet on planet, universe on universe, to which we might attain, and among whose prodigies and marvels we could dwell or wander indefinitely. In these worlds, our brains would be attuned to the comprehension of vaster and higher scientific laws, and states of entity beyond those of our present dimensional milieu.

—Clark Ashton Smith, "Beyond the Singing Flame" (1931)

I had often pondered the possibility of other worlds or material planes which may co-exist in the same space with ours, invisible and impalpable to human senses. Of course, I realized at once that I had fallen into some such dimension.

—Clark Ashton Smith, "The City of the Singing Flame" (1931)

Scientific study and reflection had taught us that the known universe of three dimensions embraces the merest fraction of the whole cosmos of substance and energy. In this case an overwhelming preponderance of evidence from numerous authentic sources pointed to the tenacious existence of certain forces of great power and, so far as the human point of view is concerned, exceptional malignancy.

—H. P. Lovecraft, "The Shunned House" (1937)

Toto, I've a feeling we're not in Kansas anymore.

—Noel Langley, Florence Ryerson, and Edgar Allan Woolf,
    The Wizard of Oz (film, 1939)

He built up impossible situations, devised great travels and adventures, accepted shaky premises and theories, dallied with metaphysical speculation. He wandered to improbable dimensions, conversed with strange beings that lived on unknown worlds, battled with vicious entities that spawned outside the pale of time and space, rescued civilizations tottering on the brink of horrible destruction.

—Clifford D. Simak, "Earth for Inspiration" (1941)

"What number are you calling, please?"
    "Charlemont 7-890," I whispered.
    "Sorry. You must have the wrong dimension."
    —Ross Rocklynne, "Sorry: Wrong Dimension" (1954)

We live in another dimension, in the suburbs of time, you might say.
   —Gore Vidal, *Visit to a Small Planet,* revised (play, 1957)

There is a fifth dimension beyond that which is known to Man. It is a dimension as vast as space and as timeless as infinity. It is the middle ground between light and shadow, between science and superstition, and it lies between the pit of man's fears and the summit of his knowledge. This is the dimension of imagination. It is an area which we call . . . *The Twilight Zone.*
   —Rod Serling, opening narration, *The Twilight Zone* (TV series, 1959)

You're traveling through another dimension, a dimension not only of sight and sound but of mind; a journey into a wondrous land whose boundaries are that of imagination. That's the signpost up ahead—your next stop, *The Twilight Zone.*
   —Rod Serling, opening narration, *The Twilight Zone* (TV series, 1961)

You unlock this door with the key of imagination. Beyond it is another dimension. A dimension of sound. A dimension of sight. A dimension of mind. You're moving into a land of both shadow and substance, of things and ideas. You've just crossed over into *The Twilight Zone.*
   —Rod Serling, opening narration, *The Twilight Zone* (TV series, 1963)

It was beyond him how someone could voluntarily let himself get involved in this game of dimension-shifting and mutant-battling. But it takes all sorts to make a continuum.
   —Robert Silverberg, "MUgwump 4" (1959)

Even if all life on our planet is destroyed, there must be other life somewhere which we know nothing of. It is impossible that ours is the only world; there must be world after world unseen by us, in some region or dimension that we simply do not perceive.
   —Philip K. Dick, *The Man in the High Castle* (1962)

These parallel worlds are a knotty problem, he realized. I wonder how many exist. Dozens? With a different human sub-species dominant on each? Weird idea. He shivered. God, how unpleasant . . . like concentric rings of hell, each with its own particular brand of torment.
   —Philip K. Dick, *The Crack in Space* (1965)

Why had the God willed that time branch and rebranch, enormous, shadowy, bearing universes like the Yggdrasil of Danskar legend? Was it so that man could realize every potentiality there was in him?

Surely not. So many of them were utter horror.

—Poul Anderson "Eutopia" (1967)

Mr. Asenion had been working on a Dimensional Redistributor. He had been seeking to open gateways to the many strange dimensions that exist around us. He had never been successful.

—Alexei Panshin, "When the Vertical World Becomes Horizontal" (1974)

You might like the desert, Dagny. There's a peculiar fascination about it. Almost like living in another dimension.

—Philip Latham, "A Drop of Dragon's Blood" (1975)

There were worlds in the jewel. There was ancient Barsoom of my childhood fairy tales; there was Middle Earth with brooding castles and sentient forests. The jewel was a window into something unimaginable, a place where there were no questions and no emotions but a vast awareness. [. . .] There was no corner of the universe that it did not reach.

—John Varley, "In the Bowl" (1975)

He believed that the so-called hallucinations caused by some of these drugs (with emphasis, he continually reminded himself, on the word "some") were not hallucinations at all, but perceptions of other zones of reality. Some of them were frightening; some appeared lovely.

—Philip K. Dick and Roger Zelazny, *Deus Irae* (1976)

We are not in the Eighth Dimension, we are over New Jersey. All is not lost.

—Earl Mac Rauch, *The Adventures of Buckaroo Banzai across the 8th Dimension* (film, 1984)

There are documented cases. Things I could tell you you wouldn't believe. Look it up. Planes of existence we can't see or not a lot. People lost and floating about in interdimensional yogurt.

—Neal Barrett, Jr., "Perpetuity Blues" (1987)

It is now known to science that there are many more dimensions than the classical four. Scientists say that these don't normally impinge on the world because the extra dimensions are very small and curve in on themselves, and that since reality is fractal most of it is tucked inside itself. This means either that the universe is more full of wonders than we can hope to understand or, more probably, that scientists make things up as they go along.

    —Terry Pratchett, *Pyramids* (1989)

"Since when did you start wearing glasses?"

    "Since I met a Buddhist street vendor who sent me on a trip to another dimension."

    —Paul Di Filippo, "Lennon Spex" (1992)

"Openers don't much care about temporal immortality," Ry Arnis said. "When we open a gate—we glimpse eternity. A hundred gates, a hundred different eternities. Coming back is just an interlude between forevers."

    —Greg Bear, "The Way of All Ghosts" (1999)

"Every meter, every second, every dimension, has its own mind here," Karn said. "Space and time are arguing, fighting."

    —Greg Bear, "The Way of All Ghosts" (1999)

DREAMS AND SLEEP

They who dream by day are cognizant of many things which escape those who dream only by night.

    —Edgar Allan Poe, "Eleanora," revised (1845)

All that we see or seem
Is but a dream within a dream.

    —Edgar Allan Poe, "A Dream within a Dream," revised (1849)

Our dreams are a second life. Not without a shudder do I pass through the gates of ivory or horn which separate us from the invisible world.

    —Gérard de Nerval, *Aurelia* (1854), translated by Richard Aldington (1932)

"If he left off dreaming about you, where do you suppose you'd be?"

"Where I am now, of course," said Alice.

"Not you!" Tweedledee retorted contemptuously. "You'd be nowhere. Why, you're only a sort of thing in his dream!"

—Lewis Carroll, *Through the Looking Glass and What Alice Found There* (1872)

How blessed are some people, whose lives have no fears, no dreads, to whom sleep is a blessing that comes nightly, and brings nothing but sweet dreams.

—Bram Stoker, *Dracula* (1897)

I have often wondered if the majority of mankind ever pause to reflect upon the occasionally titanic significance of dreams, and of the obscure world to which they belong. [. . .] We may guess that in dreams life, matter, and vitality, as the earth knows such things, are not necessarily constant; and that time and space do not exist as our waking selves comprehend them. Sometimes I believe that this less material life is our truer life, and that our vain presence on the terraqueous globe is itself the secondary or merely virtual phenomenon.

—H. P. Lovecraft, "Beyond the Wall of Sleep" (1919)

The more he withdrew from the world around him, the more wonderful became his dreams.

—H. P. Lovecraft, "Celephais" (1922)

Dreams are a serious psychic disease.

—Yevgeny Zamiatin, *We* (1924), translated by Mirra Ginsburg (1972)

At last he came to Earth, where dreams *must* come true, for there is a law against their failure.

—Robert Sheckley, "Love, Incorporated" (1956)

No live organism can continue for long to exist sanely under conditions of absolute reality; even larks and katydids are supposed, by some, to dream.

—Shirley Jackson, *The Haunting of Hill House* (1959)

Phantoms slid imperceptibly from nightmare to reality and back again, the terrestrial and psychic landscapes were now indistinguishable, as they had been at Hiroshima and Auschwitz, Golgotha and Gomorrah.

—J. G. Ballard, *The Drowned World* (1962)

In dreams, some of us walk the stars. In dreams, some of us ride the whelming brine of space, where every port is a shining one, and none are beyond our reach. Some of us, in dreams, cannot reach beyond the walls of our own little sleep.

   —Joseph Stefano and Bill S. Ballinger, "The Mice," episode of
    The Outer Limits (1964)

When dreams become more important than reality, you give up travel, building, creating.

   —Gene Roddenberry, "The Menagerie" Part 2, episode of *Star Trek* (1966)

A dream. Compensation, by the state, for reality. Night after night. It's almost worse than being awake.

   No, he decided. *Nothing* is worse than being awake.

   —Philip K. Dick, *Galactic Pot-Healer* (1969)

"Unusual and violent mental activity takes place while you sleep. First, you enter a world that to some extent is familiar. [. . .] In your mind you are where genuine personal friends, enemies, and socially-contacted figures speak and act."

   "In other words," Provoni said, "dreams."

   "This sort of dreaming forms a kind of recapitulation of the day, of what you've done, whom you've thought about, talked with. This does not alarm us. It is the next phase. You fall into a deeper interior level; you encounter personages you never knew, situations you've never been in. A disintegration of your self, of you as such, begins; you merge with primordial entities of a godlike type, possessing enormous power."

   —Philip K. Dick, *Our Friends from Frolix 8* (1970)

Everything dreams. The play of form, of being, is the dreaming of substance. Rocks have their dreams, and the earth changes . . .

   —Ursula K. Le Guin, *The Lathe of Heaven* (1971)

A realist is a man who knows both the world and his own dreams.

   —Ursula K. Le Guin, "The Word for World Is Forest" (1972)

It was only in their waking hours, Quentin let me know, that men allowed themselves to be separated by the artificial barriers of color, ethnics, politics, ideology, hunger, territorial imperatives. In their repose all men were one because all slept, and slept alike. Sleep, you might almost say, was humanity's least common denominator, because most common, indeed, universal. Sun makes men aliens to each other and, thus, themselves. Night unites. Mankind could open itself to, and assert, its true physiological community only with eyes closed.

    —Bernard Wolfe, "The Girl with Rapid Eye Movements" (1972)

"What's the basic idea, that if you make people sleep a lot you'll cut down on wars?" [. . .]

    "Mr. Rengs, well-rested people don't hit each other, asleep or awake. If we can get the insomniacs dozing off again, and improve the repose of the tossers and turners, you see how that ushers in a new epoch. The next great slogan may be, Sleepers of the world, unite!"

    —Bernard Wolfe, "The Girl with Rapid Eye Movements" (1972)

Don't dream it—be it.

    —Richard O'Brien, "Floorshow (Rose Tint My World)," *The Rocky Horror Show* (play, 1973)

The more creative and imaginative a person, the richer and more original his dreams.

    —Philip José Farmer, "Stations of the Nightmare—Part One" (1974)

"Why do they hate me?" asked Preacher Abraham.

    "Because you speak of the good that all men dream of as if it could be real."

    —Edgar Pangborn, "The Children's Crusade" (1974)

I've had my child-dreams, my naming-dreams, my hunting-dreams. Now it is time for my dying-dreams.

    —Sydney J. Van Scyoc, "Bluewater Dreams" (1981)

I'd seen enough strangers' dreams, in the mixing room at the Autonomic Pilot, to know that most people's inner monsters are foolish things, ludicrous in the calm light of one's own consciousness.

    —William Gibson, "The Winter Market" (1985)

Machine dreams hold a special vertigo.
   —William Gibson, *Count Zero* (1986)

No matter how qualified or deserving we are, we will never reach a better life until we can imagine it for ourselves and allow ourselves to have it.
   —Richard Bach, *One* (1988)

It's too bad we only had the courage to live our lives fully in dreams.
   —Kim Stanley Robinson, "Before I Wake" (1990)

EARTH

This planet doesn't need new continents, it needs new men.
— Jules Verne, *Twenty Thousand Leagues under the Sea* (1870),
    translated by Walter James Miller and Frederick Paul Walter (1993)

For what should we thank the humans of three thousand years ago? For exhausting the coal supplies of the world? For leaving us no petroleum for our chemical factories? For destroying the forests on whole mountain ranges and letting the soil erode into the valleys?
— Laurence Manning, "The Man Who Awoke" (1933)

I pray for one last landing
    On the globe that gave me birth;
Let me rest my eyes on the fleecy skies
    And the cool, green hills of Earth.

Let the sweet fresh breezes heal me
    As they rove around the girth
Of our lovely mother planet,
    Of the cool, green hills of Earth.

We've tried each spinning space mote
    And reckoned its true worth:
Take us back again to the homes of men
    On the cool, green hills of Earth.

The arching sky is calling
    Spacemen back to their trade.
All hands! Stand by! Free falling!
    And the lights below us fade.

Out ride the sons of Terra,
    Far drives the thundering jet,
Up leaps the race of Earthmen
    Out, far, and onward yet —

We pray for one last lasting
    On the globe that gave us birth;
Let us rest our eyes on the fleecy skies
    And the cool, green hills of Earth.
  —Robert A. Heinlein, "The Green Hills of Earth" (1947)

Earth hung in the after port behind and below him, a soft emerald crescent in its first thin quarter. A warm green sickle that was home, a hustling verdant young world impatient to push its way across black empty space and satisfy its lusty curiosity about its cosmic neighbors.
  —Roger Dee, "Unwelcome Tenant" (1950)

There were more beautiful planets in the Galaxy's swarming myriads—
the indigo world-ocean of Loa, jeweled with islands; the heaven-defying mountains of Sharang; the sky of Jareb, that seemed to drip light—oh, many and many, but there was only one Earth.
  —Poul Anderson, "The Chapter Ends" (1954)

Earth—it was a place where you could stop being afraid, a place where fear of suffocation was not, where fear of blowout was not, where nobody went berserk with the chokers or dreamed of poisoned air or worried about short-horn cancer or burn blindness or meteorite dust or low-gravity muscular atrophy. A place where there was wind to blow your sweat away.
  —Walter M. Miller, Jr., "The Lineman" (1957)

The biggest developments of the immediate future will take place, not on the Moon or Mars, but on Earth, and it is *inner* space, not outer, that needs to be explored. The only truly alien planet is Earth.
  —J. G. Ballard, "Which Way to Inner Space?" (1962)

He'd congratulated himself on escaping all the traps of Earth, all the snares of Man.
  —Clifford D. Simak, "All the Traps of Earth" (1960)

All my life I've wanted to go to Earth. Not to live, of course—just to see it. As everybody knows, Terra is a wonderful place to visit but not to live. Not truly suited for human habitation.
  —Robert A. Heinlein, *Podkayne of Mars: Her Life and Times* (1963)

Earth

The earth hung overhead like a rotten fruit, blue with mold, crawling, wrinkling, purulent and alive.
— Damon Knight, "Masks" (1968)

[On Earth:] "A peaceful world, certainly," said Zinin. "Rather light on the oxygen and argon, and all that nitrogen gives it a bit of odor, but on the whole a most pleasant ball of dirt."
— Alan Dean Foster, "With Friends Like These" (1971)

The Earth is beautiful, and bright, and kindly, but that is not all. The Earth is also terrible, and dark, and cruel.
— Ursula K. Le Guin, *The Tombs of Atuan* (1971)

Yours is a huge world. Only men stultified by impatience or indifference believe it to be small. Only the pitiably ignorant believe it has been explored.
— Edgar Pangborn, "Mount Charity" (1971)

She floated there in the great nothing, still warm and soft and blue-green if you could eyeball her from a few thousand miles out, still kissed under blankets of clouds.
Mama Earth. Getting old now, tired, her blankets soiled with her own secretions, her body bruised and torn by a billion forgotten passions.
Like many a mother before her, she had given birth to a monster. [. . .] Man. Big Daddy of the primates. The ape that walks like a chicken.
— Chad Oliver, "King of the Hill" (1972)

In 1979, America staged the Big Space Fuck, which was a serious effort to make sure that human life would continue to exist somewhere in the Universe, since it certainly couldn't continue much longer on Earth. Everything had turned to shit and beer cans and old automobiles and Clorox bottles.
— Kurt Vonnegut, Jr., "The Big Space Fuck" (1972)

Mother Earth.
She lived, this world of trees and rivers and rocks with deep stone thoughts. She breathed, had feelings, dreamed dreams, gave birth, laughed and grew contemplative for millennia. This great creature swimming in the sea of space.
— Harlan Ellison, "The Deathbird" (1973)

Earth really messes some people up.
— Howard Waldrop, "My Sweet Lady Jo" (1974)

The earth pulled him down, tugging at him like a burdensome friend.
— George Zebrowski, *Macrolife* (1979)

He was wrong to think he could now forget that the big, hard, oily, dirty, rainbow-hung Earth on which he lived was a microscopic dot on a microscopic dot lost in the unimaginable infinity of the Universe.
— Douglas Adams, *So Long, and Thanks for All the Fish* (1985)

Things are always going to be falling apart on Earth, you might as well get used to it.
— Kim Stanley Robinson, *Red Mars* (1992)

In a sense, the earth is mounting an immune response against the human species.
— Richard Preston, *The Hot Zone* (1994)

Beware the gifts of Earth.
— Philip C. Jennings, "The Road to Reality" (1996)

EDUCATION

To educate some to the highest degree, and leave the mass wholly uncultivated, as you did, made the gap between them almost like that between different natural species, which have no means of communication. What could be more inhuman than this consequence of a partial enjoyment of education!
— Edward Bellamy, *Looking Backward, 2000–1887* (1888)

I don't want to go to school and learn solemn things. No one is going to catch me, lady, and make me a man.
— J. M. Barrie, *Peter Pan* (play, 1904)

Education is our highest art, only allowed to our highest artists.
— Charlotte Perkins Gilman, *Herland* (1915)

Education

To the scientific mind, experimental proof is all-important and theory is merely a convenience in description, to be junked when it no longer fits. To the academic mind, authority is everything, and facts are junked when they do not fit theory laid down by authority.

It is this point of view—academic minds clinging like oysters to disproved theories—that has blocked every advance of knowledge in history.

—Robert A. Heinlein, "Life-Line" (1939)

Dad says this is the best kind of a school, that a university consists of a log with a teacher on one end and a pupil on the other. But Dad is a sort of romantic.

—Robert A. Heinlein, *Farmer in the Sky* (1950)

Teachers always tell you what you do wrong not what you do right, this is Education.

—Pauline Ashwell, "Unwillingly to School" (1958)

Alas, higher education is not necessarily a guarantee of higher virtue, or higher political wisdom.

—Aldous Huxley, *Brave New World Revisited* (1958)

You often learn more by being wrong for the right reasons than you do by being right for the wrong reasons.

—Norton Juster, *The Phantom Tollbooth* (1961)

Pompous, solemn, pedantic, devoid of originality and critical sense, intent on preserving tradition, blind and deaf to all innovation, they form the substratum of every academy. Endowed with a good memory, they learn an enormous amount by heart and from books. Then they themselves write other books, in which they repeat what they have read, thereby earning the respect of their fellow orangutans.

—Pierre Boulle, *Planet of the Apes* (1963), translated by Xan Fielding (1963)

There are things which cannot be taught in ten easy lessons, nor popularized for the masses; they take years of skull sweat. This be treason in an age when ignorance has come into its own and one man's opinion is as good as another's.

—Robert A. Heinlein, *Glory Road* (1963)

It is shocking to find how many people do not believe they can learn, and how many more believe learning to be difficult.
—Frank Herbert, *Dune* (1965)

Education, my friend, is not always a blessing. Like a gun, it depends on who has it.
—Arkady Strugatsky and Boris Strugatsky, *Prisoners of Power* (1969), translated by Helen Saltz Jacobson (1977)

Through her efforts Teachers have become the most respected of all citizens and the schools the most powerful of all institutions.
—Kate Wilhelm, "The Funeral" (1972)

Schoolteacher—lost that job when they caught me teaching the kids the raw truth, a capital offense anywhere in the Galaxy.
—Robert A. Heinlein, *Time Enough for Love* (1973)

Learning is a side-effect of joy.
—Thomas M. Disch, *334* (1974)

Wasn't the whole point of college to keep as many young people as possible occupied and out of jobs?
—Thomas M. Disch, *334* (1974)

If the liberal arts do nothing else they provide engaging metaphors for the thinking they displace.
—Roger Zelazny, "Home Is the Hangman" (1975)

Learning is finding out what you already know. Doing is demonstrating that you know it.
    Teaching is reminding others that they know just as well as you. You are all learners, doers, teachers.
—Richard Bach, *Illusions: The Adventures of a Reluctant Messiah* (1977)

You teach best what you most need to learn.
—Richard Bach, *Illusions: The Adventures of a Reluctant Messiah* (1977)

Education

How do you explain school to higher intelligence?
— Melissa Mathison, *E.T.: The Extra-Terrestrial* (film, 1982)

"The teacher usually learns more than the pupil. Isn't that true?"
"It would be hard to learn much less than my pupils," came a low growl from somewhere on the table, "without undergoing a prefrontal lobotomy."
— Douglas Adams, *Dirk Gently's Holistic Detective Agency* (1987)

She liked teaching. But she found more gratification in teaching one willing student than a dozen resentful ones.
— Octavia E. Butler, *Dawn* (1987)

"It would seem that you have no useful skill or talent whatsoever," he said. "Have you thought of going into teaching?"
— Terry Pratchett, *Mort* (1987)

An easy life doesn't teach us anything. In the end it's the learning that matters: what we've learned and how we've grown.
— Richard Bach, *One* (1988)

Human beings, who are almost unique in having the ability to learn from the experience of others, are also remarkable for their apparent disinclination to do so.
— Douglas Adams, *Last Chance to See* (1990)

"Students?" barked the Archchancellor.
"Yes, Master. You know? They're the thinner ones with the pale faces? Because we're a *university*? They come with the whole thing, like rats—"
— Terry Pratchett, *Moving Pictures* (1990)

Universities are meant to *pass the torch of civilization,* not just download data into student skulls, and the values of the academic community are strongly at odds with those of all would-be information empires. Teachers at all levels, from kindergarten up, have proven to be shameless and persistent software and data pirates. Universities do not merely "leak information" but vigorously broadcast free thought.
— Bruce Sterling, *The Hacker Crackdown* (1992)

Getting an education was a bit like a communicable sexual disease. It made you unsuitable for a lot of jobs and then you had the urge to pass it on.
— Terry Pratchett, *Hogfather* (1996)

EMOTIONS

As a consequence of foresight, some of the commonest emotions of human nature are unknown on Mars. They for whom the future has no mystery can, of course, know neither hope nor fear. Moreover, every one being assured what he shall attain to and what not, there can be no such thing as rivalship, or emulation, or any sort of competition in any respect; and therefore all the brood of heart-burnings and hatreds, engendered on Earth by the strife of man with man, is unknown to the people of Mars, save from the study of our planet.
— Edward Bellamy, "The Blindman's World" (1886)

She is not wholly heartless, but is so small that she has only room for one feeling at a time.
— J. M. Barrie, *Peter Pan* (play, 1904)

Life without emotion is meaningless.
— F. Orlon Tremaine, "True Confession" (1939)

The energy that actually shapes the world springs from emotions — racial pride, leader-worship, religious belief, love of war — which liberal intellectuals mechanically write off as anachronisms, and which they have usually destroyed so completely in themselves as to have lost all power of action.
— George Orwell, "Wells, Hitler, and the World State" (1941)

I never knew before how much of man's emotional life is bound up with his brain, how much more keenly he feels than any other animal.
— Poul Anderson, *Brain Wave* (1954)

KRETON: It took us ages to stamp out disease — scarlet fever, mumps, anxiety, the common cold and, finally, the great killer itself, the ultimate disease: passion!

ELLEN: Passion?

KRETON: Love, hate, that kind of thing. Passion — the Hydra-headed monster, so difficult to diagnose: love-nest slayings, bad temper, world wars,
verse tragedies in five acts — so many variants. But at last success crowned
our efforts. And now . . . we feel nothing. We do nothing. We are perfect.
— Gore Vidal, *Visit to a Small Planet,* revised (play, 1957)

"How is the choice determined? Is it by emotion, or by reason alone?"
"The two are in the long run the same."
— James Blish, *A Case of Conscience* (1958)

What do you despise? By this are you truly known.
— Frank Herbert, *Dune* (1965)

How often it is that the angry man rages denial of what his inner self is telling
him.
— Frank Herbert, *Dune* (1965)

Empathy, evidently, existed only within the human community, whereas
intelligence to some degree could be found throughout every phylum and
order including the arachnida.
— Philip K. Dick, *Do Androids Dream of Electric Sheep?* (1968)

HAL 9000: Dave, I can see you're really upset about this.
— Stanley Kubrick and Arthur C. Clarke, *2001: A Space Odyssey*
(film, 1968)

Pity. The most corrosive emotion endogenous to man.
— Kate Wilhelm, "The Planners" (1968)

How strange, I think objectively, that our lives are such that discomfort, pain,
sadness and hatred are so easily conveyed and so frequently felt. Love and
contentment are only soft veils which do not protect me from bludgeons; and
with the strongest loves, one can still sense the more violent undercurrents of
fear, hate and jealousy.
— Pamela Sargent, "Gather Blue Roses" (1971)

They were smart and had the goods and the money and the hatred. My God, they hated. That's who wins, who hates most.
— Kate Wilhelm, "The Funeral" (1972)

Anger was their aphrodisiac.
— Thomas M. Disch, *334* (1974)

He felt amorphous anger all through him, directed at nothing, fury without object, and he sensed that this was the quality of her own hate; it was a passion which went both nowhere and everywhere. Hate, he thought, like a flock of flies.
— Philip K. Dick, "Chains of Air, Web of Aether" (1980)

It's so easy to be temperate when one enjoys nothing, so easy to be kind when one loves nothing, so easy to be fearless when one's life is no better than one's death.
— Joanna Russ, "Souls" (1982)

After that, for a long time, nothing mattered. It wasn't like the not caring of the stillness, the crystal overdrive, and it wasn't like crashing, just this past-it feeling, the way maybe a ghost feels.
— William Gibson, *Mona Lisa Overdrive* (1988)

Some people say that love is the most powerful force in the Universe. Well, you can take it from me that it isn't. [. . .] No, the most powerful and significant force in the Universe, the one thing that gets things done and makes things happen, is aggravation.
— Tom Holt, *Ye Gods!* (1992)

Those who have strong passions, create strong self-destructions.
— Tara K. Harper, *Wolf's Bane* (1997)

Touch passion when it comes your way, Stephen. It's rare enough as it is. Don't walk away when it calls you by name.
— J. Michael Straczynski, "Lines of Communication," episode of *Babylon 5* (1997)

"My mother didn't have a heart, Kreacher," Sirius snapped. "She kept herself alive out of pure spite."
— J. K. Rowling, *Harry Potter and the Order of the Phoenix* (2003)

EVIL

All human beings, as we meet them, are commingled out of good and evil.
— Robert Louis Stevenson, *Strange Case of Dr. Jekyll and Mr. Hyde* (1886)

When I drew nigh the nameless city I knew it was accursed.
— H. P. Lovecraft, "The Nameless City" (1921)

What a world, what a world. Who would have thought a good little girl like you could destroy my beautiful wickedness?
— Noel Langley, Florence Ryerson, and Edgar Allan Woolf,
  The Wizard of Oz (film, 1939)

Gradually his mental picture of the world was transformed. No longer a world of material atoms and empty space, but a world in which the bodiless existed and moved according to its own obscure laws or unpredictable impulses. The new picture illumined with dreadful clarity certain general facts which had always bewildered and troubled him and from which he had tried to hide; the inevitability of hate and war, the diabolically timed mischances which wrecked the best of human intentions, the walls of willful misunderstanding that divided one man from another, the eternal vitality of cruelty and ignorance and greed.
— Fritz Leiber, "Smoke Ghost" (1941)

It is not our part to master all the tides of the world, but to do what is in us for the succour of those years wherein we are set, uprooting the evil in the fields that we know, so that those who live after may have clean earth to till.
— J. R. R. Tolkien, *The Return of the King* (1955)

My evil self is at that door, and I have no power to stop it.
— Cyril Hume, *Forbidden Planet* (film, 1956)

There's so little meaning in Agronski's life as it is, it won't take Egtverchi long to cut him off from any contact with reality at all. That is what evil does—it empties you.

— James Blish, *A Case of Conscience* (1958)

"Some of you are bad and kill other kinds of life. Others of you are good and protect life."

Thought I, is that all there is to *good* and *bad*?

— Cordwainer Smith, "Alpha Ralpha Boulevard" (1961)

Badness is of the self, the one, the you or me on our oddy knockies, and that self is made by old Bog or God and is his great pride and radosty. But the not-self cannot have the bad, meaning they of the government and the judges and the schools cannot allow the bad because they cannot allow the self.

— Anthony Burgess, *A Clockwork Orange* (1962)

The greatness of evil lies in its awful accuracy. Without that deadly talent for being in the right place at the right time, evil must suffer defeat. For unlike its opposite, good, evil is allowed no human failings, no miscalculations. Evil must be perfect . . . or depend upon the imperfections of others.

— Joseph Stefano, "Don't Open Till Doomsday," episode of
The Outer Limits (1964)

How little the universe knows about the nature of real cruelty!

— Frank Herbert, *Dune* (1965)

A man is an angel that has become deranged, Joe Fernwright thought. Once they—all of them—had been genuine angels, and at that time they had had a choice between good and evil, so it was easy, easy being an angel. And then something happened. Something went wrong or broke down or failed. And they had become faced with the necessity of choosing not good or evil but the lesser of two evils, and so that had unhinged them and now each was a man.

— Philip K. Dick, *Galactic Pot-Healer* (1969)

The evil are always foolish in the final analysis.

— Gene Wolfe, "The Island of Doctor Death and Other Stories" (1970)

Evil

Were wise women always evil?

    — Kate Wilhelm, "The Encounter" (1971)

A spider had spun a web, a circle delicately suspended. The silver threads caught the sunlight. In the center the spinner waited, a gray-black thing no larger than the pupil of an eye. [. . .]

    "What is evil?" asked the younger man.

    The round web, with its black center, seemed to watch them both.

    "A web we men weave," Ged answered.

    — Ursula K. Le Guin, *The Farthest Shore* (1972)

Evil breaks the rules. Good must obey the rules. Very simple.

    — Joanna Russ, "Existence" (1975)

There is no good and there is no evil, outside of what makes us happy and what makes us unhappy.

    — Richard Bach, *Illusions: The Adventures of a Reluctant Messiah* (1977)

If once you start down the dark path, forever will it dominate your destiny. Consume you it will.

    — Leigh Brackett and Lawrence Kasdan, *The Empire Strikes Back*
      (film, 1980)

He was just a little villain. An old-fashioned craftsman, making crimes one-off. The really unforgivable acts are committed by calm men in beautiful green silk rooms, who deal death wholesale, by the shipload, without lust, or anger, or desire, or any redeeming emotion to excuse them but cold fear of some pretended future. But the crimes they hope to prevent in that future are imaginary. The ones they commit in the present — they are real.

    — Lois McMaster Bujold, *Shards of Honor* (1986)

Even the most evil of men and women, if you understand their hearts, had some generous act that redeems them, at least a little, from their sins.

    — Orson Scott Card, *Speaker for the Dead* (1986)

Anyone who thinks he can draw a line between good and evil is at best mistaken, at worst demented.

    — George Turner, *Drowning Towers* (1987)

Those whose office it is to debunk the supernatural are fond of pointing out that incidences of paranormal activity most often take place in backwaters and rarely in the presence of credible witnesses, claiming that this in itself is evidence of the fraudulent character of the phenomena involved, yet it has occurred to me that the agents of the supernatural, especially those elements whose activities are directed toward evil ends, might well exhibit reticence in appearing before persons capable of verifying their existence and thus their threat to humankind.

    —Lucius Shepard, "The Ends of the Earth" (1989)

EVOLUTION

Possibly the remote ancestors of human beings were apes, though no evolutionist has made clear to me reasons for doubting the equally plausible theory that apes have either ascended, or descended, from humans.

    —Charles Fort, *Wild Talents* (1932)

There is no reason whatever to believe that the order of nature has any greater bias in favour of man than it had in favour of the ichthyosaur or the pterodactyl. In spite of all my disposition to a brave-looking optimism, I perceive that now the universe is bored with him, is turning a hard face to him, and I see him being carried less and less intelligently and more and more rapidly, suffering as every ill-adapted creature must suffer in gross and detail, along the stream of fate to degradation, suffering and death.

    —H. G. Wells, *The Fate of Homo Sapiens* (1939)

Easy times for individuals are bad times for the race. Adversity is a strainer which refuses to pass the ill equipped.

    —Robert A. Heinlein, *Beyond This Horizon* (1942)

[The Doctrine of Futility:] Sentient life on the Earth, and particularly the forecasting and introspective self-consciousness of mankind, is an evolutionary blunder or, at best, a futility, inevitably destined to be corrected by the deliberate action of its own products so soon as they should reach an intellectual maturity sufficient to enable them to recognize both their own abortion, and their power to terminate it.

    Sooner or later, it was argued, mankind must reach a maturity of thought which would recognize the vanity of the procession of life and death and, by its own deliberate and orderly extinction, restore the Harmony of the Universe, which had been momentarily disturbed by the flicker of sentient life on the planet on which we live.

— S. Fowler Wright, "Original Sin" (1946)

All life is a continuum in time. Son to father, the germ worldline runs back unbroken to the primordial ocean. For you life bowed to sex and death. For you it gasped sharp air with feeble lungs. For you it bore the pain of gravity in bones too weak to bear it. Ten thousand of your hairy fathers, each in his turn, won through this test of pain and terror to make you a man. [. . .] Two billion years beat against you like surf, Walter Cordice. The twenty thousand fists of your hairy fathers thunder on you as a door. Open the way or be shattered.

— Richard McKenna, "Mine Own Ways" (1960)

Fishes leave the water, but not as fishes. They must have the potential to change. You have lost that potential. There is your stop, your limit . . . that word you do not like. As humans, you cannot make the next step, which is co-operative intelligence. [. . .] Like the flying fish, you may glimpse, for a moment, something more, but you will have to fall back, each time.

— John T. Phillifent, "Flying Fish" (1964)

Species evolve to meet the environment. An intelligent species changes the environment to suit itself. As soon as a species becomes intelligent, it should stop evolving.

— Larry Niven and Jerry Pournelle, *The Mote in God's Eye* (1974)

This is the third stage of human social evolution. First we had the legs race. Then we had the arms race. Now we're going to have the brain race.

And if we're lucky, the final stage will be the human race.

— John Brunner, *The Shockwave Rider* (1975)

Evolution works pretty slow, is all. Couple of hundred million years to develop a thinking ape, and you want a smart one in a lousy few thousand years?

— Spider Robinson, "God Is an Iron" (1979)

In another thousand years we'll be machines, or gods.
— Bruce Sterling, "Swarm" (1982)

The infinite fullness of time brings about everything, he thought: even intelligent lobsters, even a divine octopus.
— Robert Silverberg, "Homefaring" (1983)

He stared gloomily at the gold-framed portraits of the great visionaries of space. [. . .] He could detect a common strangeness in their eyes, particularly in the eyes of the two Americans. Was it simply craziness, as he sometimes thought in his most cynical moods? Or was he able to glimpse a subtle manifestation of some weird, unbalanced force that he had often suspected of being human evolution in action?
— Bruce Sterling and William Gibson, "Red Star, Winter Orbit" (1983)

We are only the beginning of humanity, the larval stage, the species preparing for its discovery of what intelligence is for. We will survive and develop, each crest a little higher than the one before.
— George Turner, *Drowning Towers* (1987)

Extremes of any sort are a liability, in terms of evolution. Extreme intellect may be as bad for us as extreme physical size was for the dinosaurs.
— Joan Slonczewski, *The Wall around Eden* (1989)

The course of Evolution does not conform to the batrachian sluggishness of your intellect.
— William Gibson and Bruce Sterling, *The Difference Engine* (1991)

Storms of Cataclysm lashed the Cretaceous earth, vast fires raged, and cometary grit sifted through the roiling atmosphere, to blight and kill the wilting foliage, till the mighty Dinosauria, adapted to a world now shattered, fell in massed extinction, and the leaping machineries of Evolution were loosed in chaos, to re-populate the stricken Earth with strange new orders of being.
— William Gibson and Bruce Sterling, *The Difference Engine* (1991)

I'll tell you about rage. It is what you have all forgotten, or never learned. It is the motor of evolution, and evolution's end, too.
— Paul J. McAuley, "Recording Angel" (1995)

Evolution

We fondly imagine that evolution drives toward higher intelligence. But eagles would think evolution favored flight, elephants would naturally prefer the importance of great strength, sharks would feel that swimming was the ultimate desirable trait, and eminent Victorians would be quite convinced that evolution preferred Victorians.
  —Gregory Benford, *Eater* (2000)

Reverse Darwinism—survival of the most idiotic.
  —Peter Buchman, Alexander Payne, and Jim Taylor, *Jurassic Park III* (film, 2001)

Forty thousand years of evolution and we've barely even tapped the vastness of human potential.
  —David Koepp, *Spider-Man* (film, 2002)

Mutation. It is the key to our evolution. It is how we have evolved from a single-celled organism into the dominant species on the planet. This process is slow, normally taking thousands and thousands of years. But every few hundred millennia, evolution leaps forward.
  —Michael Dougherty, Dan Harris, and David Hayter, *X2: X-Men United* (film, 2003)

EXPLORATION AND ADVENTURE

I wanted to see what no one had yet observed, even if I had to pay for this curiosity with my life.
  —Jules Verne, *Twenty Thousand Leagues under the Sea* (1870), translated by Walter James Miller and Frederick Paul Walter (1993)

When we think how narrow and how devious this path of nature is, how dimly we can trace it, for all our lamps of science, and how from the darkness which girds it round great and terrible possibilities loom ever shadowly upwards, it is a bold and confident man who will put a limit to the strange by-paths into which the human spirit may wander.
  —Arthur Conan Doyle, "Lot No. 249" (1892)

Why had we come to the moon?

The thing presented itself to me as a perplexing problem. What is this spirit in man that urges him for ever to depart from happiness and security, to toil, to place himself in danger, to risk even a reasonable certainty of death? It dawned upon me up there in the moon as a thing I ought always to have known, that man is not made simply to go about safe and comfortable and well fed and amused. [. . .] Against his interest, against his happiness, he is constantly being driven to do unreasonable things. Some force not himself impels him, and go he must.

—H. G. Wells, *The First Men in the Moon* (1901)

I have ever been prone to seek adventure and to investigate and experiment where wiser men would have left well enough alone.

—Edgar Rice Burroughs, *A Princess of Mars* (1917)

Curiosity will conquer fear even more than bravery will.

—James Stephens, *The Crock of Gold* (1912)

We are plain quiet folk and have no use for adventures. Nasty disturbing uncomfortable things! Make you late for dinner! I can't think what anybody sees in them.

—J. R. R. Tolkien, *The Hobbit* (1937)

Adventure is when you toss your life on the scales of chance and wait for the pointer to stop.

—Murray Leinster, "First Contact" (1945)

"Here we are," said Carpdyke, "located in the exact hub of the Universe, located for a purpose, Pettigrew. A Purpose! Every exploding star must be investigated at once. Every new shape of a nebula must be skirted and charted. Every dark cloud must be searched for harmful material. Pettigrew, the emanations of all the Universe depend upon us."

—L. Ron Hubbard, "A Can of Vacuum" (1949)

Escape, God how we all need escape from this tiny here. The need for it has motivated just about everything man has ever done in any direction other than that of the satisfaction of his physical appetites; it has led him along weird and wonderful pathways; it has led him into art and religion, ascetism [*sic*] and astrology, dancing and drinking, poetry and insanity. All of these have been escapes because he has known only recently the true direction of escape—*outward,* into infinity and eternity, away from this little flat if rounded surface we're born on and die on. This mote in the solar system, this atom in the galaxy.

—Fredric Brown, *The Lights in the Sky Are Stars* (1953)

"Stuff your eyes with wonder," he said, "live as if you'd drop dead in ten seconds. See the world. It's more fantastic than any dream made or paid for in factories."

—Ray Bradbury, *Fahrenheit 451* (1954)

"I believe in Mars," he began, quietly. "I guess I believe some day it'll belong to us. We'll nail it down. We'll settle in. We won't turn tail and run. It came to me one day a year ago, right after we first arrived. Why did we come? I asked myself. Because, I said, because. It's the same thing with the salmon every year. The salmon don't know why they go where they go, but they go, anyway. Up rivers they don't remember, up streams, jumping waterfalls, but finally making it to where they propagate and die, and the whole thing starts again. Call it racial memory, instinct, call it nothing, but there it is. And here we are."

—Ray Bradbury, "The Strawberry Window" (1954)

It's the highest goal of man—the need to grow and advance . . . to find new things . . . to expand. To spread out, reach areas, experiences, comprehend and live in an evolving fashion. To push aside routine and repetition, to break out of mindless monotony and thrust forward. To keep moving on . . .

—Philip K. Dick, *Solar Lottery* (1955)

All explorers are seeking something they have lost. It is seldom that they find it, and more seldom still that the attainment brings them greater happiness than the quest.

—Arthur C. Clarke, *The City and the Stars* (1956)

Men with the restless natures that made them criminals on their own highly civilized Worlds, made the best pioneers.

—Charles V. De Vet and Katherine MacLean, "Second Game" (1958)

There ought not to be anything in the whole universe that man can't poke his nose into — that's the way we're built and I assume that there's some reason for it.

—Robert A. Heinlein, *Methuselah's Children,* revised (1958)

The spirit of adventure, the lure of the unknown, the thrill of a gallant quest. How very grand indeed.

—Norton Juster, *The Phantom Tollbooth* (1961)

"I went a couple of hundred miles on the Kerm Ice one autumn, years ago."
[. . .]
    "What for?"
    "Curiosity, adventure." He hesitated and smiled slightly. "The augmentation of the complexity and intensity of the field of intelligent life," he said, quoting one of my Ekumenical quotations.
    "Ah: you were consciously extending the evolutionary tendency inherent in Being; one manifestation of which is exploration."

—Ursula K. Le Guin, *The Left Hand of Darkness* (1969)

The exploration of alien worlds was just a monotonous and exhausting game.
    —Arkady Strugatsky and Boris Strugatsky, *Prisoners of Power* (1969),
        translated by Helen Saltz Jacobson (1977)

As a child I used to watch clouds, and in them, see faces, castles, animals, dragons, and giants. It was a world of escape — fantasy; something to inject wonder and adventure into the mundane, regulated life of a middle-class boy leading a middle-class life.

—Barry B. Longyear, "Enemy Mine" (1979)

If we knew exactly what to expect throughout the Solar System, we would have no reason to explore it.
    —Poul Anderson, "The Saturn Game" (1981)

These lands are not always calm. We may well have more adventures ahead of us. But we shall meet them with high hearts.
    —Poul Anderson, "The Saturn Game" (1981)

Adventures! Gone with the ravaged forests and culled beasts. We had survival, action and danger on the stock market, but no adventures. Romance was gone away.
    — George Turner, *Drowning Towers* (1987)

He liked the steady sway and rhythms of voyaging, of movement, of the perpetual mystery that lurked beyond the far horizon. This was humanity's role.
    — Gregory Benford, "At the Double Solstice" (1988)

Perhaps "because it is there" is not sufficient reason for climbing a mountain.
    — David Loughery, *Star Trek V: The Final Frontier* (film, 1989)

The world was full of locked doors, and he had to get his hands on every key.
    — Orson Scott Card, *Ender's Shadow* (1999)

Sometimes the mind needs to discover things for itself.
    — Michael Dougherty, Dan Harris, and David Hayter, *X2: X-Men United* (film, 2003)

FEAR AND HORROR

I am acutely conscious of the nearness of some mystery, of some overwhelming Presence. The very air seems pregnant with terror. I sit huddled,
and just listen, intently. Still, there is no sound. Nature, herself, seems dead.
Then, the oppressive stillness is broken by a little eldritch scream of wind,
that sweeps round the house, and dies away, remotely.
  —William Hope Hodgson, *The House on the Borderland* (1908)

They, like the subject and material, belonged to something horribly remote
and distinct from mankind as we know it; something frightfully suggestive
of old and unhallowed cycles of life in which our world and our conceptions
have no part.
  —H. P. Lovecraft, "The Call of Cthulhu" (1928)

Was I tottering on the brink of cosmic horrors beyond man's power to bear?
  —H. P. Lovecraft, "The Call of Cthulhu" (1928)

It is not so much the things we know that terrify us as it is the things we do
not know, the things that break all known laws and rules, the things that
come upon us unaware and shatter the pleasant dream of our little world.
  —Donald A. Wandrei, "Something from Above" (1930)

From even the greatest of horrors irony is seldom absent.
  —H. P. Lovecraft, "The Shunned House" (1937)

There are horrors beyond horrors, and this was one of those nuclei of all
dreamable hideousness which the cosmos saves to blast an accursed and
unhappy few.
  —H. P. Lovecraft, "The Shunned House" (1937)

I seemed able to look behind the mask which every person wears and which
is so characteristically pronounced in a congested city, and see what lay

behind—the egotistical sensitivity, the smouldering irritation, the thwarted longing, the defeat . . . and, above all, the anxiety, too ill-defined and lacking in definite object to be called fear but nonetheless infecting every thought and action, and making trivial things terrible. And it seemed to me that social, economic, or physiological factors, even Death and the War, were insufficient to explain such anxiety, and that it was in reality an upwelling from something dubious and horrible in the very constitution of the universe.
— Fritz Leiber, "The Dreams of Albert Moreland" (1945)

The idiot lived in a black and gray world, punctuated by the white lightning of hunger and the flickering of fear.
— Theodore Sturgeon, *More Than Human* (1953)

The spider was immortal. It was more than a spider. It was every unknown terror in the world fused into wriggling, poison-jawed horror. It was every anxiety, insecurity, and fear in his life given a hideous, night-black form.
— Richard Matheson, *The Shrinking Man* (1956)

The most frightening thing in this world is discovering the abnormal in that which is closest to us.
— Kobo Abé, *Inter Ice Age 4* (1959), translated by E. Dale Saunders (1970)

However selective the conscious mind may be, most biological memories are unpleasant ones, echoes of danger and terror. Nothing endures for so long as fear.
— J. G. Ballard, *The Drowned World* (1962)

I must not fear. Fear is the mind-killer. Fear is the little-death that brings total obliteration. I will face my fear. I will permit it to pass over me and through me. And when it has gone past I will turn the inner eye to see its path. Where the fear has gone there will be nothing. Only I will remain.
— Frank Herbert, *Dune* (1965)

How absolutely typical of your species—you don't understand something so you become fearful.
— Paul Schneider, "The Squire of Gothos," episode of *Star Trek* (1967)

Fire and fear, good servants, bad lords.
— Ursula K. Le Guin, *The Left Hand of Darkness* (1969)

What one fears is alien.
 —Ursula K. Le Guin, "Vaster Than Empires and More Slow" (1971)

There was horror in the earth and in the thick air, an enormity of horror.
This place was fear, was fear itself; and he was in it, and there were no paths.
 —Ursula K. Le Guin, *The Farthest Shore* (1972)

Only the unimaginative, of whom you are the king, have no fear.
 —Philip José Farmer, "Stations of the Nightmare—Part One" (1974)

Man is most human at his most frightened.
 —Ursula K. Le Guin, "Schrödinger's Cat" (1974)

The countries of love and terror border each other here and there.
 —Edgar Pangborn, "The Children's Crusade" (1974)

The Hitch-Hiker's Guide to the Galaxy [. . .] has the words "DON'T PANIC"
inscribed in large, friendly letters on the cover.
 —Douglas Adams, "Fit the First," episode of *The Hitch-Hiker's Guide to
    the Galaxy* (radio series, 1978)

The sign changed itself again. It said:
DO NOT BE ALARMED.
After a pause, it added:
BE VERY, VERY FRIGHTENED.
 —Douglas Adams, *Life, the Universe, and Everything* (1982)

Be afraid. Be very afraid.
 —Charles Edward Pogue and David Cronenberg, *The Fly* (film, 1986)

The trouble with unimaginable horrors was that they were only too easy to
imagine.
 —Terry Pratchett, *The Light Fantastic* (1986)

Lanette told her scary stuff because it was fun to be scared when you knew
you were pretty safe.
 —William Gibson, *Mona Lisa Overdrive* (1988)

FLYING

The reason birds can fly and we can't is simply that they have perfect faith, for to have faith is to have wings.

> —J. M. Barrie, *The Little White Bird, or, Adventures in Kensington Gardens* (1902)

WENDY: How lovely to fly!
PETER: I'll teach you how to jump on the wind's back and then away we go. Wendy, when you are sleeping in your silly bed you might be flying about with me, saying funny things to the stars.

> —J. M. Barrie, *Peter Pan* (play, 1904)

I pulled the covers up tight under my chin and whispered to myself, "I can so fly," and sighed heavily. Just another fun-stuff that grown-ups didn't allow, like having cake for breakfast or driving the tractor or borrowing the cow for an Indian pony on a warpath.

> —Zenna Henderson, "Gilead" (1954)

"Have you ever wondered what it would be like to be up there in the middle of the storm with clouds under your feet and over your head and lightning lacing around you like hot golden rivers?"

Dad rattled his paper. "Sounds uncomfortable," he said.

But I sat there and hugged the words to me in wonder. I knew! *I remembered!* "'And the rain like icy silver hair lashing across your lifted face.'" I recited as though it were a loved lesson.

> —Zenna Henderson, "Gilead" (1954)

"Someday—" He broke off. "I think every living thing will fly or anyhow trudge or run; some will go fast, like they do in this life, but most will fly or trudge. Up and up. Forever. Even slugs and snails; they'll go very slow but they'll make it sometime. All of them will make it eventually, no matter how slow they go. Leaving a lot behind; that has to be done."

> —Philip K. Dick, *Our Friends from Frolix 8* (1970)

I see myself streaking across the sky like a star to leave the earth forever. What holds me back?

> —William S. Burroughs, *The Wild Boys: A Book of the Dead* (1971)

Nobody burns so as when sunning himself on a cloud.
—R. A. Lafferty, "Sky" (1971)

"There is an art to flying," said Ford, "or rather a knack. The knack lies in learning how to throw yourself at the ground and miss."
—Douglas Adams, *Life, the Universe, and Everything* (1982)

Therru went, not crouching and sidling now but running freely, flying, Tenar thought, seeing her vanish in the evening light beyond the dark doorframe, flying like a bird, a dragon, a child, free.
—Ursula K. Le Guin, *Tehanu: The Last Book of Earthsea* (1990)

FOLLY AND STUPIDITY

Why do you think that foolishness is bad? If human foolishness had been as carefully nurtured and cultivated as intelligence has been for centuries, perhaps it would have turned into something extremely precious.
—Yevgeny Zamiatin, *We* (1924), translated by Mirra Ginsburg (1972)

"Men are fools," he confided to Khambee. "Trouble and misfortune are all the reward they get for their struggles."
—Raymond Z. Gallun, "Derelict" (1935)

"By proving that death is just a cyclic condition of continued individual existence, these people have conquered their last enemy."
"Last enemy but one," Verkan Vall corrected. "They still have one enemy to go, an enemy within themselves. Call it semantic confusion, or illogic, or incomprehension, or just plain stupidity."
—H. Beam Piper, "Last Enemy" (1950)

I'm impatient with stupidity. My people have learned to live without it.
—Edmund H. North, *The Day the Earth Stood Still* (film, 1951)

"I've been a fool all down the line." [. . .]
"At least you were a fool about the right things."
—Ray Bradbury, *Fahrenheit 451* (1954)

Folly and Stupidity

The first thing you learn in life is you're a fool. The last thing you learn in life is you're the same fool.
—Ray Bradbury, *Dandelion Wine* (1957)

Don't take it so hard, kid . . . "Jeder macht eine kleine Dummheit." (Everyone makes a little dumbness.)
—William S. Burroughs, *Naked Lunch* (1959)

That took more than ordinary dullness, the kind of stupidity that can only result from long practice and hard study.
—Philip K. Dick and Ray Nelson, *The Ganymede Takeover* (1967)

Terrans are known for their stupidity.
—Philip K. Dick, *Galactic Pot-Healer* (1969)

As far as Unc Kaan was concerned, everyone was an idiot, including his faculty colleagues and his assistants. And the students? The height of idiocy.
—Arkady Strugatsky and Boris Strugatsky, *Prisoners of Power* (1969), translated by Helen Saltz Jacobson (1977)

Folly springs from weakness, and weakness from ignorance, from ignorance of the correct path.
—Arkady Strugatsky and Boris Strugatsky, *Prisoners of Power* (1969), translated by Helen Saltz Jacobson (1977)

Never underestimate the power of human stupidity.
—Robert A. Heinlein, *Time Enough for Love* (1973)

There are two kinds of fool. One says, "This is old, and therefore good." And one says, "This is new, and therefore better."
—John Brunner, *The Shockwave Rider* (1975)

If stupidity kills, why aren't you dead? [. . .] Obviously stupidity is a survival trait.
—Philip K. Dick, *Valis* (1981)

If it's true that there are billions of universes stacked alongside one another, the thickness of a thought apart, then there must be people elsewhere.

But whatever they are, no matter how mightily they try, no matter how magnificent the effort, they surely can't manage to be as godawfully stupid as us.
—Terry Pratchett, *Pyramids* (1989)

A common mistake that people make when trying to design something completely foolproof was to underestimate the ingenuity of complete fools.
—Douglas Adams, *Mostly Harmless* (1992)

I used to think *I* was stupid, and then I met philosophers.
—Terry Pratchett, *Small Gods* (1992)

At times the man could be as dense as a neutron star.
—P. N. Elrod, "Fugitives" (1995)

Real stupidity beats artificial intelligence every time.
—Terry Pratchett, *Hogfather* (1996)

FOOD AND DRINK

DRACULA: I never drink—wine.
—Garrett Fort, *Dracula* (film, 1931)

They were staying the eternal gnaw of hunger that afflicts those who depend on a college commissary for sustenance. Many of them suspected a conspiracy among college cooks to see that the razor edge wasn't taken off students' and instructors' intellects by overfeeding.
—L. Sprague de Camp, "The Exalted" (1940)

The peddler came to Earth, across the empty immensities of space, after whisky.
—Jack Williamson, "The Peddler's Nose" (1951)

Martin got through all the early stages of intoxication—the eager, the uneasy, the dreamily blissful—and emerged safely into that crystal world where time almost stands still, where nothing is surer than your movements and nothing realer than your feelings, where the tight shell of personality is shattered and even dark walls and smoky sky and gray cement underfoot are sentient parts of you.

—Fritz Leiber, "I'm Looking for 'Jeff'" (1952)

It amused him to realize that he was the first human to be eaten on this planet.

—Robert Sheckley, "The Odor of Thought" (1953)

"I don't drink," Allan Garner said.

"A pity," Grandpa observed. "It is a custom that has been known to change people into human beings."

—Chad Oliver, "Pilgrimage" (1958)

The more you eat, the hungrier you get. Everyone knows that.

—Norton Juster, *The Phantom Tollbooth* (1961)

A few million years. I remember starting out as a one-celled organism and painfully becoming an amphibian, then an air-breather. From somewhere high in the treetops I heard a voice.

"He's coming around."

I evolved back into homo sapience, then a step further into a hangover.

—Roger Zelazny, "The Doors of His Face, the Lamps of His Mouth" (1965)

Nothing uses up alcohol faster than political argument.

—Robert A. Heinlein, *The Moon Is a Harsh Mistress* (1966)

What do I really yearn for? he asked himself. That for which oral gratification is a surrogate. Something vast, he decided; he felt the primordial hunger gape, huge-jawed, as if to cannibalize everything around him. To place what was outside inside.

—Philip K. Dick, *Galactic Pot-Healer* (1969)

A humanoid biped cannot maintain metabolic processes by means of plankton flour merely.

—Philip K. Dick, *Galactic Pot-Healer* (1969)

Try to go through life a little bit hungry. You never know when you'll meet someone edible.

—T. J. Bass, *Half Past Human* (1970)

He had read articles about the personality changes often suffered by alcohol addicts. How much feral cruelty often came out, a virtually psychopathic personality structure, blended with the fast moving quality of mania and the suspicious rage of paranoia.

—Philip K. Dick, *Our Friends from Frolix 8* (1970)

Cookies are better comfort than religion—more immediate and understandable, and hardly likely to do any lasting harm.

—Susanna Jacobson, "Notes from Magdalen More" (1973)

"When you're a star," she said once, half drunk, "you're not hung up about taking the last cookie on the plate."

—Edward Bryant, "Stone" (1978)

"John," I heard the woman say, "we've forgotten to take our food pills."

—William Gibson, "The Gernsback Continuum" (1981)

In twentieth-century Old Earth, a fast food chain took dead cow meat, fried it in grease, added carcinogens, wrapped it in petroleum-based foam, and sold nine hundred billion units. Human beings. Go figure.

—Dan Simmons, *Hyperion* (1989)

His philosophy was a mixture of three famous schools—the Cynics, the Stoics and the Epicureans—and summed up all three of them in his famous phrase, "You can't trust any bugger further than you can throw him, and there's nothing you can do about it, so let's have a drink."

—Terry Pratchett, *Small Gods* (1992)

I'd tried caffeine a few times; it made me believe I was focused and energetic, but it turned my judgment to shit. Widespread use of caffeine explained a lot about the twentieth century.

—Greg Egan, *Distress* (1995)

I can't believe this. I'm arguing with lunch.

—M. Night Shyamalan and Greg Brooker, *Stuart Little* (film, 1999)

FREEDOM

Those two, in paradise, were given a choice: happiness without freedom, or freedom without happiness. There was no third alternative. Those idiots chose freedom, and what came of it? Of course, for ages afterward they longed for the chains. The chains—you understand? That's what world sorrow was about.

— Yevgeny Zamiatin, *We* (1924), translated by Mirra Ginsburg (1972)

Mighty little force is needed to control a man whose mind has been hoodwinked; contrariwise, no amount of force can control a free man, a man whose mind is free. No, not the rack, not fission bombs, not anything—you can't conquer a free man; the most you can do is kill him.

— Robert A. Heinlein, "'If This Goes On . . .'" (1940)

All perfection comes from within, and the perfection that is imposed from without is as frivolous and stupid as the trimmings on gingercake. The free man may be bad, but only the free man can be good. And all the kingdom and the power and the glory—call it of God, call it of Cosmos—must arise from the free will of man.

— Anthony Boucher, "The Barrier" (1942)

Freedom is the freedom to say that two plus two make four. If that is granted, all else follows.

— George Orwell, *Nineteen Eighty-Four* (1949)

The Captain belongs to the most dangerous enemy to truth and freedom, the solid unmoving cattle of the majority. Oh, God, the terrible tyranny of the majority.

— Ray Bradbury, *Fahrenheit 451* (1954)

Poor tortured world! World of tragedy, doomed to periodic violence, priding itself on being free.

Free. Free to make each other miserable. Free to drive each other to insanity and crime. Free to kill in mass and individual slaughters. [. . .] Free to fret themselves into an early grave.

In 1950, thirty-three men out of every one hundred thousand in the United States committed suicide. That was freedom.

— James Gunn, *The Joy Makers* (1961)

Freedom was never more than a happy accident because the common jerk, all human races, hates and fears all freedom, not only for his neighbors but for himself, and stamps it out whenever possible.

    — Robert A. Heinlein, *Glory Road* (1963)

There was only the rushing wind and the flashing pillars and the dizzying lawns and musty cottages as they sped, faster and faster, toward Freelands and wild bees and wild spiders and wild tigers, and firecrackers and loud jazz and the open life and open sky and danger and spaceships and the stars.

    — Fritz Leiber, "The Crystal Prison" (1966)

She wept in pain, because she was free.

    What she had begun to learn was the weight of liberty. Freedom is a heavy load, a great and strange burden for the spirit to undertake. It is not easy. It is not a gift given, but a choice made, and the choice may be a hard one.

    — Ursula K. Le Guin, *The Tombs of Atuan* (1971)

If liberty means anything at all it means the right to tell people what they do not want to hear.

    — George Orwell, "The Freedom of the Press" (1972)

He could not show him what freedom is, that recognition of each person's solitude which alone transcends it.

    — Ursula K. Le Guin, *The Dispossessed: An Ambiguous Utopia* (1974)

Only someone who *wishes* for freedom can be free. I wish for freedom.

    — Isaac Asimov, "The Bicentennial Man" (1976)

There is no right to deny freedom to any object with a mind advanced enough to grasp the concept and desire the state.

    — Isaac Asimov, "The Bicentennial Man" (1976)

There is more than one kind of freedom, said Aunt Lydia. Freedom to and freedom from. In the days of anarchy, it was freedom to. Now you are being given freedom from. Don't underrate it.

    — Margaret Atwood, *The Handmaid's Tale* (1986)

It occurred to Teppic that the landless peasants down on the delta had more freedom than he did, although the seditious and non-kingly side of him said, yes, freedom to catch any diseases of their choice, starve as much as they wanted, and die of whatever dreadful ague took their fancy. But freedom, of a sort.

—Terry Pratchett, *Pyramids* (1989)

Even if there is no such thing as free will, we have to treat each other as if there *were* free will in order to live together in society. Because otherwise, every time somebody does something terrible, you can't punish him, because he can't help it, because his genes or his environment or God made him do it, and every time somebody does something good, you can't honor him, because he was a puppet, too. If you think that everybody around you is a puppet, why bother talking to them at all? Why even try to plan anything or create anything, since everything you plan or create or desire or dream of is just acting out the script your puppeteer built into you.

—Orson Scott Card, *Xenocide* (1991)

With the first link, a chain is forged. The first speech censured, the first thought forbidden, the first freedom denied, chains us all irrevocably.

—Jeri Taylor, "The Drumhead," episode of *Star Trek: The Next Generation* (1991)

There is no greater power in the universe than the need for freedom. Against that power governments, and tyrants, and armies can not stand.

—J. Michael Straczynski, "The Long Twilight Struggle," episode of *Babylon 5* (1995)

I demand the freedom to do what seems right to me from first principles, and not the freedom always to behave selfishly, or always to do what a man would do in the circumstances, or always to do the opposite.

—Iain M. Banks, *The Business* (1999)

FRIENDSHIP

I knew that even though you became a member of the community you would not cease to be my friend; "A warrior may change his metal, but not his heart."

—Edgar Rice Burroughs, *A Princess of Mars* (1917)

Alone: bad. Friend: good.
　—William Hurlbut, *Bride of Frankenstein* (film, 1935)

Dear George:—Remember *no* man is a failure who has *friends*.
　—Frances Goodrich, Albert Hackett, Frank Capra, and Jo Swerling,
　　It's a Wonderful Life (film, 1946)

The most fearful of monsters is the well-known friend slightly altered.
　—Kobo Abé, *Inter Ice Age 4* (1959), translated by E. Dale Saunders (1970)

The great and sudden assurance of friendship between us rose: a friendship
so much needed by us both in our exile, and already so well proved in the
days and nights of our bitter journey, that it might as well be called, now as
later, love. But it was from the difference between us, not from the affinities
and likenesses, but from the difference, that that love came; and it was itself
the bridge, the only bridge, across what divided us.
　—Ursula K. Le Guin, *The Left Hand of Darkness* (1969)

A friend is a friend, but an enemy is an enemy. Are there any questions?
　—Arkady Strugatsky and Boris Strugatsky, *Prisoners of Power* (1969),
　　translated by Helen Saltz Jacobson (1977)

Esteem is the basis of every friendship.
　—Joanna Russ, "The Soul of a Servant" (1973)

If humans have this need for companionship, why are they also ashamed to
admit it?
　—Barry B. Longyear, "Enemy Mine" (1979)

She reached out across the cathedral of space-time to those hopelessly distant
candle-furnaces, where all the material elements had been forged again and
again inside the generation of suns, where alien sunspaces were certain to
contain other humanities, however different, and she wondered if someone
there might be her friend.
　—George Zebrowski, *Macrolife* (1979)

Of my friend [Spock], I can only say this . . . of all the souls I have
encountered in my travels, his was the most—human.
　—Jack B. Sowards, *Star Trek II: The Wrath of Khan* (film, 1982)

Friendship

A friend who offers help without asking for explanations is a treasure beyond price.
  —Robert A. Heinlein, *The Cat Who Walks through Walls* (1985)

Friendship was just diplomacy by other means.
  —Kim Stanley Robinson, *Red Mars* (1992)

There are some things you can't share without ending up liking each other, and knocking out a twelve-foot mountain troll is one of them.
  —J. K. Rowling, *Harry Potter and the Sorcerer's Stone* (1997)

THE FUTURE

Whether we expect another invasion or not, our views of the human future must be greatly modified by these events. We have learned now that we cannot regard this planet as being fenced in and a secure abiding place for Man; we can never anticipate the unseen good or evil that may come upon us suddenly out of space. It may be that in the larger design of the universe this invasion from Mars is not without its ultimate benefit for men; it has robbed us of that serene confidence in the future which is the most fruitful source of decadence, the gifts to human science it has brought are enormous, and it has done much to promote the conception of the commonweal of mankind.
  —H. G. Wells, *The War of the Worlds* (1898)

The human race, to which so many of my readers belong, has been playing at children's games from the beginning, and will probably do it till the end, which is a nuisance for the few people who grow up. And one of the games to which it is most attached is called "Keep to-morrow dark," and which is also named (by the rustics in Shropshire, I have no doubt) "Cheat the Prophet." The players listen very carefully and respectfully to all that the clever men have to say about what is to happen in the next generation. They players then wait until all the clever men are dead, and bury them nicely. Then they go and do something else.
  —G. K. Chesterton, *The Napoleon of Notting Hill* (1904)

The younger lamas are naturally preoccupied with the past; it is a necessary step to envisaging the future.
  —James Hilton, *Lost Horizon* (1933)

If a man could look ahead and see some of the things that no doubt were
going to happen, how could he be happy?
  — Clifford D. Simak, "Sunspot Purge" (1940)

Is there anything to add to that preface now? Nothing except my epitaph.
That, when the time comes, will manifestly have to be: "I told you so. You
damned fools." (The italics are mine.)
  — H. G. Wells, preface to *The War in the Air, and Particularly How
    Mr. Bert Smallways Fared While It Lasted* (1941)

We have trained them to think of the Future as a promised land which
favoured heroes attain — not as something which everyone reaches at the
rate of sixty minutes an hour, whatever he does, whoever he is.
  — C. S. Lewis, *The Screwtape Letters* (1942)

Is it credible that our world should have two futures? I have seen them. Two
entirely distinct futures lie before mankind, one dark, one bright; one the
defeat of all man's hopes, the betrayal of all his ideals, the other their hard-
won triumph.
  — Olaf Stapledon, *Darkness and the Light* (1942)

We live in reference to past experience and not to future events, however
inevitable.
  — H. G. Wells, *Mind at the End of Its Tether* (1946)

How could you communicate with the future? It was of its nature impossible.
Either the future would resemble the present, in which case it would not
listen to him: or it would be different from it, and his predicament would be
meaningless.
  — George Orwell, *Nineteen Eighty-Four* (1949)

"Who controls the past," ran the Party slogan, "controls the future: who
controls the present controls the past."
  — George Orwell, *Nineteen Eighty-Four* (1949)

If you want a picture of the future, imagine a boot stamping on a human
face — for ever.
  — George Orwell, *Nineteen Eighty-Four* (1949)

The Future

In her ruddy face, surprised pleasure fought with a worry that saw the future as a suddenly treacherous thing, full of trials.
— Raymond Z. Gallun, "Prodigal's Aura" (1951)

This was a Golden Age, a time of high adventure, rich living, and hard dying ... but nobody thought so. This was a future of fortune and theft, pillage and rapine, culture and vice ... but nobody admitted it.
— Alfred Bester, *The Stars My Destination* (1956)

The less you know about the future the better off you are.
— Philip K. Dick, *The World Jones Made* (1956)

Suddenly the future was not the simple blueprint it had been until now, but seemed like some frenzied living thing that possessed a will independent of the present.
— Kobo Abé, *Inter Ice Age 4* (1959), translated by E. Dale Saunders (1970)

The greatest problem of the future is civilizing the human race.
— Arthur C. Clarke, "Aladdin's Lamp" (1962)

Do you see, then, that the important prediction is not the automobile, but the parking problem; not radio, but the soap-opera; not the income tax but the expense account; not the Bomb but the nuclear stalemate? Not the action, in short, but the reaction?
— Isaac Asimov, "Future? Tense!" (1965)

You cannot back into the future.
— Frank Herbert, *Dune* (1965)

If Jules Verne could really have looked into the future, say 1966 A.D., he would have crapped in his pants. And 2166, oh, my!
— Philip José Farmer, "Riders of the Purple Wage" (1967)

Without your existential super-self you will certainly perish in wars of the future out among the satellites, overcome by cosmic thought patterns too convoluted for the human brain to contemplate, or, if not that, torn apart by humanoids in the death throes of their own identity crises, or exploded by technological advances available not only to the future but known already to the present and, if not one or more of the above, inevitably coarsened by Earthlings of your own kind.

— Carol Emshwiller, "The Childhood of the Human Hero" (1973)

H. G. Wells [. . .] saw the obvious and foresaw the inevitable. What is really amazing and frustrating is mankind's habit of *refusing* to see the obvious and inevitable, until it is there, and then muttering about unforeseen catastrophes.

— Isaac Asimov, "How Easy to See the Future!" (1975)

Men have an extraordinary, and perhaps fortunate, ability to tune out of their consciousness the most awesome future possibilities.

— Arthur C. Clarke, *The Fountains of Paradise* (1979)

Part of human life is the need to reassure ourselves about the future that we may never live to see, rather than fool ourselves, as many did in the last century, that there won't be any future and they might as well lie down and die.

— George Zebrowski, *Macrolife* (1979)

The term "Future Perfect" has been abandoned since it was discovered not to be.

— Douglas Adams, *The Restaurant at the End of the Universe* (1980)

The designers were populists, you see; they were trying to give the public what it wanted. What the public wanted was the future.

— William Gibson, "The Gernsback Continuum" (1981)

So together they left the office and walked into the uncertainty of the rest of their lives. That, in the final analysis, is the great adventure in which each of us takes part; what more courageous thing is there, after all, than facing the unknown we all share, the danger and joy that awaits us in the unread pages of the Book of the Future . . .

— George Alec Effinger, "The World of Pez Pavilion: Preliminary to the Groundbreaking Ceremony" (1983)

I would sum up my fear about the future in one word: *boring*. And that's my one fear: that everything has happened; nothing exciting or new or interesting is ever going to happen again . . . the future is just going to be a vast, conforming *suburb of the soul.*

    —J. G. Ballard, interview with Andrea Juno and V. Vale, *Re/Search* 8–9
      (1984)

The war we fight is not against powers and principalities, it is against chaos and despair. Greater than the death of flesh is the death of hope. The death of dreams. Against this peril we can never surrender. The future is all around us, waiting in moments of transition, to be born in moments of revelation. No one knows the shape of that future, or where it will take us. We know only that it is always paved in pain.

    —J. Michael Straczynski, "Z'ha'dum," episode of *Babylon 5* (1996)

Was the Green Sun the abode of some vast Intelligence? The thought was bewildering. Visions of the Unnamable rose, vaguely. Had I, indeed, come upon the dwelling-place of the Eternal?

    — William Hope Hodgson, *The House on the Borderland* (1908)

FRANKENSTEIN: In the name of God! Now I know what it feels like to be God!

    — Garrett Fort and Francis Edward Faragoh, *Frankenstein* (film, 1931)

I've been cursed for delving into the mysteries of life. Perhaps death is sacred and I profaned it. For what a wonderful vision it was. I dreamed of being the first to give to the world the secret that God is so jealous of — the formula for life. Think of the power to create a man — and I did it. I did it! I created a man, and, who knows, in time, I could have trained him to do my will. I could have bred a race. I might even have found the secret of eternal life.

    — William Hurlbut, *Bride of Frankenstein* (film, 1935)

Virtue in the creator is not the same as virtue in the creature. For the creator, if he should love his creature, would be loving only a part of himself; but the creature, praising the creator, praises an infinity beyond himself.

    — Olaf Stapledon, *Star Maker* (1937)

His eyes were fixed upon the fleecy clouds which scurried across the moon.
    Up there —
    God?
    In a dirty bathrobe?

    — L. Ron Hubbard, "Typewriter in the Sky" (1940)

"I never thought of God as humorous," said Father Stone, coldly.
    "The Creator of the platypus, the camel, the ostrich, and Man? Oh, come now!" Father Peregrine laughed.

    — Ray Bradbury, "The Fire Balloons" (1951)

God

In those days, only God was impending, indwelling *and* transcendent all at once, and that was their hope. Today, we've given them Death instead.
  —James Blish, *A Case of Conscience* (1958)

Thou art God and I am God and all that groks is God, and I am all that I have ever been or seen or felt or experienced. I am all that I grok.
  —Robert A. Heinlein, *Stranger in a Strange Land* (1961)

You were not put on this earth just to get in touch with God.
  —Anthony Burgess, *A Clockwork Orange* (1962)

What had seemed in the Arabic poem to be death was not death but god; or rather God was death, it was one force, one hunter, one cannibal thing, and it missed again and again but, having all eternity, it could afford to miss.
  —Philip K. Dick, "Faith of Our Fathers" (1967)

THERE ARE UNIVERSES BEGGING FOR GODS
yet He hangs around this one looking for work.
  —Philip José Farmer, "Riders of the Purple Wage" (1967)

SCOTT: Captain, thank heaven!
SPOCK: Mr. Scott, there was no deity involved. It was my cross-circuiting to B that recovered them.
  —Art Wallace, "Obsession," episode of *Star Trek* (1967)

I am Ubik. Before the universe was, I am. I made the suns. I made the worlds. I created the lives and the places they inhabit; I move them here, I put them there. They go as I say, they do as I tell them. I am the word and my name is never spoken, the name which no one knows. I am called Ubik, but that is not my name. I am. I shall always be.
  —Philip K. Dick, *Ubik* (1969)

To be an atheist is to maintain God.
  —Ursula K. Le Guin, *The Left Hand of Darkness* (1969)

In a smoke-congested back room of the universe the God of my agnostic imagination oversees this crooked card game.
  —Robert Thurston, "Good-Bye, Shelley, Shirley, Charlotte, Charlene" (1972)

Sidney's damnation was complete when, his expansion finished, his size and power infinite, his dominance total over a cosmos in which there was now indeed nothing worth his stealing, he realized (in some strange fashion) that he was now God and that even his reincorporation in flesh, a matter now easily within his powers, would not change things much. It had after all been tried by his most immediate predecessor without notable success.

   —Robin Scott Wilson, "Last Train to Kankakee" (1972)

God is:

A. An invisible spirit with a long beard.
B. A small dog dead in a hole.
C. Everyman.
D. The Wizard of Oz.
   —Harlan Ellison, "The Deathbird" (1973)

I'm not talking about God as an old man with long white whiskers, either, Harry. I mean something abstract, a force, a power, a current, a reservoir of energy underlying everything and connecting everything. God is that reservoir. That reservoir is God. I think of that reservoir as being something like the sea of molten lava down beneath the earth's crust: it's there, it's full of heat and power, it's accessible for those who know the way.

   —Robert Silverberg, "Breckenridge and the Continuum" (1973)

Who is God? Who is this cloud-thing that has nothing better to do than stare on human pain and now and then poke it with his finger? Is he not bored? Will he not presently wipe it all away, or go away and forget? Or has he already gone away, forgotten?

   —Edgar Pangborn, "The Night Wind" (1974)

I have seen God creating the cosmos, watching its growth, and finally destroying it.

   —Olaf Stapledon, *Nebula Maker* (1976)

Over most of the universe, God was spread in fossil radiation, too old, too thin.

   —Brian W. Aldiss, "Non-Isotropic" (1978)

God

When she thought of Heaven here, it was small and far away, like the City. It had nothing to do with the wilderness. There was no God here; he belonged to people, and where there were no people there was no God.

    —Ursula K. Le Guin, "The Eye of the Heron" (1978)

Belief in God is apparently a psychological artifact of mammalian reproduction.

    —Arthur C. Clarke, *The Fountains of Paradise* (1979)

If a person who indulges in gluttony is a glutton, and a person who commits a felony is a felon, then God is an iron. Or else He's the dumbest designer that ever lived.

    —Spider Robinson, "God Is an Iron" (1979)

1) God does not exist.
2) And anyhow he's stupid.

    —Philip K. Dick, *Valis* (1981)

Man and the true God are identical—as the Logos and the true God are—but a lunatic blind creator and his screwed-up world separate man from God. That the blind creator sincerely imagines that he is the true God only reveals the extent of his occlusion.

    —Philip K. Dick, *Valis* (1981)

I am the Supreme Being; I'm not entirely dim.

    —Terry Gilliam and Michael Palin, *Time Bandits* (film, 1981)

If we assume the existence of an omniscient and omnipotent being, one that knows and can do absolutely anything, then to my own very limited self, it would seem that existence for it would be unbearable. Nothing to wonder about? Nothing to ponder over? Nothing to discover? Eternity in such a heaven would surely be indistinguishable from hell.

    —Isaac Asimov, introduction to *X Stands for Unknown* (1984)

He said God likes to talk to Himself . . .

    —William Gibson, *Count Zero* (1986)

"Heya, heya!" called the man in front of the trip parlor (Sojourn for Truth—Not God But An Incredible Simulation!).
  —Pat Cadigan, "Fool to Believe" (1990)

He dreamed, as he often did, of an omniscient Eye in whose infinite perspectives might be sorted every least mystery.
  —William Gibson and Bruce Sterling, *The Difference Engine* (1991)

On Stan's seventeenth birthday the Wrath of God came again, as it did every six weeks or so.
  —Frederik Pohl, "The Boy Who Would Live Forever" (1999)

One golfer a year is hit by lightning. This may be the only evidence we have of God's existence.
  —Steve Aylett, *Atom* (2000)

It is inconsistent with the nature of the universe for a severely limited, naturally emerged being such as a human to be fully acquainted with the divine, or with created beings of higher orders.
  —Gregory Benford, *Eater* (2000)

All the Johnny Appleseeds became music.
  The War Against God dates from this moment.
  —John Clute, *Appleseed* (2001)

GODS AND DEMONS

Sometimes the gods themselves forget the answers to their own riddles.
  —Edwin L. Arnold, *Lieut. Gullivar Jones: His Vacation* (1905)

I have given myself to the devil, because the devil is the only god in whom all the tribes believe.
  —Walter M. Miller, Jr., "The Soul-Empty Ones" (1951)

The gods do not speak the language of men, any more than men can speak the language of the gods.
  —Miriam Allen deFord, "The Apotheosis of Ki" (1956)

Man does not create gods, in spite of appearances. The times, the age, impose them on him.

> —Stanislaw Lem, *Solaris* (1961), translated by Joanna Kilmartin and
> Steve Cox (1970)

If there are any gods whose chief concern is man, they cannot be very important gods.

> —Arthur C. Clarke, "Rocket to the Renaissance," revised (1962)

A god cannot survive as a memory. We need love, admiration, worship as you need food.

> —Gilbert Ralston and Gene L. Coon, "Who Mourns for Adonais?"
> episode of *Star Trek* (1967)

The angel was laughing now, but he was dark, and huge, and monstrous, and I knew that angels and devils are really the same. They are angels if you are on their side and devils if you're against them.

> —Ray Nelson, "Time Travel for Pedestrians" (1972)

Even a deity needs a little recreation.

> —T. J. Bass, *The Godwhale* (1974)

There are no gods but those that are muses.

> —Charles L. Grant, "A Glow of Candles, a Unicorn's Eye" (1978)

On the disc, the Gods are not so much worshipped as blamed.

> —Terry Pratchett, *The Colour of Magic* (1983)

Demons can't call things weird. I mean, what's weird to a demon?

> —Terry Pratchett, *The Colour of Magic* (1983)

Rob McKenna was a Rain God. All he knew was that his working days were miserable and he had a succession of lousy holidays. All the clouds knew was that they loved him and wanted to be near him, to cherish him and to water him.

> —Douglas Adams, *So Long, and Thanks for All the Fish* (1985)

Only the solitary may see the gods.

> —Gene Wolfe, *Soldier of the Mist* (1986)

A god can show off once in a while can't he?
  —Douglas Adams, *The Long Dark Tea-Time of the Soul* (1988)

This interlude has been brought to you by the gods. [. . .] You may now resume your normal destinies, already in progress.
  —Arthur Byron Cover, *Stationfall* (1989)

It was extremely hard to believe in a god when you saw him at breakfast every day.
  —Terry Pratchett, *Pyramids* (1989)

People needed to believe in gods, if only because it was so hard to believe in people.
  —Terry Pratchett, *Pyramids* (1989)

Let me tell you what I think about gods. I think a *real* god is not going to be so scared or angry that he tries to keep other people down. [. . .] A real god doesn't care about control. A real god already *has* control of everything that needs controlling. Real gods would want to teach you how to be just like them.
  —Orson Scott Card, *Xenocide* (1991)

The trouble with being a god is that you've got no one to pray to.
  —Terry Pratchett, *Small Gods* (1992)

They'll make a god of her.
  I think that would please her, if she could know about it. In spite of all her protests and denials, she's always needed devoted, obedient followers— disciples—who would listen to her and believe everything she told them. And she needed large events to manipulate. All gods seem to need those things.
  —Octavia E. Butler, *Parable of the Talents* (1998)

GOVERNMENTS

In your day governments were accustomed, on the slightest international misunderstanding, to seize upon the bodies of citizens and deliver them over by hundreds of thousands to death and mutilation, wasting their treasures the while like water; and all this oftenest for no imaginable profit to the victims. We have no wars now, and our governments no war powers, but in order to protect every citizen against hunger, cold, and nakedness, and provide for all his physical and mental needs, the function is assumed of directing his industry for a term of years.

— Edward Bellamy, *Looking Backward, 2000–1887* (1888)

Patriotism, red hot, is compatible with the existence of a neglect of national interests, a dishonesty, a cold indifference to the suffering of millions. Patriotism is largely pride, and very largely combativeness.

— Charlotte Perkins Gilman, *Herland* (1915)

Government's an affair of sitting, not hitting. You rule with the brains and the buttocks, never with the fists.

— Aldous Huxley, *Brave New World* (1932)

Of all the arts that of government has been brought least to perfection.

— James Hilton, *Lost Horizon* (1933)

To govern perfectly it is necessary to avoid governing too much.

— James Hilton, *Lost Horizon* (1933)

Give the committee another hundred years and government by demagoguery will be gone. Little men with a talent for grabbing votes will have given way to men who make a profession of good government. Men who are trained for government just as doctors are trained for medicine or attorneys are trained for law. Men of science will govern, running the world scientifically in the interest of the stockholders — the little people of the world.

— Clifford D. Simak, "Lobby" (1944)

In the long run, a hierarchal society was only possible on a basis of poverty and ignorance.

— George Orwell, *Nineteen Eighty-Four* (1949)

The difference between a Welfare State and a Benevolent Despot is slight.

— Alfred Bester, "The Devil's Invention" (1950)

Any government that gets to be too big and too successful gets to be a nuisance.

  —Robert A. Heinlein, *Between Planets* (1951)

Democracy is cancerous, and bureaus are its cancer. A bureau takes root anywhere in the state, turns malignant like the Narcotic Bureau, and grows and grows, always reproducing more of its own kind, until it chokes the host if not controlled or excised. [. . .] Bureaucracy is wrong as a cancer, a turning away from the human evolutionary direction of infinite potentials and differentiation and independent spontaneous action, to the complete parasitism of a virus.

  —William S. Burroughs, *Naked Lunch* (1959)

A government is a living organism. Like every living thing its prime characteristic is the instinct to survive. You hit it, it fights back.

  —Robert A. Heinlein, *Stranger in a Strange Land* (1961)

He's not the enemy. Scott, the Joint Chiefs, even the very emotional, very illogical lunatic fringe: they're not the enemy. The enemy's an age—a nuclear age. It happens to have killed man's faith in his ability to influence what happens to him. And out of this comes a sickness, and out of sickness a frustration, a feeling of impotence, helplessness, weakness. And from this, this desperation, we look for a champion in red, white, and blue. Every now and then a man on a white horse rides by, and we appoint him to be our personal god for the duration. For some men it was a Senator McCarthy, for others it was a General Walker, and now it's a General Scott.

  —Rod Serling, *Seven Days in May* (film, 1964)

Like fire and fusion, government is a dangerous servant and a terrible master.

  —Robert A. Heinlein, *The Moon Is a Harsh Mistress* (1966)

In writing your constitution let me invite attention to the wonderful virtues of the negative! Accentuate the negative! Let your document be studded with things the government is forever forbidden to do.

  —Robert A. Heinlein, *The Moon Is a Harsh Mistress* (1966)

It may not be possible to do away with government—sometimes I think that government is an inescapable disease of human beings.

  —Robert A. Heinlein, *The Moon Is a Harsh Mistress* (1966)

There was in theory a sort of state government still at Montpelier but you never heard of it—sometimes an excellent thing in governments.
　—Edgar Pangborn, "The Children's Crusade" (1974)

ARTHUR: The Lady of the Lake, her arm clad in the purest shimmering samite, held aloft Excalibur from the bosom of the water, signifying by divine providence that I, Arthur, was to carry Excalibur. *That* is why I am your king!
DENNIS: Listen, strange women lyin' in ponds distributin' swords is no basis for a system of government! Supreme executive power derives from a mandate from the masses, not from some farcical aquatic ceremony! [. . .] You can't expect to wield supreme executive power just 'cause some watery tart threw a sword at you!
　—Graham Chapman, John Cleese, Terry Gilliam, Eric Idle, Terry Jones, and Michael Palin, *Monty Python and the Holy Grail* (film, 1975)

I wish that there had been more people interested in tending the garden of state rather than overhauling the engine of state.
　—Roger Zelazny, "Home Is the Hangman" (1975)

Ankh-Morpork had dallied with many forms of government and had ended up with that form of democracy known as One Man, One Vote. The Patrician was the Man; he had the Vote.
　—Terry Pratchett, *Mort* (1987)

Government means doing what you must, not what you would. [. . .] States will survive by doing what they must. Throw a government out and its successors will be constrained to repeat the monstrous actions they rebelled against.
　—George Turner, *Drowning Towers* (1987)

It is unusual for us to discover an imperial power-system in space. As a rule, such archaic forms of authority wither long before the relevant species drags itself off the home planet.
　—Iain M. Banks, *The Player of Games* (1988)

Even here in the Paleolithic the world is divided into a thousand little nations.
　—Robert Silverberg, "House of Bones" (1988)

Nothing upsets the citizenry more than to believe its administrators are uncertain or faltering. Doing nothing with an appearance of calm may be more important than doing the right thing in a frantic manner.
    —Sheri S. Tepper, *The Gate to Women's Country* (1988)

All of our governments are flawed, most of them disastrously. It's why history is such a bloody mess.
    —Kim Stanley Robinson, *Red Mars* (1992)

The Imperium is like a very large and disjointed symphony, composed by a committee. Over a three-hundred year period. Played by a gang of amateur volunteers. It has enormous inertia, and is fundamentally fragile. It is neither unchanging nor unchangeable. It can crush you like a blind elephant.
    —Lois McMaster Bujold, *Mirror Dance* (1994)

Lancre operated on the feudal system, which was to say, everyone feuded all the time and handed on the fight to their descendants.
    —Terry Pratchett, *Carpe Jugulum* (1998)

An elven trait, to believe that that government governs best which doesn't govern at all. Chaos is more fun. Anarchy is the ideal.
    —Glen Cook, *Angry Lead Skies* (2002)

You take a bunch of people who don't seem any different from you and me, but when you add them all together you get this sort of huge raving maniac with national borders and an anthem.
    —Terry Pratchett, *Monstrous Regiment* (2003)

HAPPINESS AND SADNESS

While his heart still beats, while his flesh still moves, I cannot accept that a being endowed with will-power can give in to despair.
> —Jules Verne, *A Journey to the Centre of the Earth* (1864), translated by William Butcher (1992)

Despair has its own calms.
> —Bram Stoker, *Dracula* (1897)

"I shall take the heart," returned the Tin Woodman; "for brains do not make one happy, and happiness is the best thing in the world."
> —L. Frank Baum, *The Wonderful Wizard of Oz* (1900)

A lifetime of happiness! No man alive could bear it: it would be hell on earth.
> —George Bernard Shaw, *Man and Superman: A Comedy and a Philosophy* (play, 1903)

You will subjugate the unknown beings on other planets, who may still be living in the primitive condition of freedom, to the beneficial yoke of reason. If they fail to understand that we bring them mathematically infallible happiness, it will be our duty to compel them to be happy.
> —Yevgeny Zamiatin, *We* (1924), translated by Mirra Ginsburg (1972)

They'll cure you, they'll stuff you full of rich, fat happiness, and, sated, you will doze off peacefully, snoring in perfect unison—don't you hear that mighty symphony of snores? Ridiculous people! They want to free you of every squirming, torturing, nagging question mark.
> —Yevgeny Zamiatin, *We* (1924), translated by Mirra Ginsburg (1972)

Earthling, it strikes me that the ancient wisdom of our race is faulty. Although we are in every way superior to you, in your puny, shortlived bodies is something that we have not. Something finer. Something that we can no more imagine than you can imagine the color of ultra-violet which does not affect your eyes. What *is* happiness?

    —R. F. Starzl, "The Planet of Despair" (1931)

That is the secret of happiness and virtue—liking what you've *got* to do. All conditioning aims at that: making people like their unescapable social destiny.

    —Aldous Huxley, *Brave New World* (1932)

Never put off till to-morrow the fun you can have to-day.

    —Aldous Huxley, *Brave New World* (1932)

Actual happiness always looks pretty squalid in comparison with the over-compensations for misery. And, of course, stability isn't nearly so spectacular as instability. And being contented has none of the glamour of a good fight against misfortune, none of the picturesqueness of a struggle with temptation, or a fatal overthrow by passion or doubt. Happiness is never grand.

    —Aldous Huxley, *Brave New World* (1932)

No news, he thought, makes a happy country but a dull breakfast.

    —Robert A. Heinlein, *Beyond This Horizon* (1942)

He was not happy. He said the words to himself. He recognized this as the true state of affairs. He wore his happiness like a mask and the girl had run off across the lawn with the mask and there was no way of going to knock on her door and ask for it back.

    —Ray Bradbury, *Fahrenheit 451* (1954)

The right to the pursuit of happiness is nothing else than the right to disillusionment phrased in another way.

    —Aldous Huxley, "Tomorrow and Tomorrow and Tomorrow" (1956)

"Did Blake not speak of the Machineries of Joy? That is, did not God promote environments, then intimidate those natures by provoking the existence of flesh, toy men and women, such as are we all? And thus happily sent forth, at our best, with good grace and fine wit, on calm noons, in fair climes, are we not God's Machineries of Joy?"

"If Blake said that," said Father Brian, "I take it all back. He never lived in Dublin!"
—Ray Bradbury "The Machineries of Joy" (1962)

He was, perhaps like Dino Watters, addicted to gloom. She felt sorry for him if that were so. It was a terrible malady to have.
—Philip K. Dick, *Clans of the Alphane Moon* (1964)

If truly ghosts haunt the scenes of tragedy and heartbreak, then the landscape of Old Earth must be home to ghosts and specters beyond all numbering.
—Jack Vance, "The Last Castle" (1966)

Isn't the measure of complexity the measure of the eternal joy?
—Ursula K. Le Guin, "Vaster Than Empires and More Slow" (1971)

Though I came to forget or regret all I have ever done, yet would I remember that once I saw the dragons aloft on the wind at sunset above the western isles; and I would be content.
—Ursula K. Le Guin, *The Farthest Shore* (1972)

Even pleasure, infinitely exquisite, infinitely realizable, becomes infinitely tedious.
—Robin Scott Wilson, "Last Train to Kankakee" (1972)

We have a bad habit, encouraged by pedants and sophisticates, of considering happiness as something rather stupid. Only pain is intellectual, only evil interesting. This is the treason of the artist: a refusal to admit the banality of evil and the terrible boredom of pain. [. . .] Happiness is based on a just discrimination of what is necessary, what is neither necessary nor destructive, and what is destructive.
—Ursula K. Le Guin, "The Ones Who Walk Away from Omelas" (1973)

There's no crime in giving yourself over to pleasure—is there?
—Richard O'Brien, *The Rocky Horror Show* (play, 1973)

A real sense of triumph must be preceded by real despair. She had unlearned despair a long time ago. There were no more triumphs. One went on.
—Ursula K. Le Guin, "The Day Before the Revolution" (1974)

Rain is a sad thing, to the human psyche. It is that, that sadness, perhaps because it recalls to unhappy people their own tears, that palliates melancholy.
— Gene Wolfe, "The Death of Doctor Island" (1974)

In the path of our happiness shall we find the learning for which we have chosen this lifetime.
— Richard Bach, *Illusions: The Adventures of a Reluctant Messiah* (1977)

If your happiness depends on what somebody else does, I guess you do have a problem.
— Richard Bach, *Illusions: The Adventures of a Reluctant Messiah* (1977)

It was the Sunday afternoons he couldn't cope with, and that terrible listlessness that starts to set in at about 2:55, when you know you've taken all the baths you can usefully take that day, that however hard you stare at any given paragraph in the newspaper you will never actually read it, or use the revolutionary new pruning technique it describes, and that as you stare at the clock the hands will move relentlessly on to four o'clock, and you will enter the long dark teatime of the soul.
— Douglas Adams, *Life, the Universe, and Everything* (1982)

"Doing what you *must* do is what living is all about" cried Amy in astonishment. "That's the perfect joy of existence!"
— Ian Watson, "Cruising" (1983)

Grief was grief, she thought. It was pain and loss and despair — an abrupt end where there should have been a continuing.
— Octavia E. Butler, *Dawn* (1987)

The secret of happiness in life is to know what you are and then be content to be that, in style, head up and proud, and not yearn to be something else. Ambition can never change a sparrow into a hawk, or a wren into a bird of paradise.
— Robert A. Heinlein, *To Sail beyond the Sunset* (1987)

It's good to have things to regret, though, isn't it? I'm sure it's an essential part of being human.
— Greg Egan, "The Cutie" (1989)

"We must live on into the new age with the spoils of our victory over evil. You with your burned child, and I with nothing at all."
Despair speaks evenly, in a quiet voice.
— Ursula K. Le Guin, *Tehanu: The Last Book of Earthsea* (1990)

Grief runs off us, Michel thought as he sat with her, like rain off a duck. In time Nadia would be well.
— Kim Stanley Robinson, *Red Mars* (1992)

What happened to "and they lived happily ever after?"
It's stuck at the end of tales in stupid Guild ballads, that's what happened to it. Real people get stuck in potholes, not platitudes.
— Mercedes Lackey, *The Robin and the Kestrel* (1993)

You accumulate grief as you go through life, and it can make you bitter, empty, cold, or wise.
— Tara K. Harper, *Grayheart* (1996)

HEROES AND SUPERHEROES

[Dejah Thoris to John Carter:] You are a queer mixture of child and man, of brute and noble. I only wish that I might read your heart.
— Edgar Rice Burroughs, *A Princess of Mars* (1917)

He was doomed, like millions, to flee from wisdom and be a hero.
— James Hilton, *Lost Horizon* (1933)

Just before the doomed planet, *Krypton,* exploded to fragments, a scientist placed his infant son within an experimental rocket-ship, launching it toward Earth!
When the vessel reached our planet, the child was found by an elderly couple, the Kents.
The infant was turned over to an orphan asylum, where it astounded the attendants with its feats of strength.
The love and guidance of his kindly foster parents was to become an important factor in the shaping of the boy's future.

As the lad grew older, he learned to his delight that he could hurdle skyscrapers . . .

. . . Leap an eighth of a mile . . .

. . . Raise tremendous weights . . .

. . . Run faster than a streamline train —

. . . And nothing less than a bursting shell could penetrate his skin!

The passing away of his foster-parents greatly grieved Clark Kent. But it strengthened a determination that had been growing in his mind.

Clark decided he must turn his titanic strength into channels that would benefit mankind. And so was created —

SUPERMAN champion of the oppressed. The physical marvel who had sworn to devote his existence to helping those in need!

— Jerry Siegel, untitled story, *Superman* #1 (comic book, 1939)

BRUCE WAYNE *(thinking):* Dad's estate left me wealthy. I am ready . . . But first I must have a disguise. Criminals are a superstitious cowardly lot. So my disguise must be able to strike terror into their hearts. I must be a creature of the night, black, terrible . . . a . . . a . . .

CAPTION: As if in answer, a huge bat flies in the open window!

BRUCE WAYNE: A bat! That's it. It's an omen . . . I shall become a *BAT*!

— Bill Finger, "The Legend of the Batman — Who He Is and How He Came to Be" (comic book, 1940)

At last, in a world torn by the hatreds and wars of men, appears a *woman* to whom the problems and feats of men are mere child's play — a woman whose identity is known to *none,* but whose sensational feats are outstanding in a fast-moving world! With a hundred times the agility and strength of our best male athletes and strongest wrestlers, she appears as though from nowhere to avenge an injustice or right a wrong! As lovely as Aphrodite — as wise as Athena — with the speed of Mercury and the strength of Hercules — she is known only as Wonder Woman, but who she is, or whence she came, nobody knows!

— William Moulton Marston, "Introducing Wonder Woman" (comic book, 1941)

"Up in the sky, look!"

"It's a bird!"

"It's a plane!"

"It's Superman!"

— Jay Morton, *Superman* (cartoon, 1941)

Faster than a speeding bullet! More powerful than a locomotive! Able to leap tall buildings at a single bound! This amazing stranger from the planet Krypton, the Man of Steel, Superman!

Empowered with X-ray vision, possessing remarkable physical strength, Superman fights a never-ending battle for truth and justice, disguised as a mild-mannered newspaper reporter, Clark Kent.

— Jay Morton, *The Mechanical Monsters* (cartoon, 1941)

Supermen are superthinkers, anything else is a side issue.

— Robert A. Heinlein, "Gulf" (1949)

I might well retort that many men on Earth have had the presentiment of a superior being who may one day succeed them but that no scientist, philosopher, or poet has ever imagined this superhuman in the guise of an ape.

— Pierre Boulle, *Planet of the Apes* (1963), translated by Xan Fielding (1963)

That which makes a man superhuman is terrifying.

— Frank Herbert, *Dune* (1965)

[The Star Child] waited, marshaling his thoughts and brooding over his still untested powers. For though he was master of the world, he was not quite sure what to do next.

But he would think of something.

— Arthur C. Clarke, *2001: A Space Odyssey* (1968)

They say people don't believe in heroes anymore. Well, damn them. You and me, Max, we're gonna give them back their heroes.

— James McCausland and George Miller, *Mad Max* (film, 1979)

To what extent are our heroisms, sacrifices, and self-aggrandizements the acting out of personae that we maintain? Some thinkers have attempted to trace this element through every aspect of society.

— Poul Anderson, "The Saturn Game" (1981)

The backside of heroism is often rather sad; women and servants know that. They know also that the heroism may be no less real for that. But achievement is smaller than men think. What is large is the sky, the earth, the sea, the soul.
—Ursula K. Le Guin, "Sur" (1982)

What he didn't like about heroes was that they were usually suicidally gloomy when sober and homicidally insane when drunk.
—Terry Pratchett, *The Colour of Magic* (1983)

What heroes like best is themselves.
—Terry Pratchett, *The Colour of Magic* (1983)

MAGNETO (*to Pyro*): You are a god among insects. Never let anyone tell you different.
—Michael Dougherty, Dan Harris, and David Hayter, *X2: X-Men United* (film, 2003)

HISTORY

History is a department of human delusion that interests us.
—Charles Fort, *The Book of the Damned* (1919)

Human history becomes more and more a race between education and catastrophe.
—H. G. Wells, *The Outline of History* (1920)

History, as [H. G. Wells] sees it is a series of victories won by the scientific man over the romantic man.
—George Orwell, "Wells, Hitler, and the World State" (1941)

The Historical Point of View, put briefly, means that when a learned man is presented with any statement in an ancient author, the one question he never asks is whether it is true. He asks who influenced the ancient writer, and how far the statement is consistent with what he said in other books, and what phase in the writer's development, or in the general history of thought, it illustrates, and how it affected later writers, and how often it has been misunderstood (specially by the learned man's colleagues) and what the general course of criticism on it has been for the last ten years, and what is the "present state of the question." To regard the ancient writer as a possible source of knowledge—to anticipate that what he said could possibly modify your thoughts or your behavior—this would be rejected as unutterably simple-minded. And since we cannot deceive the whole human race all the time, it is most important thus to cut every generation off from all others; for where learning makes a free commerce between the ages there is always the danger that the characteristic errors of one may be corrected by the characteristic truths of another. But thanks be to our Father and the Historical Point of View, great scholars are now as little nourished by the past as the most ignorant mechanic who holds that "history is bunk."

    —C. S. Lewis, *The Screwtape Letters* (1942)

People don't make history—Burkhalter thought. Peoples do that. Not the individual.

    —Henry Kuttner and C. L. Moore, "The Piper's Son" (1945)

Perhaps we do waste too much time in hankering after the past.

    —A. Bertram Chandler, "New Wings" (1948)

To an imaginative man like Denham, a teacher of advanced semantics, the last years of the Twentieth Century loomed through the mists of time with all the fascination of a vast dust bin infested with black widow spiders.

    —Frank Belknap Long, "The World of Wulkins" (1948)

You know how one feels about history, the glamour of the past; I expected to hear everybody talking about great events—battles, poets, that kind of thing—but of course you don't. You just squabble among yourselves.

    —Gore Vidal, *Visit to a Small Planet,* revised (play, 1957)

Historians list nothing but trivia.

    —Walter M. Miller, Jr., *A Canticle for Leibowitz* (1959)

I pass through Terran history this way. When the clown tumbles into the tub, I laugh. Terran history is full of clowns and tubs; at first it seems that's all there is, but you learn to see beneath the comic costumes.

    —Sonya Dorman, "When I Was Miss Dow" (1966)

The history of man is not his technical triumphs, his kills, his victories. It is a composite: a mosaic of a trillion pieces, the account of each man's accommodation with his conscience. This is the true history of the race.
  —Jack Vance, "The Last Castle" (1966)

Glogauer had no wish to change history, only to strengthen it.
  —Michael Moorcock, "Behold the Man" (1967)

Prior forms, he reflected, must carry on an invisible, residual life in every object. The past is latent, is submerged, but still there, capable of rising to the surface once the later imprinting unfortunately—and against ordinary experience—vanished. The man contains—not the boy—but earlier men.
  —Philip K. Dick, *Ubik* (1969)

No culture as yet has actually forgotten history because no culture has really possessed more than fragments of it.
  —Edgar Pangborn, "Mount Charity" (1971)

History has the relation to truth that theology has to religion—i.e., none to speak of.
  —Robert A. Heinlein, *Time Enough for Love* (1973)

The History of every major Galactic civilization has gone through three distinct and recognizable phases—those of survival, inquiry and sophistication, otherwise known as the How, Why and Where phases. For instance the first phase is characterized by the question "How can we eat?," the second by the question "Why do we eat?" and the third by the question "Where shall we have lunch?"
  —Douglas Adams, "Fit the Sixth," episode of *The Hitch-Hiker's Guide to the Galaxy* (radio series, 1978)

Did I want a world of human wolves?
  It would not be very different. Half the history of man is the history of wolf-man, which is why humanity has dominated all the other animals of the planet and his history is a history of blood.
  —Katherine MacLean, "Night-Rise" (1978)

Myths are not fiction, but history seen with a poet's eyes and recounted in a poet's terms.
— Frank Herbert and Bill Ransom, *The Jesus Incident* (1979)

"The present is never the present," Sam said. "It's layered with persistent pasts."
— George Zebrowski, *Macrolife* (1979)

Planetary history is one long dark age, he thought, *an evolving slaughterhouse.*
— George Zebrowski, *Macrolife* (1979)

History has limited use, she knew, since memory distorts.
— Suzy McKee Charnas, "The Unicorn Tapestry" (1980)

Dom Felix had gently pointed out to him something he should have known, something that had sidled up on historians since the first troglodyte grunted the tale of last month's contest with the timber wolf: History isn't only *then;* it's *now.*
— Theodore Sturgeon, "Why Dolphins Don't Bite" (1980)

"As individuals, they are hardly relevant to the course of history." [. . .]
"Of course they're relevant!" I shouted. "They *are* the history, not all these bloody numbers!"
— Connie Willis, "Fire Watch" (1982)

Tyranny is the death of history.
— Greg Bear, "Hardfought" (1983)

Any fool can foresee the past.
— Larry Niven, *The Integral Trees* (1983)

As all historians know, the past is a great darkness, and filled with echoes. Voices may reach us from it; but what they say to us is imbued with the obscurity of the matrix out of which they come; and, try as we may, we cannot always decipher them precisely in the clearer light of our own day.
— Margaret Atwood, *The Handmaid's Tale* (1986)

Romance is one thing, history another. Romance makes history palatable by making it pretty; real history is dirt and famine and plagues.

    — George Turner, *Drowning Towers* (1987)

It is too easy to fall into the trap of seeing history in terms of human movement, as though all else is ancillary, as though *we* make history. It is history that makes *us*.

    — George Turner, *Drowning Towers* (1987)

I've got news for Mr. Santayana: we're doomed to repeat the past no matter what. That's what it is to be alive.

    — Kurt Vonnegut, Jr., *Bluebeard* (1987)

History was tales and tales were a kind of lie, or else not much different from them; he knew that much. Which was enough. A practical man had to seize the moment before him, not meander through dusty tales.

    — Gregory Benford, "At the Double Solstice" (1988)

My sweet, harmless comrades were tortured, mutilated, burnt alive. History is a laboratory in which we learn that nothing works, or ever can.

    — Michael Swanwick, "The Dragon Line" (1988)

There is nothing to history. No progress, no justice. There is nothing but random horror.

    — William Gibson and Bruce Sterling, *The Difference Engine* (1991)

What was the good of being a time researcher, if you could not even learn from times past?

    — Nancy Kress, "And Wild for to Hold" (1991)

History, contrary to popular theories, *is* kings and dates and battles.

    — Terry Pratchett, *Small Gods* (1992)

History too has an inertia. In the four dimensions of spacetime, particles (or events) have directionality; mathematicians, trying to show this, draw what they call "world lines" on graphs. In human affairs, individual world lines form a thick tangle, curling out of the darkness of prehistory and stretching through time: a cable the size of Earth itself, spiraling round the sun on a

long curved course. That cable of tangled world lines is history. Seeing where it has been, it is clear where it is going—it is a matter of simple extrapolation.
—Kim Stanley Robinson, *Red Mars* (1992)

History is not evolution! It is a false analogy! Evolution is a matter of environment and chance, acting over millions of years. But history is a matter of environment and choice, acting within lifetimes, and sometimes within years, or months, or days!
—Kim Stanley Robinson, *Red Mars* (1992)

History so far had been a nightmare, a huge compendium of examples to be avoided.
—Kim Stanley Robinson, *Red Mars* (1992)

Historical analogy is the last refuge of people who can't grasp the current situation.
—Kim Stanley Robinson, *Red Mars* (1992)

Skinner had this thing he got on about history. How it was turning into plastic.
—William Gibson, *Virtual Light* (1993)

I care nothing for history, human or otherwise, Major Solomon. It has always seemed to me a mere justification for repeating the mistakes of the past.
—Adrienne Martine-Barnes, "Flambeaux" (1995)

All history begins between a woman's legs.
—Jane Yolen, "The One-Armed Queen" (1995)

RIKER: Someone once said, "Don't try to be a great man. Just be a man, and let history make its own judgments."
ZEFRAM COCHRANE: That's rhetorical nonsense. Who said that?
RIKER: You did, ten years from now.
—Brannon Braga and Ronald D. Moore, *Star Trek: First Contact* (film, 1996)

History has no laws, and all patterns that we find there are useful illusions.
—Orson Scott Card, *Children of the Mind* (1996)

Looking into history is like shining a flashlight into a cave. You can't see the whole cave, but as you play the flashlight around, a hidden shape is revealed.
  —Richard Preston, *The Cobra Event* (1997)

LONDO: So, how does it feel to make history?
G'KAR: You do not make history. You can only hope to survive it.
  —J. Michael Straczynski, "Rising Star," episode of *Babylon 5* (1997)

HUMANITY

I could not persuade myself that the men and women I met were not also another, still passably human, Beast People, animals half-wrought into the outward image of human souls, and that they would presently begin to revert, to show first this bestial mark and then that.
  —H. G. Wells, *The Island of Doctor Moreau* (1896)

A human being is like a novel: until the last page you don't know how it will end. Or it wouldn't be worth reading . . .
  —Yevgeny Zamiatin, *We* (1924), translated by Mirra Ginsburg (1972)

Nor is it to be thought [. . .] that man is either the oldest or the last of the earth's masters.
  —H. P. Lovecraft, "The Dunwich Horror" (1929)

Man himself, at the very least, is music, a brave theme that makes music also of its vast accompaniment, its matrix of storms and stars. Man himself in his degree is eternally a beauty in the eternal form of things. It is very good to have been man. And so we may go forward together with laughter in our hearts, and peace, thankful for the past, and for our own courage. For we shall make after all a fair conclusion to this brief music that is man.
  —Olaf Stapledon, *Last and First Men: A Story of the Near and Far Future* (1930)

Every word to which he had listened surfeited him with a sense of the immobility of humanity. Each individual related a cosmic circumstance to his particular case. Each individual planned to act independently not only of the rest of his fellows but of all signs and portents in the sky. Tony's mind conceived a picture of huge cities on the verge of inundation—cities in which thousands and even millions refused to budge and went about the infinitesimal affairs of their little lives selfishly, with nothing but resentment for the facts which wiser men were futilely attempting to impress upon them.

—Edwin Balmer and Philip Wylie, *When Worlds Collide* (1932)

There was something called democracy. As though men were more than physico-chemically equal.

—Aldous Huxley, *Brave New World* (1932)

All this long human story, most passionate and tragic in the living, was but an unimportant, a seemingly barren and negligible effort, lasting only for a few moments in the life of the galaxy. When it was over, the host of the planetary systems still lived on, with here and there a casualty, and here and there among the stars a new planetary birth, and here and there a fresh disaster.

—Olaf Stapledon, *Star Maker* (1937)

When you get a real sense of proportion, like mine, you realize that humanity is nothing but a sort of skin disease on a ball of dirt, and that no effort beyond subsistence, shelter, and casual amusement is worth while.

—L. Sprague de Camp, "The Exalted" (1940)

Humans are amphibians—half spirit and half animal. [. . .] As spirits they belong to the eternal world, but as animals they inhabit time.

—C. S. Lewis, *The Screwtape Letters* (1942)

All mortals tend to turn into the things they are pretending to be.

—C. S. Lewis, *The Screwtape Letters* (1942)

We are what we pretend to be, so we must be careful about what we pretend to be.

—Kurt Vonnegut, Jr., introduction to *Mother Night* (1966)

This much we have learned [about humans]; here is the race that shall rule the sevagram.

—A. E. van Vogt, *The Weapon Makers* (1943)

Man is the only creature that consumes without producing. He does not give milk, he does not lay eggs, he is too weak to pull the plough, he cannot run fast enough to catch rabbits. Yet he is lord of all the animals.
　　—George Orwell, *Animal Farm: A Fairy Story* (1945)

What is a man? A collection of living cells and tissues? A legal fiction, like this corporate "person" that would take poor Jerry's life? No, a man is none of these things. A man is a collection of hopes and fears, of human longings, of aspirations greater than himself—more than the clay from which he came; less than the Creator which lifted him up from the clay.
　　—Robert A. Heinlein, "Jerry Was a Man" (1947)

The so-called normal man is a figment of the imagination; every member of the human race, from Jojo the cave man right down to that final culmination of civilization, namely me, has been as eccentric as a pet coon—once you caught him with his mask off.
　　—Robert A. Heinlein, *The Rolling Stones* (1952)

When they had found a good world they would guide a horde of other "HEW-MEN" to it. All they had come for was to find a planet worth the trouble of taking over; if ours proved desirable they would calmly kill its present inhabitants! I caught mental glimpses of the way they imagined other forms of life. There were only two kinds in their thoughts: those that could be eaten and those that should be destroyed as inedible nuisances!
　　—Laurence Manning, "Good-Bye, Ilha!" (1952)

A man isn't really alive till he has something bigger than himself and his own little happiness, for which he'd gladly die.
　　—Poul Anderson, "Ghetto" (1954)

That's the wonderful thing about man; he never gets so discouraged or disgusted that he gives up doing it all over again, because he knows very well it is important and *worth* the doing.
　　—Ray Bradbury, *Fahrenheit 451* (1954)

People were never quite what you thought they were.
　　—William Golding, *Lord of the Flies* (1954)

With filthy body, matted hair, and unwiped nose, Ralph wept for the end of innocence, the darkness of man's heart, and the fall through the air of the true, wise friend called Piggy.
—William Golding, *Lord of the Flies* (1954)

Man is the one animal that can't be tamed. He goes along for years as peaceful as a cow, when it suits him. Then when it suits him not to be, he makes a leopard look like a tabby cat. Which goes double for the female of the species.
—Robert A. Heinlein, *Tunnel in the Sky* (1955)

We are the only conscious castaways upon the tiny raft of the Solar System, as it drifts forever along the Gulf Streams of the Galaxy.
—Arthur C. Clarke, "The Planets Are Not Enough" (1956)

My dear children, don't you know what you are? What you all are? Savages, bloodthirsty savages. That's why you're my hobby. That's why I've returned to the Dark Ages of an insignificant planet in a minor system circling a small and rather chilly sun to enjoy myself, to see you at your most typical . . .
—Gore Vidal, *Visit to a Small Planet,* revised (play, 1957)

If a machine had broken down, it would have been quickly replaced. But who can replace a man?
—Brian W. Aldiss, "Who Can Replace a Man?" (1958)

[Aliens deciding whether to destroy humanity addressing a boy:] "Have you anything more to say?" [. . .]
"Just this!" I said savagely. "It's not a defense, you don't *want* a defense. All right, take away our star—You will if you can and I guess you can. Go ahead! We'll *make* a star! Then, someday, we'll come back and hunt you down—*all of you!*"
—Robert A. Heinlein, *Have Space Suit—Will Travel* (1958)

The broken image of Man moves in minute by minute and cell by cell . . . Poverty, hatred, war, police-criminals, bureaucracy, insanity, all symptoms of The Human Virus.
The Human Virus can now be isolated and treated.
—William S. Burroughs, *Naked Lunch* (1959)

Does Man have any "right" to spread through the universe?

Man is what he is, a wild animal with the will to survive, and (so far) the ability, against all competition. Unless one accepts that, anything one says about morals, war, politics—you name it—is nonsense. Correct morals arise from knowing what Man *is*—not what do-gooders and well-meaning old Aunt Nellies would like him to be.

The universe will let us know—later—whether or not Man has any "right" to expand through it.

—Robert A. Heinlein, *Starship Troopers* (1959)

It was a species which often considered itself to be, basically, a race of divinely inspired toolmakers; any intelligent entity from Arcturus would instantly have perceived them to be, basically, a race of impassioned after-dinner speech-makers.

—Walter M. Miller, Jr., *A Canticle for Leibowitz* (1959)

Human is as human does.

—Philip José Farmer, "Prometheus" (1961)

There was one field in which man was unsurpassed; he showed unlimited ingenuity in devising bigger and more efficient ways to kill off, enslave, harass, and in all ways make an unbearable nuisance of himself to himself. Man was his own grimmest joke on himself.

—Robert A. Heinlein, *Stranger in a Strange Land* (1961)

Are we not, in the end, a clamorous prelude to the final silence, a marriage bed to engender dust, a universe for microbes, microbes that strive to circum-navigate us? We are as unfathomable, as inscrutable as That which brought us into being, and we choke on our own enigma . . .

—Stanislaw Lem, *Memoirs Found in a Bathtub* (1961), translated by
    Michael Kandel and Christine Rose (1973)

People always were puzzled about how a Space Zoologist could stand being a creature other than a human being. And Space Zoologists always were puzzled about how a human being could stand being part of that conquering race called man.

—Jack Sharkey, "Arcturus Times Three" (1961)

What they do not comprehend is man's *helplessness*. I am weak, small, of no consequence to the universe. It does not notice me; I live on unseen. But why is that bad? Isn't it better that way? Whom the gods notice they destroy. Be small . . . and you will escape the jealousy of the great.

    —Philip K. Dick, *The Man in the High Castle* (1962)

"We are all insects," he said to Miss Ephreikian. "Groping toward something terrible or divine."

    —Philip K. Dick, *The Man in the High Castle* (1962)

I needed this intellectual exercise to escape from the despair that haunted me, to prove to myself that I was a man, I mean a man from Earth, a reasoning creature who made it a habit to discover a logical explanation for the apparently miraculous whims of nature, and not a beast hunted down by highly developed apes.

    —Pierre Boulle, *Planet of the Apes* (1963), translated by Xan Fielding (1963)

Games are important; they mark that we are not just animals trying to stay alive but humans enjoying life and savoring it.

    —Robert A. Heinlein, *Farnham's Freehold* (1964)

You Homo sapiens are a treacherous lot. Probably best avoided.

    —Philip K. Dick, *The Crack in Space* (1965)

I have great confidence in Man, based on his past record. He is mean, ornery, cantankerous, illogical, emotional—and amazingly hard to kill.

    —Robert A. Heinlein, "Pandora's Box" (1966)

What is the value of a man, compared to frumpstiggle?

    —Piers Anthony, "In the Jaws of Danger" (1967)

Here I lie, surrounded by the silent flesh of my fellow human beings, he said to himself with a trace of bitterness, *and my mind goes nattering on, as if I were back at the university lecturing to some slightly dense class of undergraduates. My body is here but my mind—perhaps, students, the central problem of man is that he is never where he is, but always where he is going or where he has come from. Thus, when I am alone I am not really alone. And when I am with someone I am not really with them.*

    —Philip K. Dick and Ray Nelson, *The Ganymede Takeover* (1967)

It's always easier and more impressive to tear things down rather than to build them up or even to sustain them. A human being takes a long time to grow, to mature, but it only takes a moment to damage and destroy him.
 —Philip K. Dick and Ray Nelson, *The Ganymede Takeover* (1967)

[An alien describing a human:] Here is an entity which clings to personality survival with a ferocity unparalleled—yet faces Category Ultimate risks needlessly, in response to an abstract code of behavioral symmetry.
 —Keith Laumer, "Test to Destruction" (1967)

There was the image, for instance, of man listening, listening, listening to the silent stars, listening for an eternity, listening for signals that would never come, because—the ultimate horror—man was alone in the universe, a cosmic accident of self-awareness which needed and would never receive the comfort of companionship.
 —James Gunn, "The Listeners" (1968)

I don't think there is any question about it. It can only be attributable to human error. This sort of thing has cropped up before, and it has always been due to human error.
 —Stanley Kubrick and Arthur C. Clarke, *2001: A Space Odyssey* (film, 1968)

"Man does not change himself, according to my knowing," commented the butterfly.

"Not intentionally, perhaps, but he changes nevertheless. He is a discontented being who, not knowing the now-moment, wanders and searches for new things to know. What he finds changes him, not in the orderly manner in which he fitted you for conditions on this world, but in ways that are unplanned and sometimes undesirable. Occasionally he finds something very damaging to him, something that darkens his intelligence and causes him to forget much of his learning from previous findings."
 —Howard L. Myers, "The Creatures of Man" (1968)

Beware the beast man, for he is the Devil's pawn. Alone among God's primates, he kills for sport or lust or greed. Yea, he will murder his brother to possess his brother's land. Let him not breed in great numbers, for he will make a desert of his home and yours. Shun him, drive him back into his jungle lair, for he is the harbinger of death.
 —Michael Wilson and Rod Serling, *Planet of the Apes* (film, 1968)

Human see, human do.
> —Michael Wilson and Rod Serling, *Planet of the Apes* (film, 1968)

I have always known about man. From the evidence, I believe his wisdom must walk hand and hand with his idiocy. His emotions must rule his brain. He must be a warlike creature who gives battle to everything around him, even himself.
> —Michael Wilson and Rod Serling, *Planet of the Apes* (film, 1968)

For every Man the Crucifier, there has been a Man the Healer; for every Man the Warrior, there has been a Man the Peace-Maker; and if some men have died in an attempt to kill within reach, others have died to save them.

In the end, Man may destroy himself and all of life and his world—but he may not.

Let's give him yet another chance and perhaps in space he will find the actual nobility of which many have dreamed and which some have practiced.
> —Isaac Asimov, "That Moon Plaque: Comments by Science Fiction
>   Writers" (1969)

It gave him a strange feeling to see the wrist and leg sliced open, the chest exposed—but no bleeding. There was something wild and inhuman about that. As if bleeding were a sign of humanity. Well, he thought, perhaps it is. Perhaps the fact that we bleed to death makes us human.
> —Michael Crichton, *The Andromeda Strain* (1969)

Man, as such, is a biological error, possibly a too-large brain joined with a full set of primitive instincts that are no longer appropriate, but an error anyway, and [. . .] he will eventually destroy himself, or be destroyed by his environment, just as all non-appropriate forms of life seem to thrive for a while then die off.
> —John T. Phillifent, "That Moon Plaque: Comments by Science Fiction
>   Writers" (1969)

People are living, growing things, too. I don't know a hundredth part of what you do about bonzai but I do know this—when you start one, it isn't often the strong straight healthy ones you take. It's the twisted sick ones that can be made the most beautiful. When you get to shaping humanity, you might remember that.
> —Theodore Sturgeon, "Slow Sculpture" (1970)

Homo can truly be called sapiens when he practices his specialty of being unspecialized. His repeated attempts to freeze himself into an all-answering pattern or culture or ideology, or whatever he has named it, have repeatedly brought ruin. Give him the pragmatic business of making his living, and he will usually do rather well. He adapts, within broad limits.
  —Poul Anderson, "The Queen of Air and Darkness" (1971)

It was not lions that he feared. People were the problem, always forever.
  —Chad Oliver, "Far from This Earth" (1971)

For Man, home can never be a single country, a single world, a single Solar System, a single star cluster. While the race endures in recognizably human form, it can have no one abiding place short of the Universe itself.
  This divine discontent is part of our destiny. It is one more, and perhaps the greatest, of the gifts we inherited from the sea that rolls so restlessly around the world.
  It will be driving our descendants on toward myriad unimaginable goals when the sea is stilled forever, and Earth itself a fading legend lost among the stars.
  —Arthur C. Clarke, "Across the Sea of Stars" (1972)

She felt disgust at all mankind, mushrooming demographically and techno-logically, reaching for the moon, but spiritually degenerate.
  —David Kerr, "Epiphany for Aliens" (1972)

"You know the people you're studying are going to get plowed under, and probably wiped out. It's the way things are. It's human nature, and you must know you can't change that. Then why come and watch the process? Masochism?"
  "I don't know what 'human nature' is. Maybe leaving descriptions of what we wipe out is part of human nature."
  —Ursula K. Le Guin, "The Word for World Is Forest" (1972)

Man had come, mighty man. Oh, he was smart, he was clever. He had turned the seas into cesspools, the air into sludge, the mountains into shrieking cities.
  —Chad Oliver, "King of the Hill" (1972)

"Surely you can see that this kind of society [an all-woman society] is unnatural."

"Humanity is unnatural," said Katy.

— Joanna Russ, "When It Changed" (1972)

A human being should be able to change a diaper, plan an invasion, butcher a hog, conn a ship, design a building, write a sonnet, balance accounts, build a wall, set a bone, comfort the dying, take orders, give orders, cooperate, act alone, solve equations, analyze a new problem, pitch manure, program a computer, cook a tasty meal, fight efficiently, die gallantly. Specialization is for insects.

— Robert A. Heinlein, *Time Enough for Love* (1973)

And crawling on the planet's face
Some insects called the human race
Lost in time
And lost in space

— Richard O'Brien, *The Rocky Horror Show* (play, 1973)

If the human being actually existed, how could one believe the Central Agency's prime rule: that the universe is, in every way, logical and rational?

— Dean Koontz, "The Night of the Storm" (1974)

If the characteristic of a thing, says Little Star, *is its invariability, then surely the characteristic of a Person is passion, volition, and reason.*

— Joanna Russ, "Existence" (1975)

Most animals, when in a hopeless situation will resign themselves to fate and perish in ignominy. Man, on the other hand, does not know how to give in. He is capable of summoning up reserves of stubbornness and resilience that are without parallel on his planet. He is able to attack anything that threatens his survival, with an aggressiveness the like of which the Earth has never seen otherwise. It is this that has enabled him to sweep all before him, made him lord of all the beasts, helped him tame the winds, the rivers, the tides, and even the power of the Sun itself.

— James P. Hogan, *Inherit the Stars* (1977)

172

Her dance spoke of nothing more and nothing less than the tragedy of being alive, and being human. It spoke, most eloquently, of pain. It spoke, most knowingly, of despair. It spoke of the cruel humor of limitless ambition yoked to limited ability, of eternal hope invested in an ephemeral lifetime, of the driving need to try and create an inexorably predetermined future. It spoke of fear, and of hunger, and, most clearly, of the basic loneliness and alienation of the human animal. It described the universe through the eyes of man: a hostile environment, the embodiment of entropy, into which we are all thrown alone, forbidden by our nature to touch another mind save secondhand, by proxy. It spoke of the blind perversity which forces man to strive hugely for a peace which, once attained, becomes boredom. And it spoke of folly, of the terrible paradox by which man is simultaneously capable of reason and unreason, forever unable to cooperate even with himself.
— Spider Robinson and Jeanne Robinson, "Stardance" (1977)

This is what it is to be human: to see the essential existential futility of all action, all striving — and to act, to strive. This is what it is to be human: to reach forever beyond your grasp. This is what it is to be human: to live forever or die trying. This is what it is to be human: to perpetually ask the unanswerable questions, in the hope that the asking of them will somehow hasten the day when they will be answered. This is what it is to be human: to strive in the face of the certainty of failure.

This is what it is to be human: to persist.
— Spider Robinson and Jeanne Robinson, "Stardance" (1977)

Far out in the uncharted backwaters of the unfashionable end of the Western spiral arm of the Galaxy lies a small unregarded yellow sun. Orbiting this at a distance of roughly ninety million miles is an utterly insignificant little blue-green planet whose ape-descended life forms are so amazingly primitive that they still think digital watches are a pretty neat idea.
— Douglas Adams, "Fit the Second," episode of *The Hitch-Hiker's Guide to the Galaxy* (radio series, 1978)

Standing upright and having two hands doesn't make us human. Standing up and having ideas and ideals does! And holding fast to those ideals.
— Ursula K. Le Guin, "The Eye of the Heron" (1978)

[On humans:] The irrational appears to be not merely tolerated but highly valued among this race, and its acceptance increases as the race grows.
  —John Morressy, "The Empath and the Savages" (1979)

SAAVIK: He's so—human.
SPOCK: Nobody's perfect, Saavik.
  —Jack B. Sowards, *Star Trek II: The Wrath of Khan* (film, 1982)

Human beings are not governed by the straightforward laws of robotics. It is therefore difficult to judge the complexities of their motivations under most conditions.
  —Isaac Asimov, *The Robots of Dawn* (1983)

How would humans react to the situation he was in? More vigorously, probably. They would fight on. They always had. Even without leaders, with no discernible purpose, even in defeat. What gave them such stamina? Were they superior, more deserving?
  —Greg Bear, "Hardfought" (1983)

I was in exactly the same predicament as every other human being alive: We don't know who we are, or where we came from, or why we are here. My dilemma was merely fresher, not different.
  —Robert A. Heinlein, *Job: A Comedy of Justice* (1984)

The work of each individual contributes to a totality and so becomes an undying part of the totality. That totality of human lives—past and present and to come—forms a tapestry that has been in existence now for many tens of thousands of years and has been growing more elaborate and, on the whole, more beautiful in all that time. [. . .] An individual life is one thread in the tapestry and what is one thread compared to the whole?
  —Isaac Asimov, *Robots and Empire* (1985)

The authentic human being is one of us who instinctively knows what he should not do, and, in addition, he will balk at doing it.
  —Philip K. Dick, "How to Build a Universe That Doesn't Fall Apart Two Days Later" (1985)

Humanity is so adaptable, my mother would say. Truly amazing, what people can get used to, as long as there are a few compensations.
—Margaret Atwood, *The Handmaid's Tale* (1986)

"You [humans] have a mismatched pair of genetic characteristics. Either alone would have been useful, would have aided the survival of your species. But the two together are lethal. [. . .] You are intelligent," he said. "That's the newer of the two characteristics, and the one you might have put to work to save yourselves." [. . .]

"What's the second characteristic?"

"You are hierarchal. That's the older and more entrenched characteristic. We saw it in your closest animal relatives and in your most distant ones. It's a terrestrial characteristic. When human intelligence served it instead of guiding it, when human intelligence did not even acknowledge it as a problem, but took pride in it or did not notice it at all. [. . .] That was like ignoring cancer."
—Octavia E. Butler, *Dawn* (1987)

Human beings are more alike than different—damn sure more alike than we like to admit.
—Octavia E. Butler, *Dawn* (1987)

I found it hard to credit that men and women existed with an ingrained need to preserve essential humanity no matter what the cost in work and danger.
—George Turner, *Drowning Towers* (1987)

Humanity has the most amazing capacity for self-deception matched only by its ingenuity when trying to destroy itself.
—Ben Aaronovitch, "Remembrance of the Daleks," episode of *Doctor Who* (1988)

Stop studying humanity. Be aware of your surroundings.
—Isaac Asimov, *Prelude to Foundation* (1988)

Mechs built, that was inevitable. They sought to make of the world a place of straight lines and sharp edges, geometry made real. Eternal, rigid certainties.

Men were of a different order. They sought the curved, the flexible, the live and unenduring. They lived and died.
—Gregory Benford, "At the Double Solstice" (1988)

Those first pyramids had been built by human beings, little bags of thinking water held up briefly by fragile accumulations of calcium.
—Terry Pratchett, *Pyramids* (1989)

The great thing about being the only species that makes a distinction between right and wrong is that we can make up the rules for ourselves as we go along.
—Douglas Adams, *Last Chance to See* (1990)

Man adapts to the world, and the world adapts to man. The only thing man couldn't seem to adapt to was himself.
—Alan Dean Foster, *Cyber Way* (1990)

What horrors were humans incapable of?
—Alexander Jablokov, "The Place of No Shadows" (1990)

I remember when you knew what a human being was.
—Paul J. McAuley, "Gene Wars" (1991)

The essence of humanity is hate.
—Judith Tarr, "Sitting Shiva" (1995)

Whenever one returned from planet earth, we had to take a lot of precautions. You never know what kinds of human logic you might be infected with.
—Kalamu ya Salaam, "Buddy Bolden" (1996)

You [humans] are erratic . . . conflicted . . . disorganized. Every decision is debated . . . every action questioned . . . every individual entitled to their own small opinion. You lack harmony . . . cohesion . . . greatness. It will be your undoing.
—Brannon Braga and Joe Menosky, "Scorpion," episode of *Star Trek: Voyager* (1997)

Don't go human on me now, Wally.
—Paul Di Filippo, "Queen of the Pixies, King of the Imps" (1997)

I am nothing and nobody; atoms that have learned to look at themselves;
dirt that has learned to see the awe and the majesty of the universe.
—Geoffrey A. Landis, "Winter Fire" (1997)

Due to a cosmic administrative blunder, the human race has been given the
wrong planet to live on, so we can never quite get comfortable.
—Steve Aylett, *Slaughtermatic* (1998)

Infinite ways of being human, Solomon Gursky thought, outbound from the
sun.
—Ian MacDonald, "The Days of Solomon Gursky" (1998)

I know that you fear death, that time is still for you an unresolved enigma.
"What walks on four legs in the morning, on two at noon and on three in the
evening?" I heard myself answer, "An animal victimized by civilization."
—Élisabeth Vonarburg, "Stay Thy Flight" (1998)

You [humans] share with others (who came from primordial forces) a grave
limitation: you cannot redesign yourselves at will.
—Gregory Benford, "A Hunger for the Infinite" (1999)

You're not actually mammals. Every mammal on this planet instinctively
develops a natural equilibrium with the surrounding environment, but you
humans do not. You move to an area, and you multiply, and multiply, until
every natural resource is consumed. The only way you can survive is to
spread to another area. There is another organism on this planet that follows
the same pattern. Do you know what it is? A virus. Human beings are a
disease, a cancer of this planet, you are a plague, and we are the cure.
—Andy Wachowski and Larry Wachowski, *The Matrix* (film, 1999)

It is an historical fact: sharing the world has never been humanity's defining
attribute.
—Michael Dougherty, Dan Harris, and David Hayter, *X2: X-Men United*
(film, 2003)

HUMOR AND LAUGHTER

Laughter can be of different colors. It is only an echo of a distant explosion within you. It may be festive—red, blue, and golden fireworks; or—torn fragments of a human body flying up . . .
— Yevgeny Zamiatin, *We* (1924), translated by Mirra Ginsburg (1972)

Humor is a developed sense, stemming basically from cruelty.
— Henry Kuttner and C. L. Moore, "When the Bough Breaks" (1944)

Laff-ing spreads from mind to mind like fire in a pile of sticks. [. . .] There is a contagious sort of charm in this LAFF-ing of theirs. Oh, not the sound— that is mere cacophony—but the soft dissolving of all serious thought that goes with it.
— Laurence Manning, "Good-Bye, Ilha!" (1952)

The basic trouble with outer space, thought Van, was that a man lost his sense of humor.
— Doris Pitkin Buck, "Spanish Spoken" (1957)

Apparently the expectation of humor was enough to produce the illusion of humor, and the comedian could elicit laughter with gesture and expression, regardless of what he said.
— Walter M. Miller, Jr., *A Canticle for Leibowitz* (1959)

"Did they remember to program a sense of humor, as well, young lady?"
"We are directed to develop a sense of proportion, sir, which contributes the same effect."
— Anne McCaffrey, "The Ship Who Sang" (1961)

He was made, put on this planet, to suffer; no wonder he's a great comic. For Bunny comedy was a struggle, a fighting back against the reality of literal physical pain.
— Philip K. Dick, *Clans of the Alphane Moon* (1964)

I have wondered whether the art of being amusing, with its implied detachment from self, is not one of the most undervalued requisites of human civilization.
— Brian W. Aldiss, "The Small Stones of Tu Fu" (1978)

"You seem to have a sense of humor that most Security people lack."

"It's not a sense of humor," Afriel said sadly. "It's a sense of irony disguised as one."

— Bruce Sterling, "Swarm" (1982)

The gods gave people a sense of humour to make up for giving them sex.

— Terry Pratchett, *Pyramids* (1989)

Sometimes, Number One, you just have to bow to the absurd.

— Melinda Snodgrass, "Up the Long Ladder," episode of *Star Trek: The Next Generation* (1989)

She laugh like a dolphin leaping.

— Nalo Hopkinson, "Fisherman" (2001)

IMAGINATION AND IDEAS

What never has been cannot be imagined.
— Edgar Rice Burroughs, *Thuvia, Maid of Mars* (1920)

We must cut out imagination. In everyone . . . Extirpate imagination.
Nothing but surgery, nothing but surgery will do . . .
— Yevgeny Zamiatin, *We* (1924), translated by Mirra Ginsburg (1972)

They brought with them weapons of considerable might, not knowing that
we have a weapon truly invincible. [. . .] It took us thousands of years to learn
about the sheer invincibility of an idea. That's what we've got — a way of life,
an idea. Nothing can blast that to shreds. Nothing can defeat an idea — except
a better one.
— Eric Frank Russell, "Late Night Final" (1948)

The greatest ideas are the simplest.
— William Golding, *Lord of the Flies* (1954)

You don't put ideas in boys' heads; they grow them naturally.
— Robert A. Heinlein, *Time for the Stars* (1956)

If something is there, you can only see it with your eyes open, but if it isn't
there, you can see it just as well with your eyes closed. That's why imaginary
things are often easier to see than real things.
— Norton Juster, *The Phantom Tollbooth* (1961)

Human beings are always thinking up things they can't have, or think exist
somewhere else. It's a habit they have, although I must say I don't quite
understand it. Seems like a waste of time.
— Gregory Benford, "Stand-In" (1965)

Facts are the children of imagination. It's only through the eye of the imagination that you see the true picture of this strange universe. If imagination is strong and pure, unsullied by doubt, its truth is the only truth. Facts are simply what they're imagined to be.
    —William F. Temple, "The Legend of Ernie Deacon" (1965)

When every new idea is born an old one dies. But dies hard.
    —Burt K. Filer, "Eye of the Beholder" (1972)

Sometimes there is nothing better to do for an idea than to die for it.
    —Edgar Pangborn, "The World Is a Sphere" (1973)

It is of the nature of idea to be communicated: written, spoken, done. The idea is like grass. It craves light, likes crowds, thrives on crossbreeding, grows better for being stepped on.
    —Ursula K. Le Guin, *The Dispossessed: An Ambiguous Utopia* (1974)

You can't crush ideas by suppressing them. You can only crush them by ignoring them. By refusing to think, refusing to change.
    —Ursula K. Le Guin, *The Dispossessed: An Ambiguous Utopia* (1974)

Nitwit ideas are for emergencies. You use them when you've got nothing else to try. If they work, they go in the Book. Otherwise you follow the Book, which is largely a collection of nitwit ideas that worked.
    —Larry Niven and Jerry Pournelle, *The Mote in God's Eye* (1974)

We can only know what we can truly imagine. Finally what we see comes from ourselves.
    —Marge Piercy, *Woman on the Edge of Time* (1976)

The dimension of the imagination is much more complex than those of time and space, which are very junior dimensions indeed.
    —Terry Pratchett, *The Colour of Magic* (1983)

The idea was fantastically, wildly improbable. But like most fantastically, wildly improbable ideas it was at least as worthy of consideration as a more mundane one to which the facts had been strenuously bent to fit.
    —Douglas Adams, *The Long Dark Tea-Time of the Soul* (1988)

Imagination and Ideas

A person trusts her life to what she believes. Her ideas have to support her, they have to take the weight of her own questions and the weight of a hundred or a thousand or ten thousand critics and cynics and destroyers. Her ideas have to stand the stress of every consequence they bring!
   —Richard Bach, *One* (1988)

The exciting thing about ideas is putting them to work. The moment we try them on our own, launch them away from shore, they switch from what-if to become daring plunges down white rivers, as dangerous and as exhilarating.
   —Richard Bach, *One* (1988)

My imagination makes me human and makes me a fool; it gives me all the world and exiles me from it.
   —Ursula K. Le Guin, "The Creatures on My Mind" (1990)

So many good ideas have to be discarded simply because they won't work.
   —David Eddings, *The Sapphire Rose* (1991)

No fancy in the world is all untrue.
   —Kim Stanley Robinson, *Red Mars* (1992)

Captive imaginations do breed quite effectively, because they are protected from the terrible predator known as Thought.
   —Terry Pratchett, Jack Cohen, and Ian Stewart, *The Science of Discworld* (1999)

IMMORTALITY

Thus I have lived on for many a year—alone, and weary of myself—desirous of death, yet never dying—a mortal immortal. Neither ambition nor avarice can enter my mind, and the ardent love that gnaws at my heart, never to be returned—never to find an equal on which to expend itself—lives there only to torment me.
   —Mary Shelley, "The Mortal Immortal" (1833)

This is the price we pay, he thought, that the race must pay, for its life eternal—that we may not be able to assess in their true value the things that should be dearest to us; for a thing that has no ending, a thing that goes on forever, must have decreasing value.

— Clifford D. Simak, "Eternity Lost" (1949)

Better a life like a falling star, brief bright across the dark, than the long, long waiting of the immortals, loveless and cheerlessly wise.

— Poul Anderson, *The Broken Sword* (1954)

Everyone must leave something behind when he dies, my grandfather said. A child or a book or a painting or a house or a wall built or a pair of shoes made. Or a garden planted. Something your hand touched some way so your soul has somewhere to go when you die, and when people look at that tree or that flower you planted, you're there.

— Ray Bradbury, *Fahrenheit 451* (1954)

To be immortal is commonplace; except for man, all creatures are immortal, for they are ignorant of death; what is divine, terrible, incomprehensible, is to know that one is immortal.

— Jorge Luis Borges, "The Immortal" (1962), translated by James E. Irby (1962)

Like the Eternal Man of Babylonian legend, like Gilgamesh, one thousand plus two hundred years stretches before Trent — without love, without friendship, alone, neither man nor machine, waiting — waiting for the day he will be called to free the humans who gave him mobility, movement, but not life.

— Harlan Ellison, "Demon with a Glass Hand," episode of *The Outer Limits* (1964)

Believe me, Captain, immortality consists largely of boredom.

— Gene L. Coon, "Metamorphosis," episode of *Star Trek* (1967)

Nothing is immortal. But only to us is it given to know that we must die. And that is a great gift: the gift of selfhood. For we have only what we know we must lose, what we are willing to lose . . . That selfhood, which is our torment, and our treasure, and our humanity, does not endure. It changes; it is gone, a wave on the sea. Would you have the sea grow still and the tides cease, to save one wave, to save yourself?

— Ursula K. Le Guin, *The Farthest Shore* (1972)

Immortality

What man would not live forever, if he could?
— Ursula K. Le Guin, *The Farthest Shore* (1972)

The first ten million years were the worst. And the second ten million years, they were the worst too. The third ten million I didn't enjoy at all. After that I went into a bit of a decline.
— Douglas Adams, "Fit the Fifth," episode of *The Hitch-Hiker's Guide to the Galaxy* (radio series, 1978)

Life incorporeal, immortal, was on him now; it had him as it had her. His flesh, his body was beginning to attenuate, to dematerialise out into the great current of sentience that flowed on its mysterious purposes among the stars.
— James Tiptree, Jr., "Slow Music" (1980)

You can't achieve immortality by living forever.
— Arthur Byron Cover, *Stationfall* (1989)

The best definition of an immortal is someone who hasn't died yet.
— Tom Holt, *Ye Gods!* (1992)

If these aging treatments work, and we are living decades longer than previously, it will certainly cause a social revolution. Shortness of life was a primary force in the permanence of institutions, strange though it is to say it.
— Kim Stanley Robinson, *Red Mars* (1992)

PICARD: Someone once told me that time was a predator that stalked us all our lives. And I rather believe that time is a companion who goes with us on the journey and reminds us to cherish every moment, because they'll never come again. What we leave behind is not as important as how we've lived. After all, Number One, we're only mortal.
RIKER: Speak for yourself, sir. I plan to live forever.
— Ronald D. Moore and Brannon Braga, *Star Trek: Generations* (film, 1994)

"We could live forever, if we were willing to be stupid the whole time."
"Surely you're not saying that God had to choose between long life and intelligence for human beings!"
"It's there in your own Bible, Carlotta. Two trees — knowledge and life. You

eat of the tree of knowledge, and you will surely die. You eat of the tree of life, and you remain a child in the garden forever, undying."
  —Orson Scott Card, *Ender's Shadow* (1999)

We strive for immortality, all of us, in our myriad ways. Some of us run for public office, in the hopes that we will change the course of the world. Some of us teach, in hopes that out of the thousands of students we encounter, one will blossom. Some of us get married and have children, so that a little bit of us will survive in a fellow human being's DNA. And some of us create, whether it be art, music, poetry, or stories, in hopes of communicating to the future that once we were here, and that once we mattered.
  —Michael A. Burstein, "Paying It Forward" (2003)

IMPOSSIBILITY

"There's no use trying," she said: "one *ca'n't* believe impossible things."
  "I daresay you haven't had much practice," said the Queen. "When I was your age, I always did it for half-an-hour a day. Why, sometimes I've believed as many as six impossible things before breakfast."
  —Lewis Carroll, *Through the Looking Glass and What Alice Found There* (1872)

Everything is theoretically impossible, until it's done. One could write a history of science in reverse by assembling the solemn pronouncements of highest authority about what could not be done and could never happen.
  —Robert A. Heinlein, *Between Planets* (1951)

As you've discovered, so many things are possible just as long as you don't know they're impossible.
  —Norton Juster, *The Phantom Tollbooth* (1961)

A dear friend, a great scientist, now dead, used to tease me by saying that because politics is the art of the possible, it appeals only to second-rate minds. The *first*-raters, he claimed, were only interested in the *impossible*.
  —Arthur C. Clarke, *The Fountains of Paradise* (1979)

Impossibility

Let us leave this festering hellhole. Let us think the unthinkable, let us do the undoable. Let us prepare to grapple with the ineffable itself, and see if we may not eff it after all.

    —Douglas Adams, *Dirk Gently's Holistic Detective Agency* (1987)

The impossible often has a kind of integrity to it which the merely improbable lacks.

    —Douglas Adams, *The Long Dark Tea-Time of the Soul* (1988)

First, something is inconceivable, and that means exactly that. You can't think about it, can't say yes or no because it is altogether taboo. Then there is the conceivable but deniable. At that point the inconceivable becomes just impossible, you see. Although you still deny it, now you can think of it, and it may return again and again, each time eroding the denial a little bit more until impossible becomes possible, something you can consider. That's how the system works.

    —Kate Wilhelm, "Isosceles" (1988)

WESLEY: He wants the impossible.
LA FORGE: That's the short definition of "captain."

    —Cliff Bole, "The Ensigns of Command," episode of *Star Trek: The Next Generation* (1989)

"Impossible" is a word that humans use far too often.

    —Brannon Braga and Joe Menosky, "Hope and Fear," episode of *Star Trek: Voyager* (1998)

The impossible is only barely less likely than the normal around here.

    —Glen Cook, *Angry Lead Skies* (2002)

INDIVIDUALISM AND IDENTITY

Individualism, which in your day was the animating idea of society, not only was fatal to any vital sentiment of brotherhood and common interest among living men, but equally to any realization of the responsibility of the living for the generation to follow.

    —Edward Bellamy, *Looking Backward, 2000–1887* (1888)

No planet, no universe, is greater to a man than his own ego, his own observing self.
   —Theodore Sturgeon, "Thunder and Roses" (1947)

They say no *one* human being ever did *anything.* They say it takes a hundred pairs of hands to build a house, ten thousand pairs to build a ship. They say a single pair is not only useless—it's *evil.* All humanity is a thing made up of many parts. No part is good by itself. Any part that wants to go off by itself hurts the whole main thing—the thing that has become so great.
   —Theodore Sturgeon, "Mr. Costello, Hero" (1953)

He had returned to the group—but he carried with him the seeds of individualism, the deadly, contagious germ we Terrans spread everywhere.
   —Robert Silverberg, "Alaree" (1958)

I'm not much but I'm all I have.
   —Philip K. Dick, *Martian Time-Slip* (1964)

Everyone says "we" these days, Paul thought absently. *Nobody says "I." Everyone represents some formless, irresponsible group and nobody represents themselves.*
   —Philip K. Dick and Ray Nelson, *The Ganymede Takeover* (1967)

All these political movements and philosophies and ideals, all these wars—only illusions. Don't trouble your inner peace; there's no right and wrong, no win or lose. There're only individual men and each one is completely—completely!—alone.
   —Philip K. Dick and Ray Nelson, *The Ganymede Takeover* (1967)

I will not make any deals with you. I've resigned. I will not be pushed, filed, stamped, indexed, briefed, debriefed, or numbered. My life is my own.
   —George Markstein and David Tomblin, "Arrival," episode of *The Prisoner* (1968)

He didn't know who he was when she met him—well, not many people did.
   —Theodore Sturgeon, "Slow Sculpture" (1970)

Individualism and Identity

The duty of the individual is to accept *no* rule, to be the initiator of his own acts, to be responsible. Only if he does so will the society live, and change, and adapt, and survive.

— Ursula K. Le Guin, *The Dispossessed: An Ambiguous Utopia* (1974)

If one thing had been learned from the bloody history of mankind, it was that only individual human beings mattered: however eccentric their beliefs might be, they must be safeguarded, so long as they did not conflict with wider but equally legitimate interests.

— Arthur C. Clarke, *The Fountains of Paradise* (1979)

Nothing in those years matched the impact of the equable, incontrovertible statement that I did not matter, that my life was of no moment to anyone but myself. We accept that only one person in a million has real importance to the race but each of us remains the centre of his universe, the pivot of energy and mind. That man told me in a single sentence that the world would not flicker if I ceased to exist, that it would have affected nothing if I had never existed and that my continued existence would affect nothing in the stream of time.

— George Turner, *Drowning Towers* (1987)

"You," said Sally Mills, "are very strange."

"Only," said Dirk, "as strange as I need to be."

— Douglas Adams, *The Long Dark Tea-Time of the Soul* (1988)

She felt as though she'd had three lives, each walled away from the others by something she couldn't name, and no hope of wholeness, ever.

— William Gibson, *Mona Lisa Overdrive* (1988)

Human beings *do* metamorphose. They change their identity constantly. However, each new identity thrives on the delusion that it was always in possession of the body it has just conquered.

— Orson Scott Card, *Xenocide* (1991)

What makes you think human beings are sentient and aware? There's no evidence for it. Human beings never think for themselves, they find it too uncomfortable. For the most part, members of our species simply repeat what they are told — and become upset if they are exposed to any different

view. The characteristic human trait is not awareness but conformity, and the characteristic result is religious warfare. Other animals fight for territory or food; but, uniquely in the animal kingdom, human beings fight for their "beliefs." The reason is that beliefs guide behavior, which has evolutionary importance among human beings. But at a time when our behavior may well lead us to extinction, I see no reason to assume we have any awareness at all. We are stubborn, self-destructive conformists. Any other view of our species is just a self-congratulatory delusion.
— Michael Crichton, *The Lost World* (1995)

INTELLIGENCE

Intellectual versatility is the compensation for change, danger, and trouble. An animal perfectly in harmony with its environment is a perfect mechanism. Nature never appeals to intelligence until habit and instinct are useless. There is no intelligence where there is no change and no need of change. Only those animals partake of intelligence that have to meet a huge variety of needs and dangers.
— H. G. Wells, *The Time Machine: An Invention* (1895)

The last battle of brains against brutality had been fought on the bosom of the earth. And the intelligence of man had conquered his primeval ruthlessness.
— Edwin Balmer and Philip Wylie, *When Worlds Collide* (1932)

My mother used to say to me, "In this world, Elwood" — she always called me Elwood — she'd say, "In this world, Elwood, you must be oh, so smart or oh, so pleasant." For years I was smart. I recommend pleasant. You may quote me.
— Mary Chase, *Harvey* (play, 1944)

The brainier you are, the less stable you are, usually.
— Henry Kuttner and C. L. Moore, "Time Enough" (1946)

In general, the greater the understanding, the greater the delusion; the more intelligent, the less sane.
— George Orwell, *Nineteen Eighty-Four* (1949)

Intelligence is like candy. It comes in an endless variety of shapes, sizes and colors, no one of which is less delectable than the others.
— Eric Frank Russell, "Fast Falls the Eventide" (1952)

Twentieth-century man had both intelligence and instinct; he chose, unfortunately, to rely upon intelligence.
— Shirley Jackson, "Bulletin" (1954)

Life, *all* life, has the twin drives to survive and to reproduce. Intelligence is an aimless byproduct except as it serves these basic drives.
— Robert A. Heinlein, *Tunnel in the Sky* (1955)

"What made them realize that we were rational beings?"
  Hawkins' face darkened.
  "Only rational beings," he said, "put other beings in cages."
— A. Bertram Chandler, "The Cage" (1957)

Dr. Strauss says I shud rite down what I think and evrey thing that happins to me from now on. I dont know why but he says its important so they will see if they will use me. I hope they use me. Miss Kinnian says maybe they can make me smart. I want to be smart.
— Daniel Keyes, "Flowers for Algernon" (1959)

He was one of those unfortunate persons who have just enough intelligence to disapprove of the *status quo* but not quite enough to do anything about it.
— Robert F. Young, "There Was an Old Woman Who Lived in a Shoe" (1962)

Human intelligence was more trouble than it was worth. It was more destructive than creative, more confusing than revealing, more discouraging than satisfying, more spiteful than charitable.
— Michael Crichton, *The Andromeda Strain* (1969)

That's how people with brains operate: they don't believe a damn thing or feel sorry for anyone.
— Arkady Strugatsky and Boris Strugatsky, *Prisoners of Power* (1969), translated by Helen Saltz Jacobson (1977)

Intellectualism tends to foster negative thinking and may lead to psychosis, and those suffering from it should ideally be treated, as Professor Arca was treated, and released if still competent.
— Ursula K. Le Guin, "The Diary of the Rose" (1976)

There were moments in which he would have been glad to rid himself of that intelligence, like a crippling thing, not a privilege or gift, for continual thought must have tormented him.
— Stanislaw Lem, "The Mask" (1976), translated by Michael Kandel (1977)

"D'you mean clever or intelligent?"
 "Aren't they the same?"
 "No. Cleverness requires humor. Intelligence does not."
— Alfred Bester, "Galatea Galante" (1979)

Dear Benson, you are so mercifully free of the ravages of intelligence.
— Terry Gilliam and Michael Palin, *Time Bandits* (film, 1981)

Brainpower is the scarcest commodity and the only one of real value. Any human organization can be rendered useless, impotent, a danger to itself, by selectively removing its best minds while carefully leaving the stupid ones in place.
— Robert A. Heinlein, *Friday* (1982)

This is one of those uncomfortable periods when galactic intelligence is rife. Intelligence is a great bother. It makes all kinds of trouble for us.
— Bruce Sterling, "Swarm" (1982)

Intelligence is not a survival trait.
— Bruce Sterling, "Swarm" (1982)

Intelligence does enable you to deny facts you dislike.
— Octavia E. Butler, *Dawn* (1987)

High intelligence tends to remove itself from general considerations as though they can be left to the service classes and only the abstruse is worth its attention.
— George Turner, *Drowning Towers* (1987)

Intelligence

What, anyway, was he to say? That intelligence could surpass and excel the blind force of evolution, with its emphasis on mutation, struggle and death? That conscious cooperation was more efficient than feral competition?
— Iain M. Banks, *The Player of Games* (1988)

We must all be alike. Not everyone born free and equal, as the Constitution says, but everyone *made* equal. Each man the image of every other; then all are happy, for there are no mountains to make them cower, to judge themselves against.
— Ray Bradbury, *Fahrenheit 451* (1954)

"In a society of criminals," Shaeffer offered, "the innocent man goes to jail."
— Philip K. Dick, *Solar Lottery* (1955)

Right and wrong can sometimes be determined only through hindsight.
— Robert A. Heinlein, *Tunnel in the Sky* (1955)

Many that live deserve death. And some die that deserve life. Can you give that to them? Then be not too eager to deal out death in the name of justice, fearing for your own safety. Even the wise cannot see all ends.
— J. R. R. Tolkien, *The Two Towers* (1955)

It was right and proper to pity children, but Ruiz-Sanchez was beginning to believe that adults generally deserve any misfortune that they get.
— James Blish, *A Case of Conscience* (1958)

Be just and if you can't be just be arbitrary.
— William S. Burroughs, *Naked Lunch* (1959)

The year was 2081, and everybody was finally equal. They weren't only equal before God and the law, they were equal every which way. Nobody was smarter than anybody else; nobody was better looking than anybody else; nobody was stronger or quicker than anybody else.
— Kurt Vonnegut, Jr., "Harrison Bergeson" (1961)

UNFAIR Term applied to advantages enjoyed by other people which we tried to cheat them out of and didn't manage.
　—John Brunner, *Stand on Zanzibar* (1968)

You will be required to do wrong no matter where you go. It is the basic condition of life, to be required to violate your own identity. At some time, every creature which lives must do so. It is the ultimate shadow, the defeat of creation; this is the curse at work, the curse that feeds on all life. Everywhere in the universe.
　—Philip K. Dick, *Do Androids Dream of Electric Sheep?* (1968)

In a chaotic universe, who expects justice?
　—Raylyn Moore, "Trigononomy" (1973)

Whenever someone uses the word "justice," sooner or later there's going to be a split head or a broken heart.
　—William Tenn, "On Venus, Have We Got a Rabbi" (1974)

No one is innocent. All are guilty.
　—Ward Moore, "Durance" (1975)

There was a time you didn't have to *earn* the right to live! You had it—as a human being!
　—Mary Gentle, "The Harvest of Wolves" (1984)

We were being told: the world isn't the place you think it is; it is neither rational nor just.
　—George Turner, *Drowning Towers* (1987)

A wrong that cannot be repaired must be transcended.
　—Ursula K. Le Guin, *Tehanu: The Last Book of Earthsea* (1990)

It's the love of right lures men to wrong.
　—Kim Stanley Robinson, *Red Mars* (1992)

The *world* isn't fair, the universe isn't fair. Physics, chemistry and mathematics, they aren't fair. Or unfair, for that matter. Fairness is an idea, and only conscious creatures have ideas. That's us. We have ideas about right and wrong. We invent the idea of justice so that we can judge whether something is good or bad. We develop morality. We create rules to live by and call them laws, all to make life more fair.

—Iain M. Banks, *The Business* (1999)

KINDNESS

"I say, you do have a heart!"

"Sometimes," he replied. "When I have the time."

—Jules Verne, *Around the World in Eighty Days* (1873), translated by
William Butcher (1995)

Generous deed should not be checked by cold counsel.

—J. R. R. Tolkien, *The Return of the King* (1955)

If a man gets lost in the mountains, hundreds will search and often two or
three searchers are killed. But the next time somebody gets lost just as many
volunteers turn out.

Poor arithmetic . . . but very human. It runs through all our folklore, all
human religions, all our literature—a racial conviction that when one human
needs rescue, others should not count the price.

Weakness? It might be the unique strength that wins us a Galaxy.

—Robert A. Heinlein, *Starship Troopers* (1959)

If a man is able to help his neighbors and does not, then he ends up something less than a man.

—Michael Shaara, "Citizen Jell" (1959)

Isn't it odd how we misunderstand the hidden unity of kindness and cruelty?

—Frank Herbert, *Dune* (1965)

He thought no more of performing the lesser arts of magic than a bird thinks
of flying. Yet a greater, unlearned skill he possessed, which was the art of
kindness.

—Ursula K. Le Guin, *A Wizard of Earthsea* (1968)

It is a terrible thing, this kindness that human beings do not lose. Terrible,
because when we are finally naked in the dark and cold, it is all we have. We

who are so rich, so full of strength, we end up with that small change. We have nothing else to give.
— Ursula K. Le Guin, *The Left Hand of Darkness* (1969)

The measure of a man is not his intelligence. It is not how high he rises in the freak establishment. The measure of a man is this: how swiftly can he react to another person's need? And how much of himself can he give?
— Philip K. Dick, *Our Friends from Frolix 8* (1970)

Man, despite his enormous shortcomings, is nevertheless possessed of a greater number of kindly impulses than all the other beings where instincts are the larger part of life. These impulses, I believe, are owed directly to this capacity for guilt. It is involved in both the worst and the best of man.
— Roger Zelazny, "Home Is the Hangman" (1975)

Kindness is more pro-survival than cruelty. But which *feels* better? Which provides more pleasure? Poll any hundred people at random and you'll find at least twenty or thirty who know all there is to know about psychological torture and psychic castration—and maybe two that know how to give a terrific back rub.
— Spider Robinson, "God Is an Iron" (1979)

Being nice all the time can be very, very boring.
— Charles L. Grant, "Secrets of the Heart" (1980)

SPOCK: In any case, were I to invoke logic, logic clearly dictates that the needs of the many outweigh the needs of the few.
KIRK: Or the one.
— Jack B. Sowards, *Star Trek II: The Wrath of Khan* (film, 1982)

Because the needs of the one outweighed the needs of the many.
— Harve Bennett, *Star Trek III: The Search for Spock* (film, 1984)

When it comes to a choice between kindness and honesty, my vote is for kindness, every time—giving or receiving.
— Robert A. Heinlein, *The Cat Who Walks through Walls* (1985)

Kindness

His curtness she could meet and match with her own flippancy, guarding herself as with a fencer's foil. His kindness was like fencing with the sea, her strokes going soft and losing all volition.
  —Lois McMaster Bujold, *Shards of Honor* (1986)

"Gratitude": An imaginary emotion that rewards an imaginary behavior, "altruism." Both imaginaries are false faces for selfishness, which is a real and honest emotion.
  —Robert A. Heinlein, *To Sail beyond the Sunset* (1987)

A gentle touch;
A smile;
Kind words
By such small things
Are lives changed.
  —Tara K. Harper, *Shadow Leader* (1991)

KNOWLEDGE AND INFORMATION

He who increaseth knowledge, increaseth sorrow.
  —H. Rider Haggard, *Allan Quatermain* (1887)

People who knew too little and people who knew too much were equally a bore.
  —Edgar Rice Burroughs, *The Chessmen of Mars* (1922)

We walk in darkness with phantoms and specters we know not of, and our little world plunges blindly through abysses toward a goal of which we have no conception. That thought itself is a blow at our beliefs and comprehension. We used to content ourselves by thinking we knew all about our world, at least; but now it is different, and we wonder if we really know anything, or if there can be safety and peace anywhere in the wide universe.
  —Donald A. Wandrei, "Something from Above" (1930)

There is no knowledge, other than knowledge of oneself, and that should be free to every man who has the wit to learn.
  —Robert A. Heinlein, "Lost Legacy" (1941)

Knowledge and understanding aren't props for one another. Knowledge is a pile of bricks, and understanding is a way of building.
  —Theodore Sturgeon, "The Sex Opposite" (1952)

Do not despise the lore that has come down from distant years; for oft it may chance that old wives keep in memory word of things that once were needful for the wise to know.
  —J. R. R. Tolkien, *The Fellowship of the Ring* (1954)

There's a price to be paid for everything you learn about what's in the universe. It has to hurt, or it isn't a real price.
  —Algis Budrys, "Lower Than Angels" (1956)

It shocked Kingsbury how small man and man's knowledge were in the illimitable universe.
  —Poul Anderson, "Life Cycle" (1957)

Almost all knowledge, after all, fell into that category. It was either perfectly simple once you understood it, or else it fell apart into fiction.
  —James Blish, *A Case of Conscience* (1958)

One can lead a child to knowledge but one *cannot* make him think.
  —Robert A. Heinlein, *Starship Troopers* (1959)

During the last age of reason, certain proud thinkers had claimed that valid knowledge was indestructible—that ideas were deathless and truth immortal.
  —Walter M. Miller, Jr., *A Canticle for Leibowitz* (1959)

Words and numbers are of equal value, for, in the cloak of knowledge, one is warp and the other woof. It is no more important to count the sands than it is to name the stars.
  —Norton Juster, *The Phantom Tollbooth* (1961)

Whenever you learn something new, the whole world becomes that much richer.
  —Norton Juster, *The Phantom Tollbooth* (1961)

Knowledge and Information

The more complex a civilization, the more vital to its existence is the maintenance of the flow of information; hence the more vulnerable it becomes to any disturbance in that flow.
— Stanislaw Lem, *Memoirs Found in a Bathtub* (1961), translated by Michael Kandel and Christine Rose (1973)

Our knowledge of our own limitations is one of our most powerful weapons against the universe.
— John Brunner, "Puzzle for Spacemen," revised (1962)

Knowledge creates a craving for further knowledge. Where is the harm in knowledge?
— Jack Vance, "Green Magic" (1963)

A process cannot be understood by stopping it. Understanding must move with the flow of the process, must join it and flow with it.
— Frank Herbert, *Dune* (1965)

These dwarfs amass knowledge as others do treasure; for this reason they are called Hoarders of the Absolute.
Their wisdom lies in the fact that they collect knowledge but never use it.
— Stanislaw Lem, "How Erg the Self-Inducing Slew a Paleface" (1965), translated by Michael Kandel (1977)

The left hand knows not what the right hand is doing. As a matter of fact, the right hand doesn't know what the right hand is doing.
— Philip José Farmer, "Riders of the Purple Wage" (1967)

Man's knowing had no completeness — no limits — because Man did not even know himself.
Breathing hard in the thin mountain air, the butterfly marveled at the boundless wonder of Man.
— Howard L. Myers, "The Creatures of Man" (1968)

Information is only meaningful when it is shared.
— Samuel R. Delany, "Time Considered as a Helix of Semi-Precious Stones" (1969)

"No creature knows itself," Glimmung said. "You don't know yourself; you don't have any knowledge, none at all, of your most basic potentials."
— Philip K. Dick, *Galactic Pot-Healer* (1969)

When action grows unprofitable, gather information; when information grows unprofitable, sleep.
— Ursula K. Le Guin, *The Left Hand of Darkness* (1969)

What is man but a mote of dust to the universe? Why, he *is* the universe! All we ever can know is ourselves.
— Susanna Jacobson, "Notes from Magdalen More" (1973)

There were times, he said, when human effort appeared to generate nothing but suffering, error, confusion — but maybe even these times add a little to the sum of human understanding.
— Edgar Pangborn, "The World Is a Sphere" (1973)

You don't have to be able to swim to know a fish, you don't have to shine to recognize a star.
— Ursula K. Le Guin, *The Dispossessed: An Ambiguous Utopia* (1974)

He sure wished he knew what people were talking about, at least some of the time.
— Tom Reamy, "San Diego Lightfoot Sue" (1975)

Isn't it strange how much we know if only we ask ourselves instead of somebody else?
— Richard Bach, *Illusions: The Adventures of a Reluctant Messiah* (1977)

The chances of finding out what really is going on are so absurdly remote that the only thing to do is to say hang the sense of it and just keep yourself occupied.
— Douglas Adams, "Fit the Fourth," episode of *The Hitch-Hiker's Guide to the Galaxy* (radio series, 1978)

The main reason he had had such a wild and successful life was that he never really understood the significance of anything he did.
— Douglas Adams, *The Hitchhiker's Guide to Galaxy* (1979)

Knowledge and Information

Like a man carrying a balloon filled with acid, Fallon carried his knowledge tenderly.
—John Kessel, "Another Orphan" (1982)

We Investors deal in energy, and precious metals. To prize and pursue mere knowledge is an immature racial trait.
—Bruce Sterling, "Swarm" (1982)

What you know, you cannot hate.
—Greg Bear, "Hardfought" (1983)

I am sick to death of people who *know*. I want people who aren't sure.
—Mary Gentle, "The Harvest of Wolves" (1984)

In the moment when I truly understand my enemy, understand him well enough to defeat him, then in that very moment I also love him. I think it's impossible to really understand somebody, what they want, what they believe, and not love them the way they love themselves.
—Orson Scott Card, *Ender's Game* (1985)

"But why do we *wish* to exchange information?"
"Because we feed on information. Information is necessary for our survival. Without information we die."
—Carl Sagan, *Contact* (1985)

Knowledge lit him like an arcade game.
—William Gibson, *Count Zero* (1986)

They both savoured the strange warm glow of being much more ignorant than ordinary people, who were only ignorant of ordinary things.
—Terry Pratchett, *Equal Rites* (1987)

How harmful overspecialization is. It cuts knowledge at a million points and leaves it bleeding.
—Isaac Asimov, *Prelude to Foundation* (1988)

"Knowledge is camouflage," he was told. "It merely disguises what lies beneath."
—Alan Dean Foster, *Cyber Way* (1990)

You can't see the universe clearly until you know who you are.
—Alexander Jablokov, "The Place of No Shadows" (1990)

The bosses, the big'uns, they can take all manner of things away from us. With their bloody laws and factories and courts and banks . . . They can make the world to their pleasure, they can take away your home and kin and even the work you do. [. . .] But they can't ever take what you *know*.
—William Gibson and Bruce Sterling, *The Difference Engine* (1991)

The more time he spent away out in the Galaxy the more it seemed that the number of things he didn't know anything about actually increased.
—Douglas Adams, *Mostly Harmless* (1992)

All information looks like noise until you break the code.
—Neal Stephenson, *Snow Crash* (1992)

Any information system of sufficient complexity will inevitably become infected with viruses—viruses generated from within itself.
—Neal Stephenson, *Snow Crash* (1992)

Knowledge is just opinion that you trust enough to act upon.
—Orson Scott Card, *Children of the Mind* (1996)

Why must the existence of something inexplicable and ineffably different make people want to claim they know what it is?
—L. Timmel Duchamp, "Dance at the Edge" (1998)

So high, so low, so many things to know.
—Vernor Vinge, *A Deepness in the Sky* (1999)

There is a difference between knowing the path and walking the path.
—Andy Wachowski and Larry Wachowski, *The Matrix* (film, 1999)

Most people will never know anything beyond what they see with their own two eyes.
—Michael Dougherty, Dan Harris, and David Hayter, *X2: X-Men United* (film, 2003)

L

LANGUAGE

The words which make up human language are inadequate for those who
venture into the depths of the Earth. [. . .] New words were needed for new
sensations and my imagination could not provide them.
   —Jules Verne, *A Journey to the Centre of the Earth* (1864), translated by
      William Butcher (1992)

Take care of the sense, and the sounds will take care of themselves.
   —Lewis Carroll, *Alice's Adventures in Wonderland* (1865)

"When *I* use a word," Humpty Dumpty said in rather a scornful tone,
"it means just what I choose it to mean—neither more nor less."
   —Lewis Carroll, *Through the Looking Glass and What Alice Found There*
      (1872)

He had an idea, I believe, that to gabble about names that meant nothing was
the proper use of speech. [. . .] He had developed in the most wonderful way
the distinctive silliness of man without losing one jot of the natural folly of a
monkey.
   —H. G. Wells, *The Island of Doctor Moreau* (1896)

Human language is naturally wanting in words that are adequate for the
delineation of events and sensations beyond the normal scope of human
experience.
   —Clark Ashton Smith, "The City of the Singing Flame" (1931)

Words can be like X-rays, if you use them properly—they'll go through
anything.
   —Aldous Huxley, *Brave New World* (1932)

He liked the serene world that Shangri-La offered him, pacified rather than
dominated by its single tremendous idea. He liked the prevalent mood in

which feelings were sheathed in thoughts, and thoughts softened into felicity by their transference into language.
—James Hilton, *Lost Horizon* (1933)

Words were subtle, and frequently had little connection with the facts they were supposed to represent.
—A. E. van Vogt, *The Players of Null-A* (1948)

Don't you see that the whole aim of Newspeak is to narrow the range of thought? In the end we shall make thoughtcrime literally impossible, because there will be no words in which to express it.
—George Orwell, *Nineteen Eighty-Four* (1949)

"I never knew words could be so confusing," Milo said to Tock as he bent down to scratch the dog's ear.
"Only when you use a lot to say a little."
—Norton Juster, *The Phantom Tollbooth* (1961)

[Human] communication is rendered more complex by the use of differing sets of sound-symbols, called languages and by the fact that a given set of symbols tends to change with the passage of years to become an entirely new language.
—Howard L. Myers, "The Creatures of Man" (1968)

There is a treachery in words that somehow cuts out sincerity, albeit by accident, and makes the deepest feelings seem shallow and distant.
—John DeCles, "Cruelty" (1970)

Others have developed cries, songs, words as weapons. Words that cut like buzz saws. Words that vibrate the entrails to jelly. Cold strange words that fall like icy nets on the mind. Virus words that eat the brain to muttering shreds.
—William S. Burroughs, *The Wild Boys: A Book of the Dead* (1971)

Very little thinking was ever done in English; it is not a language suitable to logical thought.
—Robert A. Heinlein, *Time Enough for Love* (1973)

Language

With them [the phytolinguist and the critic], or after them, may there not come that even bolder adventurer—the first geolinguist, who, ignoring the delicate, transient lyrics of the lichen, will read beneath it the still less communicative, still more passive, wholly atemporal, cold, volcanic poetry of the rocks; each one a word spoken, how long ago, by the earth itself, in the immense solitude, the immenser community, of space.

> —Ursula K. Le Guin, "The Author of the Acacia Seeds and Other Extracts from the *Journal of the Association of Therolinguistics*" (1974)

"Why do people always make such a tremendous thing about words?" [. . .]

"They may be the best means we have for probing certain kinds of darkness. As for communication, Jesse, we might survive for a while without it but I'm not sure the survival would be worth having. Words weren't invented *only* to conceal thoughts as the old wheeze has it. They create thoughts, give thoughts, and are thoughts. People live by honest words, and die by the other kind."

> —Edgar Pangborn, "The Children's Crusade" (1974)

The original purpose of language was to ritualize men's threats and curses, his spells to compel the gods; communication came later. Words can be a safety valve.

> —Gene Wolfe, "The Death of Doctor Island" (1974)

They knew nothing of this world, their world, only that they must walk in it in silence, until they had learned a language fitting to be spoken here.

> —Ursula K. Le Guin, "The Eye of the Heron" (1978)

The world is a message from God written in Egyptian picture letters in an unknown tongue. A language half remembered. The shapes whispered meanings, and they seemed to mean more away from the brightest lights.

> —Katherine MacLean, "Night-Rise" (1978)

I am not certain what is meant by the smell of a rose, but if a rose on Earth is the common flower that is called a rose on Aurora, and if by its "smell" you mean a property that can be detected, sensed, or measured by human beings, then surely calling a rose by another sound-combination—and holding all else equal—would not affect the smell or any other of its intrinsic properties.

> —Isaac Asimov, *The Robots of Dawn* (1983)

They spoke in Interlingua, the language of space.
— Mack Reynolds, *Chaos in Lagrangia* (1983)

There are many creatures, but only one language, which all speak with greater or lesser skill, according to their destinies.
— Robert Silverberg, "Homefaring" (1983)

The basic tool for the manipulation of reality is the manipulation of words. If you can control the meaning of words, you can control the people who must use the words.
— Philip K. Dick, "How to Build a Universe That Doesn't Fall Apart Two Days Later" (1985)

Words used carelessly, as if they did not matter in any serious way, often allowed otherwise well-guarded truths to seep through.
— Douglas Adams, *The Long Dark Tea-Time of the Soul* (1988)

In every language, from Arabic to Zulu to calligraphy to shorthand to math to music to art to wrought stone, everything from the Unified Field Theory to a curse to a sixpenny nail to an orbiting satellite, anything expressed is a net around some idea.
— Richard Bach, *One* (1988)

Where I come from the men and women hardly speak to each other. First of all, they don't speak the same language. They don't here either, but you don't recognize that as clearly. Where I come from there's men's English and there's women's English.
— Karen Joy Fowler, "Game Night at the Fox and Goose" (1989)

That is the tragedy of language, my friend. Those who know each other only through symbolic representations are forced to imagine each other. And because their imagination is imperfect, they are often wrong.
— Orson Scott Card, *Xenocide* (1991)

In the dim, high hollow of the great station a thousand voices seemed to mingle, the constituent elements of language reduced to the aural equivalent of fog, homogeneous and impenetrable.
— William Gibson and Bruce Sterling, *The Difference Engine* (1991)

Language

Language, Jason realised, was a large part of the problem, because words say what they want to say, not what you want them to say.

    —Tom Holt, *Ye Gods!* (1992)

"Medicine is a *language*?" Drake felt that his mind must be slowed by the long sleep and thawing treatment.

    "Of course. Like Music, or Chemistry, or Astronautics. But surely this was already true in your own time. Did you not have languages specific to each— what is your word?—discipline?"

    —Charles Sheffield, "At the Eschaton" (1995)

The universe speaks in many languages, but only one voice. The language is not narn or human or centauri or gaim or minbari. It speaks in the language of hope. It speaks in the language of trust. It speaks in the language of strength and the language of compassion. It is the language of the heart and the language of the soul. But always it is the same voice. It is the voice of our ancestors speaking through us and the voice of our inheritors waiting to be born. The small, still voice that says: "We are one. No matter the blood, no matter the skin, no matter the world, no matter the star . . . We are one. No matter the pain, no matter the darkness, no matter the loss, no matter the fear . . . We are one." Here, gathered together in common cause, we begin to realize this singular truth and this singular rule that we must be kind to one another. Because each voice enriches us and ennobles us and each voice lost diminishes us. We are the voice of the universe, the soul of creation, the fire that will light our way to a better future. We are one.

    —J. Michael Straczynski, "The Paragon of Animals," episode of *Babylon 5* (1998)

He luxuriated in the sound of high language well spoken.

    —Orson Scott Card, *Ender's Shadow* (1999)

LAWS AND CRIMES

"We do without the lawyers, certainly," was Doctor Leete's reply. "It would not seem reasonable to us, in a case where the only interest of the nation is to

find out the truth, that persons should take part in the proceedings who had an acknowledged motive to color it."
—Edward Bellamy, *Looking Backward, 2000–1887* (1888)

In one respect at least the Martians are a happy people; they have no lawyers.
—Edgar Rice Burroughs, *A Princess of Mars* (1917)

Freedom and crime are linked as indivisibly as . . . well, as the motion of the aero and its speed: when its speed equals zero, it does not move; when man's freedom equals zero, he commits no crimes. That is clear. The only means of ridding man of crime is ridding him of freedom.
—Yevgeny Zamiatin, *We* (1924), translated by Mirra Ginsburg (1972)

Which is more important—to punish criminals or to end crime?
—Fredric Brown, "Crisis, 1999" (1949)

Public Officers must at all times remember that the criminal is merely a person at odds with his society. [. . .] The criminal must make amends for the results of his crime, and this might be called punishment, but the chief duty of the police is to see that he is brought in for therapy. A criminal cured is a citizen saved.
—Kendell Foster Crossen, "Public Enemy" (1952)

"The rules!" shouted Ralph, "you're breaking the rules!"
"Who cares?"
Ralph summoned his wits.
"Because the rules are the only thing we've got!"
—William Golding, *Lord of the Flies* (1954)

I don't hold with the idea that to understand all is to forgive all; you follow that and first thing you know you're sentimental over murderers and rapists and kidnappers and forgetting their victims. That's wrong.
—Robert A. Heinlein, *Have Space Suit—Will Travel* (1958)

The laws of society are what makes something a crime or not a crime.
—Walter M. Miller, Jr., *A Canticle for Leibowitz* (1959)

Laws and Crimes

What sort of a world is it at all? Men on the moon and men spinning round the earth like it might be midges round a lamp, and there's not no attention paid to earthy law nor order no more.

— Anthony Burgess, *A Clockwork Orange* (1962)

The Government cannot be concerned any longer with outmoded penological theories. Cram criminals together and see what happens. You get concentrated criminality, crime in the midst of punishment.

— Anthony Burgess, *A Clockwork Orange* (1962)

When law and duty are one, united by religion, you never become fully conscious, fully aware of yourself. You are always a little less than an individual.

— Frank Herbert, *Dune* (1965)

Must be a yearning deep in human heart to stop other people from doing as they please. Rules, laws — always for *other* fellow. A murky part of us, something we had before we came down out of trees, and failed to shuck when we stood up.

— Robert A. Heinlein, *The Moon Is a Harsh Mistress* (1966)

We live in a universe of murderers.

— Philip K. Dick and Ray Nelson, *The Ganymede Takeover* (1967)

There are very few successful thieves in this world. Still less on the other five. The will to steal is an impulse towards the absurd and the tasteless. (The talents are poetic, theatrical, a certain reverse charisma . . .) But it is a will, as the will to order, power, love.

— Samuel R. Delany, "Time Considered as a Helix of Semi-Precious Stones" (1969)

If it's all the rest of us who are killed by the suicide, it's himself whom the murderer kills; only he has to do it over, and over, and over.

— Ursula K. Le Guin, "The Word for World Is Forest" (1972)

Every impossible rule has its loopholes; every general prohibition creates its bootleggers.

— Robert A. Heinlein, *Time Enough for Love* (1973)

Some people love illegality for its own sake. Men, more often than women. It's men who make laws, and enforce them, and break them, and think the whole performance is wonderful. Most women would rather just ignore them.
   —Ursula K. Le Guin, "The New Atlantis" (1975)

The street finds its own uses for things.
   —William Gibson, "Burning Chrome" (1982)

He knew this kind of room, this kind of building; the tenants would operate in the interzone where art wasn't quite crime, crime not quite art.
   —William Gibson, *Neuromancer* (1984)

Jungle law is an accumulation of practical behaviours. Beasts of a dozen species gather at sundown at the waterhole, each in its protective group, without conflict or fear; by day, predators and prey congregate in view of each other until the moment comes for just one to be cut out and killed. There is order, understood.
   —George Turner, *Drowning Towers* (1987)

It is almost impossible for anyone to be in a street without breaking the law.
   —Terry Pratchett, *Men at Arms* (1993)

United Earth is a collection of nations whose concept of justice is a game of lawyers. A jury does not decide who is right and who has been wrong, but whose lawyer better played the game. Truth never enters into it.
   —R. M. Meluch, "Traitor" (1995)

That's why there's rules, understand? So that you *think* before you break 'em.
   —Terry Pratchett, *Thief of Time* (2001)

THE LAWS OF SCIENCE FICTION

[H. G. Wells's Law of the Beast-Men:]
Not to go on all-Fours; *that* is the Law. Are we not Men?
Not to suck up Drink; *that* is the Law. Are we not Men?
Not to eat Flesh nor Fish; *that* is the Law. Are we not Men?

The Laws of Science Fiction

Not to claw Bark of Trees; *that* is the Law. Are we not Men?
Not to chase other Men; *that* is the Law. Are we not Men?
    —H. G. Wells, *The Island of Doctor Moreau* (1896)

[George Orwell's Seven Commandments of Animals:]
1. Whatever goes upon two legs is an enemy.
2. Whatever goes upon four legs, or has wings, is a friend.
3. No animal shall wear clothes.
4. No animal shall sleep in a bed.
5. No animal shall drink alcohol.
6. No animal shall kill any other animal.
7. All animals are equal.
    —George Orwell, *Animal Farm: A Fairy Story* (1945)

[George Orwell's Revised Seventh Commandment:]
All animals are equal
but some animals are more equal than others.
    —George Orwell, *Animal Farm: A Fairy Story* (1945)

[Robert A. Heinlein's Rules for Writers:]
1. You must *write.*
2. You must *finish* what you start.
3. You must refrain from rewriting except to editorial order.
4. You must put it on the market.
5. You must keep it on the market until sold.
    —Robert A. Heinlein, "On the Writing of Speculative Fiction" (1947)

[Isaac Asimov's Three Laws of Robotics:]
[First Law:] A robot may not injure a human being, or, through inaction, allow a human being to come to harm.

[Second Law:] A robot must obey the orders given it by human beings except where such orders would conflict with the First Law.

[Third Law:] A robot must protect its own existence as long as such protection does not conflict with the First or Second Law.
    —Isaac Asimov, *I, Robot* (1950)

[Isaac Asimov's Zeroth Law:]
A robot may not injure humanity or, through inaction, allow humanity to
come to harm.

    —Isaac Asimov, *Robots and Empire* (1985)

[Arthur Byron Cover's Laws of Robotics:]
"The Singlemost Law, remember? The one that says no robot shall through
action or lack of action permit a sentient organism of an officially registered
species to come to harm!"

    "Sorry, but that's the Thirdfolded Law. The real Singlemost Law says
that under no circumstances shall a robot place his own private person in
jeopardy!"

    —Arthur Byron Cover, *Planetfall* (1988)

[Theodore Sturgeon's Law:]
It is in this vein that I repeat Sturgeon's Revelation, which was wrung out
of me after twenty years of wearying defense of science fiction against the
attacks of people who used the worst examples of the field for ammunition,
and whose conclusion was that ninety percent of sf is crud. The Revelation:

    Ninety percent of *everything* is crud.

    Corollary 1: The existence of immense quantities of trash in science fic-
tion is admitted and it is regrettable; but it is no more unnatural than the
existence of trash anywhere.

    Corollary 2: The best science fiction is as good as the best fiction in any
field.

    —Theodore Sturgeon, "On Hand: A Book" (1958)

When people talk about the mystery novel, they mention *The Maltese Falcon*
and *The Big Sleep*. When they talk about the western, they say there's *The
Way West* and *Shane*. But when they talk about science fiction, they call it
"that Buck Rogers stuff," and they say, "ninety percent of science fiction is
crud." Well, they're right. Ninety percent of science fiction is crud. But then
ninety percent of everything is crud, and it's the ten percent that isn't crud
that is important, and the ten percent of science fiction that isn't crud is as
good or better than anything being written anywhere.

    —Theodore Sturgeon, from his 1953 speech at the World Science Fiction
      Convention, cited by James Gunn, "Addendum" to review of
      The Ultimate Egoist (1995)

The Laws of Science Fiction

[Arthur C. Clarke's Three Laws:]
[First Law:] When a distinguished but elderly scientist states that something is possible, he is almost certainly right. When he states that something is impossible, he is very probably wrong.
> —Arthur C. Clarke, "Hazards of Prophecy: The Failure of Imagination" (1962)

[Second Law:] The only way of discovering the limits of the possible is to venture a little way past them into the impossible.
> —Arthur C. Clarke, "Hazards of Prophecy: An Arresting Inquiry into the Limits of the Possible: Failures of Nerve and Failures of Imagination" (1962)

[Third Law:] Any sufficiently advanced technology is indistinguishable from magic.
> —Arthur C. Clarke, "Clarke's Third Law on UFO's" (letter), *Science,* January 19 (1968)

[Isaac Asimov's Corollary to Clarke's First Law:]
When, however, the lay public rallies round an idea that is denounced by distinguished but elderly scientists—and supports that idea with great fervor and emotion—the distinguished but elderly scientists are then, after all, probably right.
> —Isaac Asimov, "Asimov's Corollary" (1977)

[Gregory Benford's Corollary to Clarke's Third Law:]
Any technology distinguishable from magic is insufficiently advanced.
> —Gregory Benford, *Foundation's Fear* (1994)

[*Star Trek*'s Prime Directive:]
SPOCK: Then the Prime Directive is in full force, Captain?
KIRK: No identification of self or mission. No interference with the social development of said planet.
McCOY: No references to space or the fact that there *are* other worlds or more advanced civilizations.
> —Gene L. Coon and Gene Roddenberry, "Bread and Circuses," episode of *Star Trek* (1968)

[Isaac Asimov's Three Laws of Futurics:]
[First Law:] What is happening will continue to happen.
  [Second Law:] Consider the obvious seriously, for few people will see it.
  [Third Law:] Consider the consequences.
  —Isaac Asimov, "Oh, Keen-Eyed Peerer into the Future" (1974)

LIFE

If he could get the hang of the thing his cry might become "To live would be an awfully big adventure!" but he can never quite get the hang of it, and so no one is as gay as he.
  —J. M. Barrie, *Peter Pan* (play, 1904)

I didn't care what it was they talked about, so long as it connected with human life, somehow. There are few things that don't.
  —Charlotte Perkins Gilman, *Herland* (1915)

They had no theory of the essential opposition of good and evil; life to them was Growth; their pleasure was in growing, and their duty also.
  —Charlotte Perkins Gilman, *Herland* (1915)

"I think of Life!" he roared. "The dead are dead, and what has passed is done! I have a ship and a fighting crew and a girl with lips like wine, and that's all I ever asked. Lick your wounds, bullies, and break out a cask of ale. You're going to work ship as she never was worked before. Dance and sing while you buckle to it, damn you! To the devil with empty seas! We're bound for waters where the seaports are fat, and the merchant ships are crammed with plunder!"
  —Robert E. Howard, "The Pool of the Black One" (1933)

We know now why all the galaxies in the cosmos are fleeing from our own, know that ours is held an accursed galaxy, leprous with the disease of life.
  —Edmond Hamilton, "The Accursed Galaxy" (1935)

Nothing is important in life but the little bit of love and laughter and sunshine that we can have before we die.
  —Edmond Hamilton, "The Ephemerae" (1938)

You see, George, you really had a wonderful life.
  —Frances Goodrich, Albert Hackett, Frank Capra, and Jo Swerling,
    It's a Wonderful Life (film, 1946)

Life could be as ugly as an open field latrine in midsummer.
  —William Tenn, "Child's Play" (1947)

He looked uncertain and suspicious of life, like a man who finds a newly-
hatched octopus in his breakfast orange juice.
  —William Tenn, "Child's Play" (1947)

What did a man live for? All Dodge's instincts jostled and shoved forward to
point to one answer: that in the last analysis a man lived to live.
  —Jerome Bixby, "Angels in the Jets" (1952)

The realization of the Principle of Sufficient Irritation came to me. Here
was the origin of life. Eons ago, in the remote past, a bit of inanimate matter had become so irritated by something that it crawled away, moved by
indignation.
  —Philip K. Dick, "The Short Happy Life of the Brown Oxford" (1954)

Everything in the universe has collapsed . . . shifting, random, purposeless
gray smoke you can't put your hands on. The only thing that's left is people;
your family, your friends, your mistress, your protector. You can touch them,
be close to them . . . breathing *life* that's warm and solid. Perspiration, skin
and hair, saliva, breath, bodies. Taste, touch, smell, colors. Good God, there
has to be something you can grab hold of! What is there, beyond people?
  —Philip K. Dick, *Solar Lottery* (1955)

It had just dawned on him, with the dazzling glow of revelation, that the
whole course of anybody's life was determined by improbable accidents.
  —Damon Knight, "You're Another" (1955)

What is life but organized energy?
  —Arthur C. Clarke, "Out of the Sun" (1958)

Logically—for what had a more gloomy prognosis than life?—every morning one should say to one's friends: "I grieve for your irrevocable death," as to anyone suffering from an incurable disease.
  —J. G. Ballard, *The Drowned World* (1962)

"If you find your life tangled up with somebody else's life for no very logical reason," writes Bokonon, "that person may be a member of your *karass*."
  —Kurt Vonnegut, Jr., *Cat's Cradle* (1963)

There is no perfect defense. *There is no protection.* Being alive means being exposed; it's the nature of life to be hazardous—it's the stuff of living.
  —Philip K. Dick, *Clans of the Alphane Moon* (1964)

There's magic and enchantment in regular life, if you look at it right.
  —Richard McKenna, "The Secret Place" (1966)

Live long, T'Pau, and prosper.
  —Theodore Sturgeon, "Amok Time," episode of *Star Trek* (1967)

Your life from birth to death resembles the progress of a hopeless drunk tightrope walker whose act has been so bad up till now that he's being bombarded with rotten eggs and broken bottles.
  —John Brunner, *Stand on Zanzibar* (1968)

There are no small matters. Just as there is no small life. The life of an insect, a spider; his life is as large as yours, and yours is as large as mine. Life is life.
  —Philip K. Dick, *Galactic Pot-Healer* (1969)

The Book made a pool ball out of me, an object set in motion, as in Aristotle's view of the world. One moving pool ball hits the next; it hits a third; that is the essence of life.
  —Philip K. Dick, *Galactic Pot-Healer* (1969)

There's meaning everywhere, Harry. For Sam Smith as well as for Beethoven. For Noel Breckenridge as well as for Michelangelo. Dawn after dawn, simply being alive, being part of it all, part of the cosmic dance of life—that's the meaning, Harry.
  —Robert Silverberg, "Breckenridge and the Continuum" (1973)

The garden of life never seems to confine itself to the plots philosophers have laid out for its convenience. Maybe a few more tractors would do the trick.
— Roger Zelazny, "Home Is the Hangman" (1975)

In the wastes of nonbeing it is born, flickers out, is born again and holds together, swells and spreads. In lifelessness it lives, against the gray tide of entropy it strives, improbably persists, gathering itself into ever richer complexities until it grows as a swelling wave. [. . .] Following it into being came its dark twin, its Adversary, the shadow which ceaselessly devours it from within. Pitilessly pursued, attacked in every vital, the living wave foams upward, its billion momentary crests blooming into the light above the pain and death that claims them. Over uncounted aeons the mortal substance strives, outreaches. Death-driven, it flees ever more swiftly before its Enemy until it runs, leaps, soars into flashing flight. [. . .] But it bears its Enemy within it, for Death is the power of its uprush.
— James Tiptree, Jr., "She Waits for All Men Born" (1976)

Why should I want to make anything up? Life's bad enough as it is without wanting to invent any more of it.
— Douglas Adams, "Fit the Fifth," episode of *The Hitch-Hiker's Guide to the Galaxy* (radio series, 1978)

She had to face life. Even if all life had to show her was a locked door, and behind the locked door, no room.
— Ursula K. Le Guin, "The Eye of the Heron" (1978)

There are so many things we can't do, any of us, for whatever the reasons — time, talent, life's callous whims. We're all on a one-way trip into infinity.
— Joan D. Vinge, "View from a Height" (1978)

"Life," said Marvin dolefully, "loathe it or ignore it, you can't like it."
— Douglas Adams, *The Hitchhiker's Guide to the Galaxy* (1979)

Life is wasted on the living.
— Douglas Adams, "Fit the Ninth," episode of *The Hitch-Hiker's Guide to the Galaxy* (radio series, 1980)

One definition of life, albeit not a particularly useful one, might run something like this: "Life is that property which a being will lose as a result of falling out of a cold and mysterious cave thirteen miles above ground level."
—Douglas Adams, "Fit the Tenth," episode of *The Hitch-Hiker's Guide to the Galaxy* (radio series, 1980)

We're all trying to fulfill ourselves, understand ourselves, get in touch with ourselves, face the reality of ourselves, explore ourselves, expand ourselves. Ever since we dispensed with God, we've got nothing but our selves to explain this meaningless horror of life.
—Paddy Chayefsky, *Altered States* (film, 1980)

Most of what matters in our lives takes place in our absence.
—Salman Rushdie, *Midnight's Children* (1980)

Life is just a process of picking up scars and experience.
—Michael Swanwick, "Ginungagap" (1980)

He hadn't realized that life speaks with a voice to you, a voice that brings you answers to the questions you continually ask of it, had never consciously detected it or recognized its tones until it now said something it had never said to him before, which was "yes."
—Douglas Adams, *So Long, and Thanks for All the Fish* (1985)

Nothing gives life more zest than running for your life.
—Robert A. Heinlein, *The Cat Who Walks through Walls* (1985)

If you haven't got a past to fall back on then you haven't got a real life at all.
—George Turner, *Drowning Towers* (1987)

He had learned the sorcery of woven things from his mother, learned of spiders and caterpillars, of nesting birds, of twining snakes, of thread and cloth. And then he had moved beyond that knowledge, to perceive the structure of living things, to recognize that they, too, were patterned, but on some level deeper than the surface, deeper than the human eye could see. Life itself was woven of a multitude of twisting strands, of interlocking pieces, as surely as a tapestry, as surely as a suit of chain mail.
—Phyllis Eisenstein, *The Crystal Palace* (1988)

The culture of the river kingdom had a lot to say about death and what happened afterwards. In fact it had very little to say about life, regarding it as a sort of inconvenient prelude to the main event and something to be hurried through as politely as possible.

—Terry Pratchett, *Pyramids* (1989)

One of the extraordinary things about life is the sort of places it's prepared to put up with living. Anywhere it can get some kind of a grip, whether it's the intoxicating seas of Santraginus V, where the fish never seem to care whatever the heck kind of direction they swim in, the fire storms of Frastra, where, they say, life begins at 40,000 degrees, or just burrowing around in the lower intestine of a rat for the sheer unadulterated hell of it, life will always find a way of hanging on in somewhere.

It will even live in New York, though it's hard to know why.

—Douglas Adams, *Mostly Harmless* (1992)

Sometimes life seems like a kind of game to me.

John shook his head. In games there are rules, but in life the rules keep changing. You could put your bishop out there to mate the other guy's king, and he could lean down and whisper in your bishop's ear, and suddenly it's playing for him, and moving like a rook. And you're fucked.

—Kim Stanley Robinson, *Red Mars* (1992)

All life feeds on destruction and death.

—Paul J. McAuley, "Recording Angel" (1995)

I'm not Chinese. I thrive in interesting times.

—Charles De Lint, *Someplace to Be Flying* (1998)

Here was my life, a mess with a few good things. Now how do I pull out the good things and step away from the mess?

—Rebecca Ore, "Half in Love with Easeful Rock and Roll" (1998)

SHERIDAN: What does the candle represent?
DELENN: Life.
SHERIDAN: Whose life?
DELENN: All life, every life. We're all born as molecules in the hearts of a
    billion stars, molecules that do not understand politics, policies, and

differences. In a billion years we, foolish molecules, forget who we are and where we came from. Desperate acts of ego. We give ourselves names, fight over lines on maps. And pretend our light is better than everyone else's. The flame reminds us of the piece of those stars that live inside us. A spark that tells us: you should know better. The flame also reminds us that life is precious, as each flame is unique. When it goes out, it's gone forever. And there will never be another quite like it. So many candles will go out tonight.

—J. Michael Straczynski, "And All My Dreams, Torn Asunder," episode of *Babylon 5* (1998)

LOGIC

Could it be that there were other things more desirable than cold logic and undefiled brain power?

—Edgar Rice Burroughs, *The Chessmen of Mars* (1922)

I hope we shall conquer. More than that—I am certain we shall conquer. Because Reason must prevail.

—Yevgeny Zamiatin, *We* (1924), translated by Mirra Ginsburg (1972)

What system do men follow if not that of logic?

—A. E. van Vogt, "Vault of the Beast" (1940)

The commonest weakness of our race is our ability to rationalize our most selfish purposes.

—Robert A. Heinlein, *The Star Beast* (1954)

I know the value of the cold light of reason. But I also know the deep shadows that light can cast—the shadows that can blind men to truth.

—Charles Bennett and Hal E. Chester, *Curse of the Demon* (film, 1957)

In a short-term argument it is helpful to have pure reason on your side— even though such an ally could be depended upon to stab you to the heart if you depended upon him too long.

—James Blish, *A Case of Conscience* (1958)

Since human reason isn't capable of understanding everything, it's irrelevant whether or not this explanation makes sense.
　—Stanislaw Lem, *The Investigation* (1959), translated by Adele Milch (1974)

Every time you decide something without having a good reason, you jump to Conclusions whether you like it or not. It's such an easy trip to make that I've been here hundreds of times.
　—Norton Juster, *The Phantom Tollbooth* (1961)

Ape is of course the only rational creature, the only one possessing a mind as well as a body. The most materialistic of our scientists recognize the supernatural essence of the simian mind.
　—Pierre Boulle, *Planet of the Apes* (1963), translated by Xan Fielding (1963)

"Logic" proved that airplanes can't fly and that H-bombs won't work and that stones don't fall out of the sky. Logic is a way of saying that anything which didn't happen yesterday won't happen tomorrow.
　—Robert A. Heinlein, *Glory Road* (1963)

How can you expect one species to follow the logic of another?
　—Philip K. Dick, *The Crack in Space* (1965)

He's a king, and does not see things rationally, but as a king.
　—Ursula K. Le Guin, *The Left Hand of Darkness* (1969)

Here we are entering the philosophical realm of Spinoza when he saw, and I think with great profundity, that if a falling stone could reason, it would think, "I *want* to fall at the rate of thirty-two feet per second per second." Freewill for us—that is, when we feel desire, when we are conscious of wanting to do what we do—may be even for us an illusion.
　—Philip K. Dick, "The Android and the Human" (1972)

For a mind once honestly wedded to reason there is no divorce.
　—Edgar Pangborn, "The Children's Crusade" (1974)

It sounded logical—but I could not forget Kettering's Law: "Logic is an organized way of going wrong with confidence."
　—Robert A. Heinlein, *The Number of the Beast* (1980)

Assumptions are the things you don't know you're making.
   —Douglas Adams, *Last Chance to See* (1990)

Descartes' immortal conclusion *cogito ergo sum* was recently subjected to destruction testing by a group of graduate researchers at Princeton led by Professors Montjuic and Lauterbrunnen, and now reads, in the revised version to be found in the *Shorter Harvard Orthodoxy:*

(a) I think, therefore I am; or
(b) Perhaps I thought, therefore I was; but
(c) These days, I tend to leave all that side of things to my wife.
   —Tom Holt, *Ye Gods!* (1992)

Logic is the beginning of wisdom, Valeris, not the end.
   —Nicholas Meyer and Denny Martin Flinn, *Star Trek VI: The Undiscovered Country* (film, 1992)

Logic is a wonderful thing but doesn't always beat actual thought.
   —Terry Pratchett, *The Last Continent* (1998)

LONELINESS AND SOLITUDE

PETER: No one must ever touch me.
WENDY: Why?
PETER: I don't know.
   —J. M. Barrie, *Peter Pan* (play, 1904)

No human soul should be denied the privilege of solitude, for only in solitude can the mind resolve its intake with its wealth.
   —Theodore Sturgeon, "The Perfect Host" (1948)

He felt as though he were wandering in the forests of the sea bottom, lost in a monstrous world where he himself was the monster. He was alone. The past was dead, the future was unimaginable.
   —George Orwell, *Nineteen Eighty-Four* (1949)

He felt the cold silence between worlds, the thrust of rocketships, the harsh, glamorous loneliness.
  —Raymond Z. Gallun, "Prodigal's Aura" (1951)

You live in your world, I live in my world, a hundred people, a hundred worlds.
  —Theodore Sturgeon, "The Clinic" (1953)

There is in certain living souls
A quality of loneliness unspeakable,
So great it must be shared
As company is shared by lesser beings.
Such a loneliness is mine; so know by this
That in immensity,
There is one lonelier than you.
  —Theodore Sturgeon, "Saucer of Loneliness" (1953)

It was as if a light came from her, more light and far less shadow than ever the practical moon could cast. Among the many things it meant was that even to loneliness there is an end, for those who are lonely enough, long enough.
  —Theodore Sturgeon, "Saucer of Loneliness" (1953)

There are times when you must walk by yourself because it hurts so much to be alone.
  —Samuel R. Delany, "Aye, and Gomorrah" (1967)

Eternity is a terrible place to endure alone.
  —Stephen Goldin, "The Last Ghost" (1971)

The distances between the stars seem brief by contrast to the distances between each of us and his fellows.
  —Thomas M. Disch, "Things Lost" (1972)

Privacy is as necessary as company; you can drive a man crazy by depriving him of either.
  —Robert A. Heinlein, *Time Enough for Love* (1973)

Without loneliness and strangeness this world would not be this world at all and maybe not worth having.
—Edgar Pangborn, "The Children's Crusade" (1974)

My loneliness was a cancer—a growth that I fed with hate: hate for the planet with its endless cold, endless winds, and endless isolation; hate for the helpless yellow child with its clawing need for care, food, and an affection that I couldn't give; and hate for myself.
—Barry B. Longyear, "Enemy Mine" (1979)

The loneliness became an awful panic, a soundless inner groping for some-one/something/somewhere she could grasp and hold, but her fingers always locked on empty air.
—Alan Brennert, "Queen of the Magic Kingdom" (1980)

Nor did Lawson miss him terribly. He had grown accustomed to the strange richness of his own company.
—Michael Bishop, "The Quickening" (1981)

Even for the most self-sufficient of men, being isolated from the flow of humanity must be the worst form of torture!
—Stephen King, "The Man Who Would Not Shake Hands" (1981)

For the first time I was in the presence of someone who had nothing—even less than the beggars of Rio, for they at least were linked to the material world by their longings for it. Scranton embodied the absolute loneliness of the human being in space and time, a situation which in many ways I shared.
—J. G. Ballard, "The Man Who Walked on the Moon" (1985)

How solitary we are, Verdit thought, each one of us with our layered histories floating in the sea of time.
—Joan Slonczewski, *Daughter of Elysium* (1993)

It's easier to desire and pursue the attention of tens of millions of total strangers than it is to accept the love and loyalty of the people closest to us.
—William Gibson, *Idoru* (1996)

LOVE AND ROMANCE

A man's way with women is in inverse ratio to his prowess among men. The weakling and the saphead have often great ability to charm the fair sex, while the fighting man who can face a thousand real dangers unafraid, sits hiding in the shadows like some frightened child.
— Edgar Rice Burroughs, *A Princess of Mars* (1917)

You love it because you cannot subdue it to your will. Only the unsubduable can be loved.
— Yevgeny Zamiatin, *We* (1924), translated by Mirra Ginsburg (1972)

"Love? What is that?"
"It's tomorrow and yesterday. It's hoping and happiness and pain, the complete self because it's selfless, the chain that binds you to life and makes living it worth while."
— Leigh Brackett, "The Vanishing Venusians" (1945)

Love can make man a beast. Love can beautify ugliness.
— Jean Cocteau, *Beauty and the Beast* (film, 1946), translated by
    Francis Howard (1946)

The Klantheid was not built to dislike, or indeed to do anything but love. Love was the deep-rooted instinct of its nature, the inner strength and meaning of its existence. Deeply, passionately, it longed to love, not merely the man and the woman, but all things, all humans, all life forms, all planets, all suns, all universes, all time and space.
— Gordon R. Dickson, "The Three" (1953)

Love and hate are so confused in your savage minds and the vibrations of the one are so very like those of the other that I can't always distinguish. You see, we neither love nor hate in my world. We simply have hobbies.
— Gore Vidal, *Visit to a Small Planet* (TV play, 1955)

The new worlds were austere, carefully planned, sterile in their perfections. Something had been lost in the dead reaches of space, and only Earth knew love.
— Robert Sheckley, "Love, Incorporated" (1956)

Leading psychologists say that *real* love is a fortifier and a restorer of sanity, a balm for damaged egos, a restorer of hormone balance, and an improver of the complexion.
— Robert Sheckley, "Love, Incorporated" (1956)

What is "love"? [. . .] I'll give an exact definition. "Love" is that condition in which the happiness of another person is essential to your own.
— Robert A. Heinlein, *Stranger in a Strange Land* (1961)

Love is not, as some poets say, a raging brush fire, but a hearthfire, which burns hotly, it is true, but in order to warm the cold sea-caves of the heart and light its pools with anemones of radiance.
— Thomas Burnett Swann, *Day of the Minotaur* (1966)

Love and joy are incredibly habitforming; often a single exposure is enough to cause permanent addiction.
— John Brunner, *Stand on Zanzibar* (1968)

Love doesn't just sit there, like a stone; it has to be made, like bread; re-made all the time, made new.
— Ursula K. Le Guin, *The Lathe of Heaven* (1971)

"A single human brain can perceive pattern on the scale of stars and galaxies," Tomiko said, "and interpret it as Love."
— Ursula K. Le Guin, "Vaster Than Empires and More Slow" (1971)

In this love he now felt there was compassion: without which love is untempered, and is not whole, and does not last.
— Ursula K. Le Guin, *The Farthest Shore* (1972)

Divine love is at worst an illusion, at best a dream for some imaginary future time. Human love is here and now.
— Edgar Pangborn, "The Children's Crusade" (1974)

I will go into the world and find my way, I will not die by my own hand, I will regret no act of love. [. . .] Any manner of love is good if there's kindness in it.
— Edgar Pangborn, "The Night Wind" (1974)

"Did you love him? Was he your lover?" [. . .]
  "There's not exactly the same thing, but, yes to both."
  —Tom Reamy, "San Diego Lightfoot Sue" (1975)

When love cannot possess, it is content to serve.
  —Spider Robinson, "Soul Search" (1979)

Hate is an attracting force, just like love.
  —Terry Pratchett, *The Colour of Magic* (1983)

He never saw Molly again.
  —William Gibson, *Neuromancer* (1984)

Nobody dies from lack of sex. It's lack of love we die from.
  —Margaret Atwood, *The Handmaid's Tale* (1986)

The more difficult it was to love the particular man beside us, the more we
believed in Love, abstract and total. We were waiting, always, for the incarna-
tion. That word, made flesh.
  —Margaret Atwood, *The Handmaid's Tale* (1986)

Love was always a word that covered too much territory, from loving a spouse
to loving a hobby or abstract justice, and the emotion-mongers of popular
entertainment portrayed it as everlasting and exclusive. In a culture under
stress the truth could not be concealed by sentimental fluff. The Greenhouse
people learned to appreciate love without glorifying it.
  —George Turner, *Drowning Towers* (1987)

Among all men—those who value beauty, money, success, prestige—those
of us who value love are the most dangerous of all. More than any others, we
will compromise morals, ethics, our lives, and the lives of those around us—
all for the sake of love.
  —Tara K. Harper, *Grayheart* (1996)

Love isn't something that one throws off like an old hat. Love clings to the
soul like cockleburs to the hair.
  —Richard A. Bamberg, "Love's Last Farewell" (1998)

Falling in love is like inscribing a map on one's vision. There's just the map, and everything that isn't on it is meaningless.

—L. Timmel Duchamp, "Dance at the Edge" (1998)

That was the first thing I had to learn about her, and maybe the hardest I've ever learned about anything—that she is her own, and what she gives me is of her choosing, and the more precious because of it. Sometimes a butterfly will come to sit in your open palm, but if you close your hand, one way or the other, it—and its choice to be there—are gone.

—Barbara Hambly, *Dragonsbane* (1999)

Just as men and women sometimes lie when they say they love and will return, so they sometimes lie also when they believe they will not.

—Tanith Lee, "Rapunzel" (2000)

Love isn't a cage, or if it is, a pretty one, with the door undone, and the birds out and sitting on the roof.

—Tanith Lee, "Rapunzel" (2000)

If I love no one I am free. So long as I love no one, I can travel where I wish. I can become anyone I wish.

—Joyce Carol Oates, "You, Little Match Girl" (2000)

She had hated being so transparent, hated that everyone could see. Love had snuck into her heart and lightened it, made it clear, easy to see through.

—Nalo Hopkinson, "Under Glass" (2001)

MACHINES AND TECHNOLOGY

INVENTOR, n. A person who makes an ingenious arrangement of wheels, levers and springs, and believes it civilization.
— Ambrose Bierce, *The Devil's Dictionary* (1906)

Why should you sweat yourselves to death to benefit the Lord of Metropolis?
  Who keeps the machines going?
  Who are the slaves of the machines?
  Let the machines stop.
  Destroy the machines.
— Fritz Lang and Thea von Harbou, *Metropolis* (film, 1926), translator unknown (1926)

Can you appreciate the crushing hopelessness it brought to me? I, who love science, who see in it, or have seen in it, the salvation, the raising of mankind — to see those wondrous machines, of man's triumphant maturity, forgotten and misunderstood. The wondrous, perfect machines that tended, protected, and cared for those gentle, kindly people who had — forgotten.
— John W. Campbell, Jr., "Twilight" (1934)

There's an affinity between men and the machines they make. They make them out of their own brains, really, a sort of mental conception and gestation, and the result responds to the mind that created them, and to all human minds that understand and manipulate them.
— C. L. Moore, "No Woman Born" (1944)

Too darned good a machine can be a menace, not a help.
— John W. Campbell, Jr., introduction to *Cloak of Aesir* (1951)

The machinery of civilization was a living body, with organismic Man as its brain.
— Walter M. Miller, Jr., "Way of a Rebel" (1954)

A man could change his politics, his friends, his religion, his country, but Men's tools were a part of his body. Having used a high-powered rifle, the man subsumed the weapon, made it a part of himself. Trading it for a stone axe would be like cutting off his arm. Man was a user of tools, a shaper of environments.

—Walter M. Miller, Jr., "Way of a Rebel" (1954)

When your life has depended for a long while upon machines—upon tubes and wires and gadgets of all kinds—you must come to trust these things as a part of yourself.

—Michael Shaara, "The Holes" (1954)

You can see from this that the world started going to pot right from the beginning. Things would be going along fine—law and order and all that and the elders in charge—and then, some smart aleck would invent something and spoil the whole business.

—John Steinbeck, "The Short-Short Story of Mankind" (1958)

The machines didn't tire and the medi-techs never made computational errors but both lacked an essential something. Something only one human being, no matter how inadequate, could give to another.

—Leo P. Kelley, "The Handyman" (1965)

We've been slaves to our tools since the first caveman made the first knife to help him get his supper. After that there was no going back, and we built till our machines were ten million times more powerful than ourselves. We gave ourselves cars when we might have learned to run; we made airplanes when we might have grown wings; and then the inevitable. We made a machine our God.

—John Brunner, "Judas" (1967)

These machines had become old and worn-out, had begun making mistakes; therefore they began to seem almost human.

—Philip K. Dick and Ray Nelson, *The Ganymede Takeover* (1967)

Only a free society, he thought, *can produce the technology that makes tyranny possible . . .*

—Keith Laumer, "Test to Destruction" (1967)

Machines and Technology

First you use machines, then you wear machines, and then . . .?

Then you serve machines. It was obvious. It followed so logically it was almost comforting.

— John Brunner, *Stand on Zanzibar* (1968)

"One of these days," Joe said wrathfully, "people like me will rise up and overthrow you, and the end of tyranny by the homeostatic machine will have arrived. The day of human values and compassion and simple warmth will return, and when that happens someone like myself who has gone through an ordeal and who genuinely needs hot coffee to pick him up and keep him functioning when he has to function will get the hot coffee whether he happens to have a poscred readily available or not."

— Philip K. Dick, *Ubik* (1969)

Man has reached the stage where he evolves through his machines.

— Gene Wolfe, "Alien Stones" (1972)

There was no easy way to heaven, or nirvana, or whatever it was that the faithful sought. Merit was acquired solely by one's own efforts, not with the aid of machines. An interesting doctrine, and one containing much truth; but there were also times when only machines could do the job.

— Arthur C. Clarke, *The Fountains of Paradise* (1979)

So the five appliances lived and worked, happy and fulfilled, serving their dear mistress and enjoying each other's companionship, to the end of their days.

— Thomas M. Disch, "The Brave Little Toaster" (1980)

He also saw a certain sense in the notion that burgeoning technologies require outlaw zones, that Night City wasn't there for its inhabitants, but as a deliberately unsupervised playground for technology itself.

— William Gibson, *Neuromancer* (1984)

Most people who sneer at technology would starve to death if the engineering infrastructure were removed.

— Robert A. Heinlein, *Job: A Comedy of Justice* (1984)

The Hitchhiker's Guide to the Galaxy, in a moment of reasoned lucidity which is almost unique among its current tally of five million, nine hundred and

seventy-three thousand, five hundred and nine pages, says of the Sirius Cybernetics Corporation products that [. . .] "*Their fundamental design flaws are completely hidden by their superficial design flaws.*"
— Douglas Adams, *So Long, and Thanks for All the Fish* (1985)

You know what your trouble is? [. . .] You're the kind who *always reads the handbook.* Anything people build, any kind of technology, it's going to have some specific purpose. It's for doing something that somebody already understands. But if it's new technology, it'll open areas nobody's ever thought of before. You read the manual, man, and you won't play around with it, not the same way. And you get all funny when somebody else uses it to do something you never thought of.
— William Gibson, "The Winter Market" (1985)

Out of order? *Fuck!* Even in the future, nothing works!
— Mel Brooks, Thomas Meehan, and Ronny Graham, *Spaceballs* (film, 1987)

The truck seemed so easy to drive, it had so much power, that you sometimes forgot how dangerous one slip might be. One of the drawbacks to advanced technology, and to evolution. It made you reckless; it became too easy to lose control over the power.
— Steve Rasnic Tem, "Dinosaur" (1987)

The late twentieth century, and the early years of our own millennium, form, in retrospect, a single era. This was the Age of the Normal Accident, in which people cheerfully accepted technological risks that today would seem quite insane.
— Bruce Sterling, "Our Neural Chernobyl" (1988)

"It is a concatenation of synergistic interactions; the whole system is on the period-doubling route to Chaos!"
"What does that mean, pray?"
"Essentially," Mallory said, smiling behind his kerchief, "in layman's terms, it means that everything gets twice as bad, twice as fast, until everything falls completely apart!"
— William Gibson and Bruce Sterling, *The Difference Engine* (1991)

Machines and Technology

The major difference between a thing that might go wrong and a thing that cannot possibly go wrong is that when a thing that cannot possibly go wrong goes wrong it usually turns out to be impossible to get at or repair.
— Douglas Adams, *Mostly Harmless* (1992)

Somewhere in its history, every technological species will make the tools to become godlike. Immortal citizens will be capable of building worlds, or obliterating them. How a species responds to the challenge . . . well, that's what determines its fate, more often than not.
— Robert Reed, "Sister Alice" (1993)

He had to get off the ship, away from the manufactured things of man, and find a contact with his soul.
— P. J. Beese, "White Wings" (1995)

We have never developed a sinister view of technology, Mr. Laney. It is an aspect of the natural, of oneness.
— William Gibson, *Idoru* (1996)

Everything happens twice, first as theology, then as technology.
— Howard V. Hendrix, "The Body Apocalyptic: Theology and Technology in Films and Fictions of the MIME Era" (2002)

MADNESS AND SANITY

Men have called me mad; but the question is not yet settled, whether madness is or is not the loftiest intelligence — whether much that is glorious — whether all that is profound — does not spring from disease of thought — from *moods* of mind exalted at the expense of the general intellect.
— Edgar Allan Poe, "Eleanora" (1841)

Everyone must lose his mind, everyone must! The sooner the better! It is essential.
— Yevgeny Zamiatin, *We* (1924), translated by Mirra Ginsburg (1972)

The whole world is mad just now, and if you want help you must come to a madman to get it.
— Hamilton Deane and John L. Balderston, *Dracula* (play, 1927)

It is the normal lot of people who must live this life [in space] to be—by terrestrial standards—insane. Insanity under such conditions is a useful and logical defense mechanism, an invaluable and salutary retreat from reality.
    —Charles L. Harness, *The Paradox Men* (1949)

In an asylum, the only lunatic is the psychologist.
    —Charles L. Harness, *The Paradox Men* (1949)

I rather pride myself on the way I manage hysteria.
    —Doris Pitkin Buck, "Two-Bit Oracle" (1954)

The mind was a tricky mechanism after all—it could break down when you least expected it.
    —Richard Matheson, "The Curious Child" (1954)

He saw Eternity with great clarity as a sink of deepening psychoses, a writhing pit of abnormal motivation, a mass of desperate lives torn brutally out of context.
    —Isaac Asimov, *The End of Eternity* (1955)

Insanity, gentlemen, is not a catchall for every human action that involves motives we don't understand. Insanity has its own structure, its own internal logic.
    —Stanislaw Lem, *The Investigation* (1959), translated by Adele Milch
      (1974)

His own withdrawal was symptomatic not of a dormant schizophrenia, but of a careful preparation for a radically new environment, with its own internal landscape and logic, where old categories of thought would merely be an encumbrance.
    —J. G. Ballard, *The Drowned World* (1962)

Perhaps if you know you are insane then you are not insane. Or you are becoming sane, finally.
    —Philip K. Dick, *The Man in the High Castle* (1962)

There's nothing more potentially explosive than a society in which psychotics dominate, define the values, control the means of communication.
    —Philip K. Dick, *Clans of the Alphane Moon* (1964)

Merely knowing that you are mentally sick won't make you well, any more than knowing you have a heart condition provides a suddenly sound heart.
  —Philip K. Dick, *Clans of the Alphane Moon* (1964)

People talk about mental illness as an escape! He shuddered. It was no escape; it was a narrowing, a contracting of life into, at last, a moldering, dank tomb, a place where nothing came or went; a place of total death.
  —Philip K. Dick, *Martian Time-Slip* (1964)

If you can keep your head whilst all around are losing theirs, maybe you haven't grasped the true facts of the event.
  —John T. Phillifent, "Flying Fish" (1964)

There was a madness to it all, but perhaps it was a divine madness. And is not that madness that which sustains man in his terrible self-knowledge, the driving madness which demands reason of a casual universe, the awful aloneness which seeks among the stars for companionship.
  —James Gunn, "The Listeners" (1968)

Crazy—a nonscientific term meaning that the person to whom one applies that label has a world picture differing from the accepted one.
  —Robert A. Heinlein, *Time Enough for Love* (1973)

What we call psychosis is sometimes simply realism.
  —Ursula K. Le Guin, "The Diary of the Rose" (1976)

If I were a madwoman, then everything would end well. From insanity, as from a dream, one could free oneself—in both cases there was hope.
  —Stanislaw Lem, "The Mask" (1976), translated by Michael Kandel (1977)

Would it save you all this bother if I just gave up and went mad now?
  —Douglas Adams, "Fit the Third," episode of *The Hitch-Hiker's Guide to the Galaxy* (radio series, 1978)

The asylum is the haven of mental health—the place of cure, where the anxious gain peace, where the weak gain strength, where the prisoners of inadequate reality assessment win their way to freedom!
  —Ursula K. Le Guin, "SQ" (1978)

The mad are sane!
   —Nigel Kneale, *Quatermass* (TV miniseries, 1979)

[On humans:] Yes, they are mad. But there is splendor in such madness.
   —John Morressy, "The Empath and the Savages" (1979)

One of the first symptoms of psychosis is that the person feels perhaps he is becoming psychotic. It is another Chinese fingertrap. You cannot think about it without becoming part of it.
   —Philip K. Dick, *Valis* (1981)

1) Those who agree with you are insane.
2) Those who do not agree with you are in power.
   —Philip K. Dick, *Valis* (1981)

Not like Armitage's madness, which he now imagined he could understand; twist a man far enough, then twist him as far back, in the opposite direction, reverse and twist again. The man broke. Like breaking a length of wire.
   —William Gibson, *Neuromancer* (1984)

The basis of psychosis, in a nutshell, is the chronic inability to see the easy way out. All the behavior, all that constitutes psychotic activity and the psychotic lifestyle, stems from this perceptual flaw.
   —Philip K. Dick, "Strange Memories of Death" (1985)

Maybe we all secretly will everything that happens to us. In that case, does the psychotic person will his own ultimate kinetic death, his own dead end path? Does he play to lose?
   —Philip K. Dick, "Strange Memories of Death" (1985)

Sanity is a valuable possession; I hoard it the way people once hoarded money. I save it, so I will have enough, when the time comes.
   —Margaret Atwood, *The Handmaid's Tale* (1986)

The Deftmenes are mad and the Dumii are sane, thought Snibril, and that's just the same as being mad except that it's quieter.
   —Terry Pratchett, *The Carpet People,* revised (1992)

Believing oneself to be perfect is often the sign of a delusional mind.
　—Brannon Braga and Ronald D. Moore, *Star Trek: First Contact*
　(film, 1996)

MARRIAGE

I demand a creature of another sex, but as hideous as myself: the gratification is small, but it is all that I can receive, and it shall content me. It is true, we shall be monsters, cut off from all the world; but on that account we shall be more attached to one another. Our lives will not be happy, but they will be harmless, and free from the misery I now feel.
　—Mary Shelley, *Frankenstein, or, The Modern Prometheus* (1818)

Women were more than any other class the victims of your civilization. There is something which, even at this distance of time, penetrates one with pathos in the spectacle of their ennuied, undeveloped lives, stunted at marriage, their narrow horizon, bounded so often, physically, by the four walls of home, and morally by a petty circle of personal interests.
　—Edward Bellamy, *Looking Backward, 2000–1887* (1888)

Marriage made people old and familiar, while still young.
　—Ray Bradbury, "Ylla" (1950)

"Drink your coffee," she said, grotesquely wifelike. "You won't get any coffee on Mars, you know."
　—Judith Merril, "So Proudly We Hail" (1953)

Marriage is like alchemy. It served an important purpose once, but I hardly feel it's here to stay.
　—Roger Zelazny, "He Who Shapes" (1965)

Every so often some idiot tries to abolish marriage. Such attempts work as well as repealing the law of gravity, making pi equal to three point zero, or moving mountains by prayer. Marriage is not something thought up by priests and inflicted on mankind; marriage is as much a part of mankind's evolutionary equipment as his eyes, and as useful to the race as eyes are to an individual.
　—Robert A. Heinlein, *Time Enough for Love* (1973)

I read the Bible for my own reasons but it never occurred to me that Jacob would. We always marry strangers.
  —Robert A. Heinlein, *The Number of the Beast* (1980)

Marriage can sometimes stand up against twin beds but almost never against twin addresses.
  —Robert A. Heinlein, *The Cat Who Walks through Walls* (1985)

Two husbands had been wonderful. Three had been even more wonderful. Five had been a bit more than she'd bargained for, and she'd determined she would take no more husbands. But then she'd had to decide on Stefet—and his eyes were the blue of an autumn sky, and his hair was the russet of a prize stag.
  Thus she came to discover that six husbands were entirely too many.
  —Holly Lisle, "A Few Good Men" (1995)

"What was it like, being dead?" [. . .]
  "It was wonderful," she said without hesitation.
  He got that hurt little boy look she had found so appealing in the early stages of their relationship, but which now made her want to puke.
  "You mean you'd rather be dead than be with me?"
  —James Stevens-Arce, "Scenes from a Future Marriage" (1995)

Sam Vimes could parallel process. Most husbands can. They learn to follow their own line of thought while *at the same time* listening to what their wives say. And the listening is important, because at any time they could be challenged and must be ready to quote the last sentence in full. A vital additional skill is being able to scan the dialogue for telltale phrases such as "and they can deliver it tomorrow" or "so I've invited them for dinner" or "they can do it in blue, really quite cheaply."
  —Terry Pratchett, *The Fifth Elephant* (1999)

A marriage is always made up of two people who are prepared to swear that only the *other* one snores.
  —Terry Pratchett, *The Fifth Elephant* (1999)

MATHEMATICS

The function of man's highest faculty, his reason, consists precisely of the continuous limitation of infinity, the breaking up of infinity into convenient, easily digestible portions—differentials. This is precisely what lends my field, mathematics, its divine beauty.
  —Yevgeny Zamiatin, *We* (1924), translated by Mirra Ginsburg (1972)

Neither mathematics nor death ever makes a mistake.
  —Yevgeny Zamiatin, *We* (1924), translated by Mirra Ginsburg (1972)

Figures are sharp things, Jones. Don't juggle them, you'll get cut.
  —Robert A. Heinlein, *Starman Jones* (1953)

He was well on the way to inventing differential calculus when his mother called him down to breakfast.
  —Poul Anderson, *Brain Wave* (1954)

"If you had high hopes, how would you know how high they were? And did you know that narrow escapes come in all different widths? Would you travel the whole wide world without ever knowing how wide it was? And how could you do anything at long last," he concluded, waving his arms over his head, "without knowing how long the last was? Why, numbers are the most beautiful and valuable things in the world."
  —Norton Juster, *The Phantom Tollbooth* (1961)

If everything, *everything* were known, statistical estimates would be unnecessary. The science of probability gives mathematical expression to our ignorance, not to our wisdom.
  —Samuel R. Delany, "Time Considered as a Helix of Semi-Precious Stones" (1969)

Anyone who cannot cope with mathematics is not fully human. At best he is a tolerable subhuman who has learned to wear shoes, bathe, and not make messes in the house.
  —Robert A. Heinlein, *Time Enough for Love* (1973)

If a book were written all in numbers, it would be true. It would be just. Nothing said in words ever came out quite even. Things in words got twisted and ran together, instead of staying straight and fitting together. But underneath the words, at the center, like the center of the Square, it all came out even. Everything could change, yet nothing would be lost. If you saw the numbers you could see that, the balance, the pattern. You saw the foundations of the world. And they were solid.

— Ursula K. Le Guin, *The Dispossessed: An Ambiguous Utopia* (1974)

There were vast areas of the Midwest intricately geometrized with squares, rectangles, and circles by those with agricultural or urban predilections; and, as here, vast areas of the Southwest in which the only sign of intelligent life was an occasional straight line heading between mountains and across deserts. Are the worlds of more advanced civilizations totally geometrized, entirely rebuilt by their inhabitants? Or would the signature of a *really* advanced civilization be that they left no sign at all?

— Carl Sagan, *Contact* (1985)

Magicians have calculated that million-to-one chances crop up nine times out of ten.

— Terry Pratchett, *Mort* (1987)

If we envision the entire System of Mathematics as a great Engine for proving theorems, then we must say, through the agency of the Modus, that such an Engine *lives,* and could indeed *prove* its own life, should it develop the capacity to look upon itself.

— William Gibson and Bruce Sterling, *The Difference Engine* (1991)

MEDIA

Whom the gods would destroy, they first give TV.

— Arthur C. Clarke, "Voices from the Sky" (1959)

The Fenshawes were conventional people who lifted their convictions and opinions from the pages of the *Daily Chronicle.*

— Stanislaw Lem, *The Investigation* (1959), translated by Adele Milch (1974)

"Remind me," Jubal told her, "to write an article on the compulsive reading of news. The theme will be that most neuroses can be traced to the unhealthy habit of wallowing in the troubles of five billion strangers."
—Robert A. Heinlein, *Stranger in a Strange Land* (1961)

There is nothing wrong with your television set. Do not attempt to adjust the picture. We are controlling transmission. We will control the horizontal, we will control the vertical. We can change the focus to a soft blur, or sharpen it to crystal clarity. For the next hour, sit quietly and we will control all that you see and hear. You are about to participate in a great adventure. You are about to experience the awe and mystery which reaches from the inner mind to . . . *The Outer Limits.*
—Leslie Stevens, opening narration, *The Outer Limits* (TV series, 1963)

KNBS was running an in-depth report on the rape of Carroll, California.
"My God," the man on Randall's left hoarsely whispered. "How can they show pictures like that?"
Inside Randall a delayed explosion found release. [. . .]
"Because you bastards watch them!" he screamed.
—Edward Bryant, "The 10:00 Report Is Brought to You By . . ." (1972)

The sky above the port was the color of television, tuned to a dead channel.
—William Gibson, *Neuromancer* (1984)

The sky above the Skye household was the color of a TV tuned to *The Brady Bunch.*
—Paul Di Filippo, "Earth Shoes" (1997)

We were the people who were not in the papers. We lived in the blank white spaces at the edges of print. It gave us more freedom.
We lived in the gaps between the stories.
—Margaret Atwood, *The Handmaid's Tale* (1986)

First you see video. Then you wear video. Then you eat video. Then you *be* video.
—Pat Cadigan, "Pretty Boy Crossover" (1986)

These people figure video was the Lord's preferred means of communicating, the screen itself a kind of perpetually burning bush.
—William Gibson, *Virtual Light* (1993)

It's been revealed to Reverend Fallon that virtual reality's a medium of Satan, cause you don't watch enough TV after you start doing it . . .
—William Gibson, *Virtual Light* (1993)

Time in a Federal Orphanage had a way of acquainting you with dead media platforms.
—William Gibson, *Idoru* (1996)

What is it with reporters? You take one person's tragedy and force the world to experience it. You spread it like sickness.
—Ehren Kruger, *The Ring* (film, 2002)

MEDICINE AND DISEASE

In this country if a man falls into ill health, or catches any disorder, or fails bodily in any way before he is seventy years old, he is tried before a jury of his countrymen, and if convicted is held up to public scorn and sentenced more or less severely as the case may be.
—Samuel Butler, *Erewhon, or, Over the Range* (1872)

A true physician begins his cure with a healthy man.
—Yevgeny Zamiatin, *We* (1924), translated by Mirra Ginsburg (1972)

Nurses run a hospital as if it were a nursery for backward children.
—Robert A. Heinlein, *The Puppet Masters* (1951)

Earth had become Hospital Earth, physician to a Galaxy, surgeon to a thousand worlds, midwife to those susceptible to midwifery and psychiatrist to those whose inner lives zigged when their outer lives zagged.
—Alan E. Nourse, "Contamination Crew" (1958)

Jails and hospitals have one thing in common: they can be very hard to get out of.
—Robert A. Heinlein, *Stranger in a Strange Land* (1961)

I myself went into a hospital and came out French.
    —Cordwainer Smith, "Alpha Ralpha Boulevard" (1961)

What can an old man do in a cold room without drugs in a winter that does not seem to end? Die, that was all, so he had died.
    —Harry Harrison, "Roommates" (1971)

Everyone is sick on Pergamon, it's the law.
    —Josephine Saxton, "Elouise and the Doctors of the Planet Pergamon"
      (1972)

My brief stay at the hospital had already convinced me that the medical profession was an open door to anyone nursing a grudge against the human race.
    —J. G. Ballard, *Crash* (1973)

Most young Anarresti felt that it was shameful to be ill. [. . .] They felt illness to be a crime, if an involuntary one. To yield to the criminal impulse, to pander to it by taking pain relievers, was immoral.
    —Ursula K. Le Guin, *The Dispossessed: An Ambiguous Utopia* (1974)

The government must look after him and restore him to health, because health is the inalienable right of the citizens of a democracy.
    —Ursula K. Le Guin, "The New Atlantis" (1975)

I've tolerated doctors as individuals; as a class they terrify me.
    —Edward Bryant, "Particle Theory" (1977)

All medical men are voyeurs. Why else would they become doctors?
    —Joan D. Vinge, *The Snow Queen* (1980)

Sickness and healing are in every heart. Death and deliverance are in every hand.
    —Orson Scott Card, *Speaker for the Dead* (1986)

In order to cure you must first understand.
    —Alex Garland, *28 Days Later* (film, 2002)

It's a poor sort of memory that only works backwards.
  —Lewis Carroll, *Through the Looking Glass and What Alice Found There*
    (1872)

He awoke, with the sensation of spinning up from an abyss. Little thoughts
came back, added to themselves, and presently chained themselves together
to perform that miracle called memory.
  —Ross Rocklynne, "At the Center of Gravity" (1936)

Memory is not a passive filing cabinet, but a continuous process beneath the
level of consciousness; in a way, you are always reliving your entire past.
  —Poul Anderson, "Journeys End" (1957)

We live in now. Memory isn't real. The past doesn't exist. Why should we feel
anything about the past, or care about it?
  —Katherine MacLean, "The Missing Man" (1971)

She felt the vengeful animals of memories trying to hold her back.
  —Vonda N. McIntyre, "The Genius Freaks" (1973)

Memory was only a matter of habit, of training, of handy mnemonic phrases
which easily triggered vital information.
  —Anne McCaffrey, "Prelude to a Crystal Song" (1974)

I'd never spent much time in Nighttown. Nobody there had anything to pay
me to remember, and most of them had a lot they paid regularly to forget.
  —William Gibson, "Johnny Mnemonic" (1981)

My own past had gone down years before, lost with all hands, no trace. I
understood Fox's late-night habit of emptying his wallet, shuffling through
his identification. He'd lay the pieces out in different patterns, rearrange
them, wait for a picture to form. I knew what he was looking for. You did the
same thing with your childhoods.
  In New Rose, tonight, I choose from your deck of pasts.
  —William Gibson, "New Rose Hotel" (1984)

When we think of the past it's the beautiful things we pick out. We want to believe it was all like that.
— Margaret Atwood, *The Handmaid's Tale* (1986)

One side effect of an overzealous memory was a restless need to escape.
— Sheila Finch, "Reichs-Peace" (1986)

Some things you teach yourself to remember to forget.
— William Gibson, *Count Zero* (1986)

Professor Urban Chronotis [. . .] had a memory that he himself had once compared to the Queen Alexandra Birdwing Butterfly, in that it was colorful, flitted prettily hither and thither, and was now, alas, almost completely extinct.
— Douglas Adams, *Dirk Gently's Holistic Detective Agency* (1987)

The sheer weight of memory reached some critical mass. [. . .] The burden and bulk of all those minute sensations over days and years and decades, triggering chemical changes in the brain which in turn trigger cellular changes, until the body cannot bear any more and breakdown accelerates. The cut-off point. It is our memories that kill us.
— Nancy Kress, "In Memoriam" (1988)

Their voices brought up memories like nets filled with coelacanths.
— Kim Stanley Robinson, *Red Mars* (1992)

Suddenly he was afraid; they *were* their pasts, they had to be or they were nothing at all, and whatever they felt or thought or said in the present was nothing more than an echo of the past.
— Kim Stanley Robinson, *Red Mars* (1992)

The hippo of recollection stirred in the muddy waters of the mind.
— Terry Pratchett, *Soul Music* (1994)

We live forever, we transform ourselves, we transform worlds, solar systems, we ship across interstellar space, we defy time and deny death, but the one thing we cannot recreate is memory, he thought.
— Ian MacDonald, "The Days of Solomon Gursky" (1998)

Money itself was a form of slavery.
  —James Blish, *A Case of Conscience* (1958)

These pretty pictures and bright medallions were not "money"; they were symbols for an idea which spread through these people, all through their world. But *things* were not money, any more than water shared was growing-closer. Money was an *idea,* as abstract as an Old One's thoughts—money was a great structured symbol for balancing and healing and growing closer.
  Mike was dazzled with the magnificent beauty of money.
  —Robert A. Heinlein, *Stranger in a Strange Land* (1961)

Most people think of money as something to pay the rent. But a money man thinks of money in terms of what he can do with it.
  —Robert A. Heinlein, *I Will Fear No Evil* (1970)

There would be a hearing, facts would have to be tortured by the computers, stories would have to be planted, money would be spent. The root of all evil produced a popular shrub.
  —Chad Oliver, "King of the Hill" (1972)

The only thing separating me from the Lysol Lady, who is crazy, is the money in my savings account. Money is the official seal of sanity.
  —Philip K. Dick, "Strange Memories of Death" (1985)

Virek's money was a sort of universal solvent, dissolving barriers to his will.
  —William Gibson, *Count Zero* (1986)

GILLIAN TAYLOR: Don't tell me they don't use money in the twenty-third century.
KIRK: Well, we don't.
  —Steve Meerson, Peter Krikes, Harve Bennett, and Nicholas Meyer,
    Star Trek IV: The Voyage Home (film, 1986)

"Why don't they modernize?"
  I answered, "Money. Donald, any question that starts out 'Why don't they—' the answer is always 'Money.'"
  —Robert A. Heinlein, *To Sail beyond the Sunset* (1987)

Money

Three millennia after its invention money had become the tiger which could be dismounted only in bankruptcy.
— George Turner, *Drowning Towers* (1987)

Dancing for money, the tales implied, was not a happy thing.
— William Gibson, *Mona Lisa Overdrive* (1988)

The Yen Buddhists are the richest religious sect in the universe. They hold that the accumulation of money is a great evil and burden to the soul. They therefore, regardless of personal hazard, see it as their unpleasant duty to acquire as much as possible in order to reduce the risk to innocent people.
— Terry Pratchett, *Witches Abroad* (1991)

Money equals power; power makes the law; and law makes government.
— Kim Stanley Robinson, *Red Mars* (1992)

"When we were kids, Warbaby, Marlboro, she was *money*."
"Arkady," Warbaby said, as though with enormous patience, "when *we* were kids, man, *money* was money."
— William Gibson, *Virtual Light* (1993)

MONSTERS

It was on a dreary night of November, that I beheld the accomplishment of my toils. With an anxiety that almost amounted to agony, I collected the instruments of life around me, that I might infuse a spark of being into the lifeless thing that lay at my feet. It was already one in the morning; the rain pattered dismally against the panes, and my candle was nearly burnt out, when, by the glimmer of the half-extinguished light, I saw the dull yellow eye of the creature open; it breathed hard, and a convulsive motion agitated its limbs.

How can I describe my emotions at this catastrophe, or how delineate the wretch whom with such infinite pains and care I had endeavoured to form? His limbs were in proportion, and I had selected his features as beautiful. Beautiful — Great God! His yellow skin scarcely covered the work of muscles and arteries beneath; his hair was of a lustrous black, and flowing; his teeth of a pearly whiteness; but these luxuriances only formed a more horrid contrast with his watery eyes, that seemed almost of the same colour as the dun white sockets in which they were set, his shrivelled complexion, and straight black lips.

— Mary Shelley, *Frankenstein, or, The Modern Prometheus* (1818)

Late one accursed night I compounded the elements, watched them boil and smoke together in the glass, and when the ebullition had subsided, with a strong glow of courage, drank off the potion.

The most racking pangs succeeded: a grinding in the bones, deadly nausea, and a horror of the spirit that cannot be exceeded at the hour of birth or death. Then these agonies began swiftly to subside, and I came to myself as if out of a great sickness. There was something strange in my sensations, something indescribably new, and, from its very novelty, incredibly sweet. I felt younger, lighter, happier in body; within I was conscious of a heady recklessness, a current of disordered sensual images running like a mill race in my fancy, a solution of the bonds of obligation, an unknown but not an innocent freedom of the soul. I knew myself, at the first breath of this new life, to be more wicked, tenfold more wicked, sold a slave to my original evil; and the thought, in that moment, braced and delighted me like wine.

— Robert Louis Stevenson, *Strange Case of Dr. Jekyll and Mr. Hyde* (1886)

No eyes could look unchanged on that slimy blob of liquid flesh and fungus and ichor, with its loathly tentacles and beaks, its blackness of corruption, its monstrous mixture of all that was obscene in the vegetable and animal kingdoms.

— Donald A. Wandrei, "Something from Above" (1930)

We are about to unfold the story of Frankenstein, a man of science who sought to create a man after his own image without reckoning upon God. It is one of the strangest tales ever told. It deals with the two great mysteries of creation: life and death. I think it will thrill you. It may shock you. It might even horrify you.

— Garrett Fort and Francis Edward Faragoh, *Frankenstein* (film, 1931)

FRANKENSTEIN: Look! It's moving. It's alive. It's alive . . . It's alive, it's moving, it's alive, it's alive, it's alive, it's alive, *it's alive!*

— Garrett Fort and Francis Edward Faragoh, *Frankenstein* (film, 1931)

You have created a monster, and it will destroy you!
—Garrett Fort and Francis Edward Faragoh, *Frankenstein* (film, 1931)

I'm going to show you the greatest thing your eyes have ever beheld. He was a king and a god in the world he knew, but now he comes to civilization merely a captive—a show to gratify your curiosity. Ladies and gentlemen, look at Kong, the Eighth Wonder of the World!
—James Ashmore Creelman and Ruth Rose, *King Kong* (film, 1933)

To a new world of gods and monsters!
—William Hurlbut, *Bride of Frankenstein* (film, 1935)

It crawled out of the darkness and hot damp mold into the cool of a morning. It was huge. It was lumped and crusted with its own hateful substances, and pieces of it dropped off as it went its way, dropped off and lay writhing, and stilled, and sank putrescent into the forest loam.
—Theodore Sturgeon, "It" (1940)

The creature crept. It whimpered from fear and pain, a thing, slobbering sound horrible to hear. Shapeless, formless thing yet changing shape and form with every jerky movement.

It crept along the corridor of the space freighter, fighting the terrible urge of its elements to take the shape of its surroundings. A gray blob of disintegrating stuff, it rolled, flowed, dissolved, every movement an agony of struggle against the abnormal need to become a stable shape.
—A. E. van Vogt, "Vault of the Beast" (1940)

My heart is good. But I am a monster.
—Jean Cocteau, *Beauty and the Beast* (film, 1946), translated by Francis Howard (1946)

The foghorn blew.

And the monster answered. A cry came across a million years of water and mist. A cry so anguished and alone that it shuddered in my head and my body. The monster cried out at the tower. The foghorn blew. The monster roared again. The foghorn blew. The monster opened its great toothed mouth, and the sound that came from it was the sound of the foghorn itself.
—Ray Bradbury, "The Fog Horn" (1951)

OSTROW: The Krell forgot one thing—
ADAMS: Yes, what?
OSTROW: Monsters, John. Monsters from the id!
  —Cyril Hume, *Forbidden Planet* (film, 1956)

We're all part monsters in our subconscious, so we have laws and religion.
  —Cyril Hume, *Forbidden Planet* (film, 1956)

I am a great soft jelly thing. Smoothly rounded, with no mouth, with pulsing white holes filled by fog where my eyes used to be. Rubbery appendages that were once my arms; bulks rounding down into legless humps of soft slippery matter. I leave a moist trail when I move. Blotches of diseased, evil gray come and go on my surface, as though light is being beamed from within. [. . .]
  I have no mouth. And I must scream.
  —Harlan Ellison, "I Have No Mouth, and I Must Scream" (1967)

Make all the monsters you wish. The world's already full of them.
  —Edgar Pangborn, "The Night Wind" (1974)

"It's not a man's skin that makes him a god—or a monster," Fallatha said quietly. "It's what lies beneath the skin, behind the eyes."
  —Joan D. Vinge, "The Storm King" (1980)

One, two, Freddy's coming for you!
Three, four, better lock your door!
Five, six, grab your crucifix!
Seven, eight, gotta stay up late!
Nine, ten, never sleep again!
  —Wes Craven, *A Nightmare on Elm Street* (film, 1984)

I'm a mog: half man, half dog. I'm my own best friend!
  —Mel Brooks, Thomas Meehan, and Ronny Graham, *Spaceballs*
    (film, 1987)

Some things deserved to be called "it."
  —Octavia E. Butler, *Dawn* (1987)

Monsters

I knew more than most how the mind conjures up monsters.
　—Jane Yolen, "The Quiet Monk" (1988)

I have never understood the practice in some cultures of describing ferocious creatures in an attempt to lull children to sleep.
　—Lisa Klink, "Innocence," episode of *Star Trek: Voyager* (1996)

"Monsters are *made*," Plass said with a grimace, clasping her Bible, "not born."
　—Greg Bear, "The Way of All Ghosts" (1999)

MORALITY

I'm really a very good man, but I'm a very bad Wizard.
　—L. Frank Baum, *The Wonderful Wizard of Oz* (1900)

Such high ideals as they had! Beauty, Health, Strength, Intellect, Goodness—for these they prayed and worked.
　—Charlotte Perkins Gilman, *Herland* (1915)

For these things which man purports to admire the most—the noble, the brilliant, the splendid—these are the very things he cannot tolerate when he finds them.
　—Mark Clifton, "What Have I Done?" (1952)

The Lithians did not know God. They did things rightly, and thought righteously, because it was reasonable and efficient and natural to do and to think that way. They seemed to need nothing else.
　—James Blish, *A Case of Conscience* (1958)

"Your conscience has been spoiled by constant attention; it groans at the slightest discomfort, and your reason bows before it respectfully instead of scolding it and putting it in its proper place." [. . .]
　"I can't agree with you," said Maxim coldly. "Conscience, driven by its own pain, sets the task; reason carries it out. Conscience sets ideals; reason searches for the path to fulfillment. That, precisely, is reason's function: to

find that path. Without conscience, reason works only for itself; that is, it runs idle."

"True," agreed the Wizard. "Conscience does set ideals. But ideals are called ideals because of their striking disparity with reality. [. . .] Don't let your conscience prevent you from thinking clearly, and don't let your reason be shy about pushing aside your conscience when necessary."

— Arkady Strugatsky and Boris Strugatsky, *Prisoners of Power* (1969), translated by Helen Saltz Jacobson (1977)

Idealism is a wasting disease, a cancer.

— Gardner Dozois, "Horse of Air" (1971)

There's a certain moral virtue in being materialistic.

— J. G. Ballard, *Crash* (1973)

I do not know what it is in us that (sometimes) will make us do a thing against our wishes because we know it to be good. "Conscience" is too thin a word, and "God" too misty, too spoiled by the many who mouth it constantly without any care for what they say. [. . .] The thing that I will not call Conscience or God (somewhere in the Old-Time books I think it was called Virtue, but doubtless few read them) — the thing that would never let me strike a child, or stone a criminal or a mue on the green as we are expected to do in Trempa — this mad cruel-sweet thing that may be a part of love commanded me to answer her.

— Edgar Pangborn, "The Night Wind" (1974)

Nothing is moral always, and anything is moral under the right circumstances.

— John Varley, "The Persistence of Vision" (1978)

His view of morality became more intelligible: it is something you practise when you can afford it, and I could not afford morality.

— George Turner, *Drowning Towers* (1987)

Cultural imperatives, meaning morality, change with the weather.

— George Turner, *Drowning Towers* (1987)

Character comes from following our highest sense of right, from trusting ideals without being sure they'll work. One challenge of our adventure on earth is to rise above dead systems—wars, religions, nations, destructions—to refuse to be a part of them, and express instead the highest selves we know how to be.
  —Richard Bach, *One* (1988)

MOTHERS AND FATHERS

Families can be just as oppressive as governments.
  —Robert A. Heinlein, *Between Planets* (1951)

I have been exploring this notion of parenthood. [. . .] It seems to be based on a reverence for the young, and an extremely patient and protective attitude toward their physical and mental welfare. Yet you make them live in these huge caves, utterly out of contact with the natural world, and you teach them to be afraid of death—which of course makes them a little insane, because there is nothing anybody can do about death. It is like teaching them to be afraid of the second law of thermodynamics, just because living matter sets that law aside for a very brief period. How they hate you!
  —James Blish, *A Case of Conscience* (1958)

Being a mother is an attitude, not a biological relation.
  —Robert A. Heinlein, *Have Space Suit—Will Travel* (1958)

LADY REPORTER: Are you in favor of Motherhood, Lord Ragelle?
DEFENSE MINISTER: I am sternly opposed to it, Madam. It exerts a malign influence on youth, particularly upon young recruits. The military services would have superior soldiers if our fighting men had not been corrupted by Motherhood.
  —Walter M. Miller, Jr., *A Canticle for Leibowitz* (1959)

A boy's best friend is his mother.
  —Joseph Stefano, *Psycho* (film, 1960)

He felt that sense of being necessary which is the burden and reward of parenthood.
— Ursula K. Le Guin, *The Dispossessed: An Ambiguous Utopia* (1974)

When wired *Come at once* to the sick mother's bedside, one comes. To certain moves in chess only certain responses are possible.
— Ursula K. Le Guin, "Two Delays on the Northern Line" (1979)

It says in the Book that you must honor thy father and thy mother. Not one word about loving them.
— Robert A. Heinlein, *Job: A Comedy of Justice* (1984)

No mother is ever, completely, a child's idea of what a mother should be, and I suppose it works the other way around as well.
— Margaret Atwood, *The Handmaid's Tale* (1986)

Motherhood involves a lifetime of mixed self-deception and clear sight.
— George Turner, *Drowning Towers* (1987)

We don't consider it good manners to discuss our fathers, Stavvy. It has no relevance in Women's Country.
— Sheri S. Tepper, *The Gate to Women's Country* (1988)

It is pleasant to be mothered by a daughter, and to behave as a daughter to one's daughter.
— Ursula K. Le Guin, *Tehanu: The Last Book of Earthsea* (1990)

When you lost things, it was like you only knew for the first time that you'd ever had them. Took a mother's leaving for you to know she'd ever been there, because otherwise she *was* that place, everything, like weather.
— William Gibson, *Virtual Light* (1993)

Many mothers are best.
— Jane Yolen, "The One-Armed Queen" (1995)

Not for the first time, a son knew himself to be older than his father.
— Tanith Lee, "Rapunzel" (2000)

MUSIC

If we could have devised an arrangement for providing everybody with music in their homes, perfect in quality, unlimited in quantity, suited to every mood, and beginning and ceasing at will, we should have considered the limit of human felicity already attained, and ceased to strive for further improvements.

— Edward Bellamy, *Looking Backward, 2000–1887* (1888)

The melody was piercingly sweet, and resembled at times the singing of some voluptuous feminine voice. However, no human voice could have possessed the unearthly pitch, the shrill, perpetually sustained notes that somehow suggested the light of remote worlds and stars translated into sound.

— Clark Ashton Smith, "The City of the Singing Flame" (1931)

Red-head said, "I feel like MEW-SIK," and went to a corner of the room to turn on a machine of some kind. Oh Ilha! Such a burst of overpoweringly sweet sound came from it that my probe tips quivered in ecstasy. They are masters of sound, these HEW-MEN. Not in my life have I imagined such an art. There was a mathematically regulated change of pitch, recurring with an urgent feeling of logic; there was a blending of tones in infinite variety; there was a measured rhythm. But none of these will give you the slightest idea of the effect on me, when all were put together.

— Laurence Manning, "Good-Bye, Ilha!" (1952)

Space is my harp, and I touch it lightly with fingers of steel. Space sings.

— Walter M. Miller, Jr., "The Big Hunger" (1952)

Music is the most perishable of things, fragile and delicate, easily destroyed.

— Philip K. Dick, "The Preserving Machine" (1953)

Softly, barely audible at first, the strains of the ancient song of evening and requiem swelled to the final poignant measure until black space itself echoed back the sound of the song the ship sang.

— Anne McCaffrey, "The Ship Who Sang" (1961)

Sarah Boyle thinks of music as the formal articulation of the passage of time, and of Bach as the most poignant rendering of this.

— Pamela Zoline, "The Heat Death of the Universe" (1967)

Music is a cooperative art, organic by definition, social. It may be the noblest
form of social behavior we're capable of. It's certainly one of the noblest jobs
an individual can undertake. And by its nature, by the nature of any art, it's a
sharing. The artist shares, it's the essence of his act.
　—Ursula K. Le Guin, *The Dispossessed: An Ambiguous Utopia* (1974)

Music, and in fact, art in general, is the process of consciously communicating
an emotional judgment or point of view in terms of abstract symbology.
　—Jack Vance, "Assault on a City" (1974)

Colors made sounds in his mind: Sunlight in summer was a blaring chord;
moonlight in winter a thin, mournful wail; new green in spring, a low
murmur in almost (but not quite) random rhythms; the flash of a red fox in
the leaves, a gasp of sudden startlement.
　—Orson Scott Card, "Unaccompanied Sonata" (1979)

The beauty of the universe lay not in the stars figured into it but in the music
generated by human minds, human voices, human hands.
　—Philip K. Dick, "Chains of Air, Web of Aether" (1980)

He had been listening to the music of life itself. The music of light dancing on
water that rippled with the wind and the tides, of the life that moved through
the water, of the life that moved on the land, warmed by the light.
　—Douglas Adams, *Dirk Gently's Holistic Detective Agency* (1987)

Learn a little music, so you'll know what discipline really is.
　—Elizabeth Moon, "Hand to Hand" (1995)

The whites, as conquered people will, found liberation in their music that
they could not have in life.
　—Harry Turtledove, "Must and Shall" (1995)

NATURE

We may brave the laws of humanity but we can't withstand the laws of
Nature.
—Jules Verne, *Twenty Thousand Leagues under the Sea* (1870), translated
by Walter James Miller and Frederick Paul Walter (1993)

The contrast between the dreadful scene of blood and turmoil that he had
left, and the peaceful face of Nature over which he was passing, came home
to his brain vividly. Here birds sang and cattle grazed; here the sun shone
undimmed by the smoke of cannon, only high up in the blue and silent air
long streams of vultures could be seen winging their way to the Plain of
Isandhlwana.
—H. Rider Haggard, "Black Heart and White Heart" (1896)

The study of Nature makes a man at last as remorseless as Nature.
—H. G. Wells, *The Island of Doctor Moreau* (1896)

Natural phenomena are less often produced by nature and most often
produced by man.
—Alfred Bester, "The Devil's Invention" (1950)

People have a funny habit of taking as "natural" whatever they are used to—
but there hasn't been any "natural" environment, the way they mean it, since
men climbed down out of trees.
—Robert A. Heinlein, *Farmer in the Sky* (1950)

The jungle looked back at them with a vastness, a breathing moss-and-leaf
silence, with a billion diamond and emerald insect eyes.
—Ray Bradbury, "And the Rock Cried Out" (1953)

Existence required Order and there was Order; the laws of nature, irrevocable
and immutable. [. . .] The laws *were,* and the universe moved in obedience to
them. Along the frontier were arrayed all the forces of nature and sometimes

they destroyed those who were fighting their way outward from Earth. The men of the frontier had long ago learned the bitter futility of cursing the forces that would destroy them for the forces were blind and deaf; the futility of looking to the heavens for mercy, for the stars of the galaxy swung in their long, long sweep of two hundred million years, as inexorably controlled as they by the laws that knew neither hatred nor compassion.

—Tom Godwin, "The Cold Equations" (1954)

A reverence for life does not require a man to respect Nature's obvious mistakes.

—Robert A. Heinlein, *Have Space Suit—Will Travel* (1958)

Objective evidence is the ultimate authority. Recorders may lie, but Nature is incapable of it.

—Walter M. Miller, Jr., *A Canticle for Leibowitz* (1959)

Nature is an experimenter.

—Philip José Farmer, "Prometheus" (1961)

My brothers, are we not ourselves Nature, Nature without end? Does not the rustle of her trees echo in our bones? Is our human blood less salty than the waters of the sea that carve great caverns of lime and chalk, great skeletons beneath the waves? Does not the everlasting fire of the desert burn in our hearts?

—Stanislaw Lem, *Memoirs Found in a Bathtub* (1961), translated by
    Michael Kandel and Christine Rose (1973)

He recalled another thing the old woman had said about a world being the sum of many things—the people, the dirt, the growing things, the moons, the tides, the suns—the unknown sum called *nature,* a vague summation without any sense of the *now.* And he wondered: *What is the now?*

—Frank Herbert, *Dune* (1965)

A lot of things have been said about Nature, that she's implacable, cruel, wasteful and so on. I like to think she's—reasonable. I concede that she reaches that state cruelly, at times, and wastefully and all the rest. But she has a way of coming up with the pragmatic solution, the one that works.

—Theodore Sturgeon, "If All Men Were Brothers, Would You Let One
    Marry Your Sister?" (1967)

Is there anything more contemptible than Nature? The scientists, the philosophers have always tried to understand Nature, while the thing to do is to destroy it!
> —Stanislaw Lem, "The Sanitorium of Dr. Vliperdius" (1971), translated by Michael Kandel (1977)

She always professed to adore what she called Nature, but she walked as though every blade of grass were poison ivy.
> —Chad Oliver, "King of the Hill" (1972)

What are called the laws of Nature I take as gossip.
> —Bernard Wolfe, "The Girl with Rapid Eye Movements" (1972)

This concern, feebly called "love of nature," seemed to Shevek to be something much broader than love. There are souls, he thought, whose umbilicus has never been cut. They never got weaned from the universe. They do not understand death as an enemy; they look forward to rotting and turning into humus. It was strange to see Takver take a leaf into her hand, or even a rock. She became an extension of it, it of her.
> —Ursula K. Le Guin, *The Dispossessed: An Ambiguous Utopia* (1974)

Nature was his real antagonist—the friendly enemy who never cheated, always played fair, but never failed to take advantage of the tiniest oversight or omission.
> —Arthur C. Clarke, *The Fountains of Paradise* (1979)

There is a time to battle against Nature, and a time to obey her. True wisdom lies in making the right choice.
> —Arthur C. Clarke, *The Fountains of Paradise* (1979)

When Aunt Em came there to live she was a young, pretty wife. The sun and wind had changed her, too. They had taken the sparkle from her eyes and left them a sober gray; they had taken the red from her cheeks and lips, and they were gray also. She was thin and gaunt, and never smiled, now.

—L. Frank Baum, *The Wonderful Wizard of Oz* (1900)

The first quarter-century of your life was doubtless lived under the cloud of being too young for things, while the last quarter-century would normally be shadowed by the still darker cloud of being too old for them; and between those two clouds, what small and narrow sunlight illumines a human lifetime!

—James Hilton, *Lost Horizon* (1933)

I have never seen why politeness should be the obligation of the young and rudeness the privilege of age.

—Robert A. Heinlein, *Beyond This Horizon* (1942)

Man has natural three-dimensional limits, and he also has four-dimensional ones, considering time as an extension. When he reaches those limits, he ceases to grow and mature, and forms rigidly within the mold of those limiting walls. It is stasis, which is retrogression unless all else stands still as well. A man who reaches his limits is tending toward subhumanity. Only when he becomes superhuman in time and space can immortality become practical.

—Henry Kuttner and C. L. Moore, "Time Enough" (1946)

Old men only lie in wait for people to ask them to talk. Then they rattle on like a rusty elevator wheezing up a shaft.

—Ray Bradbury, *Dandelion Wine* (1957)

Old Age

Old age is not an accomplishment; it is just something that happens to you despite yourself, like falling downstairs.
   —Robert A. Heinlein, *Podkayne of Mars: Her Life and Times* (1963)

When a tree is very old, and yet still lives, sometimes the limbs are strangely twisted. Do you understand?
   —Gene Wolfe, "The Island of Doctor Death and Other Stories" (1970)

Old age is always horrible. Only fools see anything good in it.
   —Ray Nelson, "Time Travel for Pedestrians" (1972)

The old ladies sitting on the side porch waved and called out to him, and he waved back at them. They sat like a bunch of ancient crows on a branch. Time was shooting them down, one by one.
   —Philip José Farmer, "Stations of the Nightmare—Part One" (1974)

Throughout most of the past the counsel of the old had been valued, even sought for; it was not until the 20th century that old people were declared obsolete and swept under the rug.
   —Edgar Pangborn, "The Children's Crusade" (1974)

We believe old people and children are kin. There's more space at both ends of life. That closeness to birth and to death makes a common concern with big questions and basic patterns.
   —Marge Piercy, *Woman on the Edge of Time* (1976)

The god is most fond of small children and the aged. Small boys and girls have innocence. Old people have tranquillity and wisdom. These are the things that are pleasing to the god. We should strive without effort to retain innocence, and to attain tranquillity and wisdom as soon as we can.
   —Gene Wolfe, "The Eyeflash Miracles" (1976)

Galloping around the cosmos is a game for the young.
   —Jack B. Sowards, *Star Trek II: The Wrath of Khan* (film, 1982)

A man my age is willing to accept almost anything. After the initial shock of astonishment that comes each morning when I wake up and discover that I'm still alive, I can face the day with an open mind.
   —David Eddings, *The Shining Ones* (1993)

I feel like I was walking across Nevada, like the pioneers, carrying a lot of stuff I need, but as I go along I have to keep dropping off things. I had a piano once but it got swamped at a crossing of the Platte. I had a good frypan but it got too heavy and I left it in the Rockies. I had a couple ovaries but they wore out around the time we were in the Carson Sink. I had a good memory but pieces of it keep dropping off, have to leave them scattered around in the sage brush, on the sand hills.

    — Ursula K. Le Guin, "Ether, OR" (1995)

I never asked questions, I was so busy answering them, but am sixty years old this winter and think I should have time for a question. But it's hard to ask. Here it is. It's like all the time I was working keeping house and raising the kids and making love and earning our keep I thought there was going to come a time or there would be some place where all of it came together. Like it was words I was saying, all my life, all the kinds of work, just a word here and a word there, but finally all the words would make a sentence, and I could read the sentence. I would have made my soul and know what it was for.

    But I have made my soul and I don't know what to do with it. Who wants it?

    — Ursula K. Le Guin, "Ether, OR" (1995)

OVERPOPULATION

The council refused to accept, even in principle, any form of population control. By now we're stifling under the pressure of our own numbers, we're crushed shapeless under it. Everything has had to give way to our one basic problem, how to feed an ever-increasing number of hungry mouths. Morality has dwindled into feeding ourselves.

    — Margaret St. Clair, "Brightness Falls from the Air" (1951)

There are too many of us, he thought. There are billions of us and that's too many. Nobody knows anyone. Strangers come and violate you. Strangers come and cut your heart out. Strangers come and take your blood.

    — Ray Bradbury, *Fahrenheit 451* (1954)

Overpopulation

Some troubledome just figured out that if you allow for every codder and shiggy and appleofmyeye a space one foot by two you could stand us all on the six hundred forty square mile surface of the island of Zanzibar.

  —John Brunner, *Stand on Zanzibar* (1968)

POPULATION EXPLOSION Unique in human experience, an event which happened yesterday but which everyone swears won't happen until tomorrow.

  —John Brunner, *Stand on Zanzibar* (1968)

It isn't the threat of war, or crime in the streets, or corruption in high places, or pesticides, or smog, or "education" that doesn't teach; those things are just symptoms of the underlying cancer. It's too many people. Not too many souls, or honks, or thirds—just . . . *too many.* Seven billion people sitting in each other's laps, trying to take in each other's washing, pick each other's pockets.

  —Robert A. Heinlein, *I Will Fear No Evil* (1970)

The special madness that man has invented: The ultimate predator, he removes all constraints on his own reproductivity and now he breeds to the point where he has to prey upon himself.

  —Thomas N. Scortia, "Judas Fish" (1971)

The earth was sick, blotched by hungry and desperate people from pole to shining pole. There had never been an uglier joke than pinning man's future on birth control.

  —Chad Oliver, "King of the Hill" (1972)

My world, my Earth, is a ruin. A planet spoiled by the human species. We multiplied and gobbled and fought until there was nothing left, and then we died. We controlled neither appetite nor violence; we did not adapt. We destroyed ourselves. But we destroyed the world first.

  —Ursula K. Le Guin, *The Dispossessed: An Ambiguous Utopia* (1974)

You humans spread like a disease.

  —Barry B. Longyear, "Enemy Mine" (1979)

The Four Horsemen were good at population control.

  —Kim Stanley Robinson, *Red Mars* (1992)

PAIN AND SUFFERING

Had I known such pain was in the next room, and had it been dumb, I believe—I have thought since—I could have stood it well enough. It is when suffering finds a voice and sets our nerves quivering that this pity comes troubling us.

    —H. G. Wells, *The Island of Doctor Moreau* (1896)

A mind truly opened to what science has to teach must see that it is a little thing. [. . .] Pain is simply our intrinsic medical adviser to warn us and stimulate us.

    —H. G. Wells, *The Island of Doctor Moreau* (1896)

"Human beings," said Tuffaron, familiarly known as the Mad Genii, "are stupid and willful. They derive intense enjoyment from suffering or else they would not bend all their efforts toward suffering."

    —L. Ron Hubbard, "Borrowed Glory" (1941)

In the face of pain there are no heroes, no heroes, he thought over and over as he writhed on the floor, clutching uselessly at his disabled left arm.

    —George Orwell, *Nineteen Eighty-Four* (1949)

The object of persecution is persecution. The object of torture is torture. The object of power is power.

    —George Orwell, *Nineteen Eighty-Four* (1949)

I do not understand objections to "cruel and unusual" punishment. While a judge should be benevolent in purpose, his awards should cause the criminal to suffer, else there is no punishment—and pain is the basic mechanism built into us by millions of years of evolution which safeguards us by warning when something threatens our survival. Why should society refuse to use such a highly perfected survival mechanism?

    —Robert A. Heinlein, *Starship Troopers* (1959)

Pain and Suffering

Pain is the only evil I know about. It's the only one I can fight.
— Walter M. Miller, Jr., *A Canticle for Leibowitz* (1959)

Sometimes pain can drive a man harder than pleasure.
— Don Ingalls, "The Alternative Factor," episode of *Star Trek* (1967)

He was wise to the ways of pain. He had to be, for he felt none.
— James Tiptree, Jr., "Painwise" (1972)

It is our suffering that brings us together. It is not love. Love does not obey the mind, and turns to hate when forced. The bond that binds us is beyond choice. We are brothers. We are brothers in what we share. In pain, which each of us must suffer alone, in hunger, in poverty, in hope, we know our brotherhood.
— Ursula K. Le Guin, *The Dispossessed: An Ambiguous Utopia* (1974)

The best way of handling pain was to study it objectively.
— Arthur C. Clarke, *The Fountains of Paradise* (1979)

He enters pain's cold regions as an explorer, an objective visitor. It is a country of ice and glass, monochromatic plains and valleys filled with wash-blue shards of ice, crystal pyramids and pinnacles, squares, oblongs, and all manner of polyhedron — block upon block of painted blue pain.
— Jack Dann, "Camps" (1979)

Pain can be controlled, you just disconnect it.
— James Cameron and Gale Anne Hurd, *The Terminator* (film, 1984)

Who can remember pain, once it's over? All that remains of it is a shadow, not in the mind even, in the flesh. Pain marks you, but too deep to see.
— Margaret Atwood, *The Handmaid's Tale* (1986)

Pain is the universe unguarded.
— Steve Aylett, "Angel Dust"(1998)

The future is always born in pain. The history of war is the history of pain. If we are wise, what is born of that pain matures into the promise of a better world, because we learn that we can no longer afford the mistakes of the past.
— J. Michael Straczynski, *Babylon 5: In the Beginning* (TV movie, 1998)

As a species, human beings define their reality through misery and suffering. The perfect world was a dream that your primitive cerebrum kept trying to wake up from.

— Andy Wachowski and Larry Wachowski, *The Matrix* (film, 1999)

PARADOXES

It is our tradition, if I may permit myself the paradox, that we are never slaves to tradition. We have no rigidities, no inexorable rules.

— James Hilton, *Lost Horizon* (1933)

War is peace
Freedom is slavery
Ignorance is strength

— George Orwell, *Nineteen Eighty-Four* (1949)

Less is more
Mars is Earth
Tomorrow is yesterday

— George Alec Effinger, *The Nick of Time* (1985)

The oftener a thing happens the more uniquely wonderful it is.

— William S. Burroughs, *Naked Lunch* (1959)

To attempt an understanding of Muad'Dib without understanding his mortal enemies, the Harkonnens, is to attempt seeing Truth without knowing Falsehood. It is the attempt to see the Light without knowing Darkness.

— Frank Herbert, *Dune* (1965)

Only in silence the word, only in dark the light, only in dying life: bright the hawk's flight on the empty sky.

— Ursula K. Le Guin, *A Wizard of Earthsea* (1968)

To oppose something is to maintain it.

— Ursula K. Le Guin, *The Left Hand of Darkness* (1969)

Paradoxes

Light is the left hand of darkness
and darkness the right hand of light.
Two are one, life and death, lying
together like lovers in kemmer,
like hands joined together,
like the end and the way.
   —Ursula K. Le Guin, *The Left Hand of Darkness* (1969)

In the Enacraotic scheme of things, things are not only what they scheme to be, but are, or can be (among other things), precisely the opposite.
   —John Heidenry, "The Counterpoint of View" (1972)

"I suppose," he says aloud, "it's possible that in some sense we are not here."
   —James Tiptree, Jr., "Houston, Houston, Do You Read?" (1976)

To fight the Empire is to be infected by its derangement. This is a paradox; whoever defeats a segment of the Empire becomes the Empire; it proliferates like a virus, imposing its form on its enemies. Thereby it becomes its enemies.
   —Philip K. Dick, *Valis* (1981)

PARANOIA

Big Brother is watching you.
   —George Orwell, *Nineteen Eighty-Four* (1949)

Watch the skies, everywhere! Keep looking. Keep watching the skies!
   —Charles Lederer, *The Thing (from Another World)* (film, 1951)

There are times when I think we're all figments of a paranoid's dream.
   —Fritz Leiber, "X Marks the Pedwalk" (1963)

The paranoid *seemed* rational. The formal pattern of logical reasoning appeared undisturbed. Underneath, however, the paranoid suffered from the greatest mental disfigurement possible for a human being. He was incapable of empathy, unable to imagine himself in another person's role. Hence for him others did not actually exist—except as objects in motion that did or did not affect his well-being.
   —Philip K. Dick, *Clans of the Alphane Moon* (1964)

The paranoid experienced love fully, both as something given to him by others and as a feeling on his part toward them. But there was a slight catch to this.

The paranoid experienced it as a variety of hate.

—Philip K. Dick, *Clans of the Alphane Moon* (1964)

Paranoia loses its meaning on the Moon. You *are* being threatened.

—John Brunner, *Stand on Zanzibar* (1968)

I am suddenly catapulted into a paranoid world where the walls not only have ears, but probably eyes, and long, claw-tipped fingers.

—Samuel R. Delany, "Time Considered as a Helix of Semi-Precious Stones" (1969)

At a certain level in my line of work, paranoia's just an occupational disease.

—Samuel R. Delany, "Time Considered as a Helix of Semi-Precious Stones" (1969)

To the paranoid, nothing is a surprise; everything happens exactly as he expected, and sometimes even more so. It all fits into his system. For us, though, there can be no system; maybe *all* systems—that is, any theoretical, verbal, symbolic, semantic, etc. formulation that attempts to act as an all-encompassing, all-explaining hypothesis of what the universe is about—are manifestations of paranoia. We should be content with the mysterious, the meaningless, the contradictory, the hostile, and most of all the unexplainably warm and giving.

—Philip K. Dick, "The Android and the Human" (1972)

Being paranoid doesn't mean we're not being followed.

—Peter Hyams and Stirling Silliphant, *Telefon* (film, 1977)

ARTHUR: All through my life I've had this strange unaccountable feeling that something was going on in the world, something big, even sinister, and no one would tell me what it was.

SLARTIBARTFAST: No, that's just perfectly normal paranoia. Everyone in the Universe has that.

—Douglas Adams, "Fit the Fourth," episode of *The Hitch-Hiker's Guide to the Galaxy* (radio series, 1978)

Paranoia is the number-one killer of fourteen-year-old girls.
    —Connie Willis, "A Letter from the Clearys" (1982)

The cultivation of a certain tame paranoia was something Case took for granted. The trick lay in not letting it get out of control.
    —William Gibson, *Neuromancer* (1984)

Paranoia is the only rational approach to a conspiracy world.
    —Robert A. Heinlein, *Job: A Comedy of Justice* (1984)

[The Grand Sphere] was, he often thought, a paranoid's paradise; somebody really *was* plotting against him all the time.
    —William Jon Watkins, *The Centrifugal Rickshaw Dancer* (1985)

Have you ever considered the relationship of clinical paranoia to the phenomenon of religious conversion?
    —William Gibson, *Mona Lisa Overdrive* (1988)

You may think you're paranoid, but are you paranoid *enough*?
    —Pat Cadigan, "Fool to Believe" (1990)

PERCEPTION AND VISION

The morphine had its customary effect—that of enduing all the external world with an intensity of interest. In the quivering of a leaf—in the hue of a blade of grass—in the shape of a trefoil—in the humming of a bee—in the gleaming of a dew-drop—in the breathing of the wind—in the faint odors that came from the forest—there came a whole universe of suggestion—a gay and motley train of rhapsodical and immethodical thought.
    —Edgar Allan Poe, "A Tale of the Ragged Mountains" (1844)

The human mind delights in grand visions of supernatural beings.
    —Jules Verne, *Twenty Thousand Leagues under the Sea* (1870),
       translated by Walter James Miller and Frederick Paul Walter (1993)

Besotted Being! You think yourself the perfection of existence, while you are in reality the most imperfect and imbecile.
    —Edwin A. Abbott, *Flatland: A Romance of Many Dimensions* (1884)

At times I suffer from the strangest sense of detachment from myself and the world about me; I seem to watch it all from the outside, from somewhere inconceivably remote, out of time, out of space, out of the stress and tragedy of it all.

   —H. G. Wells, *The War of the Worlds* (1898)

Spite of the infinite danger in which we were between starvation and a still more terrible death, we could yet struggle bitterly for that horrible privilege of sight.

   —H. G. Wells, *The War of the Worlds* (1898)

Human heads are opaque, with only tiny windows in them—the eyes.

   —Yevgeny Zamiatin, *We* (1924), translated by Mirra Ginsburg (1972)

The mind of man is not adjusted for a close observation of phenomena that belong to the cosmos.

   —Edwin Balmer and Philip Wylie, *When Worlds Collide* (1932)

Pay no attention to that man behind the curtain.

   —Noel Langley, Florence Ryerson, and Edgar Allan Woolf,
     The Wizard of Oz (film, 1939)

"Sight," Metzger said, "is the most highly civilized of the senses. It was the last to come. The other senses tie us in closely with the very roots of life; I think we perceive with them more keenly than we know. The things we realize through taste and smell and feeling stimulate directly, without a detour through the centers of conscious thought. You know how often a taste or odor will recall a memory to you so subtly you don't know exactly what caused it? We need those primitive senses to tie us in with nature and the race. [. . .] Sight is a cold, intellectual thing compared with the other senses."

   —C. L. Moore, "No Woman Born" (1944)

I'm a reliable witness, you're a reliable witness, practically all God's children are reliable witnesses in their own estimation—which makes it funny how such different ideas of the same affair get about.

   —John Wyndham, *Out of the Deeps* (1953)

Beneath lay the elevated station. There myriad experiences and lives jostled each other like waves. It was like the sea, which, seen from a mountaintop, appears calm. There is always order in the distant view.
   —Kobo Abé, *Inter Ice Age 4* (1959), translated by E. Dale Saunders (1970)

So-called common sense relies on programmed nonperception, concealment, or ridicule of everything that doesn't fit into the conventional nineteenth century vision of a world that can be explained down to the last detail.
   —Stanislaw Lem, *The Investigation* (1959), translated by Adele Milch
      (1974)

The way you see things depends a great deal on where you look at them from.
   —Norton Juster, *The Phantom Tollbooth* (1961)

I saw myself, I saw both of us, from a long way off, as if through the wrong end of a telescope, and everything looked meaningless, trivial, and slightly ridiculous.
   —Stanislaw Lem, *Solaris* (1961), translated by Joanna Kilmartin and
      Steve Cox (1970)

We peep out, but what do we see, really? Mirror reflections of our own selves, our bloodless, feeble countenances, devoted to nothing in particular, insofar as I can fathom it.
   —Philip K. Dick, *Galactic Pot-Healer* (1969)

"Much of what you see in perceiving me—" He pointed to himself for emphasis. "—is a projection from your own mind. To another percept-system I would appear quite different. To the police, for instance. There're as many worldviews as there are sentient creatures."
   —Philip K. Dick, *Galactic Pot-Healer* (1969)

"If you can see a thing whole," he said, "it seems that it's always beautiful. Planets, lives . . . But close up, a world's all dirt and rocks. And day to day, life's a hard job, you get tired, you lose the pattern. You need distance, interval. The way to see how beautiful the earth is, is to see it as the moon. The way to see how beautiful life is, is from the vantage point of death."
   —Ursula K. Le Guin, *The Dispossessed: An Ambiguous Utopia* (1974)

You can only perceive in terms of the impulses your own brain generates.
Yet you fall into the trap of believing that you perceive reality.
  —Thomas N. Scortia, "The Armageddon Tapes—Tape 1" (1974)

A star is a stone to the blind. She saw him through crippled eyes.
  —Craig Strete, "Time Deer" (1974)

How can I tell that the past isn't a fiction designed to account for the
discrepancy between my immediate physical sensations and my state of
mind?
  —Douglas Adams, "Fit the Twelfth," episode of *The Hitch-Hiker's Guide to
    the Galaxy* (radio series, 1980)

I want you to learn to look behind the mask of events.
  —Michael Swanwick, "Ginungagap" (1980)

In the tradition of young girls and windows, the young girl looks out of this
one. It is difficult to see anything.
  —Tanith Lee, "Bite-Me-Not, or, Fleur de Fur" (1984)

We lived, as usual, by ignoring. Ignoring isn't the same as ignorance, you
have to work at it.
  —Margaret Atwood, *The Handmaid's Tale* (1986)

Seeing, contrary to popular wisdom, isn't believing. It's where belief stops,
because it isn't needed any more.
  —Terry Pratchett, *Pyramids* (1989)

It does highlight the irony that everything you go to see is changed by the
very action of going to see it, which is the sort of problem which physicists
have been wrestling with for most of this century.
  —Douglas Adams, *Last Chance to See* (1990)

There is a way of looking far into the distant past and seeing everything that
happened there. The same method can be used to observe distant events
while they are actually happening—and also, of course, events that took place
both long ago and far away. It is even possible to spy upon what is occurring

in the alternative universes—those parts of the polycosmos which, unreified in our own time-line, exist for us only as the sites of dreams.
  —John Grant, *The World* (1992)

Separated at Birth was a police program you used in missing persons cases. You scanned a photo of the person you wanted, got back the names of half a dozen celebrities who looked vaguely like the subject, then went around asking people if they'd seen anybody lately who reminded them of A, B, C . . . The weird thing was, it worked better than just showing them a picture of the subject. The instructor at the Academy in Knoxville had told Rydell's class that that was because it tapped into the part of the brain that kept track of celebrities.
  —William Gibson, *Virtual Light* (1993)

There comes a time when you look into the mirror and realize that what you see is all that you will ever be. Then you accept it, or you kill yourself. Or you stop looking into mirrors.
  —J. Michael Straczynski, "Chrysalis," episode of *Babylon 5* (1994)

PLANTS

The soul of a flower is its scent, and splendid as they may look, sea flowers have no soul.
  —Jules Verne, *Twenty Thousand Leagues under the Sea* (1870), translated
    by Walter James Miller and Frederick Paul Walter (1993)

[On an alien:] An intellectual carrot. The mind boggles.
  —Charles Lederer, *The Thing (from Another World)* (film, 1951)

Tom's words laid bare the hearts of trees and their thoughts, which were often dark and strange, and filled with a hatred of things that go free upon the earth, gnawing, biting, breaking, hacking, burning: destroyers and usurpers.
  —J. R. R. Tolkien, *The Fellowship of the Ring* (1954)

He laid his hand upon the tree beside the ladder; never before had he been so suddenly and so keenly aware of the feel and texture of a tree's skin and

of the life within it. He felt a delight in wood and the touch of it, neither as forester nor as carpenter; it was the delight of the living tree itself.
— J. R. R. Tolkien, *The Fellowship of the Ring* (1954)

The silence seemed to carry as much weight as that deep mass of foliage which covered all the land on the day side of the planet. It was a silence built of millions upon millions of years, intensifying as the sun overhead poured forth more and more energy in the first stages of its decline. Not that the silence signified lack of life. Life was everywhere, life on a formidable scale. But the increased solar radiation that had brought the extinction of most of the animal kingdom had spelt the triumph of plant life. Everywhere, in a thousand forms and guises, the plants ruled. And vegetables have no voices.
— Brian W. Aldiss, "Nomansland" (1961)

That which submits rules. [. . .] The willow submits to the wind and prospers until one day it is many willows — a wall against the wind. This is the willow's purpose.
— Frank Herbert, *Dune* (1965)

Earth, terra, tellus mean both the soil and the planet, two meanings and one. But to the Athsheans soil, ground, earth was not that to which the dead return and by which the living live; the substance of their world was not earth, but forest. Terran man was clay, red dust. Athshean man was branch and root. They did not carve figures of themselves in stone, only in wood.
— Ursula K. Le Guin, "The Word for World Is Forest" (1972)

He could sense, too, the thrill of being a tree, which was something he hadn't expected. He knew that it felt good to curl your toes in the earth, but he'd never realized it could feel quite as good as that.
— Douglas Adams, *So Long, and Thanks for All the Fish* (1985)

The power of growing things confounded imagination. Little fresh top soil had formed on this man-made clearing but the roadway had for all practical purposes vanished under weeds, shrubs, trees, native grasses.
— George Turner, *Drowning Towers* (1987)

Plants

Plant breeding is not an enterprise for impatient people. It *is* a gesture of faith in the (personal) future.
— Judith Moffett, "Tiny Tango" (1989)

Wind swept the grass in waves, the golden blades swaying as if to pipe music. No smell on earth is like that one, a sweetness more delicate than any perfumed oil, richer than any scent of flower.
— Jim Grimsley, "Free in Asveroth" (1998)

POLITICS

This is entirely unlike the disorderly, disorganized elections of the ancients, when — absurd to say — the very results of the election were unknown beforehand. Building a state on entirely unpredictable eventualities, blindly — what can be more senseless?
— Yevgeny Zamiatin, *We* (1924), translated by Mirra Ginsburg (1972)

It had never occurred to me before that twentieth century politicians had meant, or had thought they meant, what they said; that indeed, they had in their own minds attached a sense of meaning or relevancy to what seem to us meaningless or irrelevant phrases.
— John R. Pierce, "Invariant" (1944)

Any collocation of persons, no matter how numerous, how scant, how even their homogeneity, how firmly they profess common doctrine, will presently reveal themselves to consist of smaller groups espousing variant versions of the common creed; and these sub-groups will manifest sub-sub-groups, and so to the final limit of the single individual, and even in this single person conflicting tendencies will express themselves.
— Jack Vance, *The Languages of Pao* (1958)

To be elected President is the greatest misfortune and disgrace that can befall an Islander.
— William S. Burroughs, *Naked Lunch* (1959)

There is an old song which asserts that "the best things in life are free." Not true! Utterly false! This was the tragic fallacy which brought on the decadence and collapse of the democracies of the twentieth century; those noble experiments failed because the people had been led to believe that they could simply vote for whatever they wanted . . . and get it, without toil, without sweat, without tears.

    —Robert A. Heinlein, *Starship Troopers* (1959)

Politics is just a name for the way we get things done . . . without fighting. We dicker and compromise and everybody thinks he has received a raw deal, but somehow after a tedious amount of talk we come up with some jury-rigged way to do it without getting anybody's head bashed in.

    —Robert A. Heinlein, *Podkayne of Mars: Her Life and Times* (1963)

When religion and politics travel in the same cart, the riders believe nothing can stand in their way. Their movements become headlong—faster and faster and faster. They put aside all thought of obstacles and forget that a precipice does not show itself to the man in a blind rush until it's too late.

    —Frank Herbert, *Dune* (1965)

What's the use of arguing about politics these days? Isn't such a thing as politics. There's just a choice between the ways you're going to cave in through force of circumstances.

    —John Brunner, *Stand on Zanzibar* (1968)

Even in a bisexual society the politician is very often something less than an integral man.

    —Ursula K. Le Guin, *The Left Hand of Darkness* (1969)

I don't mean love, when I say patriotism. I mean fear. The fear of the other. And its expressions are political, not poetical: hate, rivalry, aggression.

    —Ursula K. Le Guin, *The Left Hand of Darkness* (1969)

The purpose of diplomacy is to prolong a crisis.

    —George F. Slavin and Stanley Adams, "The Mark of Gideon," episode of *Star Trek* (1969)

"Part dreamer," continued the prosecutor, "part adventurer."

    "That's no longer a profession," replied Mac. "It is, if I may say so, simply a trait possessed by any decent scientist."

"And decent politician."

"A rare combination of words," quipped Mac.

— Arkady Strugatsky and Boris Strugatsky, *Prisoners of Power* (1969),
translated by Helen Saltz Jacobson (1977)

Journalists and politicians have generally been the worst of the race, not the
best.

— Hank Davis, "To Plant a Seed" (1972)

Fascism was a fairly popular political philosophy which made sacred
whatever nation and race the philosopher happened to belong to.

— Kurt Vonnegut, Jr., *Breakfast of Champions, or, Goodbye, Blue Monday!*
(1973)

Yesterday's politics are not worth the paper wasted on its promises, its
threats.

— Roger Zelazny, "The Engine at Heartspring's Corner" (1974)

"Ideology," growled one of his new friends. "It's a virus. The world is dying
of it."

— Brian W. Aldiss, "Three Ways" (1978)

Anyone who is capable of getting themselves made President should on no
account be allowed to do the job.

— Douglas Adams, "Fit the Twelfth," episode of *The Hitch-Hiker's Guide to
the Galaxy* (radio series, 1980)

"On its world, the people are people. The leaders are lizards. The people hate
the lizards and the lizards rule the people."

"Odd," said Arthur. "I thought you said it was a democracy."

"I did," said Ford. [. . .]

"You mean they actually *vote* for the lizards?"

"Oh, yes," said Ford with a shrug, "of course."

"But," said Arthur, going for the big one again, "why?"

"Because if they didn't vote for a lizard," said Ford, "the wrong lizard might
get in."

— Douglas Adams, *So Long, and Thanks for All the Fish* (1985)

I think you'd like politics, at least on Barrayar. Maybe because it's so similar to what we call war, elsewhere.
   —Lois McMaster Bujold, *Shards of Honor* (1986)

You got to help me. I don't know what to do. I can't make decisions. I'm a president!
   —Mel Brooks, Thomas Meehan, and Ronny Graham, *Spaceballs* (film, 1987)

Species at this stage of their development tend to be territorial, Memory reminded Drill. *Their political mentality is based around the concept of borders. The idea of a borderless community of species may be perceived as a threat.*
   —Walter Jon Williams, "Dinosaurs" (1987)

Conflicts are not won on battlefields, General, but in boardrooms.
   —Gay Marshall, "The Heart of the Hydra" (1995)

VIR: I thought the purpose of filing these reports was to provide accurate intelligence.
LONDO: Vir, intelligence has nothing to do with politics.
   —J. Michael Straczynski, "Point of No Return," episode of *Babylon 5* (1996)

POWER

"It is a wonderful thing," he cried, "to feel that one can command powers of good and of evil—a ministering angel or a demon of vengeance."
   —Arthur Conan Doyle, "Lot No. 249" (1892)

It was the law of Hadden's existence never to deny himself anything that he desired if it lay within his power to take it—a law which had led him always deeper into sin.
   —H. Rider Haggard, "Black Heart and White Heart" (1896)

The greater a man's talents, the greater his power to lead astray. It is better that one should suffer than that many should be corrupted.
   —Aldous Huxley, *Brave New World* (1932)

Man has always dreamed of power. But damn it, man has always dreamed of love, too, and of the rights of his fellow man. The only power worthy of man is the power of all mankind struggling together toward a goal of unobtainable perfection.

— Anthony Boucher, "The Barrier" (1942)

Meanwhile, as should be, the clever will rule the stupid for their own good. The realists will rule the dreamers. Those with free hands will rule those who have deliberately handcuffed themselves with taboos.

— Fritz Leiber, "Poor Superman" (1951)

He had opened the gates of infinity, and now felt awe — even fear — for all that he had done.

— Arthur C. Clarke, *The City and the Stars* (1956)

The lust for power is a part of human life. As long as people want power badly enough, they'll use any means to get it — fair or foul! Peaceful or otherwise!

— Frank Herbert, "Cease Fire" (1958)

"A world is supported by four things . . ." She held up four big-knuckled fingers. ". . . the learning of the wise, the justice of the great, the prayers of the righteous and the valor of the brave. But all of these are as nothing . . ." She closed her fingers into a fist. ". . . without a ruler who knows the art of ruling."

— Frank Herbert, *Dune* (1965)

The struggle between life elements is the struggle for the free energy of a system.

— Frank Herbert, *Dune* (1965)

Ged crouched among the dripping bushes wet and sullen, and wondered what was the good of having power if you were too wise to use it.

— Ursula K. Le Guin, *A Wizard of Earthsea* (1968)

Power has become so subtle and complex a thing in the ways taken by the Ekumen that only a subtle mind can watch it work; here it is still limited, still visible. In Estraven, for instance, one feels the man's power as an augmentation of his character; he cannot make an empty gesture or say a word that is not listened to. He knows it, and the knowledge gives him more reality than most people own: a solidness of being, a substantiality, a human grandeur.

—Ursula K. Le Guin, *The Left Hand of Darkness* (1969)

The vaster the power gained, the vaster the appetite for more.

—Ursula K. Le Guin, *The Lathe of Heaven* (1971)

Coercion is the least efficient means of obtaining order.

—Ursula K. Le Guin, *The Dispossessed: An Ambiguous Utopia* (1974)

We have lost what is Random, we have banished the Arbitrary, Mistress Christia. With our power rings and our gene banks we can, if we desire, change the courses of the planets, populate them with any kind of creature we wish, make our old sun burst with fresh energy or fade completely from the firmament. We control All. Nothing controls us!

—Michael Moorcock, "Pale Roses" (1974)

Within each of us lies the power of our consent to health and to sickness, to riches and to poverty, to freedom and to slavery. It is we who control these, and not another.

—Richard Bach, *Illusions: The Adventures of a Reluctant Messiah* (1977)

The very powerful and the very stupid have one thing in common, they don't alter their views to fit the facts, they alter the facts to fit the views, which can be uncomfortable, if you happen to be one of the facts that needs altering.

—Chris Boucher, "The Face of Evil," episode of *Doctor Who* (1977)

The Force is what gives a Jedi his power. It's an energy field created by all living things. It surrounds us and penetrates us. It binds the galaxy together.

—George Lucas, *Star Wars* (film, 1977)

The Force will be with you, always.

—George Lucas, *Star Wars* (film, 1977)

Beware of small men, he had often told himself, because they are the movers and shakers of the world.

—Arthur C. Clarke, *The Fountains of Paradise* (1979)

Power

The insistence of the weak, he thought; their dreadful power. It is so much easier to throw a body-block against the strong!
— Philip K. Dick, "Chains of Air, Web of Aether" (1980)

A commanding officer's "unlimited" authority isn't freedom; it's a strait-jacket. She can't do as *she* pleases; she *never* can — because every minute, awake and asleep, she must protect those under her command.
— Robert A. Heinlein, *The Number of the Beast* (1980)

Perhaps he's reached that stage of intoxication which power is said to inspire, the state in which you believe you are indispensable and can therefore do anything, absolutely anything you feel like, anything at all.
— Margaret Atwood, *The Handmaid's Tale* (1986)

When power is scarce, a little of it is tempting.
— Margaret Atwood, *The Handmaid's Tale* (1986)

That's what authority is, isn't it? The power to make people afraid?
— George Turner, *Drowning Towers* (1987)

It was the seat of government; it held the power. It was the powerhouse, the powder magazine, the bomb. Power had been compressed, jammed into those old reddish walls, packed and forced into them over years, over centuries, till if it exploded it would burst with horrible violence, hurling pointing shards of stone.
— Ursula K. Le Guin, "Unlocking the Air" (1990)

When you can flatten entire cities at a whim, a tendency towards quiet reflection and seeing-things-from-the-other-fellow's-point-of-view is seldom necessary.
— Terry Pratchett, *Small Gods* (1992)

Power wasn't a matter of job titles, after all. Power was a matter of vision, persuasiveness, freedom of movement, fame, influence.
— Kim Stanley Robinson, *Red Mars* (1992)

You can tear people like him apart like a piece of paper, but it doesn't change anything.
  — M. John Harrison, "Isobel Avens Returns to Stepney in the Spring" (1994)

Kathy thought of celebrity as a subtle fluid, a universal element, like the phlogiston of the ancients, something spread evenly at creation through all the universe, but prone now to accrete, under specific conditions, around certain individuals and their careers.
  — William Gibson, *Idoru* (1996)

A bit of what you call weakness would do you a world of good. Put some softness in your voice once in a while. Strength shouldn't be a shield, woman, but a sword.
  — Tara K. Harper, *Wolf's Bane* (1997)

Virtue was only the vice of whoever happened to be in control.
  — Ralph A. Sperry, "On Vacation" (1998)

PROBLEMS

Sure we had trouble building Space Station One—but the trouble was people.
  — Robert A. Heinlein, "Delilah and the Space Rigger" (1949)

Why shouldn't the boy have trouble? Trouble is the normal condition for the human race. We were raised on it. We thrive on it.
  — Robert A. Heinlein, *Red Planet: A Colonial Boy on Mars* (1949)

What is fire? It's a mystery. Scientists give us gobbledegook about friction and molecules. But they don't really know. Its real beauty is that it destroys responsibility and consequences. A problem gets too burdensome, then into the furnace with it.
  — Ray Bradbury, *Fahrenheit 451* (1954)

When faced with a problem you do not understand, do any part of it you do understand, then look at it again.
  — Robert A. Heinlein, *The Moon Is a Harsh Mistress* (1966)

Given a problem that must be solved and no possible solution, almost all individuals were forced into madness.

—Lester del Rey, *Pstalemate* (1971)

There are those who see social/economic/ecological problems as malfunctions which can be corrected by simple repair, replacement or streamlining—a kind of linear outlook where even innovations are considered to be merely additive. Then there are those who sometimes hesitate to move at all, because their awareness follows events in the directions of secondary and tertiary effects as they multiply and cross-fertilize throughout the entire system.

—Roger Zelazny, "Home Is the Hangman" (1975)

There is no such thing as a problem without a gift for you in its hands. You seek problems because you need their gifts.

—Richard Bach, *Illusions: The Adventures of a Reluctant Messiah* (1977)

Mankind has never solved its problems. It has just substituted larger ones.

—Theodore Sturgeon, "Why Dolphins Don't Bite" (1980)

It is a mistake to think you can solve any major problems just with potatoes.

—Douglas Adams, *Life, the Universe, and Everything* (1982)

Tests are a gift. And great tests are a great gift. To fail the test is a misfortune. But to refuse the test is to refuse the gift, and something worse, more irrevocable, than misfortune.

—Lois McMaster Bujold, *Shards of Honor* (1986)

What we are concerned with here is the fundamental interconnectedness of all things. I do not concern myself with such petty things as fingerprint powder, telltale pieces of pocket fluff and inane footprints. I see the solution to each problem as being detectable in the pattern and web of the whole.

—Douglas Adams, *Dirk Gently's Holistic Detective Agency* (1987)

No one can solve problems for someone whose problem is that they don't want problems solved.

—Richard Bach, *One* (1988)

The existence of a well-defined problem does not imply the existence of a solution.
　—Gregory Benford, *Tides of Light* (1989)

PROGRESS

The Count merely said that Great Movements were awfully common things in his day, and as for Progress, it was at one time quite a nuisance, but it never progressed.
　—Edgar Allan Poe, "Some Words with a Mummy," revised (1845)

He, I know—for the question had been discussed among us long before the Time Machine was made—thought but cheerlessly of the Advancement of Mankind, and saw in the growing pile of civilization only a foolish heaping that must invariably fall back upon and destroy its makers in the end. If that is so, it remains for us to live as though it were not so. But to me the future is still black and blank—is a vast ignorance, lit at a few casual places by the memory of his story. And I have by me, for my comfort, two strange white flowers—shrivelled now, and brown and flat and brittle—to witness that even when mind and strength had gone, gratitude and a mutual tenderness still lived on in the heart of man.
　—H. G. Wells, *The Time Machine: An Invention* (1895)

It is possible to believe that all the past is but the beginning of a beginning, and that all that is and has been is but the twilight of the dawn. It is possible to believe that all the human mind has ever accomplished is but the dream before the awakening.
　—H. G. Wells, *The Discovery of the Future* (1902)

What will not be forgotten, and what will and should continue to obsess our imaginations, is this revelation of the possibilities of the universe, this destruction of our ignorant self-complacency, and this demonstration of how narrow is the path of our material existence, and what abysses may lie upon either side of it. Solemnity and humility are at the base of all our emotions to-day. May they be the foundations upon which a more earnest and reverent race may build a more worthy temple.
　—Arthur Conan Doyle, *The Poison Belt* (1913)

They had early observed the value of certain improvements, had easily inferred that there was room for more, and took the greatest pains to develop two kinds of minds — the critic and inventor. Those who showed an early tendency to observe, to discriminate, to suggest, were given special training for that function; and some of their highest officials spent their time in the most careful study of one or another branch of work, with a view to its further improvement.
   — Charlotte Perkins Gilman, *Herland* (1915)

Everything in human society is being continually perfected — and should be.
   — Yevgeny Zamiatin, *We* (1924), translated by Mirra Ginsburg (1972)

If human thought is a growth, like all other growths, its logic is without foundation of its own, and is only the adjusting constructiveness of all other growing things. A tree cannot find out, as it were, how to blossom, until comes blossom-time. A social growth cannot find out the use of steam engines, until comes steam-engine-time.
   — Charles Fort, *Lo!* (1931)

We must move with the times, you know, even at Shangri-La.
   — James Hilton, *Lost Horizon* (1933)

RAYMOND PASSWORTHY: Oh, God, is there ever to be any age of happiness? Is there never to be any rest?

OSWALD CABAL: Rest enough for the individual man — too much, and too soon — and we call it death. But for Man, no rest and no ending. He must go on, conquest beyond conquest. First this little planet with its winds and ways, and then all the laws of mind and matter that restrain him. Then the planets about him and at last out across immensity to the stars. And when he has conquered all the deeps of space and all the mysteries of time, still he will be beginning.

PASSWORTHY: But . . . we're such little creatures. Poor humanity's so fragile, so weak. Little . . . little animals.

CABAL: Little animals. If we're no more than animals, we must snatch each little scrap of happiness and live and suffer and pass, mattering no more than all the other animals do or have done. It is this, or that. All the universe, or nothingness. Which shall it be, Passworthy? Which shall it be?
   — H. G. Wells, *Things to Come* (film, 1936)

They were men who built the city; they were not gods or demons. They were men. I remember the dead man's face. They were men who were here before us. We must build again.

—Stephen Vincent Benét, "By the Waters of Babylon" (1937)

It reminded him of other days, when weather was something to be experienced rather than to be planned. Life had lost some of its flavor, in his estimation, when the weather engineers had finally harnessed the elements.

—Robert A. Heinlein, *Methuselah's Children* (1941)

Speed, is that progress? Anyway, why progress? Why not enjoy what one has? Men have never exhausted present pleasures.

—Austin Tappan Wright, *Islandia* (1942)

Only the fittest should survive. Differential breeding. How else can we have a better race, eh? Progress is built on death.

—Katherine MacLean, "The Fittest" (1951)

I shall not shape humanity's future. I do not even imagine it. It is so rich in possibilities and potentialities that it is, strictly speaking, unimaginable.

—Margaret St. Clair, *Agent of the Unknown* (1952)

I thought of the distant future and the things we'd have, and discounted my wildest guesses as inadequate. Immortality? Achieved in the nineteenth millennium X. R. and discarded in the twenty-third because it was no longer necessary. Reverse entropy to rewind the universe? Obsolete with the discovery of nolanism and the concurrent cognate in the quadrate decal. Sounds wild? How would the word *quantum* or the concept of a matter-energy transformation sound to a Neanderthaler? *We're* Neanderthalers, to our descendants of a hundred thousand years from now. You'll sell them short to make the wildest guess as to what they'll do and what they'll be.

The stars? Hell, yes. They'll have the stars.

—Fredric Brown, *The Lights in the Sky Are Stars* (1953)

People don't really want change, any change at all—and xenophobia is very deep-rooted. But we progress, as we must—if we are to go out to the stars.

—Robert A. Heinlein, *Double Star* (1956)

Between 1800 and 1900 the doctrine of Pie in the Sky gave place, in a majority of Western minds, to the doctrine of Pie on the Earth. The motivating and compensatory Future came to be regarded, not as a state of disembodied happiness, to be enjoyed by me and my friends after death, but as a condition of terrestrial well-being for my children or (if that seemed a bit too optimistic) my grandchildren, or maybe my great-grandchildren.
 —Aldous Huxley, "Tomorrow and Tomorrow and Tomorrow" (1956)

Why is it always — *always* — so costly for man to move from the present to the future?
 —Robert Creighton Williams and Christopher Knopf, *20 Million Miles to Earth* (film, 1957)

Every passing hour brings the Solar System forty-three thousand miles closer to Globular Cluster M13 in Hercules — and still there are some misfits who insist that there is no such thing as progress.
 —Kurt Vonnegut, Jr., *The Sirens of Titan* (1959)

Anything that is theoretically possible will be achieved in practice, no matter what the technical difficulties, if it is desired greatly enough.
 —Arthur C. Clarke, "Hazards of Prophecy: An Arresting Inquiry into the Limits of the Possible: Failures of Nerve and Failures of Imagination" (1962)

The concept of progress acts as a protective mechanism to shield us from the terrors of the future.
 —Frank Herbert, *Dune* (1965)

You don't think progress goes in a straight line, do you? Do you recognize that it is an ascending, accelerating, maybe even exponential curve? It takes hell's own time to get started, but when it goes it goes like a bomb.
 —Frederik Pohl, "Day Million" (1966)

Faced with the challenge of the endless universe, Man will be forced to mature further, just as the Neanderthal — faced with an entire planet — had no choice but to grow away from the tradition of savagery.
 —Dean Koontz, "That Moon Plaque: Comments by Science Fiction Writers" (1969)

So long as man can see himself as a destructive, aggressive creature, who in the killing of his fellow beings can be compared only with mice, and so long as there are countries in this world where his opinion can be discussed and voiced freely, there is still hope that mankind will overcome in its pursuit of the far stars.

   — Josef Nesvadba, "That Moon Plaque: Comments by Science Fiction
      Writers" (1969)

A capsule description of most human "progress": By the time you learn how, it's too late.

   — Robert A. Heinlein, *Time Enough for Love* (1973)

Little mirrors were affixed to the front of their cars, at which they glanced to see where they had been; then they stared ahead again. I had thought that only beetles had this delusion of Progress.

   — Ursula K. Le Guin, "The Direction of the Road" (1973)

We fret about how to keep going the same old way when we should be casting around for another way that's better.

   — John Brunner, *The Shockwave Rider* (1975)

People don't die from the old diseases any more. They die from new ones, but that's Progress, isn't it?

   Isn't it?

   — Harlan Ellison, "Jeffty Is Five" (1977)

Progress is a tension between the notion of perfection and the notion that striving, not finding, is important.

   — George Zebrowski, *Macrolife* (1979)

Her grandparents, believers in progress, had always told her things were better now. Human minds had been darker when people couldn't read late at night, their prejudices greater when they had lacked television's images of other places, their work harder without the appliances many took for granted. Nina was not so sure; technical civilization had isolated people from the basics of life, and had fooled them into believing that they controlled the world.

   — Pamela Sargent, "The Old Darkness" (1983)

The present tumult in our world is the natural and understandable result of a vigorous intelligence moving out of the savagery of our life form's childhood. Instead of humanity's demise, our era seems to be filled with evidence that we were meant to survive and evolve much further.

   —Gene Roddenberry, "A Letter to the Next Generation" (1988)

The Tezumen had realised long ago that everything was steadily getting worse and, having a terrible literal-mindedness, had developed a complex system to keep track of how much worse each succeeding day was.

   —Terry Pratchett, *Eric* (1990)

"Will the world be a better place?" Jason asked.

   Prometheus shook his head. "I doubt it," he said. "It always amazes me, the way the old place quickly gets back to normal no matter what you do to try and improve it. No, you can make it worse, no problem, but it's virtually impossible to improve it. I tried, remember. I gave them fire, and yet millions of people are still cold. I taught them agriculture, and millions of them are still starving. I gave them laughter, and yet the majority of them are still as miserable as income tax. I can only imagine it's how they like it, deep down."

   —Tom Holt, *Ye Gods!* (1992)

Among all the many things we transform on Mars, ourselves and our social reality should be among them. We must terraform not only Mars, but ourselves.

   —Kim Stanley Robinson, *Red Mars* (1992)

Terraforming is an ancient profession.

   Making your world more habitable began on the Earth itself, with the first dancing fire that warmed its builder's cave; and everything since—every green world and asteroid and comet—is an enlargement on that first cozy cave.

   —Robert Reed, "A Place with Shade" (1995)

"I'm sure we can pull together, sir."

   Lord Vetinari raised his eyebrows. "Oh, I do hope not, I really do hope not. Pulling together is the aim of despotism and tyranny. Free men pull in all kinds of directions." He smiled. "It's the only way to make progress."

   —Terry Pratchett, *The Truth* (2000)

PSYCHIC POWERS

Among the mind-readers, politeness never can extend to the point of insincerity, as among talking nations, seeing that it is always one another's real and inmost thought that they read.
  —Edward Bellamy, "To Whom This May Come" (1889)

A shallow rectangular pool held goldfish, who gulped hopefully as they swam to the surface and flipped down again. The little minds of the fish lay open to Cody, minds thoughtless as so many bright, tiny, steady flames on little birthday candles, as he walked past the pool.
  —Henry Kuttner and C. L. Moore, "Humpty Dumpty" (1953)

Telepathy transmits delicate shades of meaning quite lost in spoken language.
  —Robert Sheckley, "Carrier" (1954)

You can't have a strategy against telepaths; you have to act randomly. You have to not know what you're going to do next.
  —Philip K. Dick, *Solar Lottery* (1955)

A telepathic society would be more rational. When every little wound in the child's soul could be felt and healed . . . when the thick burden of guilt was laid down, because everyone knew that everyone else had done the same . . . when men could not kill, because soldier and murderer felt the victim die . . .
  —Poul Anderson, "Journeys End" (1957)

And the creature spoke.
  Hi, pal, it said. *I trade with you my mind.*
  —Clifford D. Simak, *Time Is the Simplest Thing* (1961)

I'm still picking up your mentational processes by way of your cephalic transmitter. [. . .] So I have to warn you: anything you think may be held against you.
  —Philip K. Dick, "We Can Remember It for You Wholesale" (1966)

Plainly it was one thing to read a mind and another to understand it.
  —Philip K. Dick and Ray Nelson, *The Ganymede Takeover* (1967)

Like most telepaths, he had learned to ignore the great body of inchoate thoughts in people: hostility, boredom, outright disgust, envy. Thoughts, many of which the person himself was unaware of. A telepath had to learn to have a thick skin. In essence, he had to learn to relate to a person's conscious, positive thoughts, not the vaguely-defined mixture of his unconscious processes.

—Philip K. Dick, *Our Friends from Frolix 8* (1970)

"What is it, exactly, that you pick up with your empathic sensitivity?"

"Muck," the man answered in his high, exasperated voice. "The psychic excreta of the animal kingdom. I wade through your faeces."

—Ursula K. Le Guin, "Vaster Than Empires and More Slow" (1971)

Lasten could hear people's minds. Not their thoughts, for people don't have thoughts inside; Lasten heard emotions and mind-pictures, whatever was strongest in the consciousness of those around him. Red hate, boiling and exploding; sometimes pure fear, blue-white, rigid; sex fantasies that echoed disturbingly in Lasten's own mind.

—Terry Carr, "Ozymandias" (1972)

"Can you read my mind?" [. . .]

"Minds aren't *read*. See, you've still got the paradigms print gave you, and you're barely print-literate. I can *access* your memory, but that's not the same as your mind."

—William Gibson, *Neuromancer* (1984)

PSYCHOLOGY

The most merciful thing in the world, I think, is the inability of the human mind to correlate all its contents. We live on a placid island of ignorance in the midst of black seas of infinity, and it was not meant that we should voyage far.

—H. P. Lovecraft, "The Call of Cthulhu" (1928)

Subconscious minds are no less fallible than the objective mind.

—Edgar Rice Burroughs, *Pirates of Venus* (1934)

A psychiatrist is the last man to see about a thing like that. They know everything about a man, except what he is and what makes him tick. Besides, did
you ever see a worry-doctor that was sane himself?
　—Robert A. Heinlein, *Beyond This Horizon* (1942)

The function of a psychiatrist is to tell the difference between those who are
reasonable and those who merely talk and act reasonably.
　—Mary Chase, *Harvey* (play, 1944)

Yardsticks of scientific psychology are used to measure a man, and yet they
give no indication at all of the inner spirit of him. [. . .] Knowing about a
man, and knowing a man are two entirely different things.
　—Mark Clifton, "What Have I Done?" (1952)

A lot of human thinking occurred beneath the level of consciousness, down
in the darker regions of the mind where it was not allowed to become
conscious lest it bring shame to the thinker. And perhaps he had reasoned it
all out in that mental half-world where thoughts are inner ghosts, haunting
the possessed man with vague stirrings of uneasiness, leading him into
inexplicable behavior.
　—Walter M. Miller, Jr., "Way of a Rebel" (1954)

Thanks to technology, the reasons for many of the old social problems have
passed, and along with them went many of the reasons for psychic distress.
But between the black of yesterday and the white of tomorrow is the great
gray of today, filled with nostalgia and fear of the future, which cannot be
expressed on a purely material plane, is now being represented by a willful
seeking after historical anxiety-modes . . .
　—Roger Zelazny, "He Who Shapes" (1965)

While psychologists drink and only grow angry, psychiatrists have been
known to drink, grow angry, and break things.
　—Roger Zelazny, "He Who Shapes" (1965)

The waking brain is perpetually lapped by the unconscious.
　—Brian W. Aldiss, "Man in His Time" (1966)

Psychology

The unconscious is the ocean of the unsayable, of what has been expelled from the land of language, removed as a result of ancient prohibitions.
— Italo Calvino, "Cybernetics and Ghosts" (1967), translated by
   Patrick Creagh (1987)

I—I'm afraid, Excellency! We're tampering with the mightiest instrument in the universe: a human brain!
— Keith Laumer, "Test to Destruction" (1967)

"It bedevils me sometimes why I am the only one to notice the analogy between historical geology and depth psychology," Terrence Burdock mused as they grew lightly profound around the campfire. "The isostatic principle applies to the mind and the under-mind as well as it does to the surface and undersurface of the earth. The mind has its erosions and weatherings going on along with its deposits and accumulations. It also has its upthrusts and its stresses. It floats on a similar magma. In extreme cases it has its volcanic eruptions and its mountain building."
"And it has its glaciations," Ethel Burdock said, and perhaps she was looking at her husband in the dark.
— R. A. Lafferty, "Continued on Next Rock" (1970)

My knowledge of the human psyche is as yet imperfect. Certain areas won't yield to computation.
— Poul Anderson, "Goat Song" (1972)

Everyone, after all, is always "psychoanalysing" everyone else; it is part of our culture, the basic form of modern romance, in which one party tries to invade the psyche of another, the victim agreeing provisionally to assist the invader. Rather, in a way, like an old vampire movie.
— Thomas M. Disch, "Things Lost" (1972)

We have treatments for disturbed persons, Nicholas. But, at least for the time being, we have no treatment for disturbing persons.
— Gene Wolfe, "The Death of Doctor Island" (1974)

The best maze is the mind.
— Ursula K. Le Guin, "Mazes" (1975)

It is amazing how banal most people's minds are. [. . .] I used to think how wonderful other people's minds would be, how wonderful it was going to be to share in all the different worlds, the different colors of their passions and ideas. How naïve I was!
— Ursula K. Le Guin, "The Diary of the Rose" (1976)

In politics the authorities must lead and be followed, but in psychological medicine it is a little different, a doctor cannot "cure" the patient, the patient "cures" himself with our help, this is not contradictory to Positive Thinking.
— Ursula K. Le Guin, "The Diary of the Rose" (1976)

You know the simple psychological truth, Charles, we're always accusing others of our own flaws.
— Alfred Bester, "Galatea Galante" (1979)

Warning: Therapy can be dangerous to your health. Especially if you are the therapist.
— Suzy McKee Charnas, "The Unicorn Tapestry" (1980)

Psychotherapy has become a branch of applied biochemistry.
— Poul Anderson, "The Saturn Game" (1981)

GILLIAN TAYLOR: Sure you won't change your mind?
SPOCK: Is there something wrong with the one I have?
— Steve Meerson, Peter Krikes, Harve Bennett, and Nicholas Meyer,
Star Trek IV: The Voyage Home (film, 1986)

Looking into the capacities of my own mind was like peering into some parallel universe where the laws of sense did not operate and anything was possible.
— George Turner, *Drowning Towers* (1987)

Until you confront the dark things inside you, they make you helpless. They are your weaknesses.
— Storm Constantine, "Immaculate" (1991)

Every therapist on Earth was also in therapy; it was part of the job.
— Kim Stanley Robinson, *Red Mars* (1992)

Psychology

There was a fridge-magnet on the thermos that said I'M NOT OKAY, YOU'RE NOT OKAY — BUT HEY, THAT'S OKAY.
   — William Gibson, *Virtual Light* (1993)

The mind is not a box that can be simply unlocked and opened; it's a beehive with a million different departments.
   — Michael Dougherty, Dan Harris, and David Hayter, *X2: X-Men United* (film, 2003)

QUESTIONS AND ANSWERS

Your mind will answer most questions if you learn to relax and wait for the answer.
—William S. Burroughs, *Naked Lunch* (1959)

Why was *he* there, what failure was *he* trying to expiate? And why choose Cocoa Beach as his penitential shore? For three years he had asked himself these questions so often that they had ceased to have any meaning, like a fossilised catechism or the blunted self-recrimination of a paranoic [*sic*].
—J. G. Ballard, "The Cage of Sand" (1962)

Prof was interested in questions rather than answers, which baffled her.
—Robert A. Heinlein, *The Moon Is a Harsh Mistress* (1966)

questions
are a burden to others
answers
a prison for oneself
—George Markstein and David Tomblin, "Arrival," episode of
The Prisoner (1968)

I have something in my head that just won't quit. It's a way I have of asking the next question: why is so-and-so the way it is? Why can't it be such-and-such instead? There is always another question to be asked about anything or any situation—especially you shouldn't quit when you like an answer because there's always another one after it. And we live in a world where people just don't want to ask the next question!
—Theodore Sturgeon, "Slow Sculpture" (1970)

That's one of those meaningless and unanswerable questions the mind keeps returning to endlessly, like the tongue exploring a broken tooth.
—Arthur C. Clarke, "Transit of Earth" (1971)

"Knowledge is what man is all about. [. . .] Man needs to know."

"Maybe," Sanders said, "But is that the *only* thing man needs? I don't think so. I think he also needs mystery, and poetry, and romance. I think he needs a few unanswered questions, to make him brood and wonder."

— George R. R. Martin, "With Morning Comes Mistfall" (1973)

They argued because they liked argument, liked the swift run of the unfettered mind along the paths of possibility, liked to question what was not questioned.

— Ursula K. Le Guin, *The Dispossessed: An Ambiguous Utopia* (1974)

Do not on any account give the same answer tomorrow as you give today.

— John Brunner, *The Shockwave Rider* (1975)

Her dance addressed reality, gave successive expression to the Three Eternal Questions asked by every human being who ever lived.

Her dance observed her *self,* and asked, "*How have I come to be here?*"

Her dance observed the universe in which self existed, and asked, "*How did all this come to be here with me?*"

And at last, observing her self in relation to its universe, "*Why am I so alone?*" [. . .]

The dance ended, leaving her three questions unanswered, the tension of their asking unresolved.

— Spider Robinson and Jeanne Robinson, "Stardance" (1977)

Often the simple answers are the hardest to find.

— Poul Anderson, "The Saturn Game" (1981)

Why, he wondered, did so many people spend their lives not trying to find answers to questions — not even thinking of questions to begin with? Was there anything more exciting in life than seeking answers?

— Isaac Asimov, *Prelude to Foundation* (1988)

Todd used to say that we never ask ourselves questions we can't answer. "You don't have to know the answer," he had said patiently, "but you have to know the question is answerable. You can't even ask about things you know nothing of. And most of the time, you already know the answer. You just have to

reorganize your knowledge to make it accessible. Asking a good question attests to a tremendous amount of knowledge."
—Kate Wilhelm, "Isosceles" (1988)

Asking questions was the key to people's souls, infinitely more useful than wit.
—Kim Stanley Robinson, *Red Mars* (1992)

Why try to turn everything into a big mystery? If you go around asking questions the whole time you'll never get *anything* done.
—Terry Pratchett, *The Last Continent* (1998)

Without outside stimulation it was hard to break free of his own assumptions. One mind can think only of its own questions; it rarely surprises itself.
—Orson Scott Card, *Ender's Shadow* (1999)

RACE RELATIONS

That was another very ancient lesson: that different metabolisms produce different manifestations. How boring would the universe be if all its creatures were identically the same!

    —Eric Frank Russell, "Fast Falls the Eventide" (1952)

I didn't like Martians. I did not fancy having a thing that looks like a tree trunk topped off by a sun helmet claiming the privileges of a man. [. . .] Nobody could accuse me of race prejudice. I didn't care what a man's color, race, or religion was. But men were men, whereas Martians were *things*.

    —Robert A. Heinlein, *Double Star* (1956)

It showed us, he decided, that the difference between say myself and the average Negro is so damn slight, by every truly meaningful criterion, that for all intents and purposes it doesn't exist. When something like that, a contact with a race that's not Homo sapiens, occurs, at last we can finally see this.

    —Philip K. Dick, *The Crack in Space* (1965)

"Being white; that's also a religion. I can tell you in just one word what the white religion is."

    "What?" Joan said guardedly.

    "Hypocrisy."

    —Philip K. Dick and Ray Nelson, *The Ganymede Takeover* (1967)

NEGRO Member of a sub-group of the human race who hails, or whose ancestors hailed, from a chunk of land nicknamed—not by its residents— Africa. Superior to the Caucasian in that negroes did not invent nuclear weapons, the automobile, Christianity, nerve gas, the concentration camp, military epidemics, or the megalopolis.

    —John Brunner, *Stand on Zanzibar* (1968)

I am pleased to see that we have differences. May we together become greater than the sum of both of us.

> —Gene Roddenberry and Arthur Heinemann, "The Savage Curtain," episode of *Star Trek* (1969)

We don't want the melting pot where everybody ends up with thin gruel. We want diversity, for strangeness breeds richness.

> —Marge Piercy, *Woman on the Edge of Time* (1976)

To be open is to be uncertain. The lines used to be so clear between Human and Alien, Man and Woman, Now and the Future. These days, the distinctions vanish and reappear where least expected. Barriers become connections, and vice versa. Which is Us and which is Them?

> —Ursula K. Le Guin, introduction to *Nebula Award Stories Eleven* (1977)

[A landlady addressing an alien:] "You are concealing your actual features under a headmask. I trust you are not keeping anything important from me?"

"We merely try to be discreet on first contact," Mr. Astroven said. "However, if it is a condition for renting . . ." He pulled off the mask and showed his real face. It was garish, variegated, surreal, and mostly green.

Mrs. Dogen was visibly relieved. "Perhaps it was foolish of me," she said. "I was afraid you might be black."

> —Ted Reynolds, "Boarder Incident" (1977)

It is striking, the gulf that separates races developing in different star systems. We have tried to understand the Earthpersons, and we have failed. We are aware, too, that they do not understand us and are appalled in turn by some of our customs.

> —Philip K. Dick, "Rautavaara's Case" (1980)

The Whites did not wonder about their own culture, so they liked to study ours.

> —George Florance-Guthridge, "The Quiet" (1981)

"Different *is* threatening to most species," Nikanj answered. "Different is dangerous. It might kill you. That was true to your animal ancestors and your nearest animal relatives. And it's true for you."

> —Octavia E. Butler, *Dawn* (1987)

The world is filled with petty, narrow-minded, stupid people. They wouldn't understand you. And anyone they don't understand, they want to hurt. They hurt anyone who's different.

— Pat Murphy, "Rachel in Love" (1987)

One obstacle to adulthood needs to be solved immediately: We must learn not just to accept differences between ourselves and our ideas, but to enthusiastically welcome and enjoy them. Diversity contains as many treasures as those waiting for us on other worlds. We will find it impossible to fear diversity and to enter the future at the same time.

— Gene Roddenberry, "A Letter to the Next Generation" (1988)

Racism was not a problem on the Discworld, because — what with trolls and dwarfs and so on — speciesism was more interesting. Black and white lived in perfect harmony and ganged up on green.

— Terry Pratchett, *Witches Abroad* (1991)

Just because someone's a member of an ethnic minority doesn't mean they're not a nasty small-minded little jerk.

— Terry Pratchett, *Feet of Clay* (1996)

In the past we had little to do with other races. Evolution teaches us that we must fight that which is different in order to secure land, food, and mates for ourselves, but we must reach a point when the nobility of intellect asserts itself and says: No. We need not be afraid of those we are different, we can embrace that difference and learn from it.

— J. Michael Straczynski, "The Ragged Edge," episode of *Babylon 5* (1998)

REALITY

Thus was the edifice of my brief dream of happiness dashed, broken, to the ground of reality.

— Edgar Rice Burroughs, *A Princess of Mars* (1917)

The cruelest thing is to make a person doubt his own reality.

— Yevgeny Zamiatin, *We* (1924), translated by Mirra Ginsburg (1972)

In that beginning was the same fantastic contrast that ran through the whole adventure: the mingling of everyday reality with the stark Inexplicable.

    —Jack Williamson, *The Legion of Time* (1938)

I wrestled with reality for forty years, and I am happy to state that I finally won out over it.

    —Mary Chase, *Harvey* (play, 1944)

Amnesia is the best method of escaping from reality.

    —A. E. van Vogt, *The Players of Null-A* (1948)

"Does Big Brother exist?"

    "Of course he exists. The Party exists. Big Brother is the embodiment of the Party."

    "Does he exist in the same way as I exist?"

    "You do not exist."

    —George Orwell, *Nineteen Eighty-Four* (1949)

There is no reality. There is no life, no freedom, no will. God damn. Don't you realize? We are . . . We are all characters in a book. As the book is read, we dance our dances; when the book is read again, we dance again.

    —Alfred Bester, "The Starcomber" (1954)

It seemed as if the structure of reality trembled for an instant, and that behind the world of the senses he caught a glimpse of another and totally different universe . . .

    —Arthur C. Clarke, *The City and the Stars* (1956)

He was slowly beginning to doubt the existence of the phenomenal universe itself, and he could not bring himself to care enough about the probably unreal to feel that it mattered what intellectual organization you imposed on it.

    —James Blish, *A Case of Conscience* (1958)

"The other night coming home on the bus I got a look at how things really are. I saw through the illusion. The other people in the bus were nothing but scarecrows propped up in their seats. The bus itself—" He made a sweeping motion with his hands. "A hollow shell, nothing but a few upright supports, plus my seat and the driver's seat."

— Philip K. Dick, *Time Out of Joint* (1959)

Reality? It is only the illusion we can agree upon.

— James Gunn, *The Joy Makers* (1961)

Reality's always a little dull to whoever's involved in it.

— Keith Laumer, *The Other Side of Time* (1965)

The mind selects, out of a mass of sense data, those ones of all the possible items to pay attention to, to react to, to treat as "real." But who knows what the mind may be rejecting, what lies unseen out there in the world? Perhaps these illusions are not illusions at all, but real things that ordinarily are filtered out of the streams of incoming sense data by our intellectual demand for a logical and consistent world.

— Philip K. Dick and Ray Nelson, *The Ganymede Takeover* (1967)

The whole of modern so-called existence is an attempt to deny reality insofar as it exists.

— John Brunner, *Stand on Zanzibar* (1968)

He felt all at once like an ineffectual moth, fluttering at the windowpane of reality, dimly seeing it from outside.

— Philip K. Dick, *Ubik* (1969)

In the nighttime heart of Beirut, in one of a row of general-address transfer booths, Louis Wu flicked into reality.

— Larry Niven, *Ringworld* (1970)

A man can endure the entire weight of the universe for eighty years. It is unreality that he cannot bear.

— Ursula K. Le Guin, *The Lathe of Heaven* (1971)

Reality, to me, is not so much something that you perceive, but something you make.

— Philip K. Dick, "The Android and the Human" (1972)

Reality was empty: without life or warmth or color or sound: without meaning. There were no heights or depths. All this lovely play of form and light and color on the sea and in the eyes of men, was no more than that: a playing of illusions on the shallow void.

— Ursula K. Le Guin, *The Farthest Shore* (1972)

The theory changes the reality it describes.

— Philip K. Dick, *Flow My Tears the Policeman Said* (1974)

History and reality have a way of not coinciding.

— Alan Dean Foster, "Dream Done Green" (1974)

What drives people crazy is trying to live outside reality. Reality is terrible. It can kill you. Given time, it certainly will kill you. The reality is pain — you said that! But it's the lies, the evasions of reality, that drive you crazy.

— Ursula K. Le Guin, *The Dispossessed: An Ambiguous Utopia* (1974)

For us the enemy was Reality.

— Doris Lessing, *The Memoirs of a Survivor* (1974)

Little stars had supplanted the silvery mist, nowhere near as imposing as the big blue one in the starscreen but equally as beautiful. Maybe they were reflections, and maybe they weren't. And maybe the inns Don Quixote stayed in really *were* castles. And maybe Mars, if you looked at it the right way, really *was* crisscrossed with blue canals.

— Robert F. Young, "Spacetrack" (1974)

The world is your exercise-book, the pages on which you do your sums. It is not reality, although you can express reality there if you wish.

You are also free to write nonsense, or lies, or to tear the pages.

— Richard Bach, *Illusions: The Adventures of a Reluctant Messiah* (1977)

There was no substitute for reality; one should beware of imitations.

— Arthur C. Clarke, *The Fountains of Paradise* (1979)

One desires reality. To a home-dweller, reality comes in the comforting familiarity of a neighborhood, the greeting of a friend. A traveler must seek it out, and tell tales to encourage belief in himself, what he has done and seen.

— Carter Scholz, "Travels" (1980)

Reality

The fact is that thresholds exist throughout reality, and that things on their far sides are altogether different from things on their hither sides.
—Poul Anderson, "The Saturn Game" (1981)

Reality is that which when you stop believing in it, it doesn't go away.
—Philip K. Dick, *Valis* (1981)

She had decided that reality was whatever happened, whatever she perceived.
—Octavia E. Butler, *Dawn* (1987)

A long time ago a bunch of people reached a general consensus as to what's real and what's not and most of us have been going along with it ever since.
—Charles De Lint, "Where Desert Spirits Crowd the Night" (1995)

Always remember you are a starchild. You will become any reality that you get with unless you influence that reality to become you.
—Kalamu ya Salaam, "Buddy Bolden" (1996)

Welcome to the desert of the real.
—Andy Wachowski and Larry Wachowski, *The Matrix* (film, 1999)

RELIGION

What good is religion if it collapses at calamity?
—H. G. Wells, *The War of the Worlds* (1898)

Whenever things are so that a lot of people feel they ought to be doing something, the weak, and those who go weak with a lot of complicated thinking, always make for a sort of do-nothing religion, very pious and superior, and submit to persecution and the will of the Lord.
—H. G. Wells, *The War of the Worlds* (1898)

She made a sort of chart, superimposing the different religions as I described them, with a pin run through them all, as it were; their common basis being a Dominant Power or Powers, and some Special Behavior, mostly taboos, to please or placate. There were some common features in certain groups of

religions, but the one always present was this Power, and the things which must be done or not done because of it.
— Charlotte Perkins Gilman, *Herland* (1915)

Heretics are the only (bitter) remedy against the entropy of human thought.
— Yevgeny Zamiatin, "On Literature, Revolution, Entropy, and Other Matters" (1923), translated by Mirra Ginsburg (1970)

It is possible that many religions are moderately true.
— James Hilton, *Lost Horizon* (1933)

You show me ten men who cherish some religious doctrine or political ideology, and I'll show you nine men whose minds are utterly impervious to any factual evidence which contradicts their beliefs, and who regard the producer of such evidence as a criminal who ought to be suppressed.
— H. Beam Piper, "Last Enemy" (1950)

Throughout the earlier part of its history, the human race had brought forth an endless succession of prophets, seers, messiahs, and evangelists who convinced themselves and their followers that to them alone were the secrets of the Universe revealed. [. . .] The rise of science, which with monotonous regularity refuted the cosmologies of the prophets and produced miracles which they could never match, eventually destroyed all these faiths. It did not destroy the awe, nor the reverence and humility, which all intelligent beings felt as they contemplated the stupendous Universe in which they found themselves. What it did weaken, and finally obliterate, were the countless religions, each of which claimed, with unbelievable arrogance, that it was the sole repository of the truth and that its millions of rivals and predecessors were all mistaken.
— Arthur C. Clarke, *The City and the Stars* (1956)

"The spectacle of demagogues sending millions of people to their deaths, wrecking the world with holy wars and bloodshed, tearing down whole nations to put over some religious or political 'truth' is—" He shrugged. "Obscene. Filthy."
— Philip K. Dick, *The World Jones Made* (1956)

For me, biology *is* an act of religion, because I know that all creatures are God's — each new planet, with all its manifestations, is an affirmation of God's power.

> — James Blish, *A Case of Conscience* (1958)

The trouble with being a priest was that you eventually had to take the advice you gave to others.

> — Walter M. Miller, Jr., *A Canticle for Leibowitz* (1959)

People are prone to new religions at two periods. First, in the beginning when luxuries are almost unknown, life hard and the simple virtues a necessity. [. . .] The second period when people are particularly prone to religion is during their decadence.

> — Mack Reynolds, "Russkies Go Home!" (1960)

Being religious is often a form of conceit. The faith in which I was brought up assured me that I was better than other people; I was "saved," they were "damned" — we were in a state of grace and the rest were "heathens." [. . .] Our hymns were loaded with arrogance — self-congratulation on how cozy we were with the Almighty and what a high opinion he had of us, what Hell everybody else would catch some Judgment Day.

> — Robert A. Heinlein, *Stranger in a Strange Land* (1961)

Man is so built that he cannot imagine his own death. This leads to endless invention of religions. While this conviction by no means proves immortality to be a fact, questions generated by it are overwhelmingly important. The nature of life, how ego hooks into the body, the problem of ego itself and why each ego *seems* to be the center of the universe, the purpose of life, the purpose of the universe — these are paramount questions, Ben; they can never be trivial. Science hasn't solved them — and who am I to sneer at religions for *trying,* no matter how unconvincingly to me?

> — Robert A. Heinlein, *Stranger in a Strange Land* (1961)

Repression makes a religion flourish.

> — Frank Herbert, *Dune* (1965)

Nothing about religion is simple.

> — Frank Herbert, *Dune* (1965)

Religion is but the most ancient and honorable way in which men have striven to make sense out of God's universe. Scientists seek the lawfulness of events. It is the task of Religion to fit man into this lawfulness.
    —Frank Herbert, *Dune* (1965)

"There is a Oneness from which all life stems," someone said gently behind Kirby. "The infinite variety of the universe we owe to—"
    Another voice said, "Man and woman, star and stone, tree and bird—"
    Another said, "In the strength of the spectrum, the quantum, and the holy angstrom—"
    Kirby did not remain to listen to the familiar prayers, nor did he pray himself.
    —Robert Silverberg, "Open the Sky" (1966)

Yesterday's monomaniac is tomorrow's messiah.
    —Philip José Farmer, "Riders of the Purple Wage" (1967)

Religion was the creation of fear. Knowledge destroys fear. Without fear, religion can't survive.
    —Michael Moorcock, "Behold the Man" (1967)

Religion is a reasonable substitute for knowledge. But there is no longer any need for substitutes, Karl. Science offers a sounder basis on which to formulate systems of thought and ethics.
    —Michael Moorcock, "Behold the Man" (1967)

One man's theology is another man's belly laugh.
    —Robert A. Heinlein, *Time Enough for Love* (1973)

Melissa had always liked churches. In a world filled with change and death, church was a familiar haven, a resting place for embattled innocents to prepare for fresh encounters with a hostile world.
    —P. J. Plauger, "Child of All Ages" (1975)

Churches and the Cosa Nostra have something in common: a sort of pristine indifference at the very top levels. All the malignant chores fall to the small-fries down at the bottom.
    —Philip K. Dick and Roger Zelazny, *Deus Irae* (1976)

A continuity exists between inert matter, through the grand design of the early universe, and intelligent life today. Now accepted by all, this cosmic perspective may be seen as a culmination of all the ancient religions.
　—Gregory Benford, "Starswarmer" (1978)

A religion is sometimes a source of happiness and I would not deprive anyone of happiness. But it is a comfort appropriate for the weak, not for the strong.
　—Robert A. Heinlein, *Friday* (1982)

Christians are quite as foolish as other people, you know.
　—Joanna Russ, "Souls" (1982)

The Ten Commandments are for lame brains. The first five are solely for the benefit of the priests and the powers that be; the second five are half truths, neither complete nor adequate.
　—Robert A. Heinlein, *To Sail beyond the Sunset* (1987)

The Christians as I understand them want to save mankind from sin without first understanding either sin or mankind.
　—George Turner, *Drowning Towers* (1987)

She once described Christianity as too narrow a slit through which to watch the world.
　—George Turner, *Drowning Towers* (1987)

A small war broke out between those who worshipped the Mother Goddess in her aspect of the Moon and those who worshipped her in her aspect of a huge fat woman with enormous buttocks. After that the masters intervened and explained that religion, while a fine thing, could be taken too far.
　—Terry Pratchett, *Pyramids* (1989)

All she knew was that there was more to the world than what could be perceived with the five senses and that she couldn't accept that Mystery as having its source in some power-hungry god whose church's creeds were based on denial of all secular matters, as though the beauty of this world was not a thing to be cherished for its own sake, but was rather a testing ground for how one would or would not be rewarded in the afterlife.
　—Charles De Lint, *Spiritwalk* (1992)

REVOLUTION AND REBELLION

Two dead, dark stars collide with an inaudible, deafening crash and light a new star; this is revolution. A molecule breaks away from its orbit and, bursting into a neighboring atomic universe, gives birth to a new chemical element; this is revolution. Lobachevsky cracks the walls of the millennia-old Euclidean world with a single book, opening a path to innumerable non-Euclidean spaces; this is revolution.

Revolution is everywhere, in everything. It is infinite. There is no final revolution, no final number. The social revolution is only one of an infinite number of numbers; the law of revolution is not a social law, but an immeasurably greater one. It is a cosmic, universal law—like the laws of the conservation of energy and of the dissipation of energy (entropy).

— Yevgeny Zamiatin, "On Literature, Revolution, Entropy, and Other Matters" (1923), translated by Mirra Ginsburg (1970)

No revolution, no heresy is comfortable or easy. For it is a leap, it is a break in the smooth evolutionary curve, and a break is a wound, a pain. But the wound is necessary; most of mankind suffers from hereditary sleeping sickness, and victims of this sickness (entropy) must not be allowed to sleep, or it will be their final sleep, death.

— Yevgeny Zamiatin, "On Literature, Revolution, Entropy, and Other Matters" (1923), translated by Mirra Ginsburg (1970)

The art of war is simplicity itself compared with the art of revolution. War follows well-defined principles, and analogies may be traced down through the centuries, whether the fighting is done with pilum and ballista, or with rocket and disintegrator; but each revolution is a law unto itself, a freak, a monstrosity, whose conditions may not be repeated.

— Robert A. Heinlein, "'If This Goes On—'" (1940)

Until they become conscious they will never rebel, and until after they have rebelled they cannot become conscious.

— George Orwell, *Nineteen Eighty-Four* (1949)

Everything ought to be turned upside down occasionally; it lets in air and light.

— Robert A. Heinlein, *The Star Beast* (1954)

Revolution and Rebellion

"Repent, Harlequin!" said the Ticktockman.
"Get stuffed!" the Harlequin replied, sneering.
—Harlan Ellison, "'Repent, Harlequin!' Said the Ticktockman" (1965)

Revolutions are not won by enlisting the masses. Revolution is a science only a few are competent to practice. It depends on correct organization and, above all, on communications.
—Robert A. Heinlein, *The Moon Is a Harsh Mistress* (1966)

Riots are the opium of the people.
—Philip José Farmer, "Riders of the Purple Wage" (1967)

We intend to destroy the police machine and all its records. We intend to destroy all dogmatic verbal systems. The family unit and its cancerous expansion into tribes, countries, nations we will eradicate at its vegetable roots. We don't want to hear any more family talk, mother talk, father talk, cop talk, priest talk, country talk *or* party talk. To put it country simple we have heard enough bullshit.
—William S. Burroughs, *The Wild Boys: A Book of the Dead* (1971)

The teeners had told him that all rules were evil, that all customs were neurotic repetition, that fear was a restriction, that practicality was a restriction, and mercy was a restriction.
He told himself they were children, in a passing phase of rebellion.
—Katherine MacLean, "The Missing Man" (1971)

You cannot buy the Revolution. You cannot make the Revolution. You can only be the Revolution. It is in your spirit, or it is nowhere.
—Ursula K. Le Guin, *The Dispossessed: An Ambiguous Utopia* (1974)

Only the individual, the person, had the power of moral choice—the power of change, the essential function of life. The Odonian society was conceived as a permanent revolution, and revolution begins in the thinking mind.
—Ursula K. Le Guin, *The Dispossessed: An Ambiguous Utopia* (1974)

Revolutions begin in the universities; the streets breed only riots.
—George Turner, *Drowning Towers* (1987)

Enthusiastic soldiers with no fighting to do soon get bored and start thinking dangerous thoughts, like how much better they could run the country.
— Terry Pratchett, *Pyramids* (1989)

Don't put your trust in revolutions. They always come around again. That's why they're called revolutions. People die, and nothing changes.
— Terry Pratchett, *Night Watch* (2002)

ROADS AND AUTOMOBILES

[Automobiles] contained the seeds of their own destruction. Seventy million steel juggernauts, operated by imperfect human beings at high speeds, are more destructive than war.
— Robert A. Heinlein, "The Roads Must Roll" (1940)

Even in the gloom and despite all windings of the road he knew whither he wished to go, and he did not falter, as long as there was a path that led towards his goal.
— J. R. R. Tolkien, *The Fellowship of the Ring* (1954)

A road that has once been opened cannot be closed again merely by passing a resolution.
— Arthur C. Clarke, *The City and the Stars* (1956)

Low-slung trucks with feeble headlights (useful only for warning purposes) sped mindlessly past them. [. . .] Economic corpuscles in an artery of Man, the behemoths charged heedlessly past the two monks who dodged them from lane to lane.
— Walter M. Miller, Jr., *A Canticle for Leibowitz* (1959)

There are no wrong roads to anywhere.
— Norton Juster, *The Phantom Tollbooth* (1961)

"God, how I hate Feet," he muttered, looking down at his shrunken legs. "Wheels forever!" he softly cheered.
— Fritz Leiber, "X Marks the Pedwalk" (1963)

Like a white worm devouring the world, the road thrummed on, uncaring.
　—Kenneth Bulmer, "Station HR972" (1967)

The roads, the roads were engineered beautifully. It was the stupid bastard
people who were engineered wrong.
　—Avram Davidson, "The Roads, the Roads, the Beautiful Roads" (1969)

In the world of the freeway, there was no place for a walking man.
　—Harlan Ellison, "Along the Scenic Route" (1969)

It will engender absolute selfishness in mankind if the driving of automobiles
becomes common. It will breed violence on a scale never seen before. It will
mark the end of the family as we know it, the three or four generations living
happily in one home. It will destroy the sense of neighborhood and the true
sense of nation. It will create giantized cankers of cities, false opulence of
suburbs, ruinized countryside, and unhealthy conglomeration of specialized
farming and manufacturing. It will breed rootlessness and immorality. It will
make every man a tyrant.
　—R. A. Lafferty, "Interurban Queen" (1970)

A man in an automobile is worth a thousand men on foot!
　—R. A. Lafferty, "Interurban Queen" (1970)

I dream that as I traveled the splintered skeleton of our once-proud nation
I came upon that mythic and dearly loved statistic, the pile of shattered
automobiles that stretches into the clouds, from Detroit beyond the moon.
[. . .] The automobiles stood like the solitary headstone in the planetwide
cemetery of our race, and of all the living things that we had doomed along
with ourselves.
　—George Alec Effinger, "Wednesday, November 15, 1967" (1971)

Strange roads have strange guides.
　—Ursula K. Le Guin, *The Farthest Shore* (1972)

Along the northbound motorway embankment the sluggish traffic moved
like blood in a dying artery.
　—J. G. Ballard, *Crash* (1973)

Beyond eden, obscured but not inaudible, was the freeway—a roaring, melting glacier fed by tributary streets.
— Raylyn Moore, "Trigononomy" (1973)

All roads lead to the same end. So it's not so much which road you take, as how you take it.
— Charles De Lint, *Greenmantle* (1988)

People who plan roads, bridges, sewers, and so forth are called civil engineers. Civilization happens in cities, where civil society is possible, because of civil engineers. Cities are fed by roads, drained by sewers, watered by pipes that they lay down.

There have been barbarian poets and composers, even painters and some lawyers, but never a barbarian civil engineer. You have to be civilized to care about roads.
— John Barnes, "My Advice to the Civilized" (1990)

There is a story among truckers that some roads capture a driver: land, concrete, and sky going on forever.
— Kathryn Kristine Rusch, "Heading West" (1990)

After driving 2295 all day, Karen decided that the larger the Texas highway number, the smaller and meaner the road.
— Leah Cutter, "The Red Boots" (2000)

ROBOTS, ANDROIDS, AND CYBORGS

The old crank actually wanted to make people. [. . .] He wanted to become a sort of scientific substitute for God, you know. He was a fearful materialist, and that's why he did it all. His sole purpose was nothing more or less than to supply proof that Providence was no longer necessary.
— Karel Capek, *R.U.R.* (play, 1921), translated by P. Selver (1923)

It was a thing of glistening levers and bell cranks, of flexible shafting, cams, and delicate mechanical fingers, of vacuum tubes and photo-electric cells, of relays that clicked in ordered sequence when called upon to perform their myriad functions of pumps, tanks, condensers, reactances, microphones, and loud-speakers. A robot, created by the master scientists of the twenty-third century.

    —Harl Vincent, "Rex" (1934)

Robots by their very nature are lazy, since they lack the fierce incentives thrust by Nature on the more frail and ephemeral mortal humans.

    —Malcolm Jameson, "Pride" (1942)

The robots worked untiringly, directing the destinies of mankind.

    —Henry Kuttner and C. L. Moore, "Open Secret" (1943)

It was a voice speaking out of a place where no emotion, as humanity knew the word, had ever existed. It came from a brain as alien and incomprehensible as darkness in a world of eternal light; a brain no human could ever touch or understand, except to feel the cold weight of its strength and cower as a beast cowers before the terrible mystery of fire.

    "Sleep," said the android. "Sleep, and listen to my voice."

    —Leigh Brackett, "The Jewel of Bas" (1944)

It must be that robots predated all other life. It's the only logical conclusion.

    —A. E. van Vogt, "Final Command" (1949)

[Words to activate the robot Gort:] Klaatu barada nikto.

    —Edmund H. North, *The Day the Earth Stood Still* (film, 1951)

That perfected machines may one day succeed us is, I remember, an extremely commonplace notion on Earth. It prevails not only among poets and romantics but in all classes of society. Perhaps it is because it is so widespread, born spontaneously in popular imagination, that it irritates scientific minds. Perhaps it is also for this very reason that it contains a germ of truth. Only a germ: Machines will always be machines; the most perfected robot, always a robot.

    —Pierre Boulle, *Planet of the Apes* (1963), translated by Xan Fielding (1963)

ROBOT: I do not vote. I am not programmed for free choice.

    —Norman Lessing, "Island in the Sky," episode of *Lost in Space* (1965)

He raised the steering wheel and pulled into the parking dome, stepped out onto the ramp and left the car to the parking unit, receiving his ticket from the box-headed robot which took its solemn revenge on mankind by sticking forth a cardboard tongue at everyone it served.

 —Roger Zelazny, "He Who Shapes" (1965)

Still, Candy told herself, robots can't feel.

 —Fritz Leiber, "The Crystal Prison" (1966)

As we were made more efficient, we naturally were made more human, because the human body and brain are still the most efficient machines there are. You might almost say that, while you folks were becoming more and more false-toothed and nose-jobbed and bustplastied, and more and more warped and mutated by radiation, more and more *dehumanized*, we androids were becoming more and more human. Kind of ironic.

 —Ray Russell, "The Better Man" (1966)

A humanoid robot is like any other machine; it can fluctuate between being a benefit and a hazard very rapidly.

 —Philip K. Dick, *Do Androids Dream of Electric Sheep?* (1968)

Do androids dream? Rick asked himself. Evidently; that's why they occasionally kill their employers and flee here.

 —Philip K. Dick, *Do Androids Dream of Electric Sheep?* (1968)

The dark fire waned; the life force oozed out of her, as he had so often witnessed before with other androids. The classic resignation. Mechanical, intellectual acceptance of that which a genuine organism—with two billion years of the pressure to live and evolve hagriding it—could never have reconciled itself to.

 "I can't stand the way you androids give up," he said savagely.

 —Philip K. Dick, *Do Androids Dream of Electric Sheep?* (1968)

Robots are nice to work with. They mind their own business, and they never have anything to say.

 —Roger Zelazny, "Dismal Light" (1968)

Someday, the real masters of space would be machines, not men—and he was neither. Already conscious of his destiny, he took a somber pride in his unique loneliness—the first immortal midway between two orders of creation.

He would, after all, be an ambassador; between the old and the new—between the creatures of carbon and the creatures of metal who must one day supersede them.

Both would have need of him in the troubled centuries that lay ahead.

—Arthur C. Clarke, "A Meeting with Medusa" (1971)

Becoming what I call, for lack of a better term, an android, means as I said, to allow oneself to become a means, or to be pounded down, manipulated, made into a means without one's knowledge or consent—the results are the same. But you cannot turn a human into an android if that human is going to break laws every chance he gets. Androidization requires obedience. And, most of all, *predictability*. It is precisely when a given person's response to any given situation can be predicted with scientific accuracy that the gates are open for the wholesale production of the android life form.

—Philip K. Dick, "The Android and the Human" (1972)

Robotics is not an exact art.

—Isaac Asimov, "The Bicentennial Man" (1976)

"How can they fear robots?"

"It's a disease of mankind, one which has not yet been cured."

—Isaac Asimov, "The Bicentennial Man" (1976)

MARVIN THE PARANOID ANDROID: In the beginning I was made. I didn't ask to be made, no one consulted me or considered my feelings in the matter. I don't think it even occurred to them that I might have feelings, but if it brought some passing sadistic pleasure to some mentally benighted humans as they pranced their haphazard way through life's mournful jungle then so be it.

—Douglas Adams, "Fit the Twelfth," episode of *The Hitch-Hiker's Guide to the Galaxy* (radio series, 1980)

It had the shape of a man, the brain of an electronic devil.

—Fred Saberhagen, "Adventure of the Metal Murderer" (1980)

I read some classic stories about humanoid robots. They were charming stories and many of them hinged on something called the laws of robotics, the key notion of which was that these robots had built into them an operational rule that kept them from harming human beings either directly or through inaction. It was a wonderful basis for fiction . . . but, in practice, how could you do it? What can make a self-aware, nonhuman, intelligent organism — electronic or organic — loyal to human beings?
— Robert A. Heinlein, *Friday* (1982)

C3Po: It's against my programming to impersonate a deity.
— Lawrence Kasdan and George Lucas, *Return of the Jedi* (film, 1983)

The Terminator: I'll be back!
— James Cameron and Gale Anne Hurd, *The Terminator* (film, 1984)

Though both are bound in the spiral dance, I would rather be a cyborg than a goddess.
— Donna Haraway, "A Manifesto for Cyborgs: Science, Technology, and Socialist Feminism in the 1980s" (1985)

They made us too smart, too quick, and too many. We are suffering for the mistakes they made because when the end comes, all that will be left . . . is us. That's why they hate us.
— Steven Spielberg, *A.I.: Artificial Intelligence* (film, 2001)

SCIENCE

Science, my boy, is composed of errors, but errors that it is right to make, for they lead step by step to the truth.
— Jules Verne, *A Journey to the Centre of the Earth* (1864), translated by William Butcher (1992)

If we can possibly avoid wrecking this little planet of ours, we will. But — there *must* be risks! There must be. In experimental work there always are!
— H. G. Wells, *The First Men in the Moon* (1901)

"It's this accursed Science," I cried. "It's the very Devil. The mediaeval priests and persecutors were right, and the Moderns are all wrong. You tamper with it — and it offers you gifts. And directly you take them it knocks you to pieces in some unexpected way."
— H. G. Wells, *The First Men in the Moon* (1901)

Science of to-day — the superstition of to-morrow. Science of to-morrow — superstition of to-day.
— Charles Fort, *The Book of the Damned* (1919)

The superstitions of today are the scientific facts of tomorrow.
— Hamilton Deane and John L. Balderston, *Dracula* (play, 1927)

Science is dangerous; we have to keep it most carefully chained and muzzled.
— Aldous Huxley, *Brave New World* (1932)

There are no enemies in science, professor, only phenomena to study.
— Charles Lederer, *The Thing (from Another World)* (film, 1951)

This was what the universities were turning out nowadays. The science-is-a-sacred-cow boys. People who believe you could pour mankind into a

test tube, titrate it, and come up with all the answers to the problems of the human race.
— Frank M. Robinson, "The Day the World Ended" (1953)

The men of the frontier knew — but how was a girl from Earth to fully understand? *H amount of fuel will not power an EDS with a mass of m plus x safely to its destination.* To himself and her brother and parents she was a sweet-faced girl in her teens; to the laws of nature she was *x*, the unwanted factor in a cold equation.
— Tom Godwin, "The Cold Equations" (1954)

I'm not disparaging scientists. What they do is as it should be; I grok that fully. But what they are after is *not* what *I* am looking for — you don't grok a desert by counting its grains of sand.
— Robert A. Heinlein, *Stranger in a Strange Land* (1961)

Science is *not* a sacred cow — but there are a large number of would-be sacred cowherds busily devoting quantities of time, energy and effort to the task of making it one, so they can be sacred cowherds.
— John W. Campbell, Jr., introduction to *Prologue to Analog* (1962)

I believe in logic, the sequence of cause and effect, and in science its only begotten son our law, which was conceived by the ancient Greeks, thrived under Isaac Newton, suffered under Albert Einstein . . .
That fragment of a "creed for materialism" which a friend in college had once shown to him rose through Donald's confused mind.
— John Brunner, *Stand on Zanzibar* (1968)

Scientific research was much like prospecting: you went out and you hunted, armed with your maps and your instruments, but in the end your preparations did not matter, or even your intuition. You needed your luck, and whatever benefits accrued to the diligent, through sheer, grinding hard work.
— Michael Crichton, *The Andromeda Strain* (1969)

"Archaeology is made up entirely of anomalies," said Terrence, "rearranged to make them fit in a fluky pattern. There'd be no system to it otherwise."
"Every science is made up entirely of anomalies rearranged to fit."
— R. A. Lafferty, "Continued on Next Rock" (1970)

321

When facts are insufficient, theorizing is ridiculous at best, misleading at worst.
—Poul Anderson, "The Queen of Air and Darkness" (1971)

It is only when science asks why, instead of simply describing how, that it becomes more than technology. When it asks why, it discovers Relativity. When it only shows how, it invents the atomic bomb, and then puts its hands over its eyes and says, *"My God what have I done?"*
—Ursula K. Le Guin, "The Stalin in the Soul" (1973)

Science battered everyone into submission if it was given its way.
—Thomas M. Disch, *334* (1974)

Scientific truth will out, you can't hide the sun under a stone.
—Ursula K. Le Guin, *The Dispossessed: An Ambiguous Utopia* (1974)

The real name for "science" is *magic.*
—Harlan Ellison, "Jeffty Is Five" (1977)

Science has so accustomed us to devising and accepting theories to account for the facts we observe, however fantastic, that our minds must begin their manufacture before we are aware of it.
—Gene Wolfe, "Seven American Nights" (1978)

Once the data are in, the theory has to follow along meekly.
—Michael Swanwick, "Ginungagap" (1980)

"Matter dreams," an instructor had said a decade before. "Dreams it is real, maintains the dream by shifting rules with constant results. Disturb the dreams, the shifting of the rules results in inconstant results. Things cannot hold."
—Greg Bear, "Hardfought" (1983)

Their minds sang with the ecstatic knowledge that either what they were doing was completely and utterly and totally impossible or that physics had a lot of catching up to do.
—Douglas Adams, *So Long, and Thanks for All the Fish* (1985)

Atoms have a nucleus, made of protons and neutrons bound together. Around this nucleus shells of electrons spin, and each shell is either full or trying to get full, to balance with the number of protons — to balance the positive and negative charges. An atom is like a human heart, you see.
— Kim Stanley Robinson, "The Lunatics" (1988)

Where lies the line between sorcery and science? It is only a matter of terminology, my friend.
— Alan Dean Foster, *Cyber Way* (1990)

SCIENCE: A way of finding things out and then making them work. Science explains what is happening around us the whole time. So does RELIGION, but science is better because it comes up with more understandable excuses when it's wrong.
— Terry Pratchett, *Wings* (1990)

Science was many things, Nadia thought, including a weapon with which to hit other scientists.
— Kim Stanley Robinson, *Red Mars* (1992)

I liked science. It was about the only thing that stayed the same wherever we moved.
— Ellen Klages, "Time Gypsy" (1998)

Astronomy, Benjamin mused, was a lot like a detective story with the clues revealed first, and the actual body only later — if ever.
— Gregory Benford, *Eater* (2000)

SCIENCE FICTION

[First use of term *science fiction:*] We hope it will not be long before we may have other works of Science-Fiction [like Richard Henry Horne's "The Poor Artist"], as we believe such books likely to fulfil a good purpose, and create an interest, where, unhappily, science alone might fail.

[Thomas] Campbell says, that "Fiction in Poetry is not the reverse of truth, but her soft and enchanting resemblance." Now this applies especially to Science-Fiction, in which the revealed truths of Science may be given,

interwoven with a pleasing story which may itself be poetical and true—
thus circulating a knowledge of the Poetry of Science, clothed in a garb of
the Poetry of life.

   —William Wilson, *A Little Earnest Book upon a Great Old Subject* (1851)

[On H. G. Wells:] "I do not see the possibility of comparison between his
work and mine. We do not proceed in the same manner. It occurs to me that
his stories do not repose on very scientific bases. No, there is no *rapport* between his work and mine. I make use of physics. He invents. I go to the moon
in a cannon-ball, discharged from a cannon. Here there is no invention. He
goes to Mars in an airship, which he constructs of a metal which does away
with the law of gravitation. *Ça c'est très joli,*" cried Monsieur Verne in an
animated way, "but show me this metal. Let him produce it."

   —Jules Verne, cited in Robert H. Sherard, "Jules Verne Re-Visited" (1903)

Imagine a country where the only fertile soil is asphalt, where nothing grows
but dense forests of factory chimneys, where the animal herds are of a single
breed, automobiles, and the only fragrance in the spring is that of gasoline.
This place of stone, asphalt, iron, gasoline, and machines is present-day,
twentieth-century London, and, naturally, it was bound to produce its own
iron, automobile goblins, and its own mechanical, chemical fairy tales. Such
urban tales exist; they are told by Herbert George Wells.

   —Yevgeny Zamiatin, "H. G. Wells" (1922), translated by Mirra Ginsburg
   (1970)

By "scientifiction" I mean the Jules Verne, H. G. Wells, and Edgar Allan Poe
type of story—a charming romance intermingled with scientific fact and
prophetic vision.

   —Hugo Gernsback, "A New Sort of Magazine" (1926)

[First modern use of term *science fiction:*] Remember that Jules Verne was a
sort of Shakespeare of science fiction, and we would feel derelict if we did not
give his stories in our columns.

   —T. O'Conor Sloane, "Discussions," *Amazing Stories,* January (1927)

Not only is science fiction an idea of tremendous import, but it is to be
an important factor in making the world a better place to live in, through
educating the public to the possibilities of science and the influence of sci-

ence on life which, even today, are not appreciated by the man on the street. [. . .] If every man, woman, boy and girl, could be induced to read science fiction right along, there would certainly be a great resulting benefit to the community, in that the educational standards of its people would be raised tremendously. Science fiction would make people happier, give them a broader understanding of the world, make them more tolerant.

    — Hugo Gernsback, "Science Fiction Week" (1930)

No average mind can either understand or enjoy science-fiction; it takes an amount of imagination beyond the average man.

    — John W. Campbell, Jr., "Science-Fiction" (1938)

Back in the nineteen-hundreds it was a wonderful experience for a boy to discover H. G. Wells. There you were, in a world of pedants, clergyman and golfers, with your future employers exhorting you to "get on or get out," your parents systematically warping your sexual life, and your dull-witted schoolmasters sniggering over their Latin tags; and here was this wonderful man who could tell you about the inhabitants of the planets and the bottom of the sea, and who *knew* that the future was not going to be what respectable people imagined.

    — George Orwell, "Wells, Hitler, and the World State" (1941)

One of the purposes of literature is to transport the reader. Science fiction does that. Let more ponderous branches of the art also edify, inform, and elevate. They, too, transport the reader, but rarely as far up as Sirius or as far down as the hydrogen atom. And the fact that here are ideas and dreams which man has never before thought or imagined in the written history of the world gives these tales a certain permanence.

    — Groff Conklin, introduction to *The Best of Science Fiction* (1946)

A piece of scientific fiction is a narrative of an imaginary invention or discovery in the natural sciences and consequent adventures and experiences.

    — J. O. Bailey, *Pilgrims through Space and Time* (1947)

To all the readers and the writers of that new literature called science fiction, who find mystery, wonder, and high adventure in the expanding universe of knowledge, and also sometimes seek to observe and to forecast the vast impact of science upon the lives and minds of men.

    — Jack Williamson, dedication, *The Legion of Space,* revised (1947)

325

Nothing is deader than yesterday's science-fiction.
    —Arthur C. Clarke, *The Sands of Mars* (1951)

Begotten by Imagination on the body of Technology, there springs forth the wild child, Science Fiction. [. . .] Science fiction is a kind of archaeology of the future.
    —Clifton Fadiman, introduction to *Great Stories of Science Fiction* (1951)

Science fiction is the literature of the Technological Era. It, unlike other literatures, assumes that change is the natural order of things, that there are goals ahead larger than those we know.
    —John W. Campbell, Jr., introduction to *The Astounding Science Fiction Anthology* (1952)

A science fiction story is a story built around human beings, with a human problem, and a human solution, which would not have happened at all without its scientific content.
    —Theodore Sturgeon, cited in James Blish, "Some Propositions" (1952)

Science fiction is that class of prose narrative treating of a situation that could not arise in the world we know, but which is hypothesised on the basis of some innovation in science or technology, or pseudo-science or pseudo-technology, whether human or extra-terrestrial in origin.
    —Kingsley Amis, *New Maps of Hell: A Survey of Science Fiction* (1960)

Science fiction—the fact needs emphasizing—is no more written for scientists and technologists than ghost stories were written for ghosts.
    —Brian W. Aldiss, introduction to *Penguin Science Fiction* (1961)

Science fiction is, very strictly and literally, *analogous* to science facts. It is a convenient analog system for thinking about new scientific, social, and economic ideas—and for re-examining old ideas.
    —John W. Campbell, Jr., introduction to *Prologue to Analog* (1962)

Speculative fantasy, as I prefer to call the more serious fringe of science fiction, is an especially potent method of using one's imagination to construct a paradoxical universe where dream and reality become fused together, each retaining its own distinctive quality and yet in some way assuming the role of its opposite, and where by an undeniable logic black simultaneously becomes white.

—J. G. Ballard, "Time, Memory, and Inner Space" (1963)

That group of writings which is usually referred to as "mainstream literature" is, actually, a special subgroup of the field of science fiction—for science fiction deals with all places in the Universe, and all times in Eternity, so the literature of here-and-now is, truly, a subset of science fiction.

—John W. Campbell, Jr., introduction to *Analog I* (1963)

Science fiction is a branch of fantasy identifiable by the fact that it eases the "willing suspension of disbelief" on the part of its readers by utilizing an atmosphere of scientific credibility for its imaginative speculations in physical science, space, time, social science, and philosophy.

—Sam Moskowitz, introduction to *Explorers of the Infinite* (1963)

"I love you sons of bitches [science fiction writers]," Eliot said in Milford. "You're all I read any more. You're the only ones who'll talk about the *really* terrific changes going on, the only ones crazy enough to know that life is a space voyage, and not a short one, either, but one that'll last for billions of years. You're the only ones with guts enough to *really* care about the future, who *really* notice what machines do to us, what wars do to us, what cities do to us, what big, simple ideas do to us, what tremendous misunderstandings, mistakes, accidents and catastrophes do to us. You're the only ones zany enough to agonize over time and distances without limit, over mysteries that will never die, over the fact that we are right now determining whether the space voyage for the next billion years or so is going to be Heaven or Hell."

—Kurt Vonnegut, Jr., *God Bless You, Mr. Rosewater* (1965)

Jules Verne was my father.

H. G. Wells was my wise uncle.

Edgar Allan Poe was the batwinged cousin we kept high in the back attic room.

Flash Gordon and Buck Rogers were my brothers and friends.

There you have my ancestry.

Adding, of course, the fact that in all probability Mary Wollstonecraft Shelley, author of *Frankenstein*, was my mother.

—Ray Bradbury, introduction to *S Is for Space* (1966)

It is absurd to condemn [science fiction stories] because they do not often display any deep or sensitive characterization. They oughtn't to. [. . .] Every good writer knows that the more unusual the scenes and events of his story are, the slighter, the more ordinary, the more typical his persons should be. Hence Gulliver is a commonplace little man and Alice a commonplace little girl. If they had been more remarkable they would have wrecked their books. The Ancient Mariner himself is a very ordinary man. To tell how odd things struck odd people is to have an oddity too much; he who is to see strange sights must not himself be strange.
   —C. S. Lewis, "On Science Fiction" (1966)

Everything is becoming science fiction. From the margins of an almost invisible literature has sprung the intact reality of the 20th century.
   —J. G. Ballard, "Fictions of Every Kind" (1971)

Phrased rather too simply, science fiction deals with improbable possibilities, fantasy with plausible impossibilities.
   —Miriam Allen deFord, introduction to *Elsewhere, Elsewhen, Elsehow*
     (1971)

Science has from the beginning been what is most spectacularly is now, the handmaiden of capitalism. Sf has all along been the handmaiden of, as well as the parasite on, science. This is a treason to the profession of writing, which in its serious forms can be a handmaiden of nothing but disdain for, and assault upon, that-which-is.
   —Bernard Wolfe, afterword to "Biscuit Position" and "The Girl with Rapid
     Eye Movements" (1972)

Science fiction is the search for a definition of man and his status in the universe which will stand in our advanced but confused state of knowledge (science), and is characteristically cast in the Gothic or post-Gothic mould.
   —Brian W. Aldiss, *Billion Year Spree: The True History of Science Fiction*
     (1973)

Michael Rennie was ill
The day the Earth stood still
But he told us where we stand
And Flash Gordon was there

In silver underwear
Claude Rains was the invisible man
Then something went wrong
For Fay Wray and King Kong
They got caught in a celluloid jam
Then at a deadly pace
It came from outer space
And this is how the message ran.

Science fiction—double feature
Doctor X—will build a creature
See Androids fighting—Brad and Janet
Anne Francis stars in—Forbidden Planet
Oh, at the late night double-feature
Picture show
    —Richard O'Brien, "Science Fiction," *The Rocky Horror Show* (play, 1973)

I have been a soreheaded occupant of a file drawer labeled "science fiction" ever since, and I would like out, particularly since so many serious critics regularly mistake the drawer for a urinal.
    —Kurt Vonnegut, Jr. "Science Fiction" (1974)

My briefest-ever definition of science fiction is "Hubris clobbered by Nemesis."
    —Brian W. Aldiss, *Science Fiction Art* (1975)

Science fiction and the world. They have created each other. [. . .] We live, indisputably, in a science fiction world.
    —James Gunn, *Alternate Worlds: The Illustrated History of Science Fiction*
      (1975)

All fiction is metaphor. Science fiction is metaphor. What sets it apart from older forms of fiction seems to be its use of new metaphors, drawn from certain great dominants of our contemporary life—science, all the sciences, and technology, and the relativistic and the historical outlook, among them. Space travel is one of these metaphors; so is an alternative society, an alternative biology; the future is another.
    —Ursula K. Le Guin, introduction to *The Left Hand of Darkness* (1976)

Science Fiction

One good working definition of science fiction may be the literature which, growing with science and technology, evaluates it and relates it meaningfully to the rest of human existence.

> —H. Bruce Franklin, introduction to *Future Perfect: American Science Fiction of the Nineteenth Century,* revised (1978)

I will argue for an understanding of SF as the *literature of cognitive estrangement.* [. . .] *SF is, then, a literary genre whose necessary and sufficient conditions are the presence and interaction of estrangement and cognition, and whose main formal device is an imaginative framework alternative to the author's empirical environment.*

> —Darko Suvin, *Metamorphoses of Science Fiction* (1979)

You are welcome, therefore, Stranger, to join
Our cofraternity. But please observe the rules.
Always display a cheerful disposition. Do not refer
To our infirmities. Help us to conquer the galaxy.

> —Thomas M. Disch, "On Science Fiction" (1980)

There was hardly a science fiction writer of experience who was not—at least to Ruthven's antennae—displaying signs of mental illness.

That decay, Ruthven came to think, had to do with the very nature of the genre: the megalomaniacal, expansive visions being generated by writers who increasingly saw the disparity between Spaceways and their own hopeless condition. [. . .] At a particularly bleak time, Ruthven even came to speculate that science fiction writing was a form of illness which, like syphilis, might swim undetected in the blood for years but would eventually, untreated, strike to kill.

> —Barry N. Malzberg, "Corridors" (1982)

No less a critic than C. S. Lewis has described the ravenous addiction that these [science fiction] magazines inspired in him; the same phenomenon has led me to call science fiction the only genuine consciousness-expanding drug.

> —Arthur C. Clarke, "Of Sand and Stars" (1983)

Science fiction writers, I am sorry to say, really do not know anything. We can't talk about science, because our knowledge of it is limited and unofficial, and usually our fiction is dreadful.

— Philip K. Dick, "How to Build a Universe That Doesn't Fall Apart Two Days Later" (1985)

If science fiction is the mythology of modern technology, then its myth is tragic.

— Ursula K. Le Guin, "The Carrier Bag Theory of Fiction" (1986)

Science fiction properly conceived, like all serious fiction, however funny, is a way of trying to describe what is in fact going on, what people actually do and feel, how people relate to everything else in this vast sack, this belly of the universe, this womb of things to be and tomb of things that were, this unending story.

— Ursula K. Le Guin, "The Carrier Bag Theory of Fiction" (1986)

If poets are the unacknowledged legislators of the world, science-fiction writers are its court jesters.

— Bruce Sterling, preface to *Burning Chrome* (1986)

SF looks toward an imaginary future, while fantasy, by and large, looks toward an imaginary past. Both can be entertaining. Both can possibly be, perhaps sometimes actually are, even inspiring. But as we can't change the past, and can't avoid changing the future, only one of them can be *real*.

— Frederik Pohl, "Pohlemic: Mail Call" (1992)

A revealing way of describing science fiction is to say that it is part of a literary mode which one may call "fabril." "Fabril" is the opposite of "pastoral." [. . .] Pastoral literature is rural, nostalgic, conservative. It idealizes the past and tends to convert complexities into simplicity; its central image is the shepherd. Fabril literature (of which science fiction is now by far the most prominent genre) is overwhelmingly urban, disruptive, future-oriented, eager for novelty; its central image is the "faber," the smith or blacksmith in older usage, but now extended in science fiction to mean the creator of artefacts in general — metallic, crystalline, genetic, or even social.

— Tom Shippey, introduction to *The Oxford Book of Science Fiction* (1992)

That's all science fiction was ever about. Hating the way things are, wanting to make things different.
    — Ray Bradbury, "No News, or, What Killed the Dog?" (1994)

SF has never really aimed to tell us when we might reach other planets, or develop new technologies, or meet aliens. SF speculates about why we might want to do these things, and how their consequences might affect our lives and our planet.
    — John Clute, *SF: The Illustrated Encyclopedia* (1995)

Science fiction is an argument with the universe.
    — Farah Mendlesohn, editorial in *Foundation: The International Review of Science Fiction* 88 (2003)

SCIENTISTS

For me, research is a relief, a great diversion, a lure, a passion that can make me forget everything else. Like you, I am a man ignored and unknown, living in the fragile hope that someday I can pass on to future generations the fruits of my labors.
    — Jules Verne, *Twenty Thousand Leagues under the Sea* (1870), translated by Walter James Miller and Frederick Paul Walter (1993)

That is the only way I ever heard of research going. I asked a question, devised some method of getting an answer, and got — a fresh question. Was this possible, or that possible? You cannot imagine what this means to an investigator, what an intellectual passion grows upon him. You cannot imagine the strange colourless delight of these intellectual desires.
    — H. G. Wells, *The Island of Doctor Moreau* (1896)

They were of course quite undistinguished looking men, as indeed all true Scientists are.
    — H. G. Wells, *The Food of the Gods and How It Came to Earth* (1904)

You men of the scientific world have long wanted to obtain control over mankind and its affairs.
    — Harl Vincent, "Rex" (1934)

Great laws are not divined by flashes of inspiration, whatever you may think. It usually takes the combined work of a world full of scientists over a period of centuries.
　—Isaac Asimov, "Nightfall" (1941)

A true scientist is married to his profession.
　—Robert Charles, *Return of the Ape Man* (film, 1944)

You cold-blooded characters, you scientists, are the true visionaries. [. . .] If you strip all of the intermediate steps away from the scientist's thinking, you have an artistic concept to which the scientist responds distantly and with surprise.
　—Theodore Sturgeon, "Memorial" (1946)

These physicists—they produce wonders but they never know what other wonders their wonders will beget.
　—Robert A. Heinlein, *Between Planets* (1951)

Why can't you scientists leave things alone? What about my bit of washing when there's no washing to do?
　—Roger MacDougall, John Dighton, and Alexander Mackendrick, *The Man in the White Suit* (film, 1951)

The younger generation of scientists makes me sick to my stomach. Short order fry-cooks of destruction, they hear through the little window the dim order: "Atom bomb rare, with cobalt 60!" and sing it back and rattle their stinking skillets and sling the deadly hash—just what the customer ordered, with never a notion invading their smug, too-heated havens that there's a small matter of right and wrong that takes precedence even over their haute cuisine.
　—C. M. Kornbluth, "Gomez" (1954)

The pursuit of science, despite its social benefits, is itself not a social virtue; its practitioners can be men so self-centered as to be lacking in social responsibility.
　—Robert A. Heinlein, *Starship Troopers* (1959)

Scientists

As every researcher just out of college knows, scientists of over fifty are good for nothing but board meetings, and should at all costs be kept out of the laboratory!
> —Arthur C. Clarke, "Hazards of Prophecy: The Failure of Imagination" (1962)

I'm not foolish enough to hold opinions when I have insufficient data; I'll leave that folly to scientists.
> —Robert A. Heinlein, *Farnham's Freehold* (1964)

When they [radio astronomers] grew weary at their electronic listening posts, when their eyes grew dim with looking at unrevealing dials and studying uneventful graphs, they could step outside their concrete cells and renew their dull spirits in communion with the giant mechanism they commanded, the silent, sensing instrument in which the smallest packets of energy, the smallest waves of matter, were detected in their headlong, eternal flight across the universe. It was the stethoscope with which they took the pulse of the all and noted the birth and death of stars, the probe with which, here on an insignificant planet of an undistinguished star on the edge of its galaxy, they explored the infinite.
> —James Gunn, "The Listeners" (1968)

Nothing shocks me. I'm a scientist.
> —Willard Huyck and Gloria Katz, *Indiana Jones and the Temple of Doom* (film, 1984)

"You scientists are so shy," Rankin was saying. "You love to hide your light under a bushel basket."
> —Carl Sagan, *Contact* (1985)

Naming was the power that made every human a scientist of sorts.
> —Kim Stanley Robinson, *Red Mars* (1992)

Scientists could become as fanatical as anybody else, maybe more so; educations too narrowly focused, perhaps.
> —Kim Stanley Robinson, *Red Mars* (1992)

THE SEA

You are going to tour the land of marvels. Astonishment, amazement will become your everyday state of mind. You won't get bored with the spectacles I will provide for you. I'm going on another tour of the submarine world.
> —Jules Verne, *Twenty Thousand Leagues under the Sea* (1870), translated
> by Walter James Miller and Frederick Paul Walter (1993)

The sea is everything. It covers seven-tenths of the planet. Its breath is pure and healthful. It's an immense wilderness where a man never feels lonely, for he feels life astir on every side. The sea fosters a wondrous, supernatural existence.
> —Jules Verne, *Twenty Thousand Leagues under the Sea* (1870), translated
> by Walter James Miller and Frederick Paul Walter (1993)

Look at that sea! Who can say it isn't actually alive! It expresses its anger and its tenderness! Yesterday it went to sleep as we did, and now like us it is awakening after a peaceful night.
> —Jules Verne, *Twenty Thousand Leagues under the Sea* (1870), translated
> by Walter James Miller and Frederick Paul Walter (1993)

Ocean is more ancient than the mountains, and freighted with the memories and the dreams of Time.
> —H. P. Lovecraft, "The White Ship" (1919)

Somewhere over the darkened curve of the world the sun and moon were pulling; and the film of water on the earth planet was held, bulging slightly on one side while the solid core turned. The great wave of the tide moved further along the island and the water lifted. Softly, surrounded by a fringe of inquisitive bright creatures, itself a silver shape beneath the steadfast constellations, Simon's dead body moved out towards the open sea.
> —William Golding, *Lord of the Flies* (1954)

Leaving the sea two hundred million years ago may have been a deep trauma from which we've never recovered . . .
> —J. G. Ballard, *The Drowned World* (1962)

The Sea

A few moments earlier the water had seemed cool and inviting, but now had become a closed world, the barrier of the surface like a plane between two dimensions.

— J. G. Ballard, *The Drowned World* (1962)

The idea of the sea troubled him: enormous, massive, patient, capable of wrath, a hostile beast encircling the hostile giant of the jungle and equally ready to wash away the memory of man.

— John Brunner, *Stand on Zanzibar* (1968)

The desert, the mountains: they stood still. They did not cry out forever in a great, dull voice. The sea spoke forever, but its language was foreign to her.

— Ursula K. Le Guin, *The Tombs of Atuan* (1971)

It took a sailor who was better than good to work his way past reefs, fight clear of eddies and riptides, beat around regions against which the hovering man warned him. [. . .] The air blew full of salt and strength, it lulled, it whistled, it frolicked and kissed. To sail was to dance with the world.

— Poul Anderson, "My Own, My Native Land" (1974)

On the water, aboard the *Proteus,* the crowding, the activities, the tempo, of life in the cities, on the land, are muted, slowed—fictionalized—by the metaphysical distancing a few meters of water can provide. We alter the landscape with great facility, but the ocean has always seemed unchanged, and I suppose by extension we are infected with some feelings of timelessness whenever we set out upon her.

— Roger Zelazny, "Home Is the Hangman" (1975)

Speaking now only to that Presence, to the sea, to that vast remorseless deity, bargaining with it cannily, hopefully, shrewdly, like a country housewife at market, proffering it the fine rich red gift of his death.

— Gardner Dozois, "The Peacemaker" (1983)

Fish are not the best authority on water.

— Jane Yolen, "The White Babe" (1987)

We would stop for me to name the rivers: Memory that carries remembering away, and Anger that runs so gently smoothing the pebbles round, and Terror that we swam in fearlessly.
— Ursula K. Le Guin, "Kore 87" (1988)

They wanted a bath — in their old aquatic dolphin brains, down below the cerebrums, down where desires were primal and fierce, they wanted back into water.
— Kim Stanley Robinson, *Red Mars* (1992)

SECRETS AND MYSTERIES

A secret is a weapon and a friend.
— James Stephens, *The Crock of Gold* (1912)

Shangri-La was lovely then, touched with the mystery that lies at the core of all loveliness.
— James Hilton, *Lost Horizon* (1933)

If you want to keep a secret you must also hide it from yourself.
— George Orwell, *Nineteen Eighty-Four* (1949)

Mavor looked into the viewscreen, and out across the star-blazed midnight that was the sea between the worlds. He saw splendor and loneliness, and the challenge of a universe in which man was but one tiny mystery in a darkness that had no ending.
— Chad Oliver, "North Wind" (1956)

Hammond felt with overwhelming force the mystery and wonder of the galaxy, all the magic and marvels and enigmas that could exist inside this vast pinwheel of stars that rolled forever through the infinite.
— Edmond Hamilton, *The Star of Life*, revised (1959)

Seek out mystery; what else is the whole cosmos but mystery?
— Poul Anderson, "Goat Song" (1972)

Secrets and Mysteries

Secrecy is the beginning of tyranny.
　—Robert A. Heinlein, *Time Enough for Love* (1973)

Great thing about midwifing mysteries is you don't have to boil water or wash up.
　—Ray Bradbury, "Colonel Stonesteel's Genuine Home-Made Truly Egyptian Mummy" (1981)

Life is a magic show or *should* be if people didn't go to sleep on each other. Always leave folks with a bit of mystery.
　—Ray Bradbury, "Colonel Stonesteel's Genuine Home-Made Truly Egyptian Mummy" (1981)

Passwords, things that cannot be told, people with secret identities, dark linkages; this does not seem as if it ought to be the true shape of the world.
　—Margaret Atwood, *The Handmaid's Tale* (1986)

Without mysteries, life would be very dull indeed. What would be left to strive for if everything were known?
　—Charles De Lint, "Where Desert Spirits Crowd the Night" (1995)

Some people keep their faces on the inside.
　—Steve Aylett, *Atom* (2000)

Often the secret vice that concerns you most is of no interest whatsoever to anyone whose opinion you dread.
　—Glen Cook, *Angry Lead Skies* (2002)

SEX

Homosexuality is a *political* crime in a matriarchy. No society tolerates overt rejection of its basic tenets.
　—William S. Burroughs, *Naked Lunch* (1959)

The worst thing about sex is that we use it to hurt each other. It ought *never* to hurt; it should bring happiness, or at least, pleasure.
　—Robert A. Heinlein, *Stranger in a Strange Land* (1961)

"Don't you know, Deckard, that in the colonies they have android mistresses?"

"It's illegal," Rick said, knowing the law about that.

"Sure it's illegal. But most variations in sex are illegal. But people do it anyhow."

— Philip K. Dick, *Do Androids Dream of Electric Sheep?* (1968)

Sex, whatever else it is — much else! — is an athletic skill. The more you practice, the more you can, the more you want to, the more you enjoy it, the less it tires you.

— Robert A. Heinlein, *I Will Fear No Evil* (1970)

We lie there on the magic carpet of shared bodies.

— William S. Burroughs, *The Wild Boys: A Book of the Dead* (1971)

Sex is either for making babies or making careers; not for fun.

— Ben Bova, "Zero Gee" (1972)

[On sex in space:] They were in their own world now, their private cosmos, floating freely and softly in the darkness. Touching, drifting, coupling, searching the new seas and continents, they explored their world.

— Ben Bova, "Zero Gee" (1972)

Catherine had a natural and healthy curiosity for the perverse in all its forms.

— J. G. Ballard, *Crash* (1973)

The endless highway systems along which we moved contained the formulas for an infinity of sexual bliss.

— J. G. Ballard, *Crash* (1973)

Sex is a comforting aggravation.

— Susanna Jacobson, "Notes from Magdalen More" (1973)

I'm just a sweet transvestite
From Transexual
Transylvania.

— Richard O'Brien, "Sweet Transvestite," *The Rocky Horror Show*
    (play, 1973)

Sex

It is hard to swear when sex is not dirty and blasphemy does not exist.
—Ursula K. Le Guin, *The Dispossessed: An Ambiguous Utopia* (1974)

I was taught in crèche to class coition with eating, drinking, breathing, sleeping, playing, talking, cuddling—the pleasant necessities that make life a happiness instead of a burden.
—Robert A. Heinlein, *Friday* (1982)

Sex is a better tranquilizer than any of those drugs and much better for your metabolism. I don't see why human people make such a heavy trip out of sex. It isn't anything complex; it is simply the best thing in life, even better than food.
—Robert A. Heinlein, *Friday* (1982)

There are only so many ways that a male human body and a female human body can be joined together, and all of them, it seems, had already been invented by the time the glaciers came.
—Robert Silverberg, "House of Bones" (1988)

There is no fucking in Hades.
—Sheri S. Tepper, *The Gate to Women's Country* (1988)

When sex fails for you—when it ceases to be central in your life—you enter middle age, a zone of the most unclear exits from which some of us never escape.
—M. John Harrison, "Isobel Avens Returns to Stepney in the Spring" (1994)

The marketing lie was that the suits were "consensual aids to full body aura alignment," not sex toys. Yeah, right. Psychobabble. She was being diddled by an oversized condom possessed of fuzzy logic.
—Nalo Hopkinson, "Ganger (Ball Lightning)" (2000)

SPACE

Nothing can be prettier than to see the movement, in perfectly harmonic relations, of planets round their centres, of satellites around planets, of suns, with their planets and satellites, around their centres, and of these in turn around theirs. And to persons who have loved earth as much as I do, and who, while at school there, have studied other worlds and stars, then distant, as carefully as I have, nothing, as I say, can be more charming than to see at once all this play and interplay; to see comets passing from system to system, warming themselves now at one white sun, and then at a party-colored double; to see the people on them changing customs and costumes as they change their light, and to hear their quaint discussions as they justify the new and ridicule the old.

— Edward Everett Hale, "Hands Off" (1881)

There is, though I do not know how there is or why there is, a sense of infinite peace and protection in the glittering hosts of heaven. There it must be, I think, in the vast and eternal laws of matter, and not in the daily cares and sins and troubles of men, that whatever is more than animal within us must find its solace and its hope.

— H. G. Wells, *The Island of Doctor Moreau* (1896)

Over me, around me, closing in on me, embracing me ever nearer, was the Eternal; that which was before the beginning and that which triumphs over the end; that enormous void in which all light and life and being is but the thin and vanishing splendour of a falling star, the cold, the stillness, the silence — the infinite and final Night of space.

— H. G. Wells, *The First Men in the Moon* (1901)

You know what empty space and stars do to a man. The bigness of things gives him a colossal inferiority complex, and it puts him in the mood for anything. What I mean is, a man doesn't care.

— Ross Rocklynne, "At the Center of Gravity" (1936)

Two thousand million or so years ago two galaxies were colliding; or, rather, were passing through each other.

— E. E. "Doc" Smith, *Triplanetary,* revised (1948)

He knew now where he belonged — in space, where he was born. Any planet was merely a hotel to him; space was his home.

— Robert A. Heinlein, *Between Planets* (1951)

Space

The infinite chasm of open space seemed suddenly even more dark and cold and dreadful than it was, and for an instant he hungered fiercely for the quiet peace of this forgotten world.

—Jack Williamson, "The Peddler's Nose" (1951)

Overhead wheeled the stars, the million suns of space, fire and ice and the giant sprawl of constellations, the Milky Way a rush of curdled silver, the far, mysterious glow of nebulae, hugeness and loneliness to break a human heart.

—Poul Anderson, "Garden in the Void" (1952)

Why are we trying to get into space anyhow? There's nothing out there but a lot of nothing, and some balls of rock nobody wants.

—James Blish, "First Strike" (1953)

What can there be concerning outer space *but* ignorance?

—Nigel Kneale, *The Quatermass Experiment* (TV miniseries, 1953)

Down there, lost years and miles away, some tiny dot of a woman was opening her microscopic door to listen to an atom's song. Lost, lost, and packed away in cotton wool, like a specimen slide: one spring morning on Earth.

Black miles above, so far that sixty Earths could have been piled one on another to make a pole for his perch, Wesson swung in his endless circle within a circle. Yet, vast as was the gulf beneath him, all this—Earth, Moon, orbital stations, ships; yes, the Sun and all the rest of the planets, too—was the merest sniff of space, to be pinched up between thumb and finger.

—Damon Knight, "Stranger Station" (1956)

Suddenly the friendly protecting sky seemed to have been torn open above me as the veiling cloud was torn, and through the rent the whole Outside poured in upon me, the black freezing spaces of the galaxy, the blaze and strangeness of a billion billion suns. I shrank beneath that vastness. I was nothing, nobody, an infinitesimal fleck in a cosmos too huge to be borne.

—Leigh Brackett, "The Queer Ones" (1957)

He was aware now of the turning earth that had produced him, and the immeasurably great turning of a galaxy which had produced the earth. In his own being he felt the forward thrust of star clouds; the ordered turbulence

of spiral arms ablaze with condensations of sapphire, swirling about a red
nucleus of older stars.
—Doris Pitkin Buck, "Spanish Spoken" (1957)

There were still some meteorites coming in, making bright little winks of
fire where they bit into the plain. Deadly stingers out of nowhere, heading
nowhere, impartially orbiting, random as rain, random as death. The debris
of creation.
—Walter M. Miller, Jr., "The Lineman" (1957)

Hammond had seen space before, the hosts of stars marching forever across
the black meadows of heaven, burning companies of hot gold and smoky red
and ice-blue and green, trailing bannerets of nebulosity, a maze of light so
vast that it was hard to think of each gleaming point as a mighty sun boiling
with atomic fire as it plunged falling with its planets through infinity.
—Edmond Hamilton, *The Star of Life*, revised (1959)

Here were the stars, and the constellations, and the island universes, and the
nebulae that curved and spiraled and stretched in great gaseous bands across
the heavens like fiery diamonds in some vast showcase. And here, and here,
and here were the others, all of them, all of them waiting.
Softly, he spoke their names, as though they were old friends not seen in
too long a time. It would take a million million lifetimes to visit only a small
number of them, but he had that and more.
"Which way first?" he wondered. "Which way?"
Around him, patiently, the universe waited.
—Charles E. Fritch, "The Castaway" (1963)

Space gnawed at men's minds.
—Lester del Rey, *Siege Perilous* (1966)

For years astrophysicists have been racking their brains over the reason
for the great difference in the amounts of cosmic dust in various galaxies.
The answer, I think, is quite simple: the higher a civilization is, the more
dust and refuse it produces. This is a problem more for janitors than for
astrophysicists.
—Stanislaw Lem, "Let Us Save the Universe (An Open Letter from
Ijon Tichy, Space Traveller)" (1966), translated by Joel Stern and
Maria Swiecicka-Ziemianek (1981)

Space

Space is infinite.
It is dark.
Space is neutral.
Stars occupy minute areas of space. They are clus-
tered a few billion here.   A few billion there.
Space does not threaten.
  Space does not comfort.
Space is the absence of time and of matter.
  —Michael Moorcock, *The Black Corridor* (1969)

Space is not black. It runs, shivers and spins with a thousand colors, of which
the visible spectrum is only a minute fraction.
  —Bob Shaw, *The Palace of Eternity* (1969)

Whole worlds formed in a pregnant void: not spherical worlds merely, but
dodeka-spherical, and those much more intricate than that. Not merely seven
colors to play with, but seven to the seventh and to the seventh again.
  Stars vivid in the bright light. You who have seen stars only in darkness
be silent! Asteroids that they ate like peanuts, for now they were all meta-
morphic giants. Galaxies like herds of rampaging elephants. Bridges so long
that both ends of them receded over the light-speed edges. Waterfalls, of a
finer water, that bounced off galaxy clusters as if they were boulders.
  —R. A. Lafferty, "Sky" (1971)

It was still too early in the night to lie on her back and stare at the evil
constellations, letting the infinite horror of space invade her mind.
  —George Alec Effinger, "How It Felt" (1974)

Reynolds liked the moon. If he had not, he would never have elected to
return here to stay. It was the Earth he hated. Better than the moon was space
itself, the dark endless void beyond the reach of man's ugly grasping hands.
  —Gordon Eklund and Gregory Benford, "If the Stars Are Gods" (1974)

Space [. . .] is big. Really big. You just won't believe how vastly, hugely, mind-
bogglingly big it is. I mean, you may think it's a long way down the street to
the chemist, but that's just peanuts to space.
  —Douglas Adams, "Fit the Second," episode of *The Hitch-Hiker's Guide to
    the Galaxy* (radio series, 1978)

You can't know space unless you were born there.
—Joe Haldeman, *Worlds* (1981)

One of the interesting things about space [. . .] is how dull it is.
—Douglas Adams, *Life, the Universe, and Everything* (1982)

Space is an unnatural environment, and it takes an unnatural effort from
unnatural people to prosper there.
—Bruce Sterling, "Swarm" (1982)

For all the tenure of humans on Earth, the night sky had been a companion
and an inspiration. The stars were comforting. They seemed to demonstrate
that the heavens were created for the benefit and instruction of humans. This
pathetic conceit became the conventional wisdom worldwide.
—Carl Sagan, *Contact* (1985)

Izzie scanned the blackness of space above them, broken only by the splash
of stars where planets whirled and life quickened and grew and danced and
knew nothing of this desolation.
—Sydney Long, "For the Right Reason" (1995)

We ignore the blackness of outer space and pay attention to the stars.
—Neal Stephenson, *The Diamond Age, or, A Young Lady's Illustrated Primer*
(1995)

SPACESHIPS

He looked up at the ship; and the gleaming, metallic tower that was a finger
pointing the way to the stars, that was an arm reaching out for the stars.
—A. Bertram Chandler, "New Wings" (1948)

The rocket lay on the launching field, blowing out pink clouds of fire and
oven heat. The rocket stood in the cold winter morning, making summer
with every breath of its mighty exhausts. The rocket made climates, and
summer lay for a brief moment upon the land . . .
—Ray Bradbury, "Rocket Summer" (1950)

Spaceships

The first Martian vessel descended upon Earth with the slow, stately fall of a grounded balloon.
  —Eric Frank Russell, "Dear Devil" (1950)

She went down one more step, and let herself look at the rocket. The workmen were still there. The metal dragon swallowed all they fed it, stolid, indifferent, letting itself be stuffed, for now, with bits and pieces of paraphernalia, oddments of fiber and metal, of glass and wood. But all the while it waited, knowing the feast that was coming soon, brooding and hungering for the living flesh that would feed it this night.
  —Judith Merril, "So Proudly We Hail" (1953)

Far removed indeed were these great ships of the starways from the unsteady little rockets of the Twentieth Century. Their dark hulls loomed vast as thunderclouds over the tiny men and vehicles that came and went around them. They rested now, but it was the rest of giants who had been to the far shores of infinity, who knew the ways of distant suns and worlds, whose sides were scarred by the drift of remote nebulae, and who would presently spurn this little planet Earth from beneath them and return into the cosmic glare and gloom that was their home.
  —Edmond Hamilton, *The Star of Life*, revised (1959)

The Drive, to avoid technicalities, was a device somewhat simpler than Woman and considerably more complicated than sex, which caused its vessel to cease to exist *here* while simultaneously appeared *there*, by-passing the limitations imposed by the speed of light.
  —Theodore Sturgeon, "If All Men Were Brothers, Would You Let One Marry Your Sister?" (1967)

Supercold, superdense fluid flows from those big hairy balls of the starship *Theodore Bilko* into painboxes. Molecules are energized, atoms are squeezed, electrons are sheared from their primaries, crammed m jammed m slammed, whammed m bammed, shaped, scraped, raped, nuclei ripped apart, smashed into one another, forces whirling and driving madly, something becoming something else, something less, part of that something becoming nothing, energy produced, screams out propulsion tubes crying to the echoing deaf cosmos for relief, release, dying in an attenuating blaze of hyperenergized exhaust, thrusting the *Bilko* away from N'Alabama into the dark vacuum that surrounds Alquane, thrusting, heaving, hurling her upward. [. . .] This is propulsion by agonized matter.

—Richard A. Lupoff, "With the Bentfin Boomer Boys on Little Old New Alabama" (1972)

The ships hung in the sky in much the same way that bricks don't.

—Douglas Adams, *The Hitchhiker's Guide to Galaxy* (1979)

Picture this: a mobile space colony, supporting more than a million people. No, not a colony, but an organism which can move and grow as long as it can obtain resources and maintain a food supply within its ecology. It's a living organism because it can respond to stimuli through its optical and sensory nervous system. It thinks with the intellects of its human and cybernetic intelligences. And it can reproduce, which is what we expect from a living organism.

—George Zebrowski, *Macrolife* (1979)

A rocket is the most lavishly expensive transportation ever invented. In a typical rocketship mission half the effort is spent fighting gravity to go up and the other half is spent fighting gravity in letting down—as crashing is considered an unsatisfactory end to a mission.

—Robert A. Heinlein, *The Cat Who Walks through Walls* (1985)

SPACE TRAVEL

If we are to believe certain narrow-minded people—and what else can we call them?—humanity is confined within a circle of Popilius from which there is no escape, condemned to vegetate on this globe, never able to venture into interplanetary space! That's not so! We are going to the moon, we shall go to the planets, we shall travel to the stars just as today we go from Liverpool to New York, easily, rapidly, surely, and the oceans of space will be crossed like the seas of the moon!

—Jules Verne, *From the Earth to the Moon* (1865), translated by Walter James Miller (1978)

Dim and wonderful is the vision I have conjured up in my mind of life spreading slowly from this little seed-bed of the solar system throughout the inanimate vastness of sidereal space.

— H. G. Wells, *The War of the Worlds* (1898)

There is a sense of spectral whirling through liquid gulfs of infinity, of dizzying rides through reeling universes on a comet's tail, and of hysterical plunges from the pit to the moon and from the moon back again to the pit, all livened by a cachinnating chorus of the distorted, hilarious elder gods and the green, bat-winged mocking imps of Tartarus.

— H. P. Lovecraft, "The Call of Cthulhu" (1928)

Hammond's head spun with their tales of spaceman's life, tales of the vast glooms of cosmic clouds that ships rarely dared enter, of wrecks and castaways in the unexplored fringes of the galaxy, of strange races like the thinking rocks of Rigel and the fish-cities of Arcturus' watery worlds and the unearthly tree-wizards of dark Algol.

— Edmond Hamilton, *The Star of Life* (1947)

In this universe the night was falling: the shadows were lengthening towards an east that would not know another dawn. But elsewhere the stars were still young and the light of morning lingered — and along the path he once had followed Man would one day go again.

— Arthur C. Clarke, *Against the Fall of Night* (1948)

Space was vast, the journeys through it long and lonely, landing always a stimulating experience, with its prospect of new life forms to be seen and studied.

— A. E. van Vogt, "The Monster" (1948)

"It is good to renew one's wonder," said the philosopher. "Space travel has again made children of us all."

— Ray Bradbury, epigraph to *The Martian Chronicles* (1950)

Coming out of space was like coming out of the most beautiful cathedral they had ever seen.

— Ray Bradbury, "The Fire Balloons" (1951)

We who were meant to roam the stars go now on foot upon a ravaged earth. But above us those other worlds still hang, and still they beckon. And so is the promise still given. If we make not the mistakes of the Old Ones then shall we know in time more than the winds of this earth and the trails of this earth.

   —Andre Norton, *Star Man's Son* (1952)

The "romance" of space—drivel written in the old days. When you're not blasting, you float in a cramped hotbox, crawl through dirty mazes of greasy pipe and cable to tighten a lug, scratch your arms and bark your shins, get sick and choked up because no gravity helps your gullet get the food down. [. . .] "Did you like horror movies when you were a kid?" asked the psych. And you'd damn well better answer "yes," if you want to go to space.

   —Walter M. Miller, Jr., "Death of a Spaceman" (1954)

Fragile Earthmen, venturing out here, go back to your own system! Go back to your little orderly universe, your strict civilization. Stay away from the regions you do not know! Stay away from darkness and monsters!

   —Philip K. Dick, *Solar Lottery* (1955)

The stars will never be won by little minds; we must be big as space itself.

   —Robert A. Heinlein, *Double Star* (1956)

His brain was a bright kaleidoscope and the visions evoked by Wilson's words went round in it, and round again until he was dizzy with them.

   Fantastic, splendid visions. Earth sending out her ships and mourning them and stubbornly sending out more until one of them returned and the Big Step had been made. [. . .] Then the ships going out proud and confident, taking the children of Earth to the empty planets and filling them with life, and after that like strong swimmers leaving the shallows of their youth behind, plunging into the black seas that run cold and tideless across the universe, girdling ten billion stars, until the children of Earth were spread across the galaxy. They were born now under the light of alien suns, on countless alien planets, and they had changed as Quobba and Tammas were changed to suit their environments, but still they were the children of Earth, and space belonged to them.

   —Edmond Hamilton, *The Star of Life,* revised (1959)

"Was it such a good thing to conquer space? We thought it would be, back in the Twentieth Century. But was it?"

He looked out into the blind light and darkness of the universe but there was no answer there for his question. There would never be an answer, for it was not a matter of good or ill. Man could not choose now, he had made his choice long ago when as half-man he had looked up at the stars and coveted them. He would look farther yet with desire, upon galaxies and realms beyond present thinking, and would struggle for them, falling into many a cosmic trap like the one here, and always striving pitifully to snatch individual happiness before he died in that struggle.

— Edmond Hamilton, *The Star of Life,* revised (1959)

Mankind flung its advance agents ever outward, ever outward. Eventually it flung them out into space, into the colorless, tasteless, weightless sea of outwardness without end.

It flung them like stones.

These unhappy agents found what had already been found in abundance on Earth — a nightmare of meaninglessness without end. The bounties of space, of infinite outwardness, were three: empty heroics, low comedy, and pointless death.

— Kurt Vonnegut, Jr., *The Sirens of Titan* (1959)

We take off into the cosmos, ready for anything: for solitude, for hardship, for exhaustion, death. Modesty forbids us to say so, but there are times when we think pretty well of ourselves. And yet, if we examine it more closely, our enthusiasm turns out to be all sham. We don't want to conquer the cosmos, we simply want to extend the boundaries of Earth to the frontiers of the cosmos. [. . .] We have no need of other worlds. We need mirrors.

— Stanislaw Lem, *Solaris* (1961), translated by Joanna Kilmartin and
    Steve Cox (1970)

Man has gone out to explore other worlds and other civilizations without having explored his own labyrinth of dark passages and secret chambers, and without finding what lies behind doorways that he himself has sealed.

— Stanislaw Lem, *Solaris* (1961), translated by Joanna Kilmartin and
    Steve Cox (1970)

In those days, interplanetary voyages were an everyday occurrence, and interstellar travel not uncommon. Rockets took tourists to the wondrous sites of Sirius, or financiers to the famous stock exchanges of Arcturus and Aldebaran.

— Pierre Boulle, *Planet of the Apes* (1963), translated by Xan Fielding (1963)

I'd spend the whole night just standing there and watching the stars and the planets and the galaxies whirling about the heavens, looking at the universe as though it were a great celestial circus. And I'd say to myself, "Someday, I'm going out there. Someday I'm going out there and take apart some of those flaming pinwheels and see what they're made of. I'll go farther than anyone has ever gone before, and then farther than that. I'll discover suns and worlds no one has ever known existed, and I'll find out if the universe is round after all, and if it is I'll find out what's on the outside of it."

— Charles E. Fritch, "The Castaway" (1963)

Space . . . the final frontier. These are the voyages of the starship *Enterprise*. Its five-year mission: to explore strange, new worlds; to seek out new life, and new civilizations; to boldly go where no man has gone before.

— Gene Roddenberry, opening narration, *Star Trek* (TV series, 1966)

Space . . . the final frontier. These are the continuing voyages of the starship *Enterprise*. Her ongoing mission: to explore strange, new worlds; to seek out new life forms, and new civilizations; to boldly go where no man has gone before.

— Gene Roddenberry, closing narration, *Star Trek II: The Wrath of Khan* (film, 1982)

Space . . . the final frontier. These are the voyages of the starship *Enterprise*. Its continuing mission: to explore strange, new worlds; to seek out new life, and new civilizations; to boldly go where no one has gone before.

— Gene Roddenberry, opening narration, *Star Trek: The Next Generation* (TV series, 1987)

Beyond
The rim of the star-light
My love
Is wand'ring in star-flight

Space Travel

I know
He'll find in star-clustered reaches
Love,
Strange love a star woman teaches.
I know
His journey ends never
His star trek
Will go on forever.
But tell him
While he wanders his starry sea
Remember, remember me.
  —Gene Roddenberry, "Theme from *Star Trek*" (1968)

The all but impossible glory of having walked on the moon, of proving our mind power and our brilliant technology, this cannot ever be dimmed. [. . .] We have hurled ourselves closer to the gods.
  —Emil Petaja, "That Moon Plaque: Comments by Science Fiction Writers" (1969)

It may take endless wars and unbearable population pressure to force-feed a technology to the point where it can cope with space. In the universe, space travel may be the normal birth pangs of an otherwise dying race. A test. Some races pass, some fail.
  —Robert A. Heinlein, *I Will Fear No Evil* (1970)

My descendants are going to surf light-waves in space.
  —Katherine MacLean, "The Missing Man" (1971)

Our flight must be not only to the stars but into the nature of our own beings. Because it is not merely *where* we go, to Alpha Centauri or Betelgeuse, but what we are as we make our pilgrimage there. Our natures will be going there, too.
  —Philip K. Dick, "The Android and the Human" (1972)

We're lost in an out-of-the-way section of deep space and who knows what evil lurks among the stars?
  —Carol Emshwiller, "The Childhood of the Human Hero" (1973)

We must stop this insane foraging; this conveying of our lunacies from one segment of the solar system to the next; we must, I say, stay on our home planet and work out our problems in the Arena of our birth.

—Barry N. Malzberg, "Notes Leading Down to the Conquest" (1973)

We stand undisputed masters of the Solar System and poised on the edge of interstellar space itself, just as they did fifty thousand years ago . . . And so, gentlemen, we inherit the stars.

Let us go out, then, and claim our inheritance. We belong to a tradition in which the concept of defeat has no meaning. Today the stars and tomorrow the galaxies. No force exists in the Universe that can stop us.

—James P. Hogan, *Inherit the Stars* (1977)

Far back in the mists of ancient time, in the great and glorious days of the Former Galactic Empire, life was wild, rich, and on the whole tax free. Mighty starships plied their way between exotic suns seeking adventure and reward amongst the furthest reaches of galactic space. In those days spirits were brave, the stakes were high, men were real men, women were real women, and small furry creatures from Alpha Centauri were real small furry creatures from Alpha Centauri. And all dared to brave unknown terrors, to do mighty deeds, to boldly split infinitives that no man had split before and thus was the Empire forged.

—Douglas Adams, "Fit the Third," episode of *The Hitch-Hiker's Guide to the Galaxy* (radio series, 1978)

On a dreary Tuesday in March, Mrs. Bagley told her family she was going to Mars.

—Kate Wilhelm, "Mrs. Bagley Goes to Mars" (1978)

The great human summer of time to come, he realized, would be lived out of the cradle, in free space, around the sun in space habitats, and out among the stars.

—George Zebrowski, *Macrolife* (1979)

[On space travel:] Human DNA spreading out from gravity's steep well like an oilslick.

—William Gibson, *Neuromancer* (1984)

She would, mentally, travel a multiplicity of geographies, physical and non-physical, over mountains, under oceans, even across and among galaxies. Through the flaming peripheries of stars she had passed, and through the cold reaches of a space where the last worlds hung tiny as specks of moisture on the window-panes of her rooms. Endless varieties of creatures came and went on the paths of Medra's cerebral journeys. Creatures of landscape, waterscape, airscape, and of the gaplands between the suns.
— Tanith Lee, "Medra" (1984)

Webriding. Flowing through stars, points of flame running through hands that aren't hands, the psychic You bound up in the physical You that's just a pattern sliding along the web, held together and existing only by the strength of will of the webrider. Sailing on evanescent wings of mind through the energy/matter currents of space.
— Jayge Carr, "Webrider" (1985)

Spaceflight, therefore, is subversive. If they are fortunate enough to find themselves in Earth orbit, most people, after a little meditation, have similar thoughts. The nations that had instituted spaceflight had done so largely for nationalistic reasons; it was a small irony that almost everyone who entered space received a startling glimpse of a transnational perspective, of the Earth as one world.
— Carl Sagan, *Contact* (1985)

GILLIAN TAYLOR: Don't tell me — you're from outer space!
KIRK: No, I'm from Iowa. I only work in outer space.
— Steve Meerson, Peter Krikes, Harve Bennett, and Nicholas Meyer,
    Star Trek IV: The Voyage Home (film, 1986)

The conquest of space isn't as easy as the layman might imagine.
— Neal Barrett, Jr., "Perpetuity Blues" (1987)

Science is part of a larger human enterprise, and that enterprise includes going to the stars, adapting to other planets, adapting them to us. [. . .] The whole meaning of the universe, its beauty, is contained in the consciousness of intelligent life. We are the consciousness of the universe, and our job is to spread that around, to go look at things, to live everywhere we can.
— Kim Stanley Robinson, *Red Mars* (1992)

Sooner or later, everyone comes to Babylon 5.

— J. Michael Straczynski, "The Gathering," episode of *Babylon 5* (1993)

It was the Dawn of the Third Age of Mankind, ten years after the Earth-Minbari War. The Babylon Project was a dream given form. Its goal: to prevent another war by creating a place where humans and aliens could work out their differences peacefully. It's a port of call, home away from home for diplomats, hustlers, entrepreneurs and wanderers. Humans and aliens wrapped in two million, five hundred thousand tons of spinning metal . . . all alone in the night. It can be a dangerous place, but it's our last, best hope for peace.

This is the story of the last of the Babylon stations. The year is 2258. The name of the place is Babylon 5.

— J. Michael Straczynski, opening narration, *Babylon 5* (TV series, 1994)

Lewis loved fishing in space. Yes, I know there are no fish in space, but *catching* fish is not at all the main point of fishing. Ninety percent of the activity is sitting with rod and reel just simply mulling things over. Lewis spent hours in a space suit sitting on top of the *Ray* with his line dangling, contemplating the sheer beauty of the Universe.

— Eric Idle, *The Road to Mars: A Post-Modem Novel* (1999)

STARS

What, are the stars still there? What is the use of stars when there are no human beings?

— Karel Capek, *R.U.R.* (play, 1921), translated by P. Selver (1923)

The sky was lousy with stars — nasty little pinpoints of cold hostility that had neither the remoteness of space nor the friendly warmth of Earth.

— Lester del Rey, "Over the Top" (1949)

O God, there were so many stars you *could* have used.

What was the need to give these people to the fire, that the symbol of their passing might shine above Bethlehem?

— Arthur C. Clarke, "The Star" (1955)

There, peeping among the cloud-wrack above a dark tor high up in the mountains, Sam saw a white star twinkle for a while. The beauty of it smote his heart, as he looked up out of the forsaken land, and hope returned to him. For like a shaft, clear and cold, the thought pierced him that in the end the Shadow was only a small and passing thing: there was light and high beauty for ever beyond its reach.

—J. R. R. Tolkien, *The Return of the King* (1955)

If you have only lived on Earth, you have never seen the Sun.

—Arthur C. Clarke, "Out of the Sun" (1958)

It was stunning enough, that view of the galactic wilderness. Colossal ramparts of scattered and clotted suns rose up in front of them, gleaming hotly in clusters like great hives of stars or shining out like foggy witchfires through the farflung nebulae. A dark cloud brooded to the left, with the starlight from behind it forming a shining halo around it. Close ahead to the right hung a magnificent double star whose components were pale yellow and smoky red, and the size of those two suns increased visibly as he watched.

—Edmond Hamilton, *The Star of Life,* revised (1959)

Look the stars in the eyes as you did for ten thousand years, and know them for your brothers.

—Edmond Hamilton, *The Star of Life,* revised (1959)

No man could argue with the Sun in one of its rages, even though he might ride upon its beams to the edge of space.

—Arthur C. Clarke, "The Wind from the Sun" (1964)

Whoever made the stars set them too far apart for humans.

—William F. Temple, "The Legend of Ernie Deacon" (1965)

It may be that the old astrologers had the truth exactly reversed, when they believed that the stars controlled the destinies of men.

The time may come when men control the destinies of stars.

—Arthur C. Clarke, "Epilogue: Beyond Apollo" (1969)

He walked the hills and knew what the hills had seen through geologic time. He listened to the stars and spelled out what the stars were saying.
— Clifford D. Simak, "The Thing in the Stone" (1970)

Starlight helped her to see. Orange starlight. Gold starlight. Starlight like the reddest rose. The stars were friends, she was sure.
— Doris Pitkin Buck, "The Giberel" (1971)

The sun circles us and the stars are jewels on the nightcloak of the Mother.
— Mildred Downey Broxon, "The Night Is Cold, the Stars Are Far Away" (1974)

I want you to teach me to talk to the stars.
— Gordon Eklund and Gregory Benford, "If the Stars Are Gods" (1974)

The stars had never hesitated.
Perhaps the noble certainty of their gait had been a mere effect of distance. Perhaps in fact they had hurtled wildly, enormous furnace-fragments of a primal bomb thrown through the cosmic dark; but time and distance soften all agony. If the universe, as seems likely, began with an act of destruction, the stars we had used to see told no tales of it. They had been implacably serene.
— Ursula K. Le Guin, "The New Atlantis" (1975)

Somewhere a star was going nova, a black hole was vacuuming space, a comet was combing its hair.
— Kate Wilhelm, "Mrs. Bagley Goes to Mars" (1978)

Elsewhere thronged stars, so many and so brilliant that they well-nigh drowned the blackness which held them. The Milky Way was a torrent of silver.
— Poul Anderson, "The Saturn Game" (1981)

Nothing but stars, scattered across the blackness as though the Creator had smashed the windscreen of his car and hadn't bothered to stop to sweep up the pieces.
— Terry Pratchett, *Pyramids* (1989)

STORIES AND WRITERS

When I used to read fairy tales, I fancied that kind of thing never happened, and now here I am in the middle of one!
   —Lewis Carroll, *Alice's Adventures in Wonderland* (1865)

I had this story from one who had no business to tell it to me, or to any other.
   —Edgar Rice Burroughs, *Tarzan of the Apes* (1914)

I wondered at the ancients who had never realized the utter absurdity of their literature and poetry. The enormous, magnificent power of the literary word was completely wasted. It's simply ridiculous—everyone wrote anything he pleased.
   —Yevgeny Zamiatin, *We* (1924), translated by Mirra Ginsburg (1972)

I would not look to any fiction writer, living or dead, for guidance on any subject, and therefore, if he does not entertain, he is a total loss.
   —Edgar Rice Burroughs, "Entertainment Is Fiction's Purpose" (1930)

Things that are good to have and days that are good to spend are soon told about, and not much to listen to; while things that are uncomfortable, palpitating, and even gruesome, may make a good tale, and take a deal of telling anyway.
   —J. R. R. Tolkien, *The Hobbit* (1937)

Escape is one of the main functions of fairy-stories, and since I do not disapprove of them, it is plain that I do not accept the tone of scorn or pity with which "Escape" is now so often used: a tone for which the uses of the word outside literary criticism give no warrant at all. In what the misusers are fond of calling Real Life, Escape is evidently as a rule very practical, and may even be heroic. In real life it is difficult to blame it, unless it fails; in criticism it would seem to be the worse the better it succeeds. Evidently we are faced by a misuse of words, and also by a confusion of thought. Why should a man be scorned, if, finding himself in prison, he tries to get out and go home? Or if, when he cannot do so, he thinks and talks about other topics than jailers and prison-walls?
   —J. R. R. Tolkien, "On Fairy-Stories" (1947)

There is only one thing a writer can write about: *what is in front of his senses at the moment of writing.*

—William S. Burroughs, *Naked Lunch* (1959)

I wanted the hurtling moons of Barsoom. I wanted Storisende and Poictesme, and Holmes shaking me awake to tell me, "The game's afoot!" I wanted to float down the Mississippi on a raft and elude a mob in company with the Duke of Bilgewater and the Lost Dauphin.

I wanted Prester John, and Excalibur held by a moon-white arm out of a silent lake. I wanted to sail with Ulysses and with Tros of Samothrace and eat the lotus in a land that seemed always afternoon. I wanted the feeling of romance and the sense of wonder I had known as a kid. I wanted the world to be what they had promised me it was going to be—instead of the tawdry, lousy, fouled-up mess it is.

—Robert A. Heinlein, *Glory Road* (1963)

"Your story is impossible, ridiculous, fantastic, mad, and obviously the ravings of a disordered mind," Hermann said. "And I believe every word of it."

—Keith Laumer, *The Other Side of Time* (1965)

The role of the writer today has totally changed—he is now merely one of a huge army of people filling the environment with fictions of every kind. To survive, he must become far more analytic, approaching his subject matter like a scientist or engineer. If he is to produce fiction at all, he must out-imagine everyone else, scream louder, whisper more quietly. For the first time in the history of narrative fiction, it will require more than talent to become a writer.

—J. G. Ballard, "Fictions of Every Kind" (1971)

Most things grow old and perish, as the centuries go on and on. Very few are the precious things that remain precious, or the tales that are still told.

—Ursula K. Le Guin, *The Tombs of Atuan* (1971)

Escape literature, he told me, should be an escape for the writer as well as the reader.

—Margaret Atwood, *Lady Oracle* (1976)

Stories and Writers

Who can possibly be as deeply inside a story as the person who writes it?
—Robert A. Heinlein, *The Number of the Beast* (1980)

It was a wonderful tale he told. It had enchanted castles sitting on mountains of glass, moist caverns beneath the sea, fleets of starships and shining riders astride horses that flew the galaxy. There were evil alien creatures, and others with much good in them. There were drugged potions. Scaled beasts roared out of hyperspace to devour planets.

Amid all the turmoil strode the Prince and Princess. They got into frightful jams and helped each other out of them.
—John Varley, "The Pusher" (1981)

If you have to be a character in a book, why not be the hero?
—John Kessel, "Another Orphan" (1982)

Part of it has to do with his recent insight that he is merely hanging on, that the ultimate outcome of ultimate struggle for any writer in America not hopelessly self-deluded is to hang on.
—Barry N. Malzberg, "Corridors" (1982)

No one enjoys writing. [. . .] There is no way to stop. Writers go on writing long after it becomes financially unnecessary . . . because it hurts less to write than it does not to write.
—Robert A. Heinlein, *The Cat Who Walks through Walls* (1985)

There's a biosoft dossier in there. For when you're older. It doesn't tell the whole story. Remember that. Nothing ever does . . .
—William Gibson, *Count Zero* (1986)

"What is literature, Rabo," he said, "but an insider's newsletter about affairs relating to molecules, of no importance to anything in the Universe but a few molecules who have the disease called 'thought.'"
—Kurt Vonnegut, Jr., *Bluebeard* (1987)

People think that stories are shaped by people. In fact, it's the other way around.
—Terry Pratchett, *Witches Abroad* (1991)

So I, poor instrument — poor *contrivance* of whatever being's making — I shall write. It is what I do. It is what I am. It is all to which I ought aspire. It is my poor shadow of the true creation. And perhaps it is a shadow forged of steel, in the end.
— Esther M. Friesner, *Yesterday We Saw Mermaids* (1992)

If you present me with a hardback edition of my work, I shall autograph it, "Arthur Clarke." If you present a paperback, I will sign it, "A. C. Squiggle."
— Arthur C. Clarke, cited by S. James Blackman, "The World Keeps Up with Arthur Clarke" (1999)

What's the end of a story? When you begin telling it.
— Ursula K. Le Guin, *The Telling* (2000)

The best stories come from deep within a writer's soul.
— Michael A. Burstein, "Paying It Forward" (2003)

SURREALISM

He punched the door with a code combination, and awaited face check. It came promptly; the door dilated, and a voice inside said, "Come in, Felix."
— Robert A. Heinlein, *Beyond This Horizon* (1942)

I am reminded . . . of the way in which Heinlein has always managed to indicate the greater strangeness of a culture with the most casually dropped in reference: the first time in a novel, I believe it was in *Beyond This Horizon*, that a character came through a door that . . . dilated. And no discussion. Just: "The door dilated." I read across it, and was two lines down before I realized what the image had been that the words had urged forth. A *dilating* door. It didn't open, it *irised*! Dear God, how I knew I was in a future world.
— Harlan Ellison, "A Voice from the Styx" (1968)

The door deliquesced.
Cool against my thigh, chest, and face mist from the sill-trough blew back as I lifted my foot over the — "Hey, don't step in that!" [. . .] The blue liquid, behind us now, began to foam; the foam rose, climbing at the jambs

faster than in the middle; and darkening, and shutting out light as the door's semicrystals effloresced.
  —Samuel R. Delany, *Stars in My Pocket Like Grains of Sand* (1984)

"I can't go back," said Towser.
  "Nor I," said Fowler.
  "They would turn me back into a dog," said Towser.
  "And me," said Fowler, "back into a man."
  —Clifford D. Simak, "Desertion" (1944)

The doorknob opened a blue eye and looked at him.
  —Henry Kuttner and C. L. Moore, "The Fairy Chessmen" (1946)

I know what you're thinking, but here, on Venus, the bathroom is as much a place for social gatherings as any other room in the house.
  —A. Bertram Chandler, "Coefficient X" (1950)

Pa had sent me out to get an extra pail of air. I'd just about scooped it full and most of the warmth had leaked from my fingers when I saw the thing.
  —Fritz Leiber, "A Pail of Air" (1951)

"How are we feeling, Mr. Stone?"
  It took a minute or two for Stone to move his swollen tongue enough to answer. He wrinkled his nose in disgust.
  "What smells purple?" he demanded.
  —H. L. Gold, "The Man with English" (1953)

"Damn," he said, looking at Bob and Janice. "Knew I should have taken Invisibility in college."
  —Robert Sheckley, "The King's Wishes" (1953)

Cancer is at the door with a Singing Telegram.
  —William S. Burroughs, *Naked Lunch* (1959)

Since it's only a simple case of resurrection, rather than a matter of corpses moving, standing, and walking after death, you consider everything to be perfectly clear-cut and understandable and therefore not worthy of any further investigation.
  —Stanislaw Lem, *The Investigation* (1959), translated by Adele Milch
    (1974)

The tumbleweed said "Oof!" in the surprised way they always did when something caught them.
    —James H. Schmitz, "Balanced Ecology" (1965)

He could not argue with an angry bed.
    —Philip K. Dick, *Galactic Pot-Healer* (1969)

Did I say the wrong thing? Joe asked himself. But ye gods; what are you supposed to say to your own corpse?
    —Philip K. Dick, *Galactic Pot-Healer* (1969)

The king was pregnant.
    —Ursula K. Le Guin, *The Left Hand of Darkness* (1969)

The proper Pope for our times is a robot, certainly. At some future date it may be desirable for the Pope to be a whale, an automobile, a cat, a mountain.
    —Robert Silverberg, "Good News from the Vatican" (1971)

I had reached the age of six hundred and fifty miles.
    —Christopher Priest, *The Inverted World* (1974)

Later, as he sat on his balcony eating the dog, Dr Robert Laing reflected on the unusual events that had taken place within this huge apartment building during the previous three months.
    —J. G. Ballard, *High-Rise* (1975)

Unfortunately, no one bothered to turn off the tiger.
    —Charles L. Grant, "A Glow of Candles, a Unicorn's Eye" (1978)

"Two thousand light years to Sol," the cleaning hose remarked, unsolicited, as it crawled past Janaki down the corridor.
    —Ted Reynolds, "Millennial" (1980)

Only twenty minutes ago he had decided he would go mad, and now here he was already chasing a Chesterfield sofa across the fields of prehistoric Earth.
    —Douglas Adams, *Life, the Universe, and Everything* (1982)

Surrealism

An ancient suitcase was coming to eat him.
— Terry Pratchett, *The Colour of Magic* (1983)

She would never forgive herself for not being there when her son was born.
— Sheila Finch, *Infinity's Web* (1985)

Standing alongside the big man from Florida as they monitored the descent of the nearest skycutter, the sergeant deftly and matter-of-factly clipped the universe back onto his belt.
— Alan Dean Foster, *Cyber Way* (1990)

The briefcase was changing. Its casing bulged out, flattening into a form better adapted for swimming. It extended stubby wings, lengthened and streamlined its body, and threw out a long, slender tail. Tiny clawed feet scrabbled for purchase on the stone. Extending an eyestalk, it looked up at him.
— Michael Swanwick, *Stations of the Tide* (1991)

Phoebe had enough to worry about, without consoling an overemotional fish.
— Paul Di Filippo, "Flying the Flannel" (1996)

SURVIVAL

On Earth, everywhere in the system, the necessities of survival have made enemies of life forms even closely kin.
— Jack Williamson, *The Cometeers* (1936)

I said you were a survival type. You are — except for one thing. You don't want children. From a biological standpoint that is as contra-survival as a compulsion to suicide.
— Robert A. Heinlein, *Beyond This Horizon* (1942)

Survival of the race is the first duty of every Ethical man and woman.
— Judith Merril, "Survival Ship" (1953)

A scientifically verifiable theory of morals must be rooted in the individual's instinct to survive — *and nowhere else!* — and must correctly describe the

hierarchy of survival, note the motivations at each level, and resolve all conflicts.
— Robert A. Heinlein, *Starship Troopers* (1959)

Survival is the ability to swim in strange water.
— Frank Herbert, *Dune* (1965)

When civilization became a matter of standing in lines, the British had kept queue, and so had replaced the survival of the fittest with the survival of the fair-minded.
— Ursula K. Le Guin, "Nine Lives," revised (1970)

Q: I noticed a moment of hesitation back there when he said that the drive to survive is as potent in the intellect as in the blood. Why was that?
A: He was being very careful not to say what he says in private: that the drive to survive is as strong between the ears as it is between the legs.
— Hank Davis, "To Plant a Seed" (1972)

His people taught themselves to resist a difficult land by refusing to cry, refusing to mourn, refusing to laugh. They denied themselves grief, and allowed themselves little joy, but they survived.
— Vonda N. McIntyre, "Of Mist, and Grass, and Sand" (1973)

The law of existence is struggle — competition — elimination of the weak — a ruthless war for survival.
— Ursula K. Le Guin, *The Dispossessed: An Ambiguous Utopia* (1974)

The world is sickened of attempts to save it. The world is saving itself now in the only way it has or ever can — by small, brave individual efforts at recovery now that the storm's over. It will take centuries. Institutions have never done it and never will.
— Edgar Pangborn, "The Children's Crusade" (1974)

Uniqueness always perishes. Nature works by overproducing each species; uniqueness is a fault, a failure of nature. For survival there should be hundreds, thousands, even millions of one species, all interchangeable — if all but one dies, then nature has won. Generally it loses. But himself. I am unique, he realized. So I am doomed. Every man is unique and hence doomed.
— Philip K. Dick and Roger Zelazny, *Deus Irae* (1976)

Survival

We *are* barbarians. With survival the only moral touchstone, we show what we are. We kill in order to live. Our final decency is the ability to see what we are and exercise some rational control over it. The world's survivors will be the ruthless, not the holy meek.

—George Turner, *Drowning Towers* (1987)

Mankind. That word should have new meaning for all of us today. We can't be consumed by our petty differences anymore. We will be united in our common interest. Perhaps it's fate that today is the Fourth of July, and you will once again be fighting for our freedom. Not from tyranny, oppression, or persecution . . . but from annihilation. We're fighting for our right to live. To exist. And should we win the day, the Fourth of July will no longer be known as an American holiday, but as the day when the world declared in one voice we will not go quietly into the night! We will not vanish without a fight! We're going to live on! We're going to survive! Today, we celebrate our Independence Day!

—Dean Devlin and Roland Emmerich, *Independence Day* (film, 1996)

Staying alive is as good as it gets.

—Alex Garland, *28 Days Later* (film, 2002)

T

THINKING

Brains are the only things worth having in this world, no matter whether one is a crow or a man.
—L. Frank Baum, *The Wonderful Wizard of Oz* (1900)

She does not often go out to dinner, preferring when the children are in bed to sit beside them tidying up their minds, just as if they were drawers.
—J. M. Barrie, *Peter Pan* (play, 1904)

What egoism, what stupid vanity, to suppose that a thing could not happen because you could not conceive it!
—Edwin Balmer and Philip Wylie, *When Worlds Collide* (1932)

There is wishful thinking in Hell as well as on Earth.
—C. S. Lewis, *The Screwtape Letters* (1942)

"You Earthmen think differently," Buster went on. "Your minds are limber. You never say a thing is right until you've proven it. You never say a thing's impossible until you've proven that. And one right, so far as you are concerned, isn't the only right."
—Clifford D. Simak, "Shadow of Life" (1943)

The human brain is often too complicated a mechanism to function perfectly.
—C. L. Moore, "No Woman Born" (1944)

You mean I think like a violin, one note at a time, and you think like a guitar, a lot of related notes at a time?
—Theodore Sturgeon, "The Clinic" (1953)

Insofar as thought could be governed at all, it could only be commanded to follow what reason affirmed anyhow; command it otherwise and it would not obey.
—Walter M. Miller, Jr., *A Canticle for Leibowitz* (1959)

Thinking

The mind goes on working no matter how we try to hold it back.
—Frank Herbert, *Dune* (1965)

Three champions from the race of the Selectivitites arrived, Diodius, Triodius, and Heptodius, who possessed such a perfect vacuum in their heads, their black thought was like the starless night.
—Stanislaw Lem, "How Erg the Self-Inducing Slew a Paleface" (1965), translated by Michael Kandel (1977)

Perhaps we are incapable of rationality. Perhaps all thought is a set of impulses generated by one emotion, monitored by another, ratified by a third.
—Jack Vance, "The Last Castle" (1966)

You cannot use a spear to kill a flea which is biting you, and a shield is no use against a monster that could gobble you up shield and all. There is only one way to win against both a flea and a monster: you must think better than either of them.
—John Brunner, *Stand on Zanzibar* (1968)

Thought itself is a disease of the brain, a degenerative condition of matter. [. . .] The mind defends itself against the disintegrative process of creativity. It begins to jell, notions solidify into inalterable *systems,* which simply refuse to be broken down and reformed.
—Thomas M. Disch, *Camp Concentration* (1968)

Like many intelligent men, Stone took a rather suspicious attitude toward his own brain, which he saw as a precise and skilled but temperamental machine. He was never surprised when the machine failed to perform, though he feared those moments, and hated them.
—Michael Crichton, *The Andromeda Strain* (1969)

He pondered, having many disjointed and unconnected brooding thoughts; they swam through him like silvery fish.
—Philip K. Dick, *Ubik* (1969)

Kimoe's ideas never seemed to be able to go in a straight line; they had to walk around this and avoid that, and then they ended up smack against a wall. There were walls around all his thoughts, and he seemed utterly unaware of them, though he was perpetually hiding behind them.

    —Ursula K. Le Guin, *The Dispossessed: An Ambiguous Utopia* (1974)

He was alone with his thoughts. They were extremely unpleasant thoughts and he would rather have had a chaperon.

    —Douglas Adams, *Life, the Universe, and Everything* (1982)

A stray thought, wandering through the dimensions in search of a mind to harbour it, slid into his brain.

    —Terry Pratchett, *The Colour of Magic* (1983)

The inner mind is always stronger and more resilient than the thinking process we have, desperately, termed the brain.

    —Tanith Lee, "Medra" (1984)

Human brains back then had become such copious and irresponsible generators of suggestions as to what might be done with life, that they made acting for the benefit of future generations seem one of many arbitrary games which might be played by narrow enthusiasts—like poker or polo or the bond market, or the writing of science-fiction novels.

    —Kurt Vonnegut, Jr., *Galapagos* (1985)

His brain began to buzz gently and suck its thumb. Lots of little synapses deep inside his cerebral cortex all joined hands and started dancing around and singing nursery rhymes.

    —Douglas Adams, *Dirk Gently's Holistic Detective Agency* (1987)

It was his subconscious which told him this—that infuriating part of a person's brain which never responds to interrogation, merely gives little meaningful nudges and then sits humming quietly to itself, saying nothing.

    —Douglas Adams, *The Long Dark Tea-Time of the Soul* (1988)

Cogito ergo es. I think, therefore you is.

    —Terry Gilliam and Charles McKeown, *The Adventures of Baron Munchausen* (film, 1988)

Thinking

Ptraci didn't just derail the train of thought, she ripped up the rails, burned the stations and melted the bridges for scrap.

— Terry Pratchett, *Pyramids* (1989)

The trouble with having an open mind, of course, is that people will insist on coming along and trying to put things in it.

— Terry Pratchett, *Diggers* (1990)

Your brain has an immune system, just like your body. The more you use it — the more viruses you get exposed to — the better your immune system becomes.

— Neal Stephenson, *Snow Crash* (1992)

Never trust anything that can think for itself *if you can't see where it keeps its brain.*

— J. K. Rowling, *Harry Potter and the Chamber of Secrets* (1999)

TIME

Some people who talk about the Fourth Dimension do not know they mean it. It is only another way of looking at Time. *There is no difference between Time and any of the three dimensions of Space except that our consciousness moves along it.*

— H. G. Wells, *The Time Machine: An Invention* (1895)

The whole thing started when the clock on the Metropolitan Tower began to run backward.

— Murray Leinster, "The Runaway Skyscraper" (1919)

In the land of Sona-Nyl there is neither time nor space, neither suffering nor death.

— H. P. Lovecraft, "The White Ship" (1919)

Time is what keeps everything from happening at once.

— Ray Cummings, "The Time Professor" (1921)

Most precious of all, you will have Time—that rare and lovely gift that your Western countries have lost the more they have pursued it.
— James Hilton, *Lost Horizon* (1933)

Your ancestor did not believe in a uniform, absolute time. He believed in an infinite series of times, in a growing, dizzying net of divergent, convergent and parallel times. This network of times which approached one another, forked, broke off, or were unaware of one another for centuries, embraces *all* possibilities of time.
— Jorge Luis Borges, "The Garden of Forking Paths" (1941)

Of all the energies in the universe, time is the most potent.
— A. E. van Vogt, "The Seesaw" (1941)

Space and Time aren't real, apart. And they aren't really different. They fade one into the other all around us.
— Jack Williamson, *The Legion of Space,* revised (1947)

Time on Fyon was a tangible element. It seemed to drip down lazily from the dark fronds of the palm trees, to lie in languid pools against the pink and yellow petals of the frangipani.
— Margaret St. Clair, *Agent of the Unknown* (1952)

Days went by, days in which time was as smooth as velvet, as smooth as cream, as smooth as glass.
— Margaret St. Clair, *Agent of the Unknown* (1952)

Time is the funniest thing, sir. It ties a man in knots.
— Clifford D. Simak, *Time and Again,* revised (1952)

The world rushed in a circle and turned on its axis and time was busy burning the years and the people anyway, without any help from him.
— Ray Bradbury, *Fahrenheit 451* (1954)

That was the loathsome thing. The molasses of time: it couldn't be hurried. On it dragged, with weary, elephantine steps. Nothing could urge it faster: it was monstrous and deaf.
— Philip K. Dick, *The World Jones Made* (1956)

It marked the beginning of the giant's surrender to that all-demanding system of time in which the rest of humanity finds itself, and of which, like the million twisted ripples of a fragmented whirlpool, our finite lives are the concluding products.

—J. G. Ballard, "The Drowned Giant" (1965)

And so it goes. And so it goes. And so it goes goes goes goes goes tick tock tick tock tick tock and one day we no longer let time serve us, we serve time and we are slaves of the schedule, worshippers of the sun's passing, bound into a life predicated on restrictions because the system will not function if we don't keep the schedule tight.

—Harlan Ellison, "'Repent, Harlequin!' Said the Ticktockman" (1965)

Why let them order you about? Why let them tell you to hurry and scurry like ants or maggots? Take your time! Saunter a while! Enjoy the sunshine, enjoy the breeze, let life carry you at your own pace! Don't be slaves of time, it's a helluva way to die, slowly, by degrees. Down with the Ticktockman!

—Harlan Ellison, "'Repent, Harlequin!' Said the Ticktockman" (1965)

In grasping the present, he felt for the first time the massive steadiness of time's movement everywhere complicated by shifting currents, waves, surges, and countersurges, like surf against rocky cliffs.

—Frank Herbert, *Dune* (1965)

His vessel found itself between two vortices of gravitation called Bakhrida and Scintilla; Bakhrida speeds up time, Scintilla on the other hand slows it down, and between them lies a zone of stagnation, in which the present, becalmed, flows neither backward nor forward. There Heptodius froze alive, and remains to this day, along with the countless frigates and galleons of other astromariners, pirates, and spaceswashers, not aging in the least, suspended in the silence and excruciating boredom that is Eternity.

—Stanislaw Lem, "How Erg the Self-Inducing Slew a Paleface" (1965), translated by Michael Kandel (1977)

He was independent of the enemy that, more than Death, menaced contemporary man: Time.

—Brian W. Aldiss, "Man in His Time" (1966)

I am a Tralfamadorian, seeing all time as you might see a stretch of the Rocky Mountains. All time is all time. It does not change. It does not lend itself to warnings or explanations. It simply *is*. Take it moment by moment, and you will find that we are all, as I've said before, bugs in amber.
—Kurt Vonnegut, Jr., *Slaughterhouse-Five, or, The Children's Crusade: A Duty-Dance with Death* (1969)

"This," said Timnath Obregon, "is the device I have invented to edit time."
—Edward Bryant, "Jade Blue" (1971)

You have come to the place where all times are one, where all errors can be unmade, where past and future are fluid and subject to redefinition.
—Robert Silverberg, "Breckenridge and the Continuum" (1973)

If the passage of time is a feature of human consciousness, past and future are functions of the mind.
—Ursula K. Le Guin, *The Dispossessed: An Ambiguous Utopia* (1974)

We exist in time. Time is what binds molecules to make your brown eyes, your yellow hair, your thick fingers. Time changes the structures, alters hair or fingers, dims the eyes, immutably mutating reality. Time, itself unchanging, is the cosmic glue, the universal antisolvent that holds our worlds together.
—Marta Randall, "Secret Rider" (1976)

Time is no longer a line along which history, past or future, lies neatly arranged, but a field of great mystery and complexity, in the contemplation of which the mind perceives an immense terror, and an indestructible hope.
—Ursula K. Le Guin, introduction to *Nebula Award Stories Eleven* (1977)

Time is both longer and shorter than you think, and usually all at once.
—Joan D. Vinge, "View from a Height" (1978)

Time and space were themselves players, vast lands engulfing the figures, a weave of future and past. There was no riverrun of years. The abiding loops of causality ran both forward and back. The timescape rippled with waves, roiled and flexed, a great beast in the dark sea.
—Gregory Benford, *Timescape* (1980)

All day again and again. All moanday, tearsday, wailsday in one. A paring from the fingernail of time.
　—Ian Watson, "The Bloomsday Revolution" (1984)

In some certain important sense, *time is not real.*
　—Philip K. Dick, "How to Build a Universe That Doesn't Fall Apart Two
　　Days Later" (1985)

Time has not stood still. It has washed over me, washed me away, as if I'm nothing more than a woman of sand, left by a careless child too near the water.
　—Margaret Atwood, *The Handmaid's Tale* (1986)

Time devours everything. Entire histories vanish. What matters is endurance. The spirit survives and goes onward when the palaces crumble and the kings are forgotten.
　—Robert Silverberg, *Letters from Atlantis* (1990)

"No, the answer is an *orange* and two lemons."
　"*Lemons?*"
　"If I have three lemons and three oranges and I lose two oranges and a lemon, what do I have left?"
　"Huh?"
　"Okay, so you think that time flows *that* way, do you?"
　—Douglas Adams, *Mostly Harmless* (1992)

The past and future clasp each other like knots of the same web: Tear one strand between two, but countless others still hold.
　—Joan Slonczewski, *Daughter of Elysium* (1993)

Time travels us. Uses us as its road, going on never stopping always in one direction. No exits off this freeway.
　—Ursula K. Le Guin, "Ether, OR" (1995)

Her mother's perception of time differed from her own in radical and mysterious ways. Not just in the way that a month, to Chia's mother, was not a very long time, but in the way that her mother's "now" was such a narrow and literal thing. News-governed, Chia believed. Cable-fed. A present honed to whatever very instant of a helicopter traffic report.

—William Gibson, *Idoru* (1996)

Something had gone crack in the world when the playscreen broke. [. . .] Time and history would all be crazed now, like broken windows.

—Nalo Hopkinson, "Under Glass" (2001)

TIME TRAVEL

"Upon that machine," said the Time Traveller, holding the lamp aloft, "I intend to explore time."

—H. G. Wells, *The Time Machine: An Invention* (1895)

I drew a breath, set my teeth, gripped the starting lever with both hands, and went off with a thud. The laboratory got hazy and went dark. Mrs. Watchett came in, and walked, apparently without seeing me, towards the garden door. I suppose it took her a minute or so to traverse the place, but to me she seemed to shoot across the room like a rocket. I pressed the lever over to its extreme position. The night came like the turning out of a lamp, and in another moment came to-morrow. The laboratory grew faint and hazy, then fainter and ever fainter. To-morrow night came black, then day again, night again, day again, faster and faster still. An eddying murmur filled my ears, and a strange, dumb confusedness descended on my mind.

—H. G. Wells, *The Time Machine: An Invention* (1895)

"Think of the opportunities a time machine offers a newspaper. The other papers can tell them what has happened and what is happening, but, by Godfrey, they'll have to read the *Globe* to know what is going to happen."

"I have a slogan for you," I said. "'Read the News Before It Happens.'"

—Clifford D. Simak, "Sunspot Purge" (1940)

"Time travel," Karestly said, "is the best therapy known today."

—Henry Kuttner and C. L. Moore, "The Cure" (1946)

Time Travel

I left her at her dad's time machine playfully thrusting the universe a million years into the future.
—Howard Schoenfeld, "Built Up Logically" (1949)

The Machine howled. Time was a film run backward. Suns fled and ten million moons fled after them.
—Ray Bradbury, "A Sound of Thunder" (1952)

So we say good-by to the colorful, romantic twentieth century with its many tribes, its primitive peoples and its quaint customs.
—Wilson Tucker, "The Tourist Trade" (1953)

"You can't possibly create a paradox in time, don't you see, because anything you do in the past must have been done already or you couldn't have been there to do it in the first place."
"You're quite right. [. . .] What is to be will be, since it already was."
—Roger Dee, "The Poundstone Paradox" (1954)

He jaunted up the geodesic lines of space-time to an Elsewhere and an Elsewhen. He arrived in chaos. He hung in a precarious para-Now for a moment and then tumbled back into chaos.
—Alfred Bester, *The Stars My Destination* (1956)

Never Do Yesterday What Should Be Done Tomorrow.
—Robert A. Heinlein, "'All You Zombies—'" (1959)

He swung dizzily along the line of time, as he had done so often before. He saw himself, here and here, and saw others, shadow-figures, dream-figures, lurking behind the curtains of time.
—Robert Silverberg, "Open the Sky" (1966)

In the thirty-eighth year of his life, a man traveling back from a time when the calendar said he would have been ninety-five died a few weeks after his eighteenth birthday.
—D. G. Compton, *Chronocules* (1970)

The present, as every schoolboy knows, is only the surface of the space-time sea, and a living spacewhale can dive beneath this surface and sojourn in

376

times past, can return, if it so desires, to the primordial moment when the cosmos was born.
—Robert F. Young, "Starscape with Frieze of Dreams" (1970)

Whenever he is, he is not when he was. The time-booth works.
—Andrew J. Offutt, "My Country, Right or Wrong" (1971)

All "nows" are equal; that is the basic theorem of time travel.
—Robert A. Heinlein, *Time Enough for Love* (1973)

It's just a jump to the left
And then a step to the right
With your hands on your hips
You bring your knees in tight
But it's the pelvic thrust
That really drives you insane
Let's do the Time Warp again
—Richard O'Brien, "Time Warp," *The Rocky Horror Show* (play, 1973)

Humanity, not content with having the universe for a playground, delved into past and future, and lost itself amid the ages of the stars.
—Marta Randall, "Secret Rider" (1976)

John Albion was/is/will be living/dying/dead; sucked into the dead/dying void. John Albion had been/is/will be sitting in the warmth of her home and talking of something very small, something very alien, something very much in his bones which has/is/will be killed/killing him. Conjugate the tenses of time travel.
—Marta Randall, "Secret Rider" (1976)

The only workable time machine ever invented is the science-fiction story.
—Robert Silverberg, introduction to *Trips in Time* (1977)

Travelling in time is not like taking the tube, Mr. Bartholomew.
—Connie Willis, "Fire Watch" (1982)

The past is beyond saving. Surely that was the lesson the history department sent me all this way to learn.
—Connie Willis, "Fire Watch" (1982)

I'm 20,000 years from home and there are times when it hurts more than I can stand.
— Robert Silverberg, "House of Bones" (1988)

TRAVEL

I was caught up in the happiness of those who go on journeys, a feeling of hope mixed with a sense of freedom.
— Jules Verne, *Journey to the Centre of the Earth* (1864), translated by
    William Butcher (1992)

"Would you tell me, please, which way I ought to go from here?"
    "That depends a good deal on where you want to get to," said the Cat.
    "I don't much care where—" said Alice.
    "Then it doesn't matter which way you go," said the Cat.
    "—so long as I get *somewhere*," Alice added as an explanation.
    "Oh, you're sure to do that," said the Cat, "if you only walk long enough."
    — Lewis Carroll, *Alice's Adventures in Wonderland* (1865)

The Old Man of the Earth stooped over the floor of the cave, raised a huge stone from it, and left it leaning. It disclosed a great hole that went plumb-down.
    "That is the way," he said.
    "But there are no stairs."
    "You must throw yourself in. There is no other way."
    — George MacDonald, "The Golden Key" (1867)

Here, you see, it takes all the running *you* can do, to keep in the same place. If you want to get somewhere else, you must run at least twice as fast as that!
    — Lewis Carroll, *Through the Looking Glass and What Alice Found There*
    (1872)

Above them Phileas Fogg moved in majestic indifference. He was following his own rational orbit around the world, without bothering at all about the asteroids gravitating around him.
    — Jules Verne, *Around the World in Eighty Days* (1873), translated by
    William Butcher (1995)

Phileas Fogg had won his bet. He had completed the journey round the world in 80 days. To do so, he had used every means of transport: steamship, train, carriage, yacht, cargo vessel, sled, and elephant. In all this the eccentric gentleman had displayed his marvellous qualities of composure and precision. But what was the point? What had he gained from all this commotion? What had he got out of his journey?

Nothing, comes the reply? Nothing, agreed, were it not for a lovely wife, who — however unlikely it may seem — made him the happiest of men!

In truth, wouldn't anyone go round the world for less?

— Jules Verne, *Around the World in Eighty Days* (1873), translated by
   William Butcher (1995)

When a journey begins badly it rarely ends well.

— Jules Verne, *The Floating Island* (1895), translator unknown (1896)

My! People come and go so quickly here!

— Noel Langley, Florence Ryerson, and Edgar Allan Woolf,
   The Wizard of Oz (film, 1939)

On the way he thought about coming home, and coming home he thought about going. Wherever he was he wished he were somewhere else, and when he got there he wondered why he'd bothered.

— Norton Juster, *The Phantom Tollbooth* (1961)

Being lost is never a matter of not knowing where you are; it's a matter of not knowing where you aren't — and I don't care at all about where I'm not.

— Norton Juster, *The Phantom Tollbooth* (1961)

Peculiar travel suggestions are dancing lessons from God.

— Kurt Vonnegut, Jr., *Cat's Cradle* (1963)

It is good to have an end to journey towards; but it is the journey that matters, in the end.

— Ursula K. Le Guin, *The Left Hand of Darkness* (1969)

Travel was supposed to be broadening; why did I feel narrower?

— Margaret Atwood, *Lady Oracle* (1976)

The Bistromathic Drive had revealed to him that time and distance were one, that mind and Universe were one, that perception and reality were one, and that the more one traveled the more one stayed in one place, and that what with one thing and another he would rather just stay put for a while and sort it all out in his mind, which was now at one with the Universe so it shouldn't take too long.

   —Douglas Adams, *Life, the Universe, and Everything* (1982)

No matter where you go, there you are.

   —Earl Mac Rauch, *The Adventures of Buckaroo Banzai across the 8th Dimension* (film, 1984)

Where we're going we don't need roads.

   —Robert Zemeckis and Bob Gale, *Back to the Future* (film, 1985)

So I wished—vainly, I knew—to travel this river forever with such uncertainty in my mind, to be forever with her, riding through the cemeteries of the night, on, on, on, on, until night gave way to eternity, with the presence of hate in the world only as sure as that of love.

   Of all the world's lies, that would be the best.

   —Richard Calder, *Dead Girls* (1992)

Gypsies never belong to the places they travel. They only belong to other gypsies.

   —Ellen Klages, "Time Gypsy" (1998)

TRUTH

All truths are erroneous. This is the very essence of the dialectical process: today's truths become errors tomorrow.

   —Yevgeny Zamiatin, "On Literature, Revolution, Entropy, and Other Matters" (1923), translated by Mirra Ginsburg (1970)

The inevitable mark of truth is—its cruelty.

   —Yevgeny Zamiatin, *We* (1924), translated by Mirra Ginsburg (1972)

Facts do not cease to exist because they are ignored.
— Aldous Huxley, "A Note on Dogma" (1927)

The truth is paradoxical; but man's passion for rational coherence is even stronger than his love of truth.
— Aldous Huxley, "A Note on Dogma" (1927)

Truth is a hard deer to hunt. If you eat too much truth at once, you may die of the truth.
— Stephen Vincent Benet, "By the Waters of Babylon" (1937)

Truth is a dark and deceitful thing.
— Anthony Boucher, "The Compleat Werewolf" (1942)

Facts are ventriloquist's dummies. Sitting on a wise man's knee they may be made to utter words of wisdom; elsewhere, they say nothing, or talk nonsense, or indulge in sheer diabolism.
— Aldous Huxley, *Time Must Have a Stop* (1944)

It is easy for us to forget that science is the godchild of logic when we know that truth is older and simpler than either.
— Roger Dee, "The Springbird" (1953)

People think they love truth. They really love a comforting pack of lies.
— Doris Pitkin Buck, "Two-Bit Oracle" (1954)

Don approved of social lies, the kind that permitted people to live and work together without too much friction.
— Mildred Clingerman, "The Wild Wood" (1957)

People keep going. And they need lies to help them. Lies about abstract justice, and romantic love everlasting. The belief that right always triumphs. Even our concept of democracy may be a lie. Yet we cherish these lies and do our best to live by them. And maybe, little by little, our belief helps make these things come true.
— Robert Bloch, "Word of Honor" (1958)

Truth

Tomorrow, a new prince shall rule. Men of understanding, men of science shall stand behind his throne, and the universe will come to know his might. His name is Truth. His empire shall encompass the Earth. And the mastery of Man over the Earth shall be renewed.
—Walter M. Miller, Jr., *A Canticle for Leibowitz* (1959)

Men must fumble awhile with error to separate it from truth, I think—as long as they don't seize the error hungrily because it has a pleasanter taste.
—Walter M. Miller, Jr., *A Canticle for Leibowitz* (1959)

All of the true things I am about to tell you are shameless lies.
—Kurt Vonnegut, Jr., *Cat's Cradle* (1963)

The steps Man takes across the heavens of his universe are as uncertain as those steps he takes across the rooms of his own life. And yet if he walks with an open mind, those steps must lead him eventually to that most perfect of all destinations, truth.
—William E. Bast, "The Moonstone," episode of *The Outer Limits* (1964)

Respect for the truth comes close to being the basis for all morality.
—Frank Herbert, *Dune* (1965)

On the floor.
Dead.
Struck dead.
Liar. All the lies that were her life.
Dead on a floor.
—Harlan Ellison, "Pretty Maggie Moneyeyes" (1966)

A society adapts to fact, or doesn't survive.
—Robert A. Heinlein, *The Moon Is a Harsh Mistress* (1966)

"Everything is true," he said. "Everything anybody has ever thought."
—Philip K. Dick, *Do Androids Dream of Electric Sheep?* (1968)

I'll make my report as if I told a story, for I was taught as a child on my homeworld that Truth is a matter of the imagination.
—Ursula K. Le Guin, *The Left Hand of Darkness* (1969)

One voice speaking truth is a greater force than fleets and armies, given time; plenty of time.
—Ursula K. Le Guin, *The Left Hand of Darkness* (1969)

All truths find a use somewhere, sometime.
—Larry Niven, "Not Long Before the End" (1969)

Who is true will breed true.
—Doris Pitkin Buck, "The Giberel" (1971)

In the end, the truth usually insists upon serving only the common good.
—Ursula K. Le Guin, *The Dispossessed: An Ambiguous Utopia* (1974)

She was used to hearing what sounded well, and figuring out later what it might really mean. Indeed, until she had met Lev at school, it had not occurred to her that anyone might prefer to speak a plain fact rather than a lie that sounded well.
—Ursula K. Le Guin, "The Eye of the Heron" (1978)

The truth will set us free.
But freedom is cold, and empty, and frightening, and lies can often be warm and beautiful.
—George R. R. Martin, "The Way of Cross and Dragon" (1979)

Although people talk appreciatively of honest speech they generally avoid it, and I myself have found scarcely any use for it at all.
—Suzy McKee Charnas, "The Unicorn Tapestry" (1980)

The final truth of all things is that there is no final truth! Truth is what's transitory! It's human life that is real!
—Paddy Chayefsky, *Altered States* (film, 1980)

I would like to say that it is a very great pleasure, honor and privilege for me to open this bridge, but I can't because my lying circuits are all out of commission. I hate and despise you all. I now declare this hapless cyberstructure open to the unthinking abuse of all who wantonly cross her.
—Douglas Adams, *Life, the Universe, and Everything* (1982)

A lie, for Weasel, was a mirror. It reflected truth turned the other way round.
  —Lloyd Alexander, *The Beggar Queen* (1984)

Men like Alain lied so constantly, so passionately, that some basic distinction had been lost. They were artists in their own right, Andrea said, intent on restructuring reality.
  —William Gibson, *Count Zero* (1986)

He had died of an overdose of truth.
  —George Turner, *Drowning Towers* (1987)

The road to truth is long, and lined the entire way with annoying bastards.
  —Alexander Jablokov, "The Place of No Shadows" (1990)

An untruth tends to become indistinguishable from the real thing, simply through the action of protective mimicry.
  —Tom Holt, *Ye Gods!* (1992)

I'm not gonna give up. I can't give up. Not as long as the truth is out there.
  —Chris Carter, "The Erlenmeyer Flask," episode of *The X-Files* (1994)

The truth may be out there, but lies are inside your head.
  —Terry Pratchett, *Hogfather* (1996)

You're becoming more human all the time, Data . . . now you're learning how to lie.
  —Brannon Braga and Ronald D. Moore, *Star Trek: First Contact*
  (film, 1996)

"The truth," Dumbledore sighed. "It is a beautiful and terrible thing, and should therefore be treated with great caution."
  —J. K. Rowling, *Harry Potter and the Sorcerer's Stone* (1997)

We must scrape the flies from the headlamps of truth, then switch the fuckers to high beam.
  —Steve Aylett, *Atom* (2000)

The Truth Shall Make Ye Fret.
  —Terry Pratchett, *The Truth* (2000)

The Great Architect of the universe built it of good firm stuff.
   —Jules Verne, *Journey to the Centre of the Earth* (1864), translated by
      William Butcher (1992)

In such a universe as this what significance could there be in our fortuitous,
our frail, our evanescent community?
   —Olaf Stapledon, *Star Maker* (1937)

The universe, or the maker of the universe, must be indifferent to the fate of
worlds. That there should be endless struggle and suffering and waste must of
course be accepted; and gladly, for these were the very soil in which the spirit
grew. But that all struggle should be finally, absolutely vain, that a whole
world of sensitive spirits should fail and die, must be sheer evil. In my horror
it seemed to me that Hate must be the Star Maker.
   —Olaf Stapledon, *Star Maker* (1937)

In that instant when I had seen the blazing star that was the Star Maker, I had
glimpsed, in the very eye of that splendour, strange vistas of being; as though
in the depths of the hypercosmical past and the hypercosmical future also,
yet coexistent in eternity, lay cosmos beyond cosmos.
   —Olaf Stapledon, *Star Maker* (1937)

To Waldo the universe was the enemy, which he strove to force to submit to
his will.
   —Robert A. Heinlein, "Waldo" (1942)

He looked at the woman's handsome, impassive face for a clue; at the eyes
that were black but not brilliant, the hawklike nose, the finely cut mouth. But
there was no clue in them. They held only one comment on the universe, on
all that was in it. They said, *I am tired of you.* Nothing more.
   —Doris Pitkin Buck, "Aunt Agatha" (1952)

In the endless universe there is nothing new, nothing different. What may appear exceptional to the minute mind of man may be inevitable to the infinite Eye of God. This strange second in a life, that unusual event, those remarkable coincidences of environment, opportunity, and encounter . . . all may be reproduced over and over on the planet of a sun whose galaxy revolves once in two hundred million years and has revolved nine times already.

There are and have been worlds and cultures without end, each nursing the proud illusion that it is unique in space and time. There have been men without number suffering from the same megalomania; men who imagined themselves unique, irreplaceable, irreproducible. There will be more . . . more plus infinity.

—Alfred Bester, *The Demolished Man* (1953)

Will none wipe the sneer off the face of the cosmos?

—Poul Anderson, *The Broken Sword* (1954)

He had seen too much of the cosmos to have any great faith in man's ability to understand it.

—Poul Anderson, "Ghetto" (1954)

Alvin would never grow up; to him the whole Universe was a plaything, a puzzle to be unraveled for his own amusement.

—Arthur C. Clarke, *The City and the Stars* (1956)

There was a God, and He wasn't mean. His universe was a deadly contraption, but maybe there wasn't any way to build a universe that wasn't a deadly contraption—like a square circle. He made the contraption, and He put Man in it, and Man was a fairly deadly contraption himself. But the funny part of it was, there wasn't a damn thing the universe could do to a man that a man wasn't built to endure. He could even endure it when it killed him. And gradually he could get the better of it.

—Walter M. Miller, Jr., "The Lineman" (1957)

In the long run, when we get right down to the fundamental stuff of the universe, we'll find that there's nothing there at all—just no-things moving no-place through no-time.

—James Blish, *A Case of Conscience* (1958)

He had the dim realization that the universe, like a huge sleepy animal, knew what he was trying to do and was trying to thwart him. This feeling of opposition made him determined to outmaneuver the universe—not the first guy to yield to such a temptation, of course.

　—Fritz Leiber, "Try and Change the Past" (1958)

"The universe," Omar Diamond pointed out, "possesses an infinitude of ways by which it fulfills itself."

　—Philip K. Dick, *Clans of the Alphane Moon* (1964)

If you think upon it, O King, you will see how very ludicrous is the Universe . . .

　—Stanislaw Lem, "King Globares and the Sages" (1965), translated by
　　Michael Kandel (1977)

By squandering nuclear energy, polluting asteroids and planets, ravaging the Preserve, and leaving litter everywhere we go, we shall ruin outer space and turn it into one big dump. It is high time we came to our senses and enforced the laws. Convinced that every minute of delay is dangerous, I sound the alarm: Let us save the Universe.

　—Stanislaw Lem, "Let Us Save the Universe (An Open Letter from
　　Ijon Tichy, Space Traveller)" (1966), translated by Joel Stern and
　　Maria Swiecicka-Ziemianek (1981)

You cannot program the universe you sons of bitches, there are things going on outside of all of this which you cannot envision let alone understand and there must be an end to this banality: do you understand that? It has got to end sometime. The universe is vast, man is small, you fucking sons of bitches.

　—Barry N. Malzberg, "Still Life" (1972)

No storyteller has ever been able to dream up anything as fantastically unlikely as what really does happen in this mad Universe.

　—Robert A. Heinlein, *Time Enough for Love* (1973)

If, instead of the Mother's cloak, there was unimaginable vastness speckled with tiny lonely suns, then nothing circled the earth, the Universe was cold and empty, the Mother did not live, and they were all alone.

　—Mildred Downey Broxon, "The Night Is Cold, the Stars Are Far Away"
　　(1974)

You begin to suspect that if there's any *real* truth it's that the entire multi-dimensional infinity of the Universe is almost certainly being run by a bunch of maniacs.

— Douglas Adams, "Fit the Fourth," episode of *The Hitch-Hiker's Guide to the Galaxy* (radio series 1978)

It is our station to live within laws that give us being, but offer of themselves no purpose or promise, no triumph as a species. The universe allows us a place in its systematic workings but only cares for the system itself, not us.

— Gregory Benford, "Starswarmer" (1978)

It was as if the universe itself stretched out its finger to touch me. And in touching me, singling me out, it only heightened my awareness of my own insignificance.

That was somehow very comforting. When you confront the absolute indifference of magnitudes and vistas so overwhelming, the swollen ego of your own self-important suffering is diminished . . .

— Joan D. Vinge, "View from a Height" (1978)

There is a universe out there, a universe of life, objects, and events. There are differences, but it is all the same universe, and we all must obey the same universal laws.

— Barry B. Longyear, "Enemy Mine" (1979)

We see the universe as it *is,* Father Damien, and these naked truths are cruel ones. We who believe in life, and treasure it, will die. Afterward there will be nothing, eternal emptiness, blackness, nonexistence. In our living there has been no purpose, no poetry, no meaning. Nor do our deaths possess these qualities. When we are gone, the universe will not long remember us, and shortly it will be as if we had never lived at all. Our worlds and our universe will not long outlive us. Ultimately entropy will consume all, and our puny efforts cannot stay that awful end.

— George R. R. Martin, "The Way of Cross and Dragon" (1979)

Clearly the problem on this planet had to do with some fundamental misunderstanding of the workings of the universe.

— S. P. Somtow, "The Thirteenth Utopia" (1979)

An infinity of universes swim in superspace, all passing through their own cycles of birth and death; some are novel, others repetitious; some produce macrolife, others do not; still others are lifeless. In time, macrolife will attempt to reach out from its cycles to other space-time bubbles, perhaps even to past cycles, which leave their echoes in superspace, and might be reached. In all these ambitions, only the ultimate pattern of development is unknown, drawing macrolife toward some future transformation still beyond its view. There are times when the oldest macrolife senses that vaster intelligences are peering in at it from some great beyond . . .
—George Zebrowski, *Macrolife* (1979)

The whole fabric of the space-time continuum is not merely curved, it is in fact totally bent.
—Douglas Adams, *The Restaurant at the End of the Universe* (1980)

The sky of New Niger is the sky of Old Earth; our souls are pieces of one great eggshell enclosing the universe!
—Suzy McKee Charnas, "Scorched Supper on New Niger" (1980)

This Universe never did make sense; I suspect that it was built on government contract.
—Robert A. Heinlein, *The Number of the Beast* (1980)

She wove the tapestry and was the tapestry. The pictures filled her with happiness. The universe was her lover.
—Tanith Lee, "Medra" (1984)

He shook his head sharply in the hope that it might dislodge some salient fact which would fall into place and make sense of an otherwise utterly bewildering Universe.
—Douglas Adams, *So Long, and Thanks for All the Fish* (1985)

The vision of a populated Galaxy, of a universe spilling over with life and intelligence, made her want to cry for joy.
—Carl Sagan, *Contact* (1985)

The Captain looked up at the stars, and his big brain told him that his planet was an insignificant speck of dust in the cosmos, and that he was a germ on that speck, and that nothing could matter less than what became of him. That was what those big brains used to do with their excess capacity: blather on like that.

—Kurt Vonnegut, Jr., *Galapagos* (1985)

The universe doesn't know good or bad, only less or more.

—Pat Cadigan, "Angel" (1987)

All the universe is just a dream in God's mind, and as long as he's asleep, he believes in it, and things stay real.

—Orson Scott Card, *Seventh Son* (1987)

At least I know I'm bewildered about the really fundamental and important facts of the universe.

—Terry Pratchett, *Equal Rites* (1987)

Angel, like everyone else, comes from somewhere and goes somewhere else. She lives in that linear and binary universe. However, like everyone else, she lives concurrently in another universe less simple. Trivalent, quadrivalent, multivalent. World without end, with no amen. And so, on.

—Candas Jane Dorsey, "(Learning about) Machine Sex" (1988)

There was a thoughtful pause in the conversation as the assembled Brethren mentally divided the universe into the deserving and the undeserving, and put themselves on the appropriate side.

—Terry Pratchett, *Guards! Guards!* (1989)

We humans have always seen in the universe a mirror of our selves.

—Joan Slonczewski, *The Wall around Eden* (1989)

I pity you. We live in a universe of magic, which evidently you cannot see.

—Philip Lazebnik, "Devil's Due," episode of *Star Trek: The Next Generation* (1991)

We live in strange times.

We also live in strange places: each in a universe of our own. The people with whom we populate our universes are the shadows of whole other universes intersecting with our own.

—Douglas Adams, *Mostly Harmless* (1992)

The galaxy doesn't spin on your whims.
  —Tara K. Harper, *Lightwing* (1992)

We are not lords of the universe. We're one small part of it. We may be its consciousness, but being the consciousness of the universe does not mean turning it all into a mirror image of us. It means rather fitting into it as it is, and worshiping it with our attention.
  —Kim Stanley Robinson, *Red Mars* (1992)

Perhaps the universe, too, has some heart, some mind somewhere, which can feel pride. Which can know its offspring thrive, and feel joy.
  —David Brin, "What Continues, What Fails" (1993)

The universe is none of our business.
  —Joan Slonczewski, *Daughter of Elysium* (1993)

The universe is driven by the complex interaction between three ingredients: matter, energy, and enlightened self-interest.
  —Marc Scott Zicree, "Survivors," episode of *Babylon 5* (1994)

I would like to have more trust in dying. Maybe it's worth while, like some kind of answering, coming into another place. Like I felt that winter in the Siskiyous, walking on the snow road between black firs under all the stars, that I was the same size as the universe, the same thing as the universe. And if I kept on walking ahead there was this glory waiting for me.
  —Ursula K. Le Guin, "Ether, OR" (1995)

Ponder Stibbons was one of those unfortunate people cursed with the belief that if only he found out enough things about the universe it would all, somehow, make sense. The goal is the Theory of Everything, but Ponder would settle for the Theory of Something and, late at night, when Hex appeared to be sulking, he despaired of even a Theory of Anything.
  —Terry Pratchett, *The Last Continent* (1998)

THE UNKNOWN

How do you attack the unknown, or defend yourself from it?
  —Jules Verne, *Twenty Thousand Leagues under the Sea* (1870), translated
    by Walter James Miller and Frederick Paul Walter (1993)

All unknowns are organically inimical to man, and *homo sapiens* is human in
the full sense of the word only when his grammar is entirely free of question
marks.
  —Yevgeny Zamiatin, *We* (1924), translated by Mirra Ginsburg (1972)

Sitting there on the heather, on our planetary grain, I shrank from the abysses
that opened up on every side, and in the future. The silent darkness, the
featureless unknown, were more dread than all the terrors that imagination
had mustered.
  —Olaf Stapledon, *Star Maker* (1937)

As for the Half World—How can I describe a place that has no single matching criterion with what I have known? How can I speak of things for which
no words have been invented? [. . .] All I can hope to do is tell how matters
affected my human senses, how events influenced my human emotions,
knowing that there are two falsehoods involved—the falsehood I saw and felt,
and the falsehood that I tell.
  —Robert A. Heinlein, "Magic, Inc." (1940)

The unknown is a terrible place. There are monsters out there.
  —Philip K. Dick, *Solar Lottery* (1955)

The exploration of the unknown is always a fraud.
  —James Gunn, *Station in Space* (1958)

There are people who run at the sight of the unknown, others who advance
to meet it.
  —Fredric Brown, "Puppet Show" (1962)

The unknown is always worse than the known.
  —Eando Binder, *Menace of the Saucers* (1969)

"The unknown," said Faxe's soft voice in the forest, "the unforetold, the unproven, that is what life is based on. Ignorance is the ground of thought. Unproof is the ground of action. [. . .] The only thing that makes life possible is permanent, intolerable uncertainty: not knowing what comes next."
— Ursula K. Le Guin, *The Left Hand of Darkness* (1969)

He knew the *unknown.* It was beyond all comprehension and Guy thought that it was no more than a set of words: a black, empty World preceding the appearance of the World Light; a dead, icy World when the World Light was extinguished; an endless Wasteland with many World Lights. No one could explain what this meant.
— Arkady Strugatsky and Boris Strugatsky, *Prisoners of Power* (1969),
    translated by Helen Saltz Jacobson (1977)

To rabbits, everything unknown is dangerous.
— Richard Adams, *Watership Down* (1972)

The Sioux had outlived their way of life, had turned it over to the white technicians, who would map everything. That was what he most disliked about them: that they sought to know all things, and did not realize that a forest without dark places has value only to the woodcutter.
— Jack McDevitt, *Ancient Shores* (1996)

UTOPIA

Let me compare humanity in the olden time to a rosebush planted in a swamp, watered with black bog-water, breathing miasmatic fogs by day, and chilled with poison dews at night. Innumerable generations of gardeners had done their best to make it bloom, but beyond an occasional half-opened bud with a worm at the heart, their efforts had been unsuccessful. [. . .] Finally, during a period of general despondency as to the prospects of the bush where it was, the idea of transplanting it was again mooted, and this time found favor. "Let us try it," was the general voice. "Perhaps it may thrive better elsewhere, and here it is certainly doubtful if it be worth cultivating longer." So it came about that the rosebush of humanity was transplanted, and set in sweet, warm, dry earth, where the sun bathed it, the stars wooed it, and the south wind caressed it. Then it appeared that it was indeed a rosebush. The

vermin and the mildew disappeared, and the bush was covered with the most beautiful red roses, whose fragrance filled the world.
— Edward Bellamy, *Looking Backward, 2000–1887* (1888)

The Utopia of a modern dreamer must needs differ in one fundamental aspect from the Nowheres and Utopias men planned before Darwin quickened the thought of the world. Those were all perfect and static States, a balance of happiness won for ever against the forces of unrest and disorder that inhere in things. [. . .] But the Modern Utopia must be not static but kinetic, must shape not as a permanent state but as a hopeful stage, leading to a long ascent of stages. Nowadays we do not resist and overcome the great stream of things, but rather float upon it. We build now not citadels, but ships of state.
— H. G. Wells, *A Modern Utopia* (1905)

Here was evidently a people highly skilled, efficient, caring for their country as a florist cares for his costliest orchids.
— Charlotte Perkins Gilman, *Herland* (1915)

Theirs was a civilization in which the initial difficulties had long since been overcome. The untroubled peace, the unmeasured plenty, the steady health, the large good will and smooth management which ordered everything, left nothing to overcome. It was like a pleasant family in an old established, perfectly-run country place.
— Charlotte Perkins Gilman, *Herland* (1915)

The entire history of mankind, insofar as we know it, is the history of transition from nomadic to increasingly settled forms of existence. And does it not follow that the most settled form (ours) is at the same time the most perfect (ours)?
— Yevgeny Zamiatin, *We* (1924), translated by Mirra Ginsburg (1972)

Our prevalent belief is in moderation. We inculcate the virtue of avoiding excess of all kinds — even including, if you will pardon the paradox, excess of virtue itself. In the valley which you have seen, and in which there are several thousand inhabitants living under the control of our order, we have found that the principle makes for a considerable degree of happiness. We rule with moderate strictness, and in return we are satisfied with moderate obedience.

And I think I can claim that our people are moderately sober, moderately chaste, and moderately honest.
 —James Hilton, *Lost Horizon* (1933)

He often felt the invasion of a deep spiritual emotion, as if Shangri-La were indeed a living essence, distilled from the magic of the ages and miraculously preserved against time and death.
 —James Hilton, *Lost Horizon* (1933)

A place where there isn't any trouble. Do you suppose there is such a place, Toto? There must be. It's not a place you can get to by a boat or a train. It's far, far away. Behind the moon, beyond the rain.
 —Noel Langley, Florence Ryerson, and Edgar Allan Woolf,
  The Wizard of Oz (film, 1939)

I stood long at the window in a dream. There was such quiet and peace! It was hard to believe that I was in an actual city, for in the sunlight and stillness what I saw was like a painted model.
 —Austin Tappan Wright, *Islandia* (1942)

The closer men came to perfecting for themselves a paradise, the more impatient they seemed to become with it, and with themselves as well. They made a garden of pleasure, and became progressively more miserable with it as it grew in richness and power and beauty.
 —Walter M. Miller, Jr., *A Canticle for Leibowitz* (1959)

Over and over it's been the same sad story: a plan for perfect sharing and perfect love, glorious hopes and high ideals—then persecution and failure.
 —Robert A. Heinlein, *Stranger in a Strange Land* (1961)

It was almost beyond his imagination to conceive of a place in the universe with clean, cheerful cities, billions of good, intelligent people, and mutual trust everywhere.
 —Arkady Strugatsky and Boris Strugatsky, *Prisoners of Power* (1969),
  translated by Helen Saltz Jacobson (1977)

There are no easy Utopias.
 —Gerald Jonas, "The Shaker Revival" (1970)

Utopia

Paradise is for those who make Paradise.
    —Ursula K. Le Guin, *The Dispossessed: An Ambiguous Utopia* (1974)

Every utopia has its flaw.
    —S. P. Somtow, "The Thirteenth Utopia" (1979)

V

It would be killing for the sake of killing. I know very well that's a privilege
reserved for humanity, but I don't allow such murderous pastimes.
   —Jules Verne, *Twenty Thousand Leagues under the Sea* (1870), translated
      by Walter James Miller and Frederick Paul Walter (1993)

Only what is killed can be resurrected.
   —Yevgeny Zamiatin, *We* (1924), translated by Mirra Ginsburg (1972)

No newsman in his right mind objects to a little violence, for that's what news
is made of.
   —Clifford D. Simak, "Sunspot Purge" (1940)

"Violence," came the retort, "is the last refuge of the incompetent."
   —Isaac Asimov, "Foundation" (1942)

Humans were almost as fond of exterminating other life as they were of
killing off their own kind.
   —Lester del Rey, "Over the Top" (1949)

The practical men [. . .] recognized the validity of competition, love of battle,
strength in the face of overwhelming odds. These, they felt, were admirable
traits for a race, and insurance toward its perpetuity. Without them, the race
would be bound to retrogress.
   The tendency toward violence, they found, was inextricably linked with
ingenuity, flexibility, drive.
   —Robert Sheckley, "The Seventh Victim" (1953)

Strange, he thought, how each killing was a new excitement. It was something you just didn't tire of, the way you did of French pastry or women or
drinking or anything else. It was always new and different.
   —Robert Sheckley, "The Seventh Victim" (1953)

Anyone who clings to the historically untrue — and thoroughly immoral — doctrine that "violence never settles anything" I would advise to conjure up the ghosts of Napoleon Bonaparte and of the Duke of Wellington and let them debate it. The ghost of Hitler could referee, and the jury might well be the Dodo, the Great Auk, and the Passenger Pigeon. Violence, naked force, has settled more issues in history than has any other factor, and the contrary opinion is wishful thinking at its worst. Breeds that forget this basic truth have always paid for it with their lives and freedoms.
  —Robert A. Heinlein, *Starship Troopers* (1959)

We also have knowledge of ourselves . . . of the ancient, destructive urges in us, that grow more deadly as our populations approach in size and complexity those of ancient Mars. Every war crisis, witch-hunt, race-riot, and purge . . . is a reminder and a warning. We are the Martians. If we cannot control the inheritance within us . . . this will be their second dead planet!
  —Nigel Kneale, *Quatermass and the Pit* (TV miniseries, 1959)

He was a very dispirited Poet. He had never expected the world to act in a courteous, seemly, or even sensible manner, and the world had seldom done so; often he had taken heart in the consistency of its rudeness and stupidity. But never before had the world shot the Poet in the abdomen with a musket.
  —Walter M. Miller, Jr., *A Canticle for Leibowitz* (1959)

When mass murder's been answered with mass murder, rape with rape, hate with hate, there's no longer much meaning in asking whose ax is the bloodier.
  —Walter M. Miller, Jr., *A Canticle for Leibowitz* (1959)

A person who commits a violence against another is obviously in need of medical care.
  —Mack Reynolds, "Gun for Hire" (1960)

There is another kind of violence that is much more deadly, much more defeating. It is the violence of indifference, the violence of being a caste apart from the rest of the world, the violence of being ignored, the violence of sitting alone, living on a pension, searching through the tattered, yellowed pages of old books for the lingering warmth of human understanding the writer may have been able to impart to his words.
  —Dean Koontz, "A Mouse in the Walls of the Global Village" (1972)

Even the vagal flushes that seized at my chest seemed extensions of that real world of violence calmed and tamed within our television programmes and the pages of news magazines.

   —J. G. Ballard, *Crash* (1973)

Our fear of violence may have been as destructive as the violence itself.

   —Hilary Bailey, "The Ramparts" (1974)

They had learned that the act of violence is the act of weakness, and that the spirit's strength lies in holding fast to the truth.

   —Ursula K. Le Guin, "The Eye of the Heron" (1978)

Violence gains nothing, killing wins nothing—only sometimes nothing is what people want. Death is what they want. And they get it.

   —Ursula K. Le Guin, "The Eye of the Heron" (1978)

The slaughter he had just witnessed struck him as abysmally repetitive of a great deal of recent history, and he did not wish to belong to that history anymore.

   —Michael Bishop, "The Quickening" (1981)

Plenty of people didn't care for him much, but there is a huge difference between disliking somebody—maybe even disliking them a lot—and actually shooting them, strangling them, dragging them through the fields and setting their house on fire. It was a difference which kept the vast majority of the population alive from day to day.

   —Douglas Adams, *Dirk Gently's Holistic Detective Agency* (1987)

This is what I've seen in the four weeks since infection: people killing people—which is much what I saw in the four weeks before infection and the four weeks before that and before that—as far back as I care to remember, people killing people—which to my mind puts us in a state of normality right now.

   —Alex Garland, *28 Days Later* (film, 2002)

WAR AND PEACE

They were only planning to send a projectile to the moon, a rather brutal way of opening negotiations, even with a satellite, but one much in favor among civilized nations.
  —Jules Verne, *From the Earth to the Moon* (1865), translated by
    Walter James Miller (1978)

They did unto others what they would not have others do unto them, an immoral principle that is the basic premise of the art of war.
  —Jules Verne, *From the Earth to the Moon* (1865), translated by
    Walter James Miller (1978)

The third peculiarity of aerial warfare was that it was at once enormously destructive and entirely indecisive.
  —H. G. Wells, *The War in the Air, and Particularly How Mr. Bert Smallways
    Fared While It Lasted* (1908)

Of course a war is entertaining. The immediate fear and suffering of the humans is a legitimate and pleasing refreshment for our myriads of toiling workers.
  —C. S. Lewis, *The Screwtape Letters* (1942)

"Nations which are at peace can live together," said Surgeon General Mors earnestly. "Nations which are at war only die together."
  —Murray Leinster, "Symbiosis" (1947)

All wars are founded in economic conflict, or to put it another way, a trial by arms is merely the last battle of an economic war.
  —Alfred Bester, "The Devil's Invention" (1950)

We thought space was empty and that we were automatically the lords of creation. [. . .] Well, if Man wants to be top dog—or even a respected neighbor—he'll have to fight for it. Beat the plowshares back into swords; the other was a maiden aunt's fancy.

— Robert A. Heinlein, *The Puppet Masters* (1951)

We had our atomic wars—thousands of years ago. After that we fought with bows and arrows. Then, slowly, we learned that fighting is no solution—that aggression leads to chaos.

— Edmund H. North, *The Day the Earth Stood Still* (film script, 1951)

Men would be just as calm after their cities had been reduced to rubble. The human capacity for calmness was almost unlimited, *ex post facto,* because the routine of daily living had to go on, despite the big business of governments whose leaders invoked the Deity in the cause of slaughter.

— Walter M. Miller, Jr., "Way of a Rebel" (1954)

"Love and war," he said, "are Earth's two staple commodities. We've been turning them both out in bumper crops since the beginning of time."

— Robert Sheckley, "Love, Incorporated" (1956)

Dear Conrad, war is your specialty. Historians love you for it. I love you for it. After all, not only is it fun, it's creative! Your best scientific discoveries are made in wartime: the atom bomb, radar, luncheon meat. And think of all that travel! Getting away from home, making new acquaintances, indulging in amatory dalliance with strangers. So broadening. And then: the delirium of battle, the rush of adrenalin to the head as the trumpets sound ATTACK! Conrad, war is the principal art form of your race.

— Gore Vidal, *Visit to a Small Planet,* revised (play, 1957)

"Peace" is a condition in which no civilian pays any attention to military casualties which do not achieve page-one, lead-story prominence—unless that civilian is a close relative of one of the casualties. But, if there ever was a time in history when "peace" meant that there was no fighting going on, I have been unable to find out about it.

— Robert A. Heinlein, *Starship Troopers* (1959)

For centuries we have dreamt of flying; recently we made that come true: we have always hankered for speed; now we have speeds greater than we can stand: we wanted to speak to far parts of the Earth; we can: we wanted to explore the sea bottom; we have: and so on, and so on. And, too, we wanted the power to smash our enemies utterly; we have it. If we had truly wanted peace, we should have had that as well. But true peace has never been one of the genuine dreams—we have got little further than preaching against war in order to appease our consciences.

    —John Wyndham, *The Outward Urge* (1959)

Gentlemen, you can't fight in here! This is the War Room.

    —Stanley Kubrick, Terry Southern, and Peter George, *Dr. Strangelove,*
      or, How I Learned to Stop Worrying and Love the Bomb (film, 1964)

KIRK: There it is. War. We didn't want it. But we've got it.
SPOCK: Curious how often you humans manage to obtain that which you do
    not want.

    —Gene L. Coon, "Errand of Mercy," episode of *Star Trek* (1967)

You seem to be claiming that war could be cured, like a disease, with a dose of the proper medicine.

    —John Brunner, *Stand on Zanzibar* (1968)

Primitiveness and civilization are degrees of the same thing. If civilization has an opposite, it is war.

    —Ursula K. Le Guin, *The Left Hand of Darkness* (1969)

"Translator, explain this word 'peace.'"

    Translator: "This is incredible, but the closest approximation we can get from our instruments is that the members of this species were so accustomed to slaughtering each other that they had to employ a special word to designate the intervals when the slaughter had ceased."

    —Bob Shaw, "That Moon Plaque: Comments by Science Fiction Writers"
      (1969)

When a country's economy was in rotten shape, the easiest dodge was to start a war as a pretext for gagging everyone immediately.

    —Arkady Strugatsky and Boris Strugatsky, *Prisoners of Power* (1969),
      translated by Helen Saltz Jacobson (1977)

These great planet-wide and interplanet-wide wars break out, and everyone is supposed to be thinking of the ideologies involved . . . whereas in actuality most people simply want a good, safe night's sleep.
—Philip K. Dick, *Our Friends from Frolix 8* (1970)

War brutalizes everyone involved until there is no more innocence on either side.
—Harry Harrison, "American Dead" (1971)

He had grown up in a country run by politicians who sent the pilots to man the bombers to kill the babies to make the world safe for children to grow up in.
—Ursula K. Le Guin, *The Lathe of Heaven* (1971)

Some fight war while the rest fight wars. We can use that division of labor.
—Bernard Wolfe, "Biscuit Position" (1972)

(He wants to bring us some kind of peace. What peace, Martin?)
The peace of being, of unthinking. The peace that comes from a universe ordered in a manner that men could never order it.
—Thomas N. Scortia, "The Armageddon Tapes—Tape 1" (1974)

War had become the American way of life.
—Sydney J. Van Scyoc, "Nightfire" (1978)

Peace is often only war without fighting.
—Barry B. Longyear, "Enemy Mine" (1979)

They sang a number of tuneful and reflective songs on the subjects of peace, justice, morality, culture, sport, family life and the obliteration of all other life forms.
—Douglas Adams, *Life, the Universe, and Everything* (1982)

In all wars, the first stage was to dehumanize the enemy, reduce the enemy to a lower level so that he might be killed without compunction. When the enemy was not human to begin with, the task was easier. As wars progressed, this tactic frequently led to an underestimation of the enemy, with disastrous consequences.
—Greg Bear, "Hardfought" (1983)

As long as they did not use nuclear weapons, it appeared, nobody was going to give the right name to all the killing that had been going on since the end of the Second World War, which was surely "World War Three."
　　—Kurt Vonnegut, Jr., *Galapagos* (1985)

"Women shouldn't be in combat," said Vorkosigan, grimly glum.
　　"Neither should men, in my opinion."
　　—Lois McMaster Bujold, *Shards of Honor* (1986)

War makes it very difficult to think straight.
　　—Terry Pratchett, *Pyramids* (1989)

War is not its own end, except in some catastrophic slide into absolute damnation. It's peace that's wanted. Some better peace than the one you started with.
　　—Lois McMaster Bujold, *The Vor Game* (1990)

"The key to strategy, little Vor," she explained kindly, "is not to choose *a* path to victory, but to choose so that *all* paths lead to a victory."
　　—Lois McMaster Bujold, *The Vor Game* (1990)

The consensus seemed to be that if really large numbers of men were sent to storm the mountain, then enough might survive the rocks to take the citadel. This is essentially the basis of all military thinking.
　　—Terry Pratchett, *Eric* (1990)

The place where a war starts is long before the first missile, or the first bullet, or the first spear.
　　—Nancy Kress, "And Wild for to Hold" (1991)

That was war; killing people by every means possible.
　　—Kim Stanley Robinson, *Red Mars* (1992)

The galaxy was littered with ancient worlds torn apart by warfare.
　　—Robert Reed, "Sister Alice" (1993)

War is not a game but the most repugnant atrocity committed by sapient beings, and when indulged in it must be ended in the shortest conceivable span of time.
— Gay Marshall, "The Heart of the Hydra" (1995)

Why does any advanced civilization seek to destroy less advanced ones? Because the land is strategically valuable, because there are resources that can be cultivated and exploited, but most of all, simply because they can.
— J. Michael Straczynski, "And Now for a Word," episode of *Babylon 5* (1995)

Somewhere east of here, there had been rocket attacks and rumors of chemical agents, the latest act in one of those obscure and ongoing struggles that made up the background of his world.
— William Gibson, *Idoru* (1996)

Murder's the taking of one man's life by another — war's the other way around.
— Steve Aylett, *Slaughtermatic* (1998)

He was trying to find some help in the ancient military journals of General Tacticus, whose intelligent campaigning had been so successful that he'd lent his very name to the detailed prosecution of martial endeavour, and had actually found a section headed What to Do If One Army Occupies a Well-fortified and Superior Ground and the Other Does Not, but since the first sentence read "Endeavour to be the one inside" he'd rather lost heart.
— Terry Pratchett, *Carpe Jugulum* (1998)

WEALTH AND POSSESSIONS

One who cannot cast away a treasure at need is in fetters.
— J. R. R. Tolkien, *The Two Towers* (1955)

The creation of wealth is certainly not to be despised, but in the long run the only human activities really worth-while are the search for knowledge and the creation of beauty.
— Arthur C. Clarke, "Rocket to the Renaissance" (1960)

Wealth and Possessions

Politics and economics are concerned with power and wealth, neither of which should be the primary, still less the exclusive, concern of grown-up men.

— Arthur C. Clarke, introduction to *Profiles of the Future: An Inquiry into the Limits of the Possible* (1962)

The real wealth of a planet is in its landscape, how we take part in that basic source of civilization — agriculture.

— Frank Herbert, *Dune* (1965)

Maggie, Maggie, Maggie, pretty Maggie Moneyeyes, who came from Tucson and trailers and rheumatic fever and a surge to live that was all kaleidoscope frenzy of clawing scrabbling no-nonsense. If it took laying on one's back and making sounds like a panther in the desert, then one did it, because *nothing,* but *nothing,* was as bad as being dirt-poor, itchy-skinned, soiled-underwear, scuff-toed, hairy and ashamed lousy with the no-gots. Nothing!

— Harlan Ellison, "Pretty Maggie Moneyeyes" (1966)

"Everyone takes what is necessary, Captain," she had said. *"By definition they have to. It's what is taken that could be left behind that reveals the heart."*

— Gene Wolfe, "Alien Stones" (1972)

Our men and women are free — possessing nothing, they are free. And you the possessors are possessed. You are all in jail. Each alone, solitary, with a heap of what he owns. You live in prison, die in prison. It is all I can see in your eyes — the wall, the wall!

— Ursula K. Le Guin, *The Dispossessed: An Ambiguous Utopia* (1974)

I didn't become rich, but I was usually comfortable. That is a social disease, the symptom of which is the ability to ignore it while your society develops weeping pustules and has its brains eaten out by radioactive maggots.

— John Varley, "The Persistence of Vision" (1978)

The only things that matter are those made of truth and joy, and not of tin and glass.

— Richard Bach, *There's No Such Place as Far Away* (1979)

"I'm interested in alien philosophies," Nikolai said. "The answers of other species to the great questions of existence."

"But there is only one central question," the alien said. "We have pursued its answer from star to star. We were hoping that you would help us answer it."

Nikolai was cautious. "What is the question?"

"What is it you have that we want?"

— Bruce Sterling, "Twenty Evocations" (1984)

A person's things can be a kind of exterior morphology of their mind—like a snail's shell, or something. I like to imagine what kind of person they were, from what's in their pockets.

— Lois McMaster Bujold, *Shards of Honor* (1986)

There is only the dance. These things you treasure are shells.

— William Gibson, *Count Zero* (1986)

The child's-eye view is not fixed on the things it doesn't have. That comes later.

— George Turner, *Drowning Towers* (1987)

The only skill the alchemists of Ankh-Morpork had discovered so far was the ability to turn gold into less gold.

— Terry Pratchett, *Moving Pictures* (1990)

Possess nothing and be possessed by nothing. Put away what you have in your head, give what you have in your heart.

— Kim Stanley Robinson, *Red Mars* (1992)

Money doesn't exist in the twenty-fourth century. [. . .] The acquisition of wealth is no longer the driving force in our lives. We work to better ourselves and the rest of humanity.

— Brannon Braga and Ronald D. Moore, *Star Trek: First Contact* (film, 1996)

The rich and the famous, Kathy had once said, were seldom that way by accident. It was possible to be one or the other, but very seldom, accidentally, to be both.

— William Gibson, *Idoru* (1996)

Wealth that is stored up in gold is dead. It rots and stinks. True wealth is made every day by men getting up out of bed and going to work. By schoolchildren doing their lessons, improving their minds.
— Neal Stephenson, *Cryptonomicon* (1999)

WEAPONS

The sole preoccupation of this learned society was the destruction of humanity for philanthropic reasons and the perfection of weapons as instruments of civilization.
— Jules Verne, *From the Earth to the Moon* (1865), translated by
   Walter James Miller (1978)

Science has toiled too long forging weapons for fools to use. It is time she held her hand.
— H. G. Wells, *The First Men in the Moon* (1901)

In the arts of life man invents nothing; but in the arts of death he outdoes Nature herself, and produces by chemistry and machinery all the slaughter of plague, pestilence and famine. [. . .] There is nothing in Man's industrial machinery but his greed and sloth: his heart is in his weapons.
— George Bernard Shaw, *Man and Superman: A Comedy and a Philosophy*
   (play, 1903)

No male or female Martian is ever voluntarily without a weapon of destruction.
— Edgar Rice Burroughs, *A Princess of Mars* (1917)

The knife is the strongest, the most immortal, the most brilliant of man's creations. The knife has been a guillotine; the knife is the universal means of solving all knots.
— Yevgeny Zamiatin, *We* (1924), translated by Mirra Ginsburg (1972)

The right to buy weapons is the right to be free.
— A. E. van Vogt, "The Seesaw" (1941)

An armed citizenry, willing to fight, is the foundation of civil freedom.
— Robert A. Heinlein, *Beyond This Horizon* (1942)

An armed society is a polite society. Manners are good when one may have to back up his acts with his life.
—Robert A. Heinlein, *Beyond This Horizon* (1942)

There are no dangerous weapons; there are only dangerous men. We're trying to teach you to be dangerous—to the enemy. Dangerous even without a knife. Deadly as long as you still have one hand or one foot and are still alive.
—Robert A. Heinlein, *Starship Troopers* (1959)

Destroying civilization, always a task for fools, was relatively easy with the tools constructed for the purpose in the 20th century.
—Edgar Pangborn, "The Children's Crusade" (1974)

He woke in sunlit morning, lying on his side, looking at the swords, cavalry sabres, hung crossed on the chimneypiece.

They were tools, he thought, expressing purpose as simply as a needle or a hammer, their purpose, their reason or meaning, being death; they were made to kill men with; the slightly curved and still unpolished blades were death, were in fact his own death, which he saw with clarity and relaxation.
—Ursula K. Le Guin, "Two Delays on the Northern Line" (1979)

The pen is mightier than the sword [. . .] only if the sword is very small and the pen is very sharp.
—Terry Pratchett, *The Light Fantastic* (1986)

A weapon is a device for making your enemy change his mind.
—Lois McMaster Bujold, *The Vor Game* (1990)

A man with a gun is in no need of advice.
—Steve Aylett, *Atom* (2000)

WISDOM

She generally gave herself very good advice (though she very seldom followed it).
—Lewis Carroll, *Alice's Adventures in Wonderland* (1865)

You are a wise man, Professor—for one who has not lived even a single lifetime.
    —Hamilton Deane and John L. Balderston, *Dracula* (play, 1927)

You are wiser than your friends, my dear sir, and therefore you are less impatient.
    —James Hilton, *Lost Horizon* (1933)

Perhaps the exhaustion of the passions is the beginning of wisdom.
    —James Hilton, *Lost Horizon* (1933)

He had some wits, as well as luck and a magic ring—and all three are very useful possessions.
    —J. R. R. Tolkien, *The Hobbit* (1937)

If I had followed my better judgment always, my life would have been a very dull one.
    —Edgar Rice Burroughs, *Llana of Gathol* (1948)

Too much wisdom is a bad thing. It makes one cynical, overcautious, backward-looking.
    —Malcolm Jameson, "Pride" (1942)

The trouble was, if you were a chief you had to think, you had to be wise.
    —William Golding, *Lord of the Flies* (1954)

He that breaks a thing to find out what it is has left the path of wisdom.
    —J. R. R. Tolkien, *The Fellowship of the Ring* (1954)

If you try to save wisdom until the world is wise, Father, the world will never have it.
    —Walter M. Miller, Jr., *A Canticle for Leibowitz* (1959)

A desire not to butt into other people's business is eighty percent of all human wisdom.
    —Robert A. Heinlein, *Stranger in a Strange Land* (1961)

Goodness alone is *never* enough. A hard, cold wisdom is required for goodness to accomplish good. Goodness without wisdom always accomplishes evil.
 —Robert A. Heinlein, *Stranger in a Strange Land* (1961)

Sometimes one must try anything, he decided. It is no disgrace. On the contrary, it is a sign of wisdom, of recognizing the situation.
 —Philip K. Dick, *The Man in the High Castle* (1962)

Polish comes from the cities; wisdom from the desert.
 —Frank Herbert, *Dune* (1965)

From that time on he was the ruler of the Argonautians and became a great philosopher, for he devoted himself to the study of nothingness, there being nothing less than this to meditate upon.
 —Stanislaw Lem, "The Advisers of King Hydrops" (1965), translated by
    Michael Kandel (1977)

He believed that the wise man is one who never sets himself apart from other living things, whether they have speech or not, and in later years he strove long to learn what can be learned, in silence, from the eyes of animals, the flight of birds, the great slow gestures of trees.
 —Ursula K. Le Guin, *A Wizard of Earthsea* (1968)

Age does not bring wisdom. Often it merely changes simple stupidity into arrogant conceit.
 —Robert A. Heinlein, *Time Enough for Love* (1973)

We take foul medicines to improve our health; so we must entertain foul thoughts on occasion, to strengthen wisdom.
 —Brian W. Aldiss, "The Small Stones of Tu Fu" (1978)

The wise are not wise because they make no mistakes. They are wise because they correct their mistakes as soon as they recognize them.
 —Orson Scott Card, *Xenocide* (1991)

Wisdom

When the sun was still young and men fools who worshipped war, the wise ones of Urth took for themselves the names of humble plants to teach men wisdom.

—Gene Wolfe, "Empires of Foliage and Flower" (1993)

"Those who know do not speak, those who speak do not know," it muttered. "Thus wisdom remains uninherited."

—Steve Aylett, "Angel Dust" (1998)

WOMEN AND MEN

This close resemblance of the sexes was after all what one would expect; for the strength of a man and the softness of a woman, the institution of the family, and the differentiation of occupations are mere militant necessities of an age of physical force. Where population is balanced and abundant, much child-bearing becomes an evil rather than a blessing to the State: where violence comes but rarely and offspring are secure, there is less necessity— indeed there is no necessity—of an efficient family, and the specialization of the sexes with reference to their children's needs disappears. We see some beginnings of this even in our own time, and in this future age it was complete.

—H. G. Wells, *The Time Machine: An Invention* (1895)

These women, whose essential distinction of Motherhood was the dominant note of their whole culture, were strikingly deficient in what we call "femininity." This led me very promptly to the conviction that those "feminine charms" we are so fond of are not feminine at all, but mere reflected masculinity—developed to please us because they had to please us—and in no way essential to the real fulfillment of their great process.

—Charlotte Perkins Gilman, *Herland* (1915)

We were now well used to seeing women not as females, but as people; people of all sorts, doing every kind of work.

—Charlotte Perkins Gilman, *Herland* (1915)

Fatigue makes women talk more and men talk less.

—C. S. Lewis, *The Screwtape Letters* (1942)

Girls, he reflected, were much odder than dragons. Probably another race entirely.
    —Robert A. Heinlein, *Between Planets* (1951)

After male domination had almost wrecked the world, the women established the Matriarchy for the survival of the race. Men are wicked, quarrelsome, dirty, untrustworthy and savage. Only a few picked specimens can be tolerated.
    —Alfred Coppel, "Defender of the Faith" (1952)

The Earth Powers are strong and strange in womankind.
    —Poul Anderson, "The Long Remembering" (1957)

There was no explaining the chemistry which joined men and women, locked them in embraces of hate and mutual suffering sometimes for ninety years on end.
    —Philip K. Dick, *The Crack in Space* (1965)

Women are amazing creatures—sweet, soft, gentle, and far more savage than we are.
    —Robert A. Heinlein, *The Moon Is a Harsh Mistress* (1966)

If we find a child with an aptitude for music we give him a scholarship to Julliard. If they found a child whose aptitudes were for being a woman, they made him one.
    —Frederik Pohl, "Day Million" (1966)

Strange how a man can love a woman and yet at the same time pray for her to fall under a train.
    —Bob Shaw, "Light of Other Days" (1966)

Being a man or a woman is, in a large measure, just an act, a certain culturally determined role that may have very little to do with how we really are inside.
    —Philip K. Dick and Ray Nelson, *The Ganymede Takeover* (1967)

"Must you be right, at a time like this?" he demanded. "It is unbecoming in a woman."
    —Suzette Haden Elgin, "For the Sake of Grace" (1969)

Women and Men

The most important thing, the heaviest single factor in one's life, is whether one's born male or female. In most societies it determines one's expectations, activities, outlook, ethics, manners—almost everything. Vocabulary. Semiotic usages. Clothing. Even food.

    —Ursula K. Le Guin, *The Left Hand of Darkness* (1969)

I said, "Yes, here you are," and smiled (feeling like a fool), and wondered seriously if male Earth people's minds worked so very differently from female Earth people's minds, but that couldn't be so or the race would have died out long ago.

    —Joanna Russ, "When It Changed" (1972)

"Why do you want to be a shark?"

    She ran her nails delicately along the cords of his neck. "I want to kill people, eat them."

    "Any people?"

    "Just men."

    —Edward Bryant, "Shark" (1973)

I *don't* hate men. That would be as silly as—as hating the weather.

    —James Tiptree, Jr., "The Women Men Don't See" (1973)

Women have no rights, Don, except what men allow us. Men are more aggressive and powerful, and they run the world. When the next real crisis upsets them, our so-called rights will vanish like—like that smoke. We'll be back where we always were: property. And whatever has gone wrong will be blamed on our freedom, like the fall of Rome was. You'll see.

    —James Tiptree, Jr., "The Women Men Don't See" (1973)

What women do is survive. We live by ones and twos in the chinks of your world-machine.

    —James Tiptree, Jr., "The Women Men Don't See" (1973)

The trouble with men is that they have limited minds. That's the trouble with women, too.

    —Joanna Russ, "Existence" (1975)

Where men are weak and dangerous is in their vanity. A woman has a center, is a center. But a man isn't, he's a reaching out. So he reaches out and grabs things and piles them up around him and says, I'm this, I'm that, this is me, that's me, I'll prove that I am me! And he can wreck a lot of things, trying to prove it.
—Ursula K. Le Guin, "The Eye of the Heron" (1978)

Any intelligent being is a man. That's what his people believe. Isn't that a fine concept? It binds us together instead of separating us into alien and human.
—Lee Killough, "Bête et Noir" (1980)

Men are not such bad folk when one stops expecting them to be gods.
—Joanna Russ, "Souls" (1982)

God created men to test the souls of women.
—Robert A. Heinlein, *Job: A Comedy of Justice* (1984)

Premenstrual Syndrome: Just before their periods women behave the way men do all the time.
—Robert A. Heinlein, *The Cat Who Walks through Walls* (1985)

A man is just a woman's strategy for making other women.
—Margaret Atwood, *The Handmaid's Tale* (1986)

Flynn planted her with the tomatoes in the greenhouse on the first day of spring. The instructions on the package were similar to the instructions on any seed envelope. Vegetable Wife: prefers sandy soil, sunny conditions. Plant two inches deep after all danger of frost has passed. When seedling is two feet tall, transplant. Water frequently.
—Pat Murphy, "His Vegetable Wife" (1986)

Few males have a firm grip on reality; I can't see that it matters.
—Robert A. Heinlein, *To Sail beyond the Sunset* (1987)

You'll understand when you come there at last, Achilles . . . Hades is Women's Country.
—Sheri S. Tepper, *The Gate to Women's Country* (1988)

"The universe is shaped by the struggle between two great forces. [. . .] Male and female. Minute by minute, the balance tips one way or the other. Not just here. In every universe. There are places," the woman leaned forward, "where men are not allowed to gather and drink. Places where football is absolutely illegal."
— Karen Joy Fowler, "Game Night at the Fox and Goose" (1989)

Males and females always got along best when neither actually listened fully to what the other one was saying.
— Terry Pratchett, *Pyramids* (1989)

"A man's in his skin, see, like a nut in its shell." She held up her long, bent, wet fingers as if holding a walnut. "It's hard and strong, that shell, and it's all full of him. Full of grand man-meat, man-self. And that's all. That's all there is. It's all him and nothing else, inside. [. . .] A woman's a different thing entirely. Who knows where a woman begins and ends? Listen, mistress, I have roots, I have roots deeper than this island. Deeper than the sea, older than the raising of the lands. I go back into the dark."
— Ursula K. Le Guin, *Tehanu: The Last Book of Earthsea* (1990)

They're all strange, men are. I guess if I understood them I wouldn't find them so interesting.
— Ursula K. Le Guin, "Ether, OR" (1995)

A woman is a worse hindrance to a man than anything else, even the Government. [. . .] What's wrong with women is that you can't count on them. They are not fully civilized.
— Ursula K. Le Guin, "Ether, OR" (1995)

Women send signals but men speak English.
— Steve Aylett, *Slaughtermatic* (1998)

A man should never know a woman's secret life; men cannot stand so much reality.
— Kalamu ya Salaam, "Can You Wear My Eyes" (2000)

Carl often bragged that Chaos Theory was his moral and aesthetic code. What this actually meant was that he couldn't be bothered to clean up after himself.
   —Ellen Steiber, "The Cats of San Marino" (2000)

If a man speaks in the heart of a forest and no woman is there to hear them, is he still wrong?
   —Glen Cook, *Angry Lead Skies* (2002)

WORK

Even if one has been to the moon, one has still to earn a living.
   —H. G. Wells, *The First Men in the Moon* (1901)

We rather spread ourselves, telling of the advantages of competition; how it developed fine qualities; that without it there would be "no stimulus to industry." Terry was very strong on that point.
   "No stimulus to industry," they repeated, with that puzzled look we had learned to know so well. "*Stimulus? To industry?* But don't you *like* to work?"
   —Charlotte Perkins Gilman, *Herland* (1915)

Laziness in doing stupid things can be a great virtue.
   —James Hilton, *Lost Horizon* (1933)

Very few people have the imagination and the temperament to spend a lifetime in leisure.
   —Robert A. Heinlein, *Beyond This Horizon* (1942)

The Romance of Interplanetary Travel—it looked well in print, but he knew what it was: a job, monotony, no scenery, bursts of work, tedious waits, no home life.
   —Robert A. Heinlein, "Space Jockey" (1947)

The only thing you can do easily is be wrong, and that's hardly worth the effort.
   —Norton Juster, *The Phantom Tollbooth* (1961)

If you only do the easy and useless jobs, you'll never have to worry about the important ones which are so difficult.
— Norton Juster, *The Phantom Tollbooth* (1961)

"Okay!" he said resignedly. "Another day, another world!"
— Murray Leinster, "Third Planet" (1963)

"There's a law," Chuck said, "which I call Rittersdorf's Third Law of Diminished Returns, which states that proportional to how long you hold a job you imagine that it has progressively less and less importance in the scheme of things."
— Philip K. Dick, *Clans of the Alphane Moon* (1964)

It is dangerous to disturb a magician at work.
— Randall Garrett, "The Muddle of the Woad" (1965)

Housework is never completed, the chaos always lurks ready to encroach on any area left unweeded, a jungle filled with dirty pans and the roaring of giant stuffed toy animals suddenly turned savage. Terrible glass eyes.
— Pamela Zoline, "The Heat Death of the Universe" (1967)

The Padre's weightless voice floated reassuringly back to him. "You have worked and not worked. Not working is the hardest work of all."
That's what I get for dialing Zen, Joe said to himself.
— Philip K. Dick, *Galactic Pot-Healer* (1969)

The more I want to get something done, the less I call it work.
— Richard Bach, *Illusions: The Adventures of a Reluctant Messiah* (1977)

Nikopoulis was a professional who kept his humanity in some desk drawer of his life, to be indulged secretly.
— George Turner, *Drowning Towers* (1987)

I was happy in that cluttered office, in that insignificant museum, doing work that no one on earth cared a damn about.
— Kate Wilhelm, "Isosceles" (1988)

The way to deal with an impossible task was to chop it down into a number of merely very difficult tasks, and break each one of *them* into a group of horribly hard tasks, and each of *them* into tricky jobs, and each one of them . . .
— Terry Pratchett, *Truckers* (1989)

All I understand about living is having your work to do, and being able to do it. That's the pleasure, and the glory, and all. And if you can't do the work, or it's taken from you, then what's any good? You have to have something . . .
— Ursula K. Le Guin, *Tehanu: The Last Book of Earthsea* (1990)

At the day's end there was supper together, and bed together, and sleep, and wake at dawn and back to work, and so round and so round, like the wheel of a water mill, rising full and emptying, the days like the bright water falling.
— Ursula K. Le Guin, *Tehanu: The Last Book of Earthsea* (1990)

Now the world falls into the hands of the little men, the hypocrites and clerks.
Look at them. They have not the mettle for the great work. They will botch it.
— William Gibson and Bruce Sterling, *The Difference Engine* (1991)

Whenever you see a bunch of buggers puttering around talking about truth and beauty and the best way of attacking Ethics, you can bet your sandals it's because dozens of other poor buggers are doing all the real work around the place.
— Terry Pratchett, *Small Gods* (1992)

INDEX OF AUTHORS

INDEX OF TITLES